The Essential Guide to CSS and HTML Web Design

Craig Grannell

friendsof

DESIGNER TO DESIGNER™

an Apress® company

The Essential Guide to CSS and HTML Web Design

ISBN-13 (pbk): 978-1-59059-907-5

ISBN-10 (pbk): 1-59059-907-1

Printed and bound in the United States of America 9 8 7 6 5 4 3 2 1

Distributed to the book trade worldwide by Springer-Verlag New York, Inc., 233 Spring Street, 6th Floor, New York, NY 10013. Phone 1-800-SPRINGER, fax 201-348-4505, e-mail orders-ny@springer-sbm.com, or visit www.springeronline.com.

For information on translations, please contact Apress directly at 2855 Telegraph Avenue, Suite 600, Berkeley, CA 94705. Phone 510-549-5930, fax 510-549-5939, e-mail info@apress.com, or visit www.apress.com.

The source code for this book is freely available to readers at www.friendsofed.com in the Downloads section.

Credits

Lead Editors Chris Mills, Tom Welsh	**Assistant Production Director** Kari Brooks-Copony
Technical Reviewer David Anderson	**Production Editor** Ellie Fountain
Editorial Board Steve Anglin, Ewan Buckingham, Gary Cornell, Jonathan Gennick, Jason Gilmore, Jonathan Hassell, Matthew Moodie, Jeffrey Pepper, Ben Renow-Clarke, Dominic Shakeshaft, Matt Wade, Tom Welsh	**Compositor** Dina Quan **Artist** April Milne
Project Manager Kylie Johnston	**Proofreader** Nancy Sixsmith **Indexer** Julie Grady
Copy Editor Damon Larson	**Interior and Cover Designer** Kurt Krames
Manufacturing Director Tom Debolski	

CONTENTS AT A GLANCE

CONTENTS

CONTENTS

Chapter 6: Tables: How Nature (and the W3C) Intended 233

ABOUT THE AUTHOR

 Craig Grannell is a well-known web designer and writer who's been flying the flag for web standards for a number of years. Originally trained in the fine arts, the mid-1990s saw Craig become immersed in the world of digital media, his creative projects encompassing everything from video and installation-based audio work, to strange live performances—sometimes with the aid of a computer, televisions, videos, and a PA system, and sometimes with a small bag of water above his head. His creative, playful art, which usually contained a dark, satirical edge, struck a chord with those who saw it, leading to successful appearances at a number of leading European media arts festivals.

Craig soon realized he'd actually have to make a proper living, however. Luckily, the Web caught his attention, initially as a means to promote his art via an online portfolio, but then as a creative medium in itself, and he's been working with it ever since. It was during this time that he founded Snub Communications (www.snubcommunications.com), a design and writing agency whose clients have since included the likes of Rebellion Developments (publishers of 2000 AD), IDG UK (publishers of *Macworld*, *PC Advisor*, *Digital Arts*, and other magazines), and Swim Records.

Along with writing the book you're holding right now, Craig has authored *Web Designer's Reference* (friends of ED, 2005) and various books on Dreamweaver, including *Foundation Web Design with Dreamweaver 8* (friends of ED, 2006). Elsewhere, he's written numerous articles for *Computer Arts*, *MacFormat*, *.net/Practical Web Design*, 4Talent, *MacUser*, the dearly departed *Cre@te Online*, and many other publications besides.

When not designing websites, Craig can usually be found hard at work in his quest for global superstardom by way of his eclectic audio project, the delights of which you can sample at www.projectnoise.co.uk.

ABOUT THE TECHNICAL REVIEWER

 David Anderson is a biochemistry graduate from North West England who first noticed the value of the Internet in the early 1990s while using it as a research tool to aid his academic studies. He created his first website shortly after graduating in 1997, and began to establish himself as a freelance developer while also working in a variety of roles for several major UK companies until eventually founding his own business, S2R Creations, in 2003.

David discovered the web standards movement early in his career, and quickly adapted his working practices to utilize the power and versatility of CSS and semantic HTML. Clients benefiting from his skills have included New Directions Recruitment and Rex Judd Ltd. He has been sharing his knowledge with members of various web development forums for over five years, has written for *Practical Web Design* magazine, and has established his reputation as an authority on web standards as a result.

When he isn't developing websites, he can be found taking photos of anything that will stay still long enough, as well as a few things that won't. He shares his photos on Flickr, at www.flickr.com/photos/ap4a, and also writes on his blog at www.ap4a.co.uk.

ACKNOWLEDGMENTS

Writing a book is a long process, involving many hours of effort. To see the final product is exhilarating and extremely satisfying, but it couldn't have happened without those who've supported me along the way. In particular, I'd like to thank David Anderson, whose excellent editing, reviewing, ideas, and suggestions were indispensable in the revision of the text. Special thanks also to Chris Mills for getting the ball rolling, to Tom Welsh for picking up the baton, and to Kylie Johnston for keeping everything ticking over. Thanks also to the other members of the friends of ED team for their hard work in getting this publication into the world.

I'm also extremely fortunate to have had the support of several other great designers. I particularly owe a debt of gratitude to Sarah Gay (www.stuffbysarah.net) for her highly useful, selfless contributions, and to my former partner in crime David Powers, who once again stepped in to assist with a couple of elements in the book. Thanks also to Jon Hicks, Matthew Pennell, and Lokesh Dhakar for granting permission to include elements of their work, and to the many designers whose work has been an inspiration over the years.

And, finally, thanks to Kay for once again being there for me and putting up with me while I wrote this book.

FOREWORD

Designing for the Web is a wonderful thing. The ability to publish something and have it appear immediately and globally is an empowering feeling. I'll never forget the first rush I felt when, as a print designer, I could simply "upload" some files and have them be immediately visible, rather than waiting in trepidation for the boxes to return from the printer. Back then the Web was simpler, there were fewer materials and tools, and "styling" was something you hacked together using bizarre hacks and workarounds to achieve even the simplest of tasks. The browser landscape was equally testing.

Now we're in a much better position. We have a wonderful thing called CSS that allows us to style pages with concise style rules and leave the HTML to describe the content, not the presentation. Content can be repurposed for different media.

But anyone keen to learn web design (from scratch, or to improve their existing skills) has a bewildering job on their hands. The publishing market is saturated with good books on web design, HTML, and CSS. Yet if you were asked for a single book that encompasses all three, and that someone could understand without assuming any prior "Internet knowledge," what would you recommend? Still trying to think of one?

A regular contributor to .net/Practical Web Design magazine, Craig Grannell has written The Essential Guide to CSS and HTML Web Design for this purpose. Whether you need a reference for unmemorable code like HTML entities, or need to know what on earth HTML entities are, it's all here. Laid out in an understandable and non-patronizing manner, every aspect of creating a site is covered.

There are still many challenges to face when designing sites, but the sheer fun of it is better than ever. With this guide in your hands, more so!

Jon Hicks
Hicksdesign

INTRODUCTION

The Web is an ever-changing, evolving entity, and it's easy for a designer to get left behind. As both a designer and writer, I see a lot of books on web design, and although many are well written, few are truly integrated, modular resources that any designer can find useful in his or her day-to-day work. Most web design books concentrate on a single technology (or, commonly, a piece of software), leaving the designer to figure out how to put the pieces together.

This book is different

The Essential Guide to CSS and HTML Web Design provides a modern, integrated approach to web design. Each of the chapters looks at a specific aspect of creating a web page, such as type, working with images, creating navigation, and creating layout blocks. In each case, relevant technologies are explored in context and at the appropriate times, just as in real-world projects—for example, markup is explored along with associated CSS and JavaScript, rather than each technology being placed in separate chapters, and visual design ideas are discussed so you can get a feel for how code affects page layouts. Dozens of practical examples are provided, which you can use to further your understanding of each subject. This highly modular and integrated approach means that you can dip in and out of the book as you need to, crafting along the way a number of web page elements that you can use on countless sites in the future.

Because the entire skills gamut is covered—from foundation to advanced—this book is ideal for beginners and long-time professionals alike. If you're making your first move into standards-based web design, the "ground floor" is covered, rather than an assumption being made regarding your knowledge. However, contemporary ideas, techniques, and thinking are explored throughout, ensuring that the book is just as essential for the experienced designer wanting to work on CSS layouts, or the graphic designer who wants to discover how to create cutting-edge websites.

This book's advocacy of web standards, usability, and accessibility with a strong eye toward visual design makes it of use to technologists and designers alike, enabling everyone to build better websites. An entire chapter is devoted to browser issues, which should help ensure your sites look great, regardless of the end user's setup. And for those moments when a particular tag or property value slips your mind, this book provides a comprehensive reference guide that includes important and relevant XHTML elements and attributes, XHTML entities, web colors, and CSS 2.1 properties and values.

Remember that you can visit the friends of ED support forums at www.friendsofed.com/forums to discuss aspects of this book, or just to chat with like-minded designers and developers. You can also download files associated with this book from www.friendsofed.com— just find the book in the friends of ED catalog located on the homepage, and then follow its link to access downloads and other associated resources.

Layout conventions

To keep this book as clear and easy to follow as possible, the following conventions are used throughout:

- Important words or concepts are normally highlighted on the first appearance in **bold type**.
- Code is presented in fixed-width font.
- New or changed code is normally presented in **bold fixed-width font**.
- Pseudo-code and variable input are written in *italic fixed-width font*.
- Menu commands are written in the form Menu ➤ Submenu ➤ Submenu.
- Where I want to draw your attention to something, I've highlighted it like this:

> *Ahem, don't say I didn't warn you.*

- To make it easier to work through the exercises, each one has an introductory box that lists where you can find any required files and the completed files within the downloadable file archive. A short overview of what you'll learn is also included.
- Sometimes code won't fit on a single line in a book. Where this happens, I use an arrow like this: ➡.

  ```
  This is a very, very long section of code that should be written all on
  ➡ the same line without a break.
  ```

In this chapter:

- Introducing the Internet and web design
- Working with web standards
- Working with XHTML
- Understanding and creating CSS rules
- Creating web page boilerplates
- Organizing web page content

A brief history of the Internet

Even in the wildest dreams of science fiction and fantasy writers, few envisioned anything that offers the level of potential that the Internet now provides for sharing information on a worldwide basis. For both businesses and individuals, the Internet is now the medium of choice, largely because it enables you to present your wares to the entire world on a 24/7 basis. But the technology's origins were more ominous than and very different from the ever-growing, sprawling free-for-all that exists today.

In the 1960s, the American military was experimenting with methods by which the US authorities might be able to communicate in the aftermath of a nuclear attack. The suggested solution was to replace point-to-point communication networks with one that was more akin to a net. This meant information could find its way from place to place even if certain sections of the network were destroyed. Despite the project eventually being shelved by the Pentagon, the concept itself lived on, eventually influencing a network that connected several American universities.

During the following decade, this fledgling network went international and began opening itself up to the general public. The term *Internet* was coined in the 1980s, which also heralded the invention of Transmission Control Protocol/Internet Protocol (TCP/IP), the networking software that makes possible communication between computers running on different systems. During the 1980s, Tim Berners-Lee was also busy working on HTML, his effort to weld hypertext to a markup language in an attempt to make communication of research between himself and his colleagues simpler.

Despite the technology's healthy level of expansion, the general public remained largely unaware of the Internet until well into the 1990s. By this time, HTML had evolved from a fairly loose set of rules—browsers having to make assumptions regarding coder intent and rendering output—to a somewhat stricter set of specifications and recommendations. This, along with a combination of inexpensive hardware, the advent of highly usable web browsers such as Mosaic (see the following image), and improved communications technology, saw an explosion of growth that continues to this day.

Initially, only the largest brands dipped their toes into these new waters, but soon thousands of companies were on the Web, enabling customers all over the globe to access information, and later to shop online. Home users soon got in on the act, once it became clear that the basics of web design weren't rocket science, and that, in a sense, everyone could do it—all you needed was a text editor, an FTP client, and some web space. Designers soon got in on the act, increasingly catered for by new elements within HTML; Cascading Style Sheets (CSS), which took a while to be adopted by browsers, but eventually provided a means of creating highly advanced layouts for the Web; and faster web connections, which made media-rich sites accessible to the general public without forcing them to wait ages for content to download.

Therefore, unlike most media, the Web is truly a tool for everyone, and in many countries, the Internet has become ubiquitous. For those working in a related industry, it's hard to conceive that as recently as the mid-1990s relatively few people were even aware of the Internet's existence!

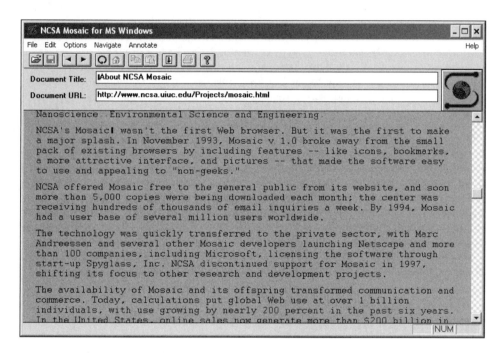

So, from obscure roots as a concept for military communications, the Internet has evolved into an essential tool for millions of people, enabling them to communicate with each other, research and gather information, telecommute, shop, play games, and become involved in countless other activities on a worldwide basis.

Why create a website?

Before putting pen to paper (and mouse to keyboard), it's important to think about the *reason* behind putting a site online. Millions already exist, so why do you need to create one yourself? Also, if you're working for a company, perhaps you already have plenty of marketing material, so why do you need a website as well?

I should mention here that I'm certainly not trying to put you off—far from it. Instead, I'm trying to reinforce the point that planning is key in any web design project, and although some people swear that "winging it" is the best way to go, most such projects end up gathering virtual dust online. Therefore, before doing anything else, think through why you should build a website and what you're trying to achieve.

Companies and individuals alike have practical and commercial reasons for setting up a website. A website enables you to communicate with like-minded individuals or potential clients on a worldwide basis. If you're a creative talent of some kind, you can use a website to showcase your portfolio, offering online photographs, music tracks for download, or poetry. If you fancy yourself as a journalist, a blog enables you to get your opinion out there. If you own or work for a business, creating a website is often the most efficient means of marketing your company. And even if you just have a hobby, a website can be a great way of finding others who share your passion—while you may be the only person in town who likes a particular movie or type of memorabilia, chances are there are thousands of people worldwide who think the same, and a website can bring you all together. This is perhaps why the paper fanzine has all but died, only to be reborn online, where development costs are negligible and worldwide distribution is a cinch.

In practical terms, a website exists online all day, every day (barring the odd hiccup with ISPs), which certainly isn't the case with printed media, which is there one minute and in the recycle trash the next. Distribution is less expensive than sending out printed material—a thousand-page website can be hosted for $10 per month or less, but sending a thousand-page document to one person (let alone a thousand or several thousand) may cost more than that. Likewise, development (particularly corrections and updates) is often significantly cheaper, too. For example, if you want to rework a print brochure, you have to redesign it and then reprint it. Reworking a section of a website often means swapping out a few files, which is efficient and affordable. So, for large companies and individuals alike, the ability to have relevant information online in a form that can often be updated in mere minutes, thereby keeping all interested parties up to date, is hard to resist!

Audience requirements

This book centers on the design and technology aspects of web design, but close attention must always be paid to your potential audience. It's no good forcing design ideas that result in inappropriate visuals, unusable navigation to all but the most technically minded of people, and huge download times on your site's unsuspecting visitors.

Prior to creating a site, you must ascertain what your audience wants and expects in terms of content, design, and how the site will work (by way of talking to the relevant people, and also, if your budget allows, by using surveys and focus groups). You don't have to take all of your audience's ideas into account (after all, many will be contradictory), but be mindful of common themes and ensure they're not ignored.

Technical considerations must be researched. If you're targeting designers, you can be fairly sure that a large proportion of the audience will be using monitors set to a high resolution and millions of colors, and you can design accordingly. If your site is aimed at business users, be mindful that much of your potential audience will likely be using laptops (or older computers, for staff at the lower end of the ladder), with screen resolutions of 1024×768 or lower.

Determining the web browsers your audience members use is another important consideration. Although use of web standards (used throughout this book) is more likely to result in a highly compatible site, browser quirks still cause unforeseen problems; therefore, always check to see what browsers are popular with a site's visitors, and ensure you test in as many as you can. Sometimes you won't have access to such statistics, or you may just be after a "sanity check" regarding what's generally popular. A couple of useful places to research global web browser statistics are www.w3schools.com/browsers/browsers_stats.asp and www.upsdell.com/BrowserNews/. Note, though, that any statistics you see online are effectively guesswork and are not a definitive representation of the Web as a whole; still, they do provide a useful, sizeable sample that's often indicative of current browser trends.

Although you might be used to checking browser usage, and then, based on the results, designing for specific browsers, we'll be adhering closely to web standards throughout this book. When doing this, an "author once, work anywhere" approach is feasible, as long as you're aware of various browser quirks (many of which are explored in Chapter 9). Of course, you should still always ensure you test sites in as many browsers as possible, just to make sure everything works as intended.

Web design overview

Web design has evolved rapidly over the years. Initially, browsers were basic, and early versions of HTML were fairly limited in what they enabled designers to do. Therefore, many older sites on the Web are plain in appearance. Additionally, the Web was originally largely a technical repository, hence the boring layouts of many sites in the mid 1990s—after all, statistics, documentation, and papers rarely need to be jazzed up, and the audience didn't demand such things anyway.

As with any medium finding its feet, things soon changed, especially once the general public flocked to the Web. It was no longer enough for websites to be text-based information repositories. Users craved—demanded, even—color! Images! Excitement! Animation! Interaction! Even video and audio managed to get a foothold as compression techniques improved and connection speeds increased.

The danger of eye candy became all too apparent as the turn of the century approached: every site, it seemed, had a Flash intro, and the phrase "skip intro" became so common that it eventually spawned a parody website.

These days, site design has tended toward being more restrained, as designers have become more comfortable with using specific types of technologies for relevant and appropriate purposes. Therefore, you'll find beautifully designed XHTML- and CSS-based sites sitting alongside highly animated Flash efforts.

Of late, special emphasis is being placed on **usability** and **accessibility**, and, in the majority of cases, designers have cottoned to the fact that content must take precedence. However, just because web standards, usability, and accessibility are key, that doesn't mean design should be thrown out the window. As we'll see in later chapters, web standards do not have to come at the expense of good design—far from it. In fact, a strong understanding of web standards helps to improve websites, making it easier for you to create cutting-edge layouts that work across platforms and are easy to update. It also provides you with a method of catering for obsolete devices.

> *If you're relatively new to web design, you may be wondering about the best platform and software for creating websites. Ultimately, it matters little which platform you choose, as long as you have access to the most popular browsers for testing purposes (a list that I'd now include Apple's Safari in, alongside Internet Explorer, Firefox, and Opera). Regarding software, there's an overview in Appendix E ("Browsers Guide"), but this isn't an exhaustive guide, so do your own research and find software to your liking.*

Why WYSIWYG tools aren't used in this book

With lots of software available and this book being design-oriented, you might wonder why I'm not using WYSIWYG web design tools. This isn't because I shun such tools—it's more that in order to best learn how to do something, you need to start from scratch, with the foundations. Many web design applications make it tempting to "hide" the underlying code from you, and most users end up relying on the graphical interface. This is fine until something goes wrong and you don't know how to fix it.

Removing software from the equation also means we concentrate on the underlying technology that drives web pages, without the distraction of working out which button does what. It also ensures that the book will be relevant to you, regardless of what software you use or your current skill level. Therefore, I suggest you install a quality text editor to work through the exercises, or set your web design application to use its code view. Once you're familiar with the concepts outlined in this book, you can apply them to your work, whatever your chosen application for web design. This level of flexibility is important, because you never know when you might have to switch applications—something that's relatively painless if you know how to design for the Web and understand technologies like CSS and HTML.

Introducing HTML and XHTML

The foundation of the majority of web pages is **HyperText Markup Language**, commonly known by its initials, HTML. A curious facet of the language is that it's easy to pick up the basics—anyone who's computer literate should be able to piece together a basic page after learning some tags—but it has enough flexibility and scope to keep designers interested and experimenting, especially when HTML is combined with Cascading Style Sheets (CSS), which we'll discuss later in this chapter. This section presents an overview of HTML tags and elements, and how HTML and XHTML relate to web standards.

Introducing the concept of HTML tags and elements

HTML documents are text files that contain tags, which are used to mark up HTML elements. These documents are usually saved with the .html file extension, although some prefer .htm, which is a holdover from DOS file name limitations, which restricted you to eight characters for the file name and three for the extension.

The aforementioned tags are what web browsers use to display pages, and assuming the browser is well behaved (most modern ones are), the display should conform to standards as laid out by the **World Wide Web Consortium (W3C)**, the organization that develops guidelines and specifications for many web technologies.

> *The W3C website is found at* www.w3.org. *The site offers numerous useful tools, including validation services against which you can check your web pages.*

HTML tags are surrounded by angle brackets—for instance, <p> is a paragraph start tag. It's good practice to close tags once the element content or intended display effect concludes, and this is done with an end tag. End tags are identical to the opening start tags, but with an added forward slash: /. A complete HTML element looks like this:

```
<p>Here is a paragraph.</p>
```

This element consists of the following:

- **Start tag**: <p>
- **Content**: Here is a paragraph.
- **End tag**: </p>

> *HTML doesn't have a hard-and-fast rule regarding the case of tags, unlike XHTML, which we'll shortly be talking about and which will be used throughout the book. If you look at the source code of HTML pages on the Web, you may see lowercase tags, uppercase tags or, in the case of pages put together over a period of time, a mixture of the two. That said, it's still good practice with any markup language to be consistent, regardless of whether the rules are more flexible.*

Nesting tags

There are many occasions when tags must be placed inside each other; this process is called nesting. One reason for nesting is to apply basic styles to text-based elements. Earlier, you saw the code for a paragraph element. We can now make the text bold by surrounding the element content with a strong element:

```
<p><strong>Here is a paragraph.</strong></p>
```

> *You might be used to using the* bold *element to make text bold, but it is a* **physical** *element that only amends the look of text rather than also conveying semantic meaning.* **Logical** *elements, such as* strong, *convey meaning and add styling to text and are therefore preferred. These will be covered in Chapter 3.*

Note that the strong tags are nested within the paragraph tags (<p></p>), not the other way around. That's because the paragraph is the parent element to which formatting is being applied. The paragraph could be made bold *and* italic by adding another element, emphasis (<em></em>), as follows:

```
<p><strong><em>Here is a paragraph.</em></strong></p>
```

In this case, the strong and em tags could be in the opposite order, as they're at the same level in the hierarchy. However, you must always close nested tags in the reverse order to that in which they're opened, as shown in the previous code block, otherwise some browsers may not display your work as intended. For instance, the following should be avoided:

```
<p><strong><em>Here is a paragraph.</strong></em></p>
```

As previously mentioned, it's good practice to close tags in HTML—even though it's not a requirement for all elements, being sloppy in this area can lead to errors. Take a look at the following:

```
<p><strong><em>Here is a paragraph.</strong></p>
```

Here, the emphasis element isn't closed, meaning subsequent text-based content on the page is likely to be displayed in italics—so take care to close all your tags.

Web standards and XHTML

As mentioned earlier, we'll be working with **Extensible HyperText Markup Language (XHTML)** rules in this book, rather than HTML. The differences between HTML and XHTML are few, but important, and largely came about because of the inconsistent way that browsers displayed HTML. XHTML is stricter than HTML and has additional rules; oddly, this actually makes it easier to learn, because you don't have to worry about things like which case to use for tags and whether they require closing. You have hard-and-fast rules in each case. XHTML-specific rules are as follows.

All tags and attribute names must be in *lowercase* and must *always* be closed. Therefore, the following is incorrect:

```
<P>This is a paragraph.
<P>This is another paragraph.
```

The preceding lines should be written like this:

```
<p>This is a paragraph.</p>
<p>This is another paragraph.</p>
```

Unlike HTML, all XHTML elements require an end tag, including empty elements (such as br, img, and hr). The HTML for a carriage return is br. In XHTML, this must be written `<br></br>` or, more usually, in a combination form that looks like this: `<br />`. The trailing slash is placed at the end of the start tag, with a space prior to it (now typical practice, this was initially done to ensure compatibility with aging browsers that would otherwise ignore the tag entirely if the space wasn't present).

Tags often have **attributes** that modify them in some way. For instance, two attributes for the table cell tag td are nowrap (to stop content wrapping) and colspan (which states how many columns this cell should span). In XHTML, attributes must be quoted and always have a value. If necessary, the attribute name itself is repeated for the value. Therefore, the following is *incorrect*:

```
<td colspan=2 nowrap>
```

Instead, in XHTML, we write this:

```
<td colspan="2" nowrap="nowrap">
```

Evolution is another aspect that we have to deal with. Just as the survival of the fittest removes some species from nature, so too are tags (and attributes) unceremoniously dumped from the W3C specifications. Such tags and attributes are referred to as **deprecated**, meaning they are marked for removal from the standard and may not be supported in future browsers. In cases when deprecated tags are used in this book, this will be highlighted (and likewise in the reference section); in most cases, these tags can be avoided.

Semantic markup

In the previous few subsections, you may have noticed specific elements being used for specific things. This is referred to as **semantic markup** and is a very important aspect of modern web design. Plenty of (X)HTML elements exist, and each one has a clearly defined purpose (although some have more than one use). Because of the flexibility of markup languages, it's often possible to "wrongly" use elements, bashing your page into shape by using elements for design tasks they're not strictly suited for and certainly weren't originally designed for.

During the course of this book, we'll talk about semantics a fair amount. Ultimately, good semantic design enables you to simplify your markup and also provides the greatest scope for being able to style it with CSS (see the following section). By thinking a little before you code and defining your content with the correct markup, you'll end up with cleaner code and make it much easier for yourself in the long run when it comes to adding presentation to your content.

Introducing CSS

CSS is the W3C standard for defining the visual presentation for web pages. HTML was designed as a structural markup language, but the demands of users and designers encouraged browser manufacturers to support and develop presentation-oriented tags. These tags "polluted" HTML, pushing the language toward one of decorative style rather than logical structure. Its increasing complexity made life hard for web designers, and source code began to balloon for even basic presentation-oriented tasks. Along with creating needlessly large HTML files, things like font tags created web pages that weren't consistent across browsers and platforms, and styles had to be applied to individual elements—a time-consuming process.

The concept behind CSS was simple, yet revolutionary: remove the presentation and separate design from content. Let HTML (and later XHTML) deal with structure, and use a separate CSS document for the application of visual presentation.

The idea caught on, albeit slowly. The initial problem was browser support. At first, most browsers supported only a small amount of the CSS standard—and badly at that. But Internet Explorer 5 for Mac made great strides with regard to CSS support, and it was soon joined by other browsers fighting for the crown of standards king. These days, every up-to-date browser supports the majority of commonly used CSS properties and values, and more besides.

Another problem has been educating designers and encouraging them to switch from old to new methods. Benefits constantly need to be outlined and proven, and the new methods taught. Most designers these days style text with CSS, but many still don't use CSS for entire web page layouts, despite the inherent advantages in doing so. This, of course, is one of the reasons for this book: to show you, the designer, how CSS can be beneficial to you—saving you (and your clients) time and money—and to provide examples for various areas of web page design and development that you can use in your sites.

In this section we'll look at separating content from design, CSS rules, CSS selectors and how to use them, and how to add styles to a web page.

Separating content from design

Do you ever do any of the following?

- Use tables for website layout
- Use invisible GIFs to "push" elements around your web page
- Hack Photoshop documents to bits and stitch them back together in a web page to create navigation elements and more
- Get frustrated when any combination of the previous leads to unwieldy web pages that are a pain to edit

If so, the idea of separating content from design should appeal to you. On one hand, you have your HTML documents, which house content marked up in a logical and semantic manner. On the other hand, you have your CSS documents, giving you site-wide control of

1

the presentation of your web page elements from a single source. Instead of messing around with stretching transparent GIFs, and combining and splitting table cells, you can edit CSS rules to amend the look of your site, which is great for not only those times when things just need subtle tweaking, but also when you decide everything needs a visual over-haul. After all, if presentation is taken care of externally, you can often just replace the CSS to provide your site with a totally new design.

Designers (and clients paying for their time) aren't the only ones to benefit from CSS. Visitors will, too, in terms of faster download times, but also with regard to **accessibility**. For instance, people with poor vision often use screen readers to surf the Web. If a site's layout is composed of complex nested tables, it might visually make sense; however, the underlying structure may not be logical. View the source of a document and look at the order of the content. A screen reader reads from the top to the bottom of the *code* and doesn't care what the page looks like in a visual web browser. Therefore, if the code com-promises the logical order of the content (as complex tables often do), the site is compromised for all those using screen readers.

Accessibility is now very important in the field of web design. Legislation is regularly passed to strongly encourage designers to make sites accessible for web users with dis-abilities. It's likely that this trend will continue, encompassing just about everything except personal web pages. (However, even personal websites shouldn't be inaccessible.)

The rules of CSS

Style sheets consist of a number of **rules** that define how various web page elements should be displayed. Although sometimes bewildering to newcomers, CSS rules are simple to break down. Each rule consists of a **selector** and a **declaration**. The selector begins a CSS rule and specifies which part of the HTML document the rule will be applied to. The dec-laration consists of a number of property/value pairs that set specific properties and determine how the relevant element will look. In the following example, p is the selector and everything thereafter is the declaration:

```
p {
  color: blue;
}
```

As you probably know, p is the HTML tag for a paragraph. Therefore, if we attach this rule to a web page (see the section "Adding styles to a web page" later on in this chapter for how to do so), the declaration will be applied to any HTML marked up as a paragraph, thereby setting the color of said paragraphs to blue.

CSS property names are not case sensitive, but it's good to be consistent in web design—it's highly recommended to always use lowercase. Note, though, that XML is case sensitive, so when using CSS with XHTML documents served with the proper XHTML MIME type, everything must be consistent. Also, the W3 specifications recommend that CSS style sheets for XHTML should use lower-case element and attribute names.

When you write CSS rules, you place the declaration within curly brackets {}. Properties and values are separated by a colon (:), and property/value pairs are terminated by a semicolon (;). Technically, you don't have to include the final semicolon in a CSS rule, but most designers consider it good practice to do so. This makes sense—you may add property/value pairs to a rule at a later date, and if the semicolon is already there, you don't have to remember to add it.

If we want to amend our paragraph declaration and define paragraphs as bold, we can do so like this:

```
p {
  color: blue;
  font-weight:bold;
}
```

You don't have to lay out CSS rules as done in this section; rather, you can add rules as one long string. However, the formatting shown here is more readable in print. Note that in the files available for download, the formatting is changed slightly again: the property/value pairs and closing curly bracket are both tabbed inward, enabling rapid vertical scanning of a CSS document's selectors.

Types of CSS selectors

In the previous example, the most basic style of selector was used: an **element selector**. This defines the visual appearance of the relevant HTML tag. In the sections that follow, we'll examine some other regularly used (and well-supported) CSS selectors: class, ID, grouped, and contextual.

Class selectors

In some cases, you may wish to modify an element or a group of elements. For instance, you may wish for your general website text to be blue, as in the examples so far, but some portions of it to be red. The simplest way of doing this is by using a **class selector**.

In CSS, a class selector's name is prefixed by a period (.), like this:

```
.warningText {
  color: red;
}
```

This style is applied to HTML elements in any web page the style sheet is attached to using the class attribute, as follows:

```
<h2 class="warningText">This heading is red.</h2>
<p class="warningText">This text is red.</p>
<p>This is a paragraph, <span class="warningText">and this text is
➥ red</span>.</p>
```

If you want a make a class specific to a certain element, place the relevant HTML tag before the period in the CSS rule:

```
p.warningText {
  color: red;
}
```

If you used this CSS rule with the HTML elements shown previously, the paragraph's text would remain red, but not the heading or span, due to the warningText class now being exclusively tied to the paragraph selector only.

Usefully, it's possible to style an element by using multiple class values. This is done by listing multiple values in the class attribute, separated by spaces:

```
<p class="warningText hugeText">
```

The previous example's content would be styled as per the rules .warningText and .hugeText.

ID selectors

ID selectors can be used only once on each web page. In HTML, you apply a unique identifier to an HTML element with the id attribute:

```
<p id="footer">&copy; 200X The Company. All rights reserved.</p>
```

To style this element in CSS, precede the ID name with a hash mark (#):

```
p#footer {
  padding: 20px;
}
```

In this case, the footer div would have 20 pixels of padding on all sides.

Essentially, then, classes can be used multiple times on a web page, but IDs cannot. Typically, IDs are used to define one-off page elements, such as structural divisions, whereas classes are used to define the style for multiple items.

Grouped selectors

Should you wish to set a property value for a number of different selectors, you can use grouped selectors, which take the form of a comma-separated list:

```
h1, h2, h3, h4, h5, h6 {
  color: green;
}
```

In the preceding example, all the website's headings have been set to be green. Note that you're not restricted to a single rule for each element—you can use grouped selectors for common definitions and separate ones for specific property values, as follows:

```
h1, h2, h3, h4, h5, h6 {
  color: green;
}

h1 {
  font-size: 1.5em;
}

h2 {
  font-size: 1.2em;
}
```

If you define a property value twice, browsers render your web element depending on each rule's position in the cascade. See the section "The cascade" later in the chapter for more information.

Contextual selectors

This selector type is handy when working with advanced CSS. As the name suggests, **contextual selectors** define property values for HTML elements depending on context. Take, for instance, the following example:

```
<p>I am a paragraph.</p>
<p>So am I.</p>
<div id="navigation">
  <p>I am a paragraph within the navigation div.</p>
  <p>Another paragraph within the navigation div.</p>
</div>
```

You can style the page's paragraphs as a whole and then define some specific values for those within the navigation div by using a standard element selector for the former and a contextual selector for the latter:

```
p {
  color: black;
}

#navigation p {
  color: blue;
  font-weight: bold;
}
```

As shown, syntax for contextual selectors (#navigation p) is simple—you just separate the individual selectors with some whitespace. The two rules shown previously have the following result:

- The p rule colors the web page's paragraphs black.
- The #navigation p rule overrides the p rule for paragraphs within the navigation div, coloring them blue and making them bold.

By working with contextual selectors, it's possible to get very specific with regard to styling things on your website; we'll be using these selectors regularly.

There are other types of selectors used for specific tasks. These will be covered as relevant later in the book.

Adding styles to a web page

The most common (and useful) method of applying CSS rules to a web page is by using **external style sheets**. CSS rules are defined in a text document, which is saved with the file suffix .css. This document is attached to an HTML document in one of two ways, both of which require the addition of HTML elements to the head section.

The first method of attaching a CSS file is to use a link tag:

```
<link rel="stylesheet" href="mystylesheet.css" type="text/css"
➥ media="screen" />
```

Remember that we're working with XHTML in this book, hence the trailing slash on the link tag, a tag that has no content.

Alternatively, import the style sheet into the style element:

```
<style type="text/css" media="screen">
/* <![CDATA[ */
@import url(mystylesheet.css);
/* ]]> */
</style>
```

The second of these methods was initially used to "hide" CSS rules from noncompliant browsers, thereby at least giving users of such devices access to the website's content, if not its design. In some browsers (notably Internet Explorer), however, this can cause a "flash" of unstyled content before the page is loaded. This flash doesn't occur when a link element is also present. In the full site designs in Chapter 10, you'll note that both methods are used—@import for importing the main style sheet for screen and link for linking to a print style sheet.

The style tag can also be used to embed CSS directly into the head section of a specific HTML document, like this:

```
<head>
<style type="text/css">
/* <![CDATA[ */
p {
  color: black;
}

#navigation p {
  color: blue;
  font-weight: bold;
}
/* ]]> */
</style>
</head>
```

You'll find that many visual web design tools create CSS in this manner, but adding rules to a style element is only worth doing if you have a one-page website, or if you want to affect tags on a specific page, overriding those in an attached style sheet (see the next section for more information). There's certainly no point in adding styles like this to every page, because updating them would then require every page to be updated, rather than just an external style sheet.

The third method of applying CSS is to do so as an **inline style**, directly in an element's HTML tag:

```
<p style="color: blue;">This paragraph will be displayed in blue.</p>
```

As you can see, this method involves using the style attribute, and it's only of use in very specific, one-off situations. There's no point in using inline styles for all styling on your website—to do so would give few benefits over the likes of archaic font tags. Inline styles also happen to be deprecated in XHTML 1.1, so they're eventually destined for the chop.

The cascade

It's possible to define the rule for a given element multiple times: you can do so in the same style sheet, and several style sheets can be attached to an HTML document. On top of that, you may be using embedded style sheets and inline styles. The **cascade** is a way of dealing with conflicts, and its simple rule is this:

The value closest to the element in question is the one that is applied.

In the following example, the second font-size setting for paragraphs takes precedence because it's closest to paragraphs in the HTML:

```
p {
   font-size: 1.1em;
}

p {
   font-size: 1.2em;
}
```

Subsequently, paragraphs on pages the preceding rule is attached to are rendered at 1.2em. If a similar rule were placed as an embedded style sheet below the imported/linked style sheet, that rule would take precedence, and if one were applied as an inline style (directly in the relevant element), then that would take precedence over all others.

> *Note that it's possible to import or link multiple style sheets in a web page's* head *section. The cascade principle still applies; in other words, any rules in a second attached style sheet override those in the one preceding it.*

CSS uses the concept of inheritance. A document's HTML elements form a strict hierarchy, beginning with html, and then branching into head and body, each of which has numerous descendant elements (such as title and meta for head, and p and img for body). When a style is applied to an element, its descendants—those elements nested within it—often take on CSS property values, unless a more specific style has been applied. However, not all CSS style properties are inherited. See the CSS reference section of this book for more details.

The CSS box model explained

The **box model** is something every designer working with CSS needs a full understanding of, in order to know how elements interact with each other and also how various properties affect an element. Essentially, each element in CSS is surrounded by a box whose dimensions are automated depending on the content. By using width and height properties in CSS, these dimensions can be defined in a specific manner.

You can set **padding** to surround the content and add a **border** and **margins** to the box. A **background image** and **background color** can also be defined. Any background image or color is visible behind the content and padding, but not the margin. The effective space an element takes up is the sum of the box dimensions (which effectively define the available dimensions for the box's contents), padding, border, and margins. Therefore, a 500-pixel-wide box with 20 pixels of padding at each side and a 5-pixel border will actually take up 550 pixels of horizontal space (5 + 20 + 500 + 20 + 5).

> *Note that in some cases, margins between two elements "collapse," leading to only the larger margin value being used.*

THE CSS BOX MODEL HIERARCHY

Content

Here's some sample content, constrained by the padding that's been applied. Here's some sample content, constrained by the padding that's been applied.

Border

Padding*

Background image

Background color

Margin*

* Transparent elements

© Jon Hicks (www.hicksdesign.co.uk)

Creating boilerplates

Every web page looks different, just as every book or magazine is different from every other one. However, under the hood there are often many similarities between sites, and if you author several, you'll soon note that you're doing the same things again and again. With that in mind, it makes sense to create some web page boilerplates—starting points for all of your projects. In the download files, available from the Downloads section of the friends of ED website (www.friendsofed.com), there are two boilerplates folders: basic-boilerplates and advanced-boilerplates. In basic-boilerplates, the XHTML-basic.html web page is a blank XHTML Strict document, and in advanced-boilerplates, XHTML-extended.html adds some handy divs that provide a basic page structure that's common in many web pages, along with some additions to the head section. (The former is used as a quick starting point for many of the tutorials in this book. The latter is perhaps a better starting point for a full website project.) The CSS-with-ToC.css document in advanced-boilerplates uses CSS comments to create sections in the document to house related CSS rules. This is handy when you consider that a CSS document may eventually have dozens of rules in it—this makes it easier for you to be able to find them quickly.

CSS comments look like this: /* this is a comment */, and can be single-line or multiple-line. In the advanced CSS boilerplate, a multiline comment is used for an introduction and table of contents:

```
/*

STYLE SHEET FOR [WEB SITE]
Created by [AUTHOR NAME]
[URL OF AUTHOR]

ToC

  1. defaults
  2. structure
  3. links and navigation
  4. fonts
  5. images

Notes

*/
```

Each section of the document is then headed by a lengthy comment that makes it obvious when a section has begun:

```
/* --------- 1. defaults  --------- */

* {
  margin: 0;
  padding: 0;
  }

body {
  }
```

As you can see, property/value pairs and the closing curly bracket are indented by two tabs in the document (represented by two spaces on this page), which makes it easier to scan vertically through numerous selectors. (Note that for the bulk of this book, the rules aren't formatted in this way, because indenting only the property/value pairs differentiates them more clearly in print; however, the download files all have CSS rules indented as per the recommendations within this section.) Comments can also be used for subheadings, which I tend to indent by one tab:

```
  /* float-clearing rules */
.separator {
  clear: both;
  }
```

Although the bulk of the style sheet's rules are empty, just having a boilerplate to work from saves plenty of time in the long run, ensuring you don't have to key in the same defaults time and time again. Use the one from the download files as the basis for your own, but if you regularly use other elements on a page (such as pull quotes), be sure to add those, too—after all, it's quicker to amend a few existing rules to restyle them than it is to key them in from scratch.

> *Along the same lines as boilerplates, you can save time by creating a snippets folder on your hard drive. Use it to store snippets of code—HTML elements, CSS rules, and so on—that you can reuse on various websites. Many applications have this functionality built in, so make use of it if your preferred application does.*

To show you the power of CSS, we're going to work through a brief exercise using the boilerplates mentioned earlier. Don't worry about understanding everything just yet, because all of the various properties and values shown will be explained later in the book.

Creating, styling, and restyling a web page

Required files	XHTML-basic.html and CSS-default.css from the basic-boilerplates folder.
What you'll learn	How to create, style, and restyle a web page.
Completed files	creating-and-styling-a-web-page.html, creating-and-styling-a-web-page.css, creating-and-styling-a-web-page-2.html, and creating-and-styling-a-web-page-2.css, in the chapter 1 folder.

1. Copy XHTML-basic.html and CSS-default.css to your hard drive and rename them creating-and-styling-a-web-page.html and creating-and-styling-a-web-page.css.

2. Attach the style sheet. Type Creating and styling a web page in the title element to give the page a title, and then amend the @import value so that the style sheet is imported:

```
<style type="text/css" media="screen">
/* <![CDATA[ */
@import url(creating-and-styling-a-web-page.css);
/* ]]> */
</style>
```

3. Add some content. Within the wrapper div, add some basic page content, as shown in the following code block. Note how the heading, paragraph, and quote are marked up using a heading element (<h1></h1>), paragraph element (<p></p>), and block quote element (<blockquote></blockquote>), rather than using styled paragraphs for all of the text-based content. This is semantic markup, as discussed briefly earlier in the chapter.

```
<div id="wrapper">
  <h1>A heading</h1>
  <p>A paragraph of text, which is very exciting&mdash;something
  ➡ that will live on through the generations.</p>
  <blockquote>
    <p>&ldquo;A quote about something, to make
    ➡ people go "hmmmm" in a thoughtful manner.&rdquo;</p>
  </blockquote>
  <p>Another paragraph, with equally exciting text; in fact, it&rsquo;s
  ➡ so exciting, we're not sure it&rsquo;s legal to print.</p>
</div>
```

The items with ampersands and semicolons, such as — and ”, are HTML entities—see Appendix C ("Entities Reference") for more details.

4. Edit some CSS. Save and close the web page and then open the CSS document. Amend the body rule within the defaults section of the CSS. This ensures the text on the page is colored black and that the page's background color is white. The padding value ensures the page content doesn't hug the browser window edges.

```
body {
  font: 62.5%/1.5 Verdana, Arial, Helvetica, sans-serif;
  color: #000000;
  background: #ffffff;
  padding: 20px;
}
```

5. Style the wrapper. Add the following property values to the #wrapper rule to define a fixed width for it and then center it (via the margin property's auto value).

```
#wrapper {
  font-size: 1.2em;
  line-height: 1.5em;
  margin: 0 auto;
  width: 500px;
}
```

6. Style the text. Add the h1 rule as shown, thereby styling the level-one heading:

```
h1 {
  font: 1.5em/1.8em Arial, sans-serif;
  text-transform: uppercase;
}
```

7. Add the blockquote and blockquote p rules as shown. The former adds margins to the sides of the block quote, thereby making the text stand out more, while the latter (a contextual selector) styles paragraphs within block quotes only, making them italic and larger than standard paragraphs. Once you've done this, save your files and preview the web page in a web browser; it should look like the following image. (Don't close the browser at this point.)

```
blockquote {
  margin: 0 100px;
}
blockquote p {
  font-style: italic;
  font-size: 1.2em;
}
```

A HEADING

A paragraph of text, which is very exciting—something that will live on through the generations.

> *"A quote about something, to make people go "hmmmm" in a thoughtful manner."*

Another paragraph, with equally exciting text; in fact, it's so exciting, we're not sure it's legal to print.

8. Duplicate creating-and-styling-a-web-page.css and rename it creating-and-styling-a-web-page-2.css. Open creating-and-styling-a-web-page.html, and amend the @import value, linking to the newly created CSS document:

```
@import url(creating-and-styling-a-web-page-2.css);
```

9. Open creating-and-styling-a-web-page-2.css and switch the values of color and background in the first body rule.

```
body {
  font: 62.5%/1.5 Verdana, Arial, Helvetica, sans-serif;
  color: #ffffff;
  background: #000000;
  padding: 20px;
}
```

10. Replace the text-transform property/value pair from the h1 rule with color: #bbbbbb;. For the blockquote rule, make the following amendments, which add a border to the left and right edges, and some horizontal padding around the block quote's contents.

```
blockquote {
  margin: 0 100px;
  border-left: 3px solid #888888;
  border-right: 3px solid #888888;
  padding: 0 20px;
}
```

11. Finally, amend the blockquote p rule as shown:

```
blockquote p {
  font-weight: bold;
  font-size: 1.0em;
}
```

Refresh the web page in the browser, and you should see it immediately change, looking like that shown in the following image. Effectively, nothing in the web page was changed (you could have overwritten the rules in `creating-and-styling-a-web-page.css` rather than creating a duplicate style sheet)—instead, the web page's design was updated purely by using CSS. (Note that in the download files, there are two sets of documents for this exercise—one with the design as per step 7, and the other as per step 11, the latter of which has the -2 suffix added to the HTML and CSS document file names.)

Although this was a very basic example, the same principle works with all CSS-based design. Create a layout in CSS and chances are that when you come to redesign it, you may not have to change much—or any—of the underlying code. A great example of this idea taken to extremes is css Zen Garden (www.csszengarden.com), whose single web page is radically restyled via dozens of submitted CSS documents.

Working with website content

Before we explore how to create the various aspects of a web page, we're going to briefly discuss working with website content and what you need to consider prior to creating your site. Technology and design aren't the only factors that affect the success of a website. The human element must also be considered. Most of the time, people use the Web to get information of some sort, whether for research purposes or entertainment. Typically, people want to be able to access this information quickly; therefore, a site must be structured in a logical manner. It's imperative that a visitor doesn't spend a great deal of time looking for information that should be easy to find. Remember, there are millions of sites out there, and if yours isn't up to scratch, it's easy for someone to go elsewhere.

> *There are exceptions to the general rule of a website having a structured and logical design—notably sites that are experimental in nature or the equivalent of online art, thereby requiring exploration. In these cases, it may actually be detrimental to present a straightforward and totally logical site, but these cases are strictly a minority.*

In this section, we'll look specifically at information architecture and site maps, page layout, design limitations, and usability.

Information architecture and site maps

Before you begin designing a website, you need to collate and logically organize the information it's going to contain. A **site map** usually forms the basis of a site's navigation, and you should aim to have the most important links immediately visible. What these links actually are depends on the nature of your website, but it's safe to say that prominent links to contact details are a common requirement across all sites. A corporate website may also need prominent links to products, services, and a press area. The resulting site map for a corporate site might resemble the following illustration.

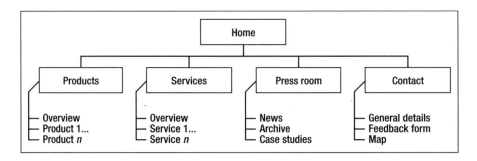

Here, the boxed links serve as the primary navigation and are effectively sections of the website. Underneath each boxed link is a list of subcategories or pages housed within that section. With this structure, it's easy for a newcomer to the site to work out where information is located. When working on site maps, try talking to people who might be interested in the site to get their reaction to your organization of the content. When working for a client, ensure that they sign off on the site map, and that you get feedback on the site map from people at all levels in the company and, if possible, from the company's customers. In all cases, seek the opinions of both the technically minded and relative computer novices, because each may have different ideas about how information should be structured. After all, most web designers are technically minded (or at least well versed in using a computer), and they often forget that most people don't use the Web as regularly as they do. In other words, what seems obvious to you might not be to the general public.

For larger sites, or those with many categories, site maps can be complex. You may have to create several versions before your site map is acceptable. Always avoid burying content too deep. If you end up with a structure in which a visitor has to click several times to access information, it may be worth reworking your site's structure.

Basic web page structure and layout

Once you've sorted out the site map, avoid firing up your graphics package. It's a good idea to sketch out page layout ideas on paper before working on your PC or Mac. Not only is this quicker than using graphics software, but it also allows you to compare many ideas side by side. At this stage, you shouldn't be too precious about the design—work quickly and try to get down as many ideas as possible. From there, you can then refine your ideas, combine the most successful elements of each, and then begin working on the computer.

Although the Web has no hard-and-fast conventions, themes run throughout successful websites, many of which are evident in the following image of a version of my Snub Communications homepage.

A website's navigation should be immediately accessible—you should never have to scroll to get to it. It's also a good idea to have a masthead area that displays the organization's corporate brand (or, if it's a personal site, whatever logo/identity you wish to be remembered by, even if it's only a URL).

The homepage should include an introduction of some sort that briefly explains what the site is about, and it should have some pull-ins to other areas of the site. These pull-ins could be in the form of news items that link to recent product launches, completed projects, and so on.

Most websites require a method for people to contact the site owner, and at least one clear link to a contact page is essential.

Avoid constantly changing the design throughout the site. In print, this sometimes works well and provides variation within a book or magazine. Online, people expect certain things to be in certain places. Constantly changing the position of your navigation, the links themselves, and even the general design and color scheme often creates the impression of an unprofessional site and makes it harder to use.

Ultimately, however your site ends up, and whatever your design, you need to ensure your creation is as usable as possible. A good checklist—even if the points may seem entirely obvious—is as follows:

- Is the site easy to navigate?
- Is it easy for users to locate content on each page?
- Is it easy for users to find what they need on the site?
- Are download times kept to a minimum?
- Is the site suitable and relevant for its target audience?
- Does the site use familiar conventions?

If you can answer yes to all these things, then you should be on the right track!

> *Regarding conventions, it's important not to go overboard. For example, some web gurus are adamant that default link colors should always be used. I think that's sweet and quaint, but somewhat archaic. As long as links are easy to differentiate from other text and styled consistently throughout the site, that's what matters.*

Limitations of web design

Depending on your viewpoint, the inherent limitations of the Web are either a challenge or a frustration. Print designers often feel the latter, and consider themselves hampered by the Web when compared to the relative freedom of print design. Resolution is low, and you can't place whopping great images everywhere, because if you did download speeds would slow to a crawl and all your visitors would go elsewhere.

Columns take on a different role online compared to in print, as they're primarily used to display several areas of content with the same level of prominence. You don't use columns online to display continuous copy, unless you use just one column. If you use several columns, the visitor has to constantly scroll up and down to read everything.

There are other limitations when it comes to rendering text online. There are few web standard fonts (detailed in Chapter 3); serifs, which work well on paper, don't work so well online; and reading text onscreen is already harder than reading print, so complex page backgrounds should be avoided.

And then there are issues like not knowing what an end user's setup is, and therefore having to consider monitor resolution and color settings, what browser is being used, and even the various potential setups of web browsers. Do you go for a **liquid design**, which stretches with the browser window, or a **fixed design**, which is flanked by blank space at larger monitor resolutions?

Don't worry, this isn't a pop quiz. These are questions that will be answered in this book, but I mention them now to get you thinking and realizing that planning is key with regard to web design. Because this is largely a book about concepts, ideas, and techniques, we won't return to talk about planning very much, hence drumming it in at this early stage.

Also, don't get disheartened by the previous limitations spiel. The Web is a truly magnificent medium, and for every downside there's something amazing to counter it. So what if the resolution's low? Nowhere else can you so effortlessly combine photography, video, sound, and text. Sure, it's all well and good to read a magazine, but the Web enables interaction, and navigation can be nonlinear, enabling you to link words within specific pieces to other articles on your website or elsewhere on the Internet. Don't get me wrong: the Web is a great thing. If it weren't, I wouldn't be interested in it, wouldn't be designing for it, and wouldn't be writing this book.

mentum, magna diam molestie sapien, n
uam iac

iverra g
Morbi a
iscing s
etium n
. Nulla

usce ult
m meti

mollis.

d pharetra gravida, orci magna rhoncus n
ullam sit amet enim. Suspendisse id velit

iquam erat volutpat. Sed quis velit. Nulla
osuere sapien. Nam consectetuer. Sed alic
ctus nunc ullamcorper orci, fermentum bi
orttitor ligula eu dolor. Maecenas vitae nul
am magna enim, accumsan eu, blandit se

uisque facilisis erat a dui. Nam malesuada
net rhoncus ornare, erat elit consectetuer
oin tincidunt, velit vel porta elementum,
iquet massa pede eu diam. Aliquam iaculis
cilisis.

In this chapter:

- Creating XHTML documents
- Understanding document type definitions
- Using meta tags
- Attaching external documents
- Working with the body section
- Using CSS for web page backgrounds
- Commenting your work

Starting with the essentials

You might wonder what's meant by this chapter's title: web page essentials. This chapter will run through everything you need to do with a web page prior to working on the layout and content, including creating the initial documents, attaching external documents to HTML files, and dealing with the head section of the web page. Little of this is a thrill with regard to visual design, which is why many designers ignore the topics we'll cover, or stick their fingers in their ears, hum loudly, and wish it would all go away (and then probably get rather odd looks from nearby colleagues). However, as the chapter's title states, everything we'll be talking about is *essential* for any quality web page, even if you don't see exciting things happening visually.

This chapter also explores web page backgrounds, which, although they should be used sparingly and with caution, often come in handy. It's worth bearing in mind that some aspects discussed here will crop up later in the book. For example, CSS techniques used to attach backgrounds to a web page can be used to attach a background to *any* web page element (be that a div, table, heading, or paragraph). But before we get into any CSS shenanigans, we'll put our CSS cheerleading team on hold and look at how to properly construct an XHTML document.

Document defaults

As mentioned in Chapter 1, we'll be working with XHTML markup in this book rather than HTML. Although XHTML markup differs slightly from HTML, the file suffix for XHTML web pages remains .html (or .htm if you swear by old-fashioned 8.3 DOS naming techniques).

Although XHTML's stricter rules make it easier to work with than HTML, you need to be aware of the differences in the basic document structure. In HTML, many designers are used to starting out with something like the following code:

```
<html>
  <head>
    <title></title>
  </head>
```

```
    <body>
    </body>
  </html>
```

But in XHTML, a basic, blank document awaiting content may well look like this (although there are variations):

```
<!DOCTYPE html PUBLIC "-//W3C//DTD XHTML 1.0 Strict//EN"
    "http://www.w3.org/TR/xhtml1/DTD/xhtml1-strict.dtd">
<html xmlns="http://www.w3.org/1999/xhtml" xml:lang="en" lang="en">
  <head>
    <meta http-equiv="content-type" content="text/html;
    ➥ charset=utf-8" />
    <title></title>
  </head>
  <body>
  </body>
</html>
```

Although this is similar to the minimal HTML document, there are important differences. The most obvious is found at the beginning of the document: a DOCTYPE **declaration** that states what **document type definition** (**DTD**) you are following (and no, I'm not shouting—DOCTYPE is spelled in all caps according to the W3C).

```
<!DOCTYPE html PUBLIC "-//W3C//DTD XHTML 1.0 Strict//EN"
    "http://www.w3.org/TR/xhtml1/DTD/xhtml1-strict.dtd">
```

The DTD indicates to a web browser what markup you're using, thereby enabling the browser to accurately display the document in question (or at least as accurately as it can—as shown in Chapter 9, browsers have various quirks, even when you're using 100% validated markup).

Next is the html start tag, which contains both a **namespace** and a **language declaration**. The first of those is intended to reduce the ambiguity of defined elements within the web page. (In XML, elements can mean different things, depending on what technology is being used.) The language declaration indicates the (default) language used for the document's contents. This can assist various devices, for example enabling a screen reader in correctly pronouncing words on a page, rather than assuming what the language is. (Also, internal content can have language declarations applied to override the default, for example when embedding some French within an English page.) The xml:lang attribute is a reserved attribute of XML, while the lang attribute is a fallback, used for browsers that lack XML support. Should the values of the two attributes differ, xml:lang outranks lang.

```
<html xmlns="http://www.w3.org/1999/xhtml" xml:lang ="en" lang="en">
```

You'll also notice that a meta tag appears in the head section of the document:

```
<meta http-equiv="content-type" content="text/html; charset=utf-8" />
```

To pass validation tests, you must declare your content type, which can be done using this meta element. Here, the defined character set is UTF-8 (Unicode), the recommended default encoding, and one that supports many languages and characters (so many characters needn't be converted to HTML entities).

There are other sets in use, too, for the likes of Hebrew, Nordic, and Eastern European languages, and if you're using them, the charset value would be changed accordingly. Although www.iana.org/assignments/character-sets provides a thorough character set listing, and www.czyborra.com/charsets/iso8859.html contains useful character set diagrams, it's tricky to wade through it all, so listed here are some common values and their associated languages:

- **ISO-8859-1 (Latin1)**: Western European and American, including Afrikaans, Albanian, Basque, Catalan, Danish, Dutch, English, Faeroese, Finnish, French, Galician, German, Icelandic, Irish, Italian, Norwegian, Portuguese, Spanish, and Swedish.
- **ISO-8859-2 (Latin2)**: Central and Eastern European, including Croatian, Czech, Hungarian, Polish, Romanian, Serbian, Slovak, and Slovene.
- **ISO-8859-3 (Latin3)**: Southern European, including Esperanto, Galician, Maltese, and Turkish. (See also ISO-8859-9.)
- **ISO-8859-4 (Latin4)**: Northern European, including Estonian, Greenlandic, Lappish, Latvian, and Lithuanian. (See also ISO-8859-6.)
- **ISO-8859-5**: Cyrillic, including Bulgarian, Byelorussian, Macedonian, Russian, Serbian, and Ukrainian.
- **ISO-8859-6**: Arabic.
- **ISO-8859-7**: Modern Greek.
- **ISO-8859-8**: Hebrew.
- **ISO-8859-9 (Latin5)**: European. Replaces Icelandic-specific characters with Turkish ones.
- **ISO-8859-10 (Latin6)**: Nordic, including Icelandic, Inuit, and Lappish.

For an overview of the ISO-8859 standard, see http://en.wikipedia.org/wiki/ISO_8859.

DOCTYPE declarations explained

XHTML 1.0 offers you three choices of DOCTYPE declaration: XHTML Strict, XHTML Transitional, and XHTML Frameset. In the initial example, the DOCTYPE declaration is the first thing in the web page. This is always how it should be—you should never have any content or HTML elements prior to the DOCTYPE declaration. (An exception is the XML declaration; see the section "What about the XML Declaration?" later in this chapter.)

XHTML Strict

For code purists, this is the DTD that does not allow the use of presentational markup or deprecated elements:

```
<!DOCTYPE html PUBLIC "-//W3C//DTD XHTML 1.0 Strict//EN"
    "http://www.w3.org/TR/xhtml1/DTD/xhtml1-strict.dtd">
```

It forces a stricter way of working, but tends to ensure greater browser compatibility when you play by its rules, and so it's used throughout this book.

XHTML Transitional

In common usage, this friendly DTD enables you to get away with using deprecated elements, and is useful for those rare occasions where you'd otherwise be banging your head against a brick wall, trying to work out how to get around using one of those few still-useful old tags:

```
<!DOCTYPE html PUBLIC "-//W3C//DTD XHTML 1.0 Transitional//EN"
    "http://www.w3.org/TR/xhtml1/DTD/xhtml1-transitional.dtd">
```

Note that even if you end up solely using strict markup, the transitional DTD still ensures browsers generally render elements correctly.

XHTML Frameset

Frames are a relic, and are rarely used online. However, for backward compatibility and for those designers who still use them, there is a frameset-specific DTD (individual pages within a frameset require one of the aforementioned DTDs):

```
<!DOCTYPE html PUBLIC "-//W3C//DTD XHTML 1.0 Frameset//EN"
    "http://www.w3.org/TR/xhtml1/DTD/xhtml1-frameset.dtd">
```

> *Note that in Gecko browsers, XHTML Transitional and Frameset are rendered in "almost standards" mode. The main difference between this and standards mode is in the formatting of tables, which is designed to largely match that of Internet Explorer, making sliced-images-in-tables layouts less likely to fall apart.*

HTML DOCTYPEs

If you wish to work with HTML markup rather than XHTML, your documents still need a DOCTYPE to pass validation. The three DOCTYPEs for HTML 4.01 more or less match those for HTML: Strict, Transitional, and Frameset.

```
<!DOCTYPE HTML PUBLIC "-//W3C//DTD HTML 4.01//EN"
    "http://www.w3.org/TR/html4/strict.dtd">
```

```
<!DOCTYPE HTML PUBLIC "-//W3C//DTD HTML 4.01 Transitional//EN"
    "http://www.w3.org/TR/html4/loose.dtd">
```

```
<!DOCTYPE HTML PUBLIC "-//W3C//DTD HTML 4.01 Transitional//EN"
    "http://www.w3.org/TR/html4/frameset.dtd">
```

Partial DTDs

Always include full DTDs. Some older web design packages and online resources provide incomplete or outdated ones that can switch browsers into "quirks" mode, displaying your site as though it were written with browser-specific, old-fashioned markup and CSS, and rendering the page accordingly (as opposed to complying strictly with web standards. The argument for quirks mode was largely down to backward-compatibility. For example, it enabled Internet Explorer 6 to display CSS layouts with the box model used by Internet Explorer 5. This type of fix is today considered archaic—see Chapter 9 for modern methods of backward compatibility, including conditional comments. For more on quirks mode, read Wikipedia's article at http://en.wikipedia.org/wiki/Quirks_mode.

For the record, an example of an incomplete DTD looks like this:

```
<!DOCTYPE html PUBLIC "-//W3C//DTD XHTML 1.0 Transitional//EN"
    "/DTD/xhtml1-transitional.dtd">
```

In this case, the URI (web address) is relative. Unless you have the DTD in the relevant place on your own website, the browser will display the page this DTD is included on in quirks mode. (And, quite frankly, if you do have the DTD on your website instead of using the one on the W3C's site, you are very odd indeed.) The same thing happens if you leave out DTDs entirely. Therefore, *always* include a DTD and *always* ensure it's complete.

What about the XML declaration?

As stated earlier, there is an exception to the DTD being the first thing on a web page. The one thing that can precede it is an **XML declaration** (often referred to as the **XML prolog**). This unassuming piece of markup looks like this (assuming you're using Unicode encoding):

```
<?xml version="1.0" encoding="utf-8"?>
```

The tag tells the browser which version of XML is being used and that the character encoding is UTF-8.

> For an overview of character sets, see the following URLs: www.w3.org/International/O-charset.html, www.w3.org/International/O-charset-lang.html, and www.w3.org/International/O-charset-list.html.

Some web design applications add this tag by default when creating new XHTML documents, and the W3C recommends using it to declare the character encoding used within your document. However, I don't, because versions of Internet Explorer before version 7 take one look at the XML declaration, recoil in horror, and then spit out your site in a way rather different from how you intended (the playfully-referred-to quirks mode discussed earlier).

Of course, Internet Explorer 6's share of the market is in decline, but it's likely to take at least a couple of years from Internet Explorer 7's release for its predecessor to become extinct. Therefore, because the XML declaration has the potential to cause havoc with a fair chunk of your likely audience, it's cause for concern. However, as mentioned earlier, there's an alternative, compliant, totally safe option that you can use instead:

```
<meta http-equiv="content-type" content="text/html; charset=utf-8" />
```

Using the preceding meta tag works fine, it does the same job as one of the main roles of the XML declaration (stating the page's character encoding), and no browsers choke on it. The net result is that everyone goes home happy, and we can finally start talking about the next part of a web page.

> *Although the* content-type meta *tag can be placed anywhere in the head of a web page, it's worth noting that some browsers don't get the right encoding unless this tag is the first element within the* head *section.*

The head section

The head section of a web page contains information about the document, the majority of which is invisible to the end user. Essentially, it acts as a container for the tags outlined in this section (which should generally be added in the same order that we run through them).

Page titles

Many designers are so keen to get pages online that they forget to provide a title for each page. Titles are added using the title element, as follows:

```
<title>IMAGES FROM ICELAND - photography by Craig Grannell</title>
```

The title is usually shown at the top of the browser window (and sometimes within the active tab, if you're using a browser that has a tabbed interface); the results of the previous code block are shown in the following image.

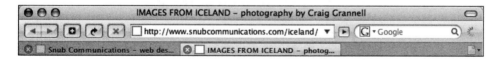

By default, web design packages usually do one of the following things with regard to the title element:

- Add no content.
- Set the title element's content as "Untitled Document."
- Set the title element's content as the application's name.

The first of these results in no title being displayed for the web page and is invalid XHTML, while the second means your page joins the legions online that have no title. The third option is just as bad: using your web page to advertise the application you used to create it. Therefore, add a title to every web page you create—in fact, make it one of the first things you do, so you don't forget.

With regard to the content of your web page titles, bear in mind that this is often the most prominent thing returned in search engine results pages. Keep titles clear, concise, and utterly to the point. Use too many words and the title will be clipped; use too few (or try to get arty with characters) and you may end up with something that stumps search engines and potential visitors, too.

Generally speaking, for the homepage at least, it's good to include the name of the site or organization, followed by an indication of the site's reason for existence (and author or location, if relevant). For instance, as shown in the following image, the Snub Communications title includes the organization's name, the primary services it offers, and its author.

Snub Communications - web design and copywriting by Craig Grannell ...
Snub Communications provides quality design and copywriting services for anyone that wants a top-notch, cost-effective solution.
www.snubcommunications.com/ - 10k - Cached - Similar pages

Some designers use the same title throughout their site. This is a bad idea—web page titles are used as visual indicators by visitors trawling bookmarks or their browser's history. This is why I generally tend to use titles as a breadcrumb navigation of sorts, showing where a page sits within the website's hierarchy, like this:

```
<title>Company name - Services - Service name</title>
```

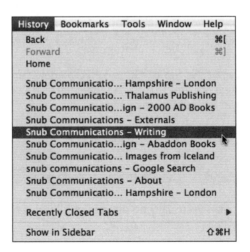

meta tags and search engines

The Web was once awash with tips for tweaking meta tags. This was because although these tags are primarily there to provide information about the document, they were initially what most search engines used to categorize web pages and return results. It didn't take long for the shortfalls in the system to become apparent and for designers to abuse them, and so many meta tags are today considered redundant.

Generally, search engines now trawl the content of the web page (including the contents of the title element), trying to match a user's search with the most important content on the page. This is why strong use of semantic markup is essential—by correctly utilizing headings, paragraphs, and other structural elements for text, and by avoiding overuse of images for text content, modern search engines get a better handle on your content and can therefore—in theory—return more accurate results to users.

Tagging and other forms of metadata are also becoming an increasingly popular search engine aid, for both internal search engines—those within the site itself—and for the search engines that return results from the whole of the Internet. Both are a means of adding information to a website to aid users. Visual tags may show a number of keywords associated with a blog posting, for example, enabling a user to see if something interests them by the size of the word; search engines will latch onto the keywords and the content of the piece itself. Metadata enables you to "embed" information in the page, aiding all manner of devices, and potentially creating networks and links to like information. A form of metadata—microformats—is explored in Chapter 8.

Despite this, it's still worth being mindful of meta tags when creating web pages, for those search engines that still make use of them—just be aware that they're not nearly as important as they once were (with the possible exception of description).

Keywords and descriptions

Unless you're totally new to web design, it's likely you'll be aware of the keywords and description meta tags:

```
<meta name="keywords" content="keywords, separated, by, commas" />
<meta name="description" content="A short description about the Web
➡ site" />
```

> *Because* meta *tags are empty tags, they must be closed using a space and trailing slash, as explained in Chapter 1.*

The first of these tags, keywords, should contain a list of words that users might type into a search engine to find your site. Because of abuse (websites including thousands of words in the meta tag content, in order to try and create a catchall in search engine results pages), such lists are rarely used these days. Instead, search engines tend to look at the entire content of a page to determine its relevance to someone's search. If you choose to include this element in your web page, 30 or fewer words and short phrases are sufficient.

The contents of the description's content attribute are returned by some search engines in a results page along with the web page's title. As with the title, keep things succinct, otherwise the description will be cropped. Most search engines display a maximum of 200 characters, so 25 well-chosen words are just about all you can afford.

revisit-after, robots, and author

Other meta tags also use name and content attributes. These tags assist search engines. In the following example, the first tag provides an indication of how often they should return (useful for regularly updated sites), and the second tag states whether the page should be indexed or not.

```
<meta name="Revisit-After" content="30 Days" />
<meta name="robots" content="all,index" />
```

The content attribute of the robots meta tag can instead include the values noindex and none, in order to block indexing, and follow or nofollow, depending on whether you want search engine robots to follow links from the current page or not.

The author meta tag is of less use to search engines, and typically includes the page author's name and home URL. Designers sometimes use it as a means to declare the author's name and details, but it has little use beyond that.

```
<meta name="author" content="Craig Grannell for
➥ www.snubcommunications.com." />
```

Attaching external documents

A web page—as in the (X)HTML document—is primarily designed to contain content that is structured in markup. Presentation should be dealt with via external CSS documents, and behavior via external scripting documents. Although it is possible to work with the likes of JavaScript and CSS within an HTML document, this goes against the modular nature of good web design. It's far easier to create, edit, and maintain a site if you work with separate files for each technology. (The exception is if your "site" is only a single page, therefore making it sensible to include everything in a single document.)

As already mentioned, XHTML documents are text files that are saved with the suffix .html (or .htm). CSS and JavaScript files are also text documents, and their file suffixes are .css and .js, respectively. When you start a project, having already set the relevant DOCTYPE and added meta tags, it's a good idea to create blank CSS and JavaScript files and to attach them to your web page, so you can then work on any element as you wish.

Attaching external CSS files: The link method

In the previous chapter, you were shown how to attach CSS to a web page (see the section "Adding styles to a web page" in Chapter 1), and we'll briefly recap the process here. There are two methods of attaching an external CSS file: the link method and the @import method.

The `link` tag specifies a relationship between the linked document and the document it's being linked to. In the context of attaching a CSS file, it looks something like this:

```
<link rel="StyleSheet" href="stylesheet.css" type="text/css"
➥ media="all" />
```

The attributes used are the following:

- `rel`: Defines the relation from the parent document to the target
- `href`: The location of the target file
- `type`: The MIME type of the target document
- `media`: The target medium of the target document

The `title` attribute is also occasionally used with the `link` element, either to provide additional information or to be used as a "hook" for the likes of a style sheet switcher (see www.alistapart.com/stories/alternate/ for more information). Any style sheet lacking a `title` attribute (and a `rel` value of stylesheet) is **persistent**—always affecting a document. These are by far the most common types of style sheets. A **preferred** style sheet also takes a `title` along with the `rel` attribute and only one such style sheet can be used at a time—typically the first, with subsequent ones ignored. On pages that offer **alternate** style sheets (typically via a style switcher), the persistent styles are always used, and the first preferred is the additional default; the preferred styles, however, can be swapped out by selecting an alternative style sheet. (Note that in Firefox, you should avoid adding a `title` attribute to any style sheet for print, because otherwise the content may not print.)

In the previous example, the `media` attribute is set to `all`, specifying that this style sheet is intended for all devices. But it's feasible to attach multiple style sheets to a web page, and set the `media` attribute of each one to a different type. For instance, in the following example, two CSS files are attached, one for screen and the other for printed output:

```
<link rel="stylesheet" href="stylesheet.css" type="text/css"
➥ media="screen" />
<link rel="stylesheet" href="printcss.css" type="text/css"
➥ media="print" />
```

There are other media types, including aural, braille, projection, and tv, but few are supported well. However, in Chapter 10, we'll look at style sheets for print, which is one of the alternatives to screen that is supported reasonably well in mainstream browsers.

Attaching CSS files: The @import method

A problem with the `link` method is that obsolete browsers see the style sheet but don't understand it. This can result in garbled layouts—and often in unusable websites for those unfortunate enough to have to deal with such arcane web browsers. The solution is to hide the CSS from such browsers by using a command that they don't understand and so will ignore. This is often referred to as the @import method.

As shown in the following example, the style element is used to do this:

```
<style type="text/css" media="all">
/* <![CDATA[ */
@import url(stylesheet.css);
/* ]]> */
</style>
```

> The CSS specifications permit the use of the style sheet location as a quoted string instead of enclosing it in url(). The method shown here is more commonly supported, though.

The following image shows the result in obsolete browsers, such as Netscape 4. The CSS is hidden, so just the content is displayed.

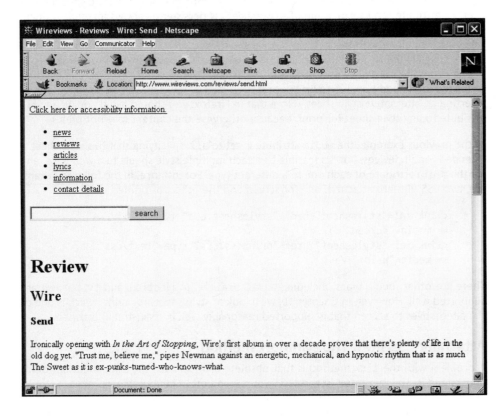

However, compliant browsers see the CSS and render the site as shown in the following image.

This method isn't perfect. Some browsers think they can deal with CSS but can't, meaning they understand @import, import the CSS, and then screw up the display anyway. Also, some versions of Internet Explorer in some cases offer a flash of unstyled content, although a workaround there is to have a link or script element in the web page's head section (which will be likely, since sites should carry a print style sheet in addition to the one for screen, or work with JavaScript). In any case, if you have to cater for obsolete and alternative devices, using @import is probably the best bet, ensuring your site is accessible to (almost) all.

Attaching favicons and JavaScript

Favicons are those little icons you often see in your browser's address bar. They are attached using the link method discussed earlier, although you only need to include three attributes: rel, href, and type. The type value can change, depending on the file type of your favicon. For example, image/png is fine if you've used a PNG.

```
<link rel="shortcut icon" href="favicon.ico" type="image/x-icon"/>
```

These days, favicons are almost ubiquitous, and they provide users with an additional visual clue to a site's identity. Although not particularly useful on their own, they can be handy when trawling through a large bookmarks list—you can look for the icon rather than the text. However, don't rely on them instead of a good web page title—they should merely be an additional tool in your arsenal.

Attaching a JavaScript file to a web page is similarly painless. You do so via the script element, as follows:

```
<script type="text/javascript" src="javascriptfile.js"></script>
```

> *You may have seen the* language *attribute used within* script *start tags, but this is deprecated and won't validate if you're using XHTML Strict.*

Checking paths

When working with external files, ensure paths between files are complete and don't become broken as files are moved around, otherwise your web page may lose track of the CSS and JavaScript, affecting its display and functionality. If you're using document-relative links (i.e., links relative to the current document), remember to amend paths accordingly.

> *If you're not sure how to work with the different types of links—absolute, relative, and root-relative—read the guide in Chapter 5, at the beginning of the "Creating and styling web page links" section.*

The body section

The body element is used to define the body of a web page, and it contains the document's content. *No document content should ever be placed outside of the* body *element.* Sorry for the italic type, but this is something I see on a regular basis, so I wanted to nip that one in the bud.

Although the body element has a number of possible attributes that can be included in its start tag, mostly for defining link state color and backgrounds, these should be avoided. This is because such things should be dealt with using CSS, which enables you to define values on a site-wide basis, rather than having to do so for each individual page. The body element attributes include the likes of alink, link, and vlink for defining link colors; text for defining the default text color; and background and bgcolor for defining a background pattern and color. There are also a number of proprietary attributes that were intended to set padding around web page content, which aren't worth mentioning further. In this next section, we'll look at the contemporary way of setting content margins and padding, default font and color, and web page backgrounds.

Content margins and padding in CSS

Page margins and padding are easy to define using CSS. By setting these values once in an external file, you can update settings site-wide by uploading an amended style sheet rather than every single page on your site that has an amended body tag.

Furthermore, in terms of page weight, CSS is more efficient. If using old methods, to cater for all browsers, you set the following body attributes:

```
<body marginwidth="0" marginheight="0" topmargin="0" leftmargin="0"
➡ bottommargin="0" rightmargin="0">
```

The equivalent in CSS is the following:

```
body {
  margin: 0;
  padding: 0;
}
```

> *If a CSS setting is 0, there's no need to state a unit such as px or em.*

The reason both `margin` and `padding` are set to 0 is because some browsers define a default padding value. Therefore, even if you set all body margins to 0, there would still be a gap around your page content. Setting both the margin and padding to 0 in the body rule ensures that all browsers display your content with no gaps around it.

Zeroing margins and padding on all elements

Although the previous block of code is clean and efficient, it isn't something I use in my websites. The reason for this is that browsers place default (and sometimes varying) margins around various elements other than the page's body, too. Therefore, my CSS boilerplates always include the following:

```
* {
  margin: 0;
  padding: 0;
}
```

The selector, *, is the **universal selector**, and the declaration therefore applies to all elements on the web page. In other words, add this rule to your CSS, and *all* default margins and padding for *all* elements are removed, enabling you to start from scratch in all browsers and define explicit values for those elements that need them.

Working with CSS shorthand for boxes

Both of the previous two code examples use CSS shorthand, and this is something that is useful to get to grips with, in order to create the most efficient and easy-to-update CSS. The previous example showed how to set *all* margins and padding values to 0, and this was done in shorthand instead of writing out every single value. How CSS shorthand works for boxes is like this:

- **A single value (**`margin: 10px;`**):** This is applied to all edges.
- **Two values (**`margin: 10px 20px;`**):** The first setting (10px) is applied to the top and bottom edges. The second setting (20px) is applied to both the left and right edges (20px each, not in total).
- **Three values (**`margin: 10px 20px 30px;`**):** The first setting (10px) is applied to the top edge. The second setting (20px) is applied to both the left and right edges. The third setting (30px) is applied to the bottom edge.
- **Four settings (**`margin: 10px 20px 30px 40px;`**):** Settings are applied clockwise from the top (i.e., top: 10px; right: 20px; bottom: 30px; left: 40px).

Shorthand's benefits become obvious when comparing CSS shorthand with the equivalent properties and values written out in full. For instance, the following shorthand

```
#box {
  margin: 0;
  padding: 0 100px;
}
```

looks like this when written out in full:

```
#box {
  margin-top: 0;
  margin-right: 0;
  margin-bottom: 0;
  margin-left: 0;
  padding-top: 0;
  padding-right: 100px;
  padding-bottom: 0;
  padding-left: 100px;
}
```

Whether or not you use shorthand is up to you. Some designers swear by it and others because of it. Some web design applications have options to "force" shorthand or avoid it entirely. I reckon it's a good thing: CSS documents are usually more logical and shorter because of shorthand. But if you don't agree, feel free to keep on defining margins and padding as relevant for every edge of every element.

Setting a default font and font color

As mentioned earlier, the body start tag was historically used to house attributes for dealing with default text and background colors, link colors, and background images. In CSS, link styles are dealt with separately (see Chapter 5). We'll look at how to apply backgrounds later in this chapter.

At this point, it's worth noting that, when working with CSS, the body selector is often used to set a default font family and color for the website. We'll discuss working with text in more depth in the next chapter, but for now, check out the following CSS:

```
body {
  font-family: Verdana, Arial, Helvetica, sans-serif;
  color: #000000;
  background-color: #ffffff;
}
```

This is straightforward. The font-family property sets a default font (in this case, Verdana) and fallback fonts in case the first choice isn't available on the user's system. The list must end with a generic family, such as sans-serif or serif, depending on your other choices. The fonts are separated by commas in the list, and if you're using multiple-word fonts, they must be quoted ("Courier New", not Courier New).

The color property's value defines the default color of text throughout the site. In the preceding example, its value is #000000, which is the hexadecimal (hex) value for black (when defining colors in CSS, it's most common to use hex values, although you can use comma-separated RGB values if you wish). It's also advisable where possible to add a background color for accessibility; in this case, the background color is #ffffff—hex for white.

> Although it's possible to set a default size (and other property values) for text in the body declaration, we'll leave that for now, and instead explore how best to do so in the following chapter.

Web page backgrounds

Web page backgrounds used to be commonplace, but they became unpopular once designers figured out that visitors to web pages didn't want their eyes wrenched out by gaudy tiled background patterns. With text being as hard to read onscreen as it is, it's adding insult to injury to inflict some nasty paisley mosaic background (or worse) on the poor reader, too.

But, as affordable monitors continue to increase in size and resolution, designers face a conundrum. If they're creating a liquid design that stretches to fit the browser window, text can become unreadable, because the eye finds it hard to scan text in wide columns. And if they're creating a fixed-width design, large areas of the screen often end up blank. It's for the latter design style that backgrounds can be useful, both in drawing the eye to the content and providing some visual interest outside of the content area.

Like most things related to design, the use and style of backgrounds is subjective, but some rules are worth bearing in mind. The most obvious is that a background should not distract from your content. If you're using background images, keep them simple, and when you're using color, ensure that the contrast and saturation with the page's background color is fairly low, but the contrast with the text content over the background is very high. Also, unless you're using a subtle watermark, it's generally bad form to put complex images underneath text (a soft gradient or simple geometric shape can sometimes be OK, however)—the low resolution of the Web means it's harder to read text than the print-based equivalent, and you don't want to make this even tougher! Also, because backgrounds are typically ancillary content, they should not significantly increase the loading time of the page.

Web page backgrounds in CSS

Backgrounds are added to web page elements using a number of properties, as described in the sections that follow.

background-color

This property sets the background color of the element. In the following example, the page's body background color has been set to #ffffff (which is hex for white):

```
body {
  background-color: #ffffff;
}
```

background-image

This property sets a background image for the relevant element:

```
body {
  background-image: url(background_image.jpg);
}
```

By using this CSS, you end up with a tiled background, as shown in the following image.

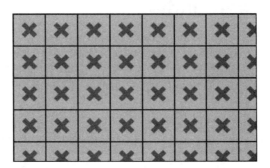

background-repeat

The properties explored so far mimic the range offered by deprecated HTML attributes, but CSS provides you with control over the background's tiling and positioning. The background-repeat property can take four values, the default of which is repeat, creating the tiled background just shown.

If background-repeat is set to no-repeat, the image is shown just once, as in the following illustration.

If this property is set to repeat-x, the image tiles horizontally only.

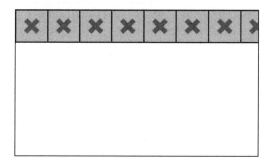

And if the property is set to repeat-y, the image tiles vertically only.

background-attachment

This property has two possible values: scroll and fixed. The default is scroll, in which the background works as normal, scrolling with the rest of the page. If you set the value to fixed, the background image remains stationary while the remainder of the page scrolls.

background-position

This property's values set the origin of the background by using two values that relate to the horizontal and vertical position. The default background-position value is 0 0 (the top left of the web page).

Along with keywords (center, left, and right for horizontal positioning; center, top, and bottom for vertical positioning), you can use percentages and pixel values. It's possible to use a combination of percentages and pixel sizes, but you cannot mix keywords with either. Therefore, it's recommended that designers stick with using percentages and pixel values—after all, keyword positioning can be emulated with numbers anyway (left top being the same as 0 0, for instance). When setting values, they should always be defined in the order horizontal-vertical.

When using keywords, it's also recommended to use the order horizontal-vertical, because both percentage- and pixel-based background positioning use this order, and it's simpler to remember a single rule. In the following example, the background would be positioned on the left of the web page and positioned in the vertical center of the content:

```
body {
  background-image: url(background_image.gif);
  background-repeat: no-repeat;
  background-position: left center;
}
```

Again, when using percentages or pixel values, the first value relates to the horizontal position and the second to the vertical. So, to create the equivalent of the keyword example, you'd use the following CSS:

```
body {
  background-image: url(background_image.gif);
  background-repeat: no-repeat;
  background-position:  0 50%;
}
```

Note, however, when using background-position with the body element, that browsers disagree slightly on where the background should be positioned vertically if the page content isn't taller than the viewing area. Internet Explorer and Safari assume the body is the full view area height when there's no content, thereby setting an image with a background-position value of 50% 50% directly in the center of the viewing area. Firefox and Opera instead assume the body has an effective height of 0, thereby placing the background vertically at the top of the view area (in fact, you only see the bottom half). For consistency across browsers in this case, you can define both background-position and background-attachment (as fixed), although this means the background will not scroll with the page content.

CSS shorthand for web backgrounds

As when defining margins and padding, you can use shorthand for web background values, bundling them into a single background property, although it's worth stating that the shorthand value overrides any previous settings in a CSS file for individual background properties. (For instance, if you use individual settings to define the background image, and then subsequently use the shorthand for setting the color, the background image will most likely not appear.)

When using shorthand, you can set the values in any order. Here's an example:

```
body {
  background: #ffffff url(background_image.gif) no-repeat fixed 50%
  ➥ 10px;
}
```

Generally speaking, it's best to use shorthand over separate background properties—it's quicker to type and easier to manage. You also don't have to explicitly define every one of the values; if you don't, the values revert to their defaults. Therefore, the following is acceptable:

```
body {
  background: #ffffff url(background_image.gif) no-repeat;
}
```

Because the background-attachment value hasn't been specified, this background would scroll with the page, and because the background-position value hasn't been defined, the background would be positioned at 0%, 0%—the top left of the browser window.

Web page background ideas

Before finishing up this section on web page backgrounds, we'll run through some examples that show the CSS and the result, along with the background image used. The files within the basic-boilerplates folder can be used as starting points for web pages and CSS documents. The images used in each case are in the chapter 2 folder of the download files, and these should be placed in the same folder as the HTML and CSS document, unless you amend path values accordingly.

Rename the files as appropriate for each example, ensuring you import the relevant CSS file via the HTML document's @import line.

For the HTML document, add several paragraphs within the existing div element that has an id value of wrapper, as in the following code block (which, for space reasons, shows only a single truncated paragraph—add more than this!):

```
<div id="wrapper">
  <p>...</p>
</div>
```

In CSS, there are also some common elements to add to the boilerplate. For the #wrapper rule, add some padding to ensure the content within doesn't hug the box's edges, and a background rule to color the box's background white. Also, the width value defines the width of the box's content, while the margin settings center the box horizontally. (The method will be discussed further in other chapters, but by setting 0 auto as the margin values, vertical margins are removed and horizontal margins are set to auto, which center the box horizontally in the browser window.)

49

```
#wrapper {
  padding: 18px;
  background: #ffffff;
  width: 500px;
  margin: 0 auto;
}
```

Note that in the download files, in order to keep things modular there are two #wrapper rules in the CSS, and that's what's assumed in the previous code block. However, if you prefer, add the property/value pairs from the previous code block to the style sheet's existing #wrapper rule. The same is true for many of the rules, such as the body rules in the following subsections.

> *Files at this point, ready for the following examples, are available in the* chapter 2 *folder of the download files (at* www.friendsofed.com/downloads.html*), named* backgrounds-default.html *and* backgrounds-default.css.

Adding a background pattern

The following CSS can be used to add a patterned, tiled background to your web page:

```
body {
  background: #ffffff url(background-tile.gif);
}
```

The following screenshot shows a page with a diagonal cross pattern, although you could alternatively use diagonal stripes, horizontal stripes, squares, or other simple shapes.

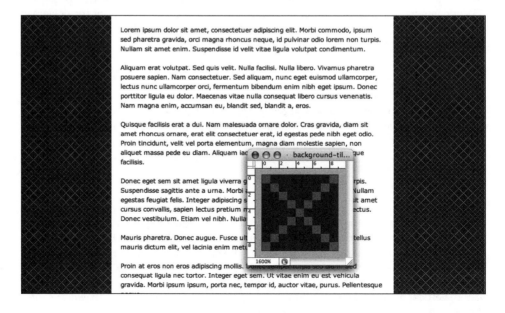

2

Note that if you remove many of the paragraphs from the web page, the white background color ends with the content, since in CSS a container's size by default only stretches to that of its content.

Drop shadows

The following image shows a page with a content area and drop shadow.

This effect was achieved by creating the depicted background image and tiling it vertically. In the body rule, the position was set to 50% 0 in order to position the background centrally on the horizontal axis. The background color of the web page is the same as the solid background on the image itself, and so the image and color seamlessly blend.

```
body {
    background: #878787 url(background-drop-shadow.gif) 50% 0 repeat-y;
}
```

Regarding the white area of the image, this is 536 pixels wide. This is because the wrapper div's width was earlier set to 500 pixels, and its padding value was set to 18 pixels. As you will remember from the box model information from the previous chapter, padding is added to the dimensions of a box, and so the overall width taken up by the wrapper div is 536 pixels (18 + 500 + 18 = 536).

A drop shadow that terminates with the content

In the previous example, the white background of the content area is part of the image. Therefore, if you remove most of the paragraphs in that example, the background stays as it is, tiling vertically to the height of the viewing area. Using a different method, you can instead have the background terminate with the content.

Some additional markup is needed, due to this method requiring two background images: one for the wrapper div (because, as per the white background in the "Adding a background pattern" section, you want the content area's background to stop when the content runs out) and one for a shadow for the bottom edge of the wrapper div (otherwise the shadows at the side will just stop dead, resulting in something like what's shown in the following image).

In terms of markup, add an empty div, as shown in the following code block:

```
    ? accumsa'n eu, blandit sed, blandit a, eros.</p>
    <div class="contentFooter"><!-- x --></div>
  </div>
 </body>
</html>
```

In CSS, for the drop shadows flanking the content area to stop where the content does, they need to be assigned to the wrapper div, not the web page's body. Therefore, you need to amend the body rule, removing the link to a background, but retaining the color setting:

```
body {
  background: #878787;
}
```

The #wrapper rule needs updating in two ways. First, the new background image needs to be applied to the div—hence the new background property/value pair. However, because the drop shadows are now shown *within* the wrapper div, it needs to take up more horizontal space. Since the dimensions of the div's content don't need changing, this is achieved by increasing the horizontal padding value. Also, because padding at the foot of the div is no longer required (the contentFooter div effectively takes care of padding at the bottom of the content area), the bottom padding value needs to be set to 0. These padding values are done in shorthand, as per the method outlined in the "Working with CSS shorthand for boxes" section earlier in this chapter.

```
#wrapper {
  padding: 18px 36px 0;
  background: url(background-drop-shadow-2.gif) 50% 0 repeat-y;
  width: 500px;
  margin: 0 auto;
}
```

Finally, the contentFooter div needs styling. Its height is defined on the basis of the height of the background image (which is a slice of the Photoshop document shown in the following image). The background is applied to the div in the same way as in previous examples.

One major change, however, is the use of *negative* margins. The contentFooter div is nested within the wrapper, which has 36 pixels of horizontal padding. This means that the contentFooter div background doesn't reach the edges of the wrapper div by default, leaving whitespace on its left and right sides. By using margins equal to the negative value of this padding, the div can be "stretched" into place.

```
.contentFooter {
  height: 20px;
  background: url(background-drop-shadow-2-footer.gif) 50% 0;
  margin: 0 -36px;
}
```

As you can see, the horizontal value for margin is -36px, the negative of the horizontal padding value assigned to #wrapper. The addition of all these new rules results in the following image (which also shows the Photoshop image and exported GIF that makes up the background).

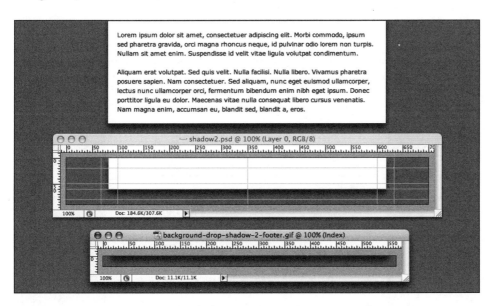

An alternate method for getting this effect would be to place the contentFooter div outside of the wrapper and then use the same method of aligning it:

```
.contentFooter {
  width: 500px;
  height: 20px;
  background: url(background-drop-shadow-2-footer.gif) 50% 0;
```

```
    padding: 0 36px;
    margin: 0 auto;
  }
```

In order to ensure the background of the wrapper joins up with the shadow on the contentFooter div, a single pixel of bottom padding needs to be applied to the #wrapper rule:

```
#wrapper {
  padding: 18px 36px 1px;
  background: url(background-drop-shadow-2.gif) 50% 0 repeat-y;
  width: 500px;
  margin: 0 auto;
}
```

Gradients

Tiled gradient images can be used to add depth and visual interest, without sapping resources (the example's image is under 2 KB in size). The depicted example is based on the page from the "Drop shadows" section. The changes are an amendment to the background pair in the #wrapper rule, tiling the gradient image horizontally on the wrapper's background, and new padding settings, so the text doesn't appear over the gradient.

```
#wrapper {
  padding: 36px 18px 18px;
  background: #ffffff url(background-gradient.gif) repeat-x;
  width: 500px;
  margin: 0 auto;
}
```

Watermarks

Although it's common for sites to be centered in the browser window, many designers choose left-aligned sites that cling to the left edge of the browser window. Both design styles are perfectly valid, but in an era of rapidly increasing monitor resolutions, you can end up with a lot of dead space to the side of a fixed-width left-aligned design. And while some of you might be saying, "Well, create flexible-width designs, then!" some designs aren't suited to that, and text-heavy sites tend to work better with fairly narrow text columns, since most users find it hard to read very wide blocks of text.

All of this brings us to the final example in this chapter, which shows how to create watermarks for a web page. In the following screenshot, the wrapper `div` is to the left, with a background image to the right of this area.

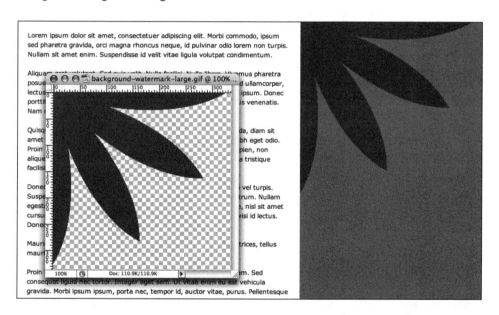

To achieve this effect, the margin property/value pair in the `#wrapper` rule has been removed, and the following rule has been added:

```
body {
    background: #878787 url(background-watermark-large.gif) no-repeat
    ➥ 536px 0;
}
```

> As mentioned earlier in the chapter, this assumes you're adding a second body rule. You can, however, just add the background property/value pair to the existing body rule in the style sheet.

The image used is a transparent GIF, so the background color setting was made a medium-gray (#878787). The reasoning behind using a transparent GIF is explained in Chapter 4, but it relates to web browsers sometimes interpreting colors differently from graphics packages. Therefore, it's often easier to make the flat background color of a graphic transparent and then use the web page background color in place of it.

The repeat setting is set to no-repeat, because we don't want the image to tile. Finally, the background's position is set to 536px 0. The 0 setting means it hugs the top of the browser window, while the 536px setting means the image is placed at 536 pixels from the left. This is because the content area was earlier defined as 500 pixels wide with 18 pixels of padding, and 18 + 500 + 18 = 536.

As mentioned earlier, backgrounds can be added to any web page element. For instance, you can add a watermark to the wrapper div by using the following CSS:

```
#wrapper {
  padding: 18px;
  background: #ffffff url(background-watermark.gif) no-repeat 20px
  ➥ 20px;
  width: 500px;
}
```

This adds the background-watermark.gif image to the background of the content div, and positions it 20 pixels from the top and 20 pixels from the left. Again, no-repeat is used to stop the image from tiling.

In either case for the watermark backgrounds, the images scroll with the page content. However, watermarks can also work well as fixed backgrounds—this can be achieved by adding the fixed value to the background property in the body and #wrapper rules.

Completed examples of all of the web pages in this section are in the chapter 2 *folder in the download files.*

Closing your document

Back at the start of this chapter, we examined basic HTML and XHTML documents. Regardless of the technology used, the end of the document should look like this:

```
    </body>
</html>
```

There are no variations or alternatives. A body end tag terminates the document's content, and an html end tag terminates the document itself. No web page content should come after the body end tag, and no HTML content should come after the html end tag (whitespace is fine, and it's common practice with server-side technologies to put functions after the html end tag—just don't put any HTML there).

Also, you must only ever have *one* body and *one* head in an HTML document, as well as a single html start tag and a single html end tag.

This is important stuff to bear in mind, and even if you think it's obvious, there are millions of pages out there—particularly those that utilize server-side includes and server-side languages—that include multiple body tags and head tags, have content outside the body tag, and have HTML outside the html tag.

Don't do this in your own work.

Naming your files

Each designer has their own way of thinking when it comes to naming files and documents. Personally, I like to keep document names succinct, but obvious enough that I can find them rapidly via a trawl of my hard drive. Certain conventions, however, are key: all file names should avoid illegal characters (such as spaces), and it's good to be consistent throughout your site. I find that naming files in lowercase and replacing spaces with hyphens—like-this-for-example.html—works well.

Web designers have historically used underscores in place of spaces, but that causes problems with some search engines, some of which run-in keywords, effectively considering the words within the file name as one string. This doesn't happen with hyphens.

Commenting your work

The rules for HTML, CSS, and JavaScript comments are simple, but the actual characters used are different in each case.

HTML comments begin with `<!--` and end with `-->`, and can run over multiple lines, as follows:

```
<!-- this is a comment in HTML -->
<!--
Multiple-line
HTML
comment
-->
```

In XHTML, double hyphens should not occur within the comment itself. Therefore, the following is not valid XHTML:

```
<!-- This is invalid -- as is the comment below -->
<!---------------------------------------------------------->
```

The multiple-hyphen comment is commonly used by designers who favor hand-coding to separate large chunks of code within a document. When working in XHTML, you can replace the hyphens with a different character:

```
<!--oooooooooooooooooooooooooooooooooooooo-->
<!--===================================-->
```

CSS comments were covered in the "Creating boilerplates" section of Chapter 1, but we'll briefly look through them again; they're opened with `/*` and closed with `*/` and, like HTML comments, can run over multiple lines, as shown here:

```
/* This is a comment in CSS */
/*
Multiple-line
CSS
comment
*/
```

Multiple-line comments in JavaScript are the same as in CSS, but single-line comments are placed after double forward slashes:

```
// This is a single-line JavaScript comment.
```

Don't use comments incorrectly. CSS comments in an HTML document won't be problematic from a rendering standpoint—but they will be displayed. HTML comments in CSS can actually cause a CSS file to fail entirely.

> *Along with enabling you to comment your work, comments can be used to disable sections of code when testing web pages.*

Web page essentials checklist

Congratulations—you made it to the end of this chapter! I'm aware that some of this one was about as much fun as trying to work out complex quadratic equations in your head, but as mentioned at the start, you need to know this stuff. Imagine designing a site and it suddenly not working the way you thought it would. It looks fine in your web design package and also in some web browsers, but it starts falling apart in others. Just removing an XML declaration might be enough to fix the site.

If you take the elements of this chapter and form them into a simple checklist, you won't have to risk displaying those wonderful "Untitled Documents" to the entire world (or inadvertently advertising the package you used to create the page). To make your life easier, you can refer to this checklist:

1. Ensure the relevant DOCTYPE declaration and namespace is in place.
2. Remove the XML declaration if it's lurking.
3. Add a title tag and some content within it.
4. Add a meta tag to define your character set.
5. If required, add keywords and description meta tags.
6. Attach a CSS file (or files).
7. Attach a JavaScript file (or files).
8. If your web editor adds superfluous body attributes, delete them.
9. Ensure there are no characters prior to the DOCTYPE declaration or after the html end tag.
10. Ensure no web page content appears outside the body element.

Georgia (24px)

Georgia (12px)

Georgia (9px)

Palatino (bold, 24px)

Palatino (24px)

Palatino (12px)

Palatino (9px)

Times New Roman (bol

Times New Roman (24p

Article heading

**Lorem ipsum dolor sit amet, consecteti
aliquet elementum erat. Integer diam n
a, hendrerit at, mi. Morbi risus mi, tinci
eleifend nec, risus.**

Quisque faucibus lorem eget sapien. In ur
et, venenatis at, velit. Ut sodales lacus sec
tristique senectus et netus et malesuada f

Curabitur sit amet risus

Lorem ipsum dolor sit amet, consectetuer
elementum erat. Integer diam mi, venena

⭐ **LIST - 1.1**

🔲 List - 2.1

🔲 List - 2.2

☐ List - 3.1

☐ List - 3.2

☐ List - 3.3

🔲 List - 2.3

In this chapter:

- Working with semantic markup
- Defining font colors, families, and other styles
- Understanding web-safe fonts
- Creating drop caps and pull quotes
- Rapidly editing styled text
- Working to a grid
- Creating and styling lists

An introduction to typography

Words are important—not just what they say, but how they look. To quote Ellen Lupton, from her book *Thinking with Type*, "Typography is what language looks like." Language has always been symbolic, although the origins of such symbols (of certain letterforms relating to, for example, animals) has largely been lost in written English; instead, we now have rather more abstract symbols designed for repetition on the page or screen.

However, from the early calligraphy that was created by hand, through the movable type (invented in Germany by Johannes Gutenberg during the 15th century) that enabled mass-production printing via molded letterform casts, to the most advanced desktop-publishing software available today, the ultimate aim of type has been one of record and information provision. In other words, type itself is important from a design standpoint because it needs to record whatever information is being written about, and that information needs to be easily retrievable by anyone who wants to understand it.

Like all aspects of design, typography has massively evolved over the years, particularly over the past couple of decades, where computers have enabled designers to more rapidly experiment with lettering. Despite this, many conventions formed much earlier still have a part to play:

- Myriad fonts exist, and each one has a different look, and therefore a different "feel;" you need to choose the most appropriate one for your purpose. (This is further complicated by there being only a certain number of web-safe fonts, as you'll see later.)
- Headings, strap-lines/stand-firsts (the introductory line that introduces a piece of text, commonly used in editorial articles), and crossheads (short subheadings that break up areas of body copy) should stand out, and the prominence of each piece of text should be related to its level of importance (in other words, a crosshead shouldn't be more prominent than a main heading).
- Footnotes often use text smaller than the main body copy text to signify their lesser significance to the main text, but nonetheless provide useful supplementary information.

- Decorative elements can be used to draw the reader's attention to specific parts of the text. Drop caps and initials—large initial letters, flamboyant in classical typography, but typically more restrained in modern work (see right)—enable a reader to rapidly navigate to the beginning of a piece of text. Pull quotes—quotes from the main body of the text, displayed in large lettering outside of context—are often used in magazine articles to draw a reader's attention to a particular article, highlighting particularly interesting quotes or information.

- Spacing is just as important as content. **Kerning**—the spacing between letter pairs—can be increased to add prominence to a heading. **Leading**—the amount of added vertical spacing between lines of text—can also be adjusted. Increasing leading from its default can make text more legible. In books, a **baseline grid** is often employed, ensuring that text always appears in the same place on each page. This means that the text on the opposite side of the paper doesn't appear in the gaps between the lines on the page you're reading. Baseline grids often make for extremely pleasing vertical rhythm, and are regularly used in print publications; they're infrequently used online, but can nonetheless be of use, making a page of text easier to read and navigate.

- Columns can be used to make a page easier to read. This is common in newspapers and magazines; online, the low resolution of monitors, and the (current) lack of being able to auto-flow columns of text makes de facto text columns impractical, but the reasoning behind columns is still handy to bear in mind. Generally, it's considered easier to read text that has fairly narrow columns (although not *too* narrow—if there are too few characters, reading and comprehension slow down)—text that, for example, spans the entire width of a 23-inch monitor rapidly becomes tiring to read. There are no hard-and-fast rules when it comes to line length, although some go by the "alphabet-and-a-half" rule (39 characters per line), some advocate the "points-times-two" rule (double the point size and use the number for the number of characters), and others recommend a dozen or so words, or about 60 characters.

A few highly useful online resources for web typography can be found at the following locations:

- **The Elements of Typographic Style Applied to the Web**: www.webtypography.net/

- **Five Simple Steps to Better Typography**: www.markboulton.co.uk/articles/detail/five_simple_steps_to_better_typography/

- **Five Simple Steps to Designing Grid Systems**: www.markboulton.co.uk/articles/detail/five_simple_steps_to_designing_grid_systems/

When it comes to web design, some conventions are used, and others are ignored. In fact, while web designers take the utmost care to get layouts right, scant few give the same thought to text, merely choosing a font and arbitrarily setting other values, if they set them at all. Once, this could be excused, but CSS has enabled web type to come a long way, and although the same degree of control as print-based type isn't possible, you can do a lot more than just choose your preferred font for headings and body copy.

In this chapter, we'll take a look at the various components available when working on web-based type (including elements and CSS properties), and provide some exercises, the results from which you can use for the basis of your own sites' type. As a final note in this introduction, it's also worth mentioning spelling and grammar. Both of these are clearly way outside of the scope of this book, but they're things designers tend to overlook. A site with a lot of grammatical and spelling errors, especially in larger text (such as headings and pull quotes) looks unprofessional. If in doubt when working on sites, consult (or get your client to consult) a copywriter.

> *There are a couple of books worth digging out for more information on typography and language. A decent primer on type design is Helen Lupton's* Thinking with Type. *For an entertaining (if not entirely accurate) history of the English language, read Bill Bryson's* The Mother Tongue.

Styling text the old-fashioned way (or, why we hate font tags)

Styling text online used to be all about font tags. When Netscape introduced the font element—complete with size and color attributes—web designers wept tears of joy. When Microsoft announced it would go further, adding a face attribute (enabling you to specify the font family), web designers were giddy with anticipation. But things didn't go according to plan. Page sizes bloated as designers created pages filled with fonts of myriad sizes and colors. Web users looked on aghast, wondering whether giant, orange body copy was really the way to go, and whether it was worth waiting twice as long for such abominations to download.

More important, it became apparent that font tags caused problems, including the following:

- Inconsistent display across browsers and platforms
- The requirement for font tags to be applied to individual elements
- Difficulty ensuring fonts were consistent site-wide, because of having to style individual elements
- HTML geared toward presentation rather than logical structure
- Large HTML documents due to all the extra elements

In addition, working with font tags is a time-consuming, boring process, and yet some (although, thankfully, increasingly few) web designers remain blissfully ignorant of such problems. In my opinion, if font tags weren't HTML elements, I'd suggest they be taken out back and shot. Today, there is no reason whatsoever to stick with them. Text can be rapidly styled site-wide with CSS and, as we'll see later in this chapter, CSS provides you with a greater degree of control than font tags ever did. More crucially, font tags encourage badly formed documents, with designers relying on inline elements to style things like headings, when there are perfectly good HTML elements better suited to that purpose.

HTML should be reserved for content and structure, and CSS for design. Web pages should be composed of appropriate elements for each piece of content. This method of working, called **semantic markup**, is what we're going to discuss next.

A new beginning: Semantic markup

Essentially, "semantic markup" means "using the appropriate tag at the relevant time," and well-formed semantic markup is an essential aspect of any website. The following is an example of the *wrong* way of doing things—relying on font tags to create a heading and double line breaks (

) for separating paragraphs:

```
<font size="7" color="red" face="Helvetica">Article heading</font>
<br /><br />
Lorem ipsum dolor sit amet, consectetuer adipiscing elit. Sed aliquet
➥ elementum erat. Integer diam mi, venenatis non, cursus a,
➥ hendrerit at, mi.
<br /><br />
Quisque faucibus lorem eget sapien. In urna sem, vehicula ut, mattis
➥ et, venenatis at, velit. Ut sodales lacus sed eros.
```

The likelihood of this displaying consistently across browsers and platforms is low. More important, the tags used don't relate to the content. Therefore, if the styling is removed, there's no indication regarding what role each element plays within the document structure and hierarchy—for instance, there would be no visual clues as to the importance of the heading. Also, the use of double line breaks (

) instead of paragraph tags means the "paragraphs" cannot be styled in CSS, because there's nothing to inform the web browser what the content actually is.

Instead, the example should be marked up like this:

```
<h1>Article heading</h1>
<p>Lorem ipsum dolor sit amet, consectetuer adipiscing elit. Sed
➥ aliquet elementum erat. Integer diam mi, venenatis non, cursus
➥ a, hendrerit at, mi.</p>
<p>Quisque faucibus lorem eget sapien. In urna sem, vehicula ut,
➥ mattis et, venenatis at, velit. Ut sodales lacus sed eros.</p>
```

Here, the heading is marked up with the relevant tags, and paragraph elements are used instead of double line breaks. This means the page's structural integrity is ensured, and the markup is logical and semantic. If attached CSS styles are removed, the default formatting still makes obvious to the end user the importance of the headings, and will visually display them as such.

In this section, we'll look at how to mark up paragraphs and headings, explore logical and physical styles, and discuss the importance of well-formed semantic markup.

Paragraphs and headings

With words making up the bulk of online content, the paragraph and heading HTML elements are of paramount importance. HTML provides six levels of headings, from h1 to h6, with h1 being the top-level heading. The adjacent image shows how these headings, along with a paragraph, typically appear by default in a browser.

```
<h1>Level one heading</h1>
<h2>Level two heading</h2>
<h3>Level three heading</h3>
<h4>Level four heading</h4>
<h5>Level five heading</h5>
<h6>Level six heading</h6>
<p>Default paragraph size</p>
```

Level one heading

Level two heading

Level three heading

Level four heading

Level five heading

Level six heading

Default paragraph size

By default, browsers put margins around paragraphs and headings. This can vary from browser to browser, but it can be controlled by CSS. Therefore, there's no excuse for using double line breaks to avoid default paragraph margins affecting web page layouts.

Despite the typical default sizes, level-five and level-six headings are not intended as "tiny text," but as a way to enable you to structure your document, which is essential, as headings help with assistive technology, enabling the visually disabled to efficiently surf the Web.

In terms of general usage, it's generally recommended to stick to just one h1 element per document, used for the page's primary heading. The next level down—and the *first* level in a sidebar—would be h2, and then h3, and so on. Take care not to use too many heading levels, though—unless you're working on complex legal documents, you really shouldn't be getting past level four. If you are, look at restructuring your document.

Logical and physical styles

Once text is in place, it's common to add inline styles, which can be achieved by way of logical and physical styles. Many designers are confused by the difference between the two, especially because equivalents (such as the logical strong and physical b) tend to be displayed the same in browsers. The difference is that **logical styles** describe what the content *is*, whereas **physical styles** merely define what the content *looks like*. This subtle difference is more apparent when you take into account things like screen readers.

In the markup I like to emphasize things, a screen reader emphasizes the text surrounded by the em tags. However, replace the em tags with i tags and the screen reader won't emphasize the word, although in a visual web browser the two pieces of markup will almost certainly look identical.

Styles for emphasis (bold and italic)

Physical styles enable you to make text bold and <i>italic</i>, and these are the most commonly used inline physical styles. However, logical styles are becoming much more widespread (the majority of web design applications, such as Dreamweaver, now default to logical styles rather than physical ones). Typically, strong emphasis emboldens text in a visual web browser and emphasis italicizes text.

Deprecated and nonstandard physical styles

Many physical elements are considered obsolete, including the infamous blink (a Netscape "innovation" used to flash text on and off, amusingly still supported in Firefox). Some physical styles are deprecated: u (underline) and s (strikethrough; also strike) have CSS equivalents using the text-decoration property (text-decoration: underline and text-decoration: line-through, respectively).

The big and small elements

The big and small elements are used to increase and decrease the size of inline text (even text defined in pixels in CSS). An example of the use of small might be in marking up text that is semantically small print. An example of big might be to denote that a drop cap is a big character, or for when adding asterisks to required form fields.

```
<input type="text" name="realname" size="30" /> <big>*</big>
```

Note, however, that the change in size depends on individual web browsers, so it's often better to use span elements with a specific class relating to a font size defined in CSS (see the section "Creating alternatives with classes and spans" later in the chapter), or ensure that you define specific values in CSS for small and big elements when used in context.

Teletype, subscript, and superscript

This leaves three useful physical styles. The first, tt, renders text in a monospace font (à la teletype text). The others, sub and sup, render text as subscript and superscript text, respectively. These are useful for scientific documents, although there is a drawback: characters are displayed at the same size, defined by the browser. You can get around this by using a CSS tag selector and defining a new font size for each element. The following code shows how to do this, and the accompanying screenshot shows a default sup element (at the top of the image) and a CSS-styled sup element (at the bottom) in use.

```
sup {
font-size: 70%;
}
```

Logical styles for programming-oriented content

Several logical styles do similar jobs, are programming-oriented, and are usually displayed in a monospace font:

```
<code>Denotes a code sample.</code>
<kbd>Indicates text entered by the user.</kbd>
<samp>Indicates a programming sample.</samp>
```

The var element also relates to programming, signifying a variable. However, it is usually displayed in italics.

Block quotes, quote citations, and definitions

The blockquote element is used to define a lengthy quotation and must be set within a block-level element. Its cite attribute can be used to define the online location of quoted material, although the cite element is perhaps more useful for this, enabling you to place a visible citation (a reference to another document, such as an article) online; this is usually displayed in italics. See the "Creating drop caps and pull quotes using CSS" section for more on using this element.

> Note that some web design applications—notably, early versions of Dreamweaver—used the blockquote element to indent blocks of text, and this bad habit is still used by some designers. Don't do this—if you want to indent some text, use CSS.

For shorter quotes that are inline, the q element can be used. This is also supposed to add language-specific quotes before and after the content between the element's tags. These quotes vary by browser—Firefox adds "smart" quotes, Safari and Opera add "straight" quotes, and Internet Explorer doesn't display anything at all. The article "Long Live the Q Tag," by Stacey Cordoni (available at A List Apart; www.alistapart.com/articles/qtag), offers a few workarounds, although none are ideal (one advises using JavaScript; another uses CSS to hide the quotes in compliant browsers, and then says to add the quotes manually, outside of the element's tags. However, another alternative is to merely ensure that the quoted content is differentiated from surrounding text, which can be done by setting font-style in CSS to italic for the q element.

Finally, to indicate the defining instance of a term, you use the dfn element. This is used to draw attention to the first use of such a term and is also typically displayed in italics.

Acronyms and abbreviations

Two logical styles assist with accessibility, enabling you to provide users with full forms of abbreviations and acronyms by way of the title attribute:

```
<abbr title="Cascading Style Sheets">CSS</abbr>
<acronym title="North Atlantic Treaty Organization">NATO</acronym>
```

This has two uses. For one, it allows users with disabilities (using screen readers) to access the full form of the words in question. But anyone using a visual web browser can access the information, too, because title attribute contents are usually displayed as a tooltip when you hover your mouse over elements they're used on.

To further draw attention to an abbreviation or acronym, style the tag in CSS (using a tag selector), thereby making all such tags consistent across an entire website. The following code is an example of this, the results of which are shown in the example to the right (including the tooltip triggered by hovering over the abbr element, which has a title attribute).

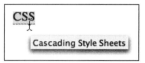

```
abbr {
   border-bottom: 1px dotted #000000;
   background-color: yellow;
}
```

> *You can provide an additional aid to users by setting cursor to help in CSS for abbr elements. This changes the cursor to a question mark while hovering over the element.*

Elements for inserted and deleted text

The del and ins elements are used, respectively, to indicate deleted text and inserted text, typically in a manner akin to the tracking features of word processing packages, although they do not include the tracking functionality. The del element usually appears in strikethrough format, whereas ins usually appears underlined. Both accept cite and datetime attributes. The former enables you to define a URL that explains why text was inserted or deleted; the latter enables you to define the time and date that the text was amended—see the <ins> and <del> entries in Appendix A (XHTML Reference) for accepted formats.

Note that these elements cannot be nested inside each other, for obvious reasons. Following is an example of their use:

```
<p>I <del>deleted this</del> and then <ins>inserted this</ins>.</p>
```

I ~~deleted this~~ and then inserted this.

The default style of the ins element can prove problematic online. Because links are underlined by default, users may attempt to click text marked up as inserted text and wonder why nothing happens. It's a good idea to amend the tag's visual appearance by changing the underline color. This can be done by removing the default underline and replacing it with a bottom border, like so:

```
ins {
   text-decoration: none;
   border-bottom: 1px solid red;
}
```

The bottom border resembles an underline, although it appears lower than the default underline, which further differentiates inserted text from hypertext links.

The importance of well-formed markup

Many logical styles are rarely used online, because they look no different from text marked up using the likes of the i element. However, as mentioned earlier, physical appearance alone misses the point of HTML. Always using the most appropriate relevant element means that you can later individually style each element in CSS, overriding the default appearance if you wish. If the likes of citations, defining instances, and variables are all marked up with i instead of cite, dfn, and var, there's no way of distinguishing each type of content and no way of manipulating their appearance on an individual basis. Well-formed markup involves more than ensuring visual flexibility, though. Use of the cite tag, for instance, enables you to manipulate the Document Object Model (DOM) to extract a bibliography or list of quotations from a page or even a full website. The ability to style logical tags like this with CSS is likely to be of increasing rather than diminishing importance.

The importance of end tags

While we're on the subject of well-formed markup, we'll revisit the importance of end tags. As mentioned earlier, XHTML demands that all tags be closed. Most browsers let you get away with ignoring some end tags, though, such as on paragraphs. Some designers may still have bad habits from working with HTML, for which many end tags are optional. Omit many others at your peril. For instance, overlook a heading element end tag and a browser considers subsequent content to be part of the heading and displays it accordingly. As shown in the following image, two paragraphs are displayed as a heading because the earlier heading element lacks an end tag.

A similar problem occurs when you accidentally omit end tags when using logical and physical elements. For instance, forget to close an emphasis element and the remainder of the web page may be displayed in italics.

Some designers when hand-coding create both start and end tags at the same time, and then populate the element with content, ensuring end tags are not forgotten.

Styling text using CSS

HTML is intended as a structural markup language, but the Web's increasing popularity meant it got "polluted" with tags designed for presentation. This made HTML more complex than it needed to be, and such tags soon became a headache for web designers trying to style page elements, such as text. In the bad ol' days (the end of the 1990s), you'd often see source code like this:

```
<font face="Helvetica" size="3" color="#333333"> This markup is
➥ <font size="+3"><small>really </small></font>bad, but it was sort of
➥ the norm in the 1990s.</font>
```

WYSIWYG tools would insert new tags to override previous ones, adding to the page weight and making it tough to ensure visual consistency site-wide. By and large, CSS eradicates these problems and enables far more control over text, as you'll see in the following sections.

This is a boon for graphic designers who used to loathe HTML's lack of typographical control. However, the level of freedom evident in print design still isn't quite so on the Web. Restrictions imposed by browsers and the screen must be taken into account, such as it being harder to read type onscreen than in print. This is largely related to resolution. Even magazines with fairly low-quality print tend to be printed at around 200 dpi or more—more than twice the resolution of a typical monitor. This means that very small text (favored by many designers, who think such small text looks neat) becomes tricky to read onscreen, because there aren't enough pixels to create a coherent image.

I'll note restrictions such as this at appropriate times during this section on styling text with CSS, thereby providing advice on striking a balance between the visual appearance and practicality of web-based text.

Defining font colors

In CSS, the color property value defines the foreground color of the relevant CSS element, which for text sets its color. This can be set using hex, keywords, or RGB. The following examples show each method in turn, and all have the same result: setting paragraphs to black.

```
p {
  color: #000000;
}
p {
  color: black;
}
p {
  color: rgb(0,0,0);
}
```

3

Declaring colors using RGB is rare in web design—hex is most popular, especially because CSS supports so few keywords (see the section "Working with hex" in Chapter 4).

Remember to test your choices on both Windows and Mac, because there are differences in the default color space for each platform. In general terms, the Mac default display settings are brighter (or Windows is darker, depending on your outlook on life); if you use subtle dark tones on the Mac, or very light tones on Windows, the result might be tricky to view on the other platform. This should cause few problems with text, but some designers insist on rendering text with very little contrast to the background color, and this ends up being even harder to read on a different platform from the one on which it was created.

> *The main tip to keep in mind for color with regard to web-based text is simple: always provide plenty of contrast so that your text remains readable.*

Defining fonts

The font-family property enables you to specify a list of font face values, starting with your preferred first choice, continuing with alternates (in case your choice isn't installed on the user's machine), and terminating in a generic font family, which causes the browser to substitute a similar font (think of it as a last resort).

```
selector {
  font-family: preferred, alterate 1, alterate 2, generic;
}
```

The most common generic font family names are serif and sans-serif, although when you're using monospace fonts (such as Courier New), you should end your list with monospace.

Multiple-word font family names must be quoted (such as "Trebuchet MS" and "Times New Roman"). You can use single or double quotes—just be consistent. Single-word font family names should never be quoted. Examples of font-family in use are as follows:

```
h1 {
  font-family: Arial, Helvetica, sans-serif;
}
p {
  font-family: Georgia, "Times New Roman", Times, serif;
}
pre {
  font-family: Courier, "Courier New", Monaco, monospace;
}
```

> pre *is the element for preformatted text, used to display monospace text in an identical fashion to how it's formatted in the original HTML document. It's commonly used for online FAQs, film scripts, and the like.*

Web-safe fonts

Print designers have a world of fonts at their disposal, but the same isn't true online. Rather than being limited by installed fonts, you're restricted by common fonts across various platforms. If end users don't have the same fonts installed as you, they won't see your design like you do, rendering your choices pointless.

Over the next few pages, I'll provide an overview of different available fonts for the Web, but there are some handy online references that you should also bookmark. A page comparing fonts common to the Mac and Windows is available at `www.ampsoft. net/webdesign-l/WindowsMacFonts.html`, and `www.codestyle.org/css/font-family/ sampler-Monospace.shtml` details available monospace fonts for various systems.

Sans-serif fonts for the Web

Arial is a common font choice, largely because of its dominance on Windows. Its poor design makes it unreadable at small sizes and a poor choice for body copy, although it can be of use for headings. Mac users should be wary of choosing Helvetica—it's an excellent font, but it's not generally shipped with Windows. Although you can specify fallback fonts in CSS, again, there's little point in making your first choice something that the majority of people won't see.

> *Despite its lack of penetration on Windows, Helvetica is often used as a fallback sans-serif font, due to its prevalence on Linux.*

Better choices for body copy are Verdana or Trebuchet MS. The former is typically a good choice, because its spacious nature makes it readable at any size. Its bubbly design renders it less useful for headings, though. Trebuchet MS is perhaps less readable, but it has plenty of character, and is sometimes an interesting alternative, simply because it isn't used all that much online.

In recent times, Lucida variants have become popular, due to Apple using it not only as the default font in Mac OS X, but also on its website. Despite Lucida Grande not being available for Windows, Lucida Sans Unicode is common and similar enough to be used as a first fallback. Usefully, Lucida is common on UNIX systems, meaning that sites using Lucida variants can look fairly similar text-wise across all three major operating systems. Another pairing—albeit one that's less common—is Tahoma and Geneva, so use those with care, providing more generic fallbacks.

See the following images for a comparison of several sans-serif fonts on Mac (left) and Windows (right).

Arial (bold, 24px) Arial (24px) Arial (12px) Arial (9px)	**Arial (bold, 24px)** Arial (24px) Arial (12px) Arial (9px)
Lucida Grande (bold, 24px) Lucida Grande (24px) Lucida Grande (12px) Lucida Grande (9px)	**Lucida Grande (bold, 24px)** Lucida Grande (24px) Lucida Grande (12px) Lucida Grande (9px)
Trebuchet MS (bold, 24px) Trebuchet MS (24px) Trebuchet MS (12px) Trebuchet MS (9px)	**Trebuchet MS (bold, 24px)** Trebuchet MS (24px) Trebuchet MS (12px) Trebuchet MS (9px)
Verdana (bold, 24px) Verdana (24px) Verdana (12px) Verdana (9px)	**Verdana (bold, 24px)** Verdana (24px) Verdana (12px) Verdana (9px)

Serif fonts for the Web

Although popular in print, serif fonts fare less well online. If using serifs, ensure you render them large enough so that they don't break down into an illegible mess. Georgia is perhaps the best available web-safe serif, especially when used at sizes equivalent to 12 pixels and above, and it can be more suitable than a sans-serif if you're working with traditional subject matter, or if you're attempting to emulate print articles (such as in the following screenshot of the online column Revert to Saved; www.reverttosaved.com).

reverttosaved
craig grannell

21. PLAIN ENGLISH (DOT COM)

navigate:
now / then / contact

Even with the dying echoes of the 'boom' from the web's recentish 'boom and bust' still ringing in many people's ears, there's no denying that the Internet remains a fast-moving place. However, while technology has changed, words and language seem to have evolved even faster. Therefore, Revert to Saved is proud to present the 'Dumbass-techie-speak-to-plain-English phrasebook'. Print it out and take it with you wherever you go, as many of these phrases have spread beyond the confines of your monitor, and you don't want to look stupid, do you? (Unlike, for instance, the people that actually use these phrases...)

Dumbass techie speak	Plain English
We must be proactive in having a	I've just read an Internet magazine

The other commonly available serif font, Times New Roman (Times being a rough equivalent on Linux systems), is inferior to Georgia, but worth using as a fallback. Like Arial, its popularity is the result of its prevalence as a system font.

Elsewhere, Palatino is fairly common—installed by default on Windows (as Palatino Linotype), and available on Mac systems that have Classic or iWork installed. Mac owners with Office will also have the virtually identical Book Antiqua. That said, if using these fonts, you'll still need to fall back to safer serifs, as mentioned earlier.

See the following illustration for a comparison of serif fonts on Mac (left) and Windows (right).

Fonts for headings and monospace type

The remaining "safe" fonts are typically display fonts (for headings) or monospace fonts for when each character needs to be the same width—for example, when adding code examples to a web page.

Arial Black and Impact are reasonable choices for headings, although they must be handled with care. The bold version of Impact looks terrible (and isn't displayed at all in some browsers), and some browsers by default render headings in bold, so this must be overridden in CSS. Often, large versions of fonts mentioned in the previous two sections are superior.

Courier New is more useful and a good choice when you need a monospace font. Note that falling back to Courier for Linux is recommended. The pairing of Lucida Console (Windows) and Lucida Sans Typewriter or Monaco (Mac) may also be suitable for monospace work, if you're looking for a less "computery" feel.

Few other fonts are worth a mention, barring perhaps Comic Sans MS, which is inexplicably popular with novice web designers. To give the font its due, it is readable, but its quirky and unprofessional nature makes it unsuitable for most purposes (even comic artists eschew it in favor of personalized fonts).

The following image shows several of the fonts mentioned in this section, again with Mac versions on the left and Windows versions on the right.

While Windows Vista arrived with six great new "C" fonts (the serifs Cambria and Constantia; the sans-serifs Calibri, Candara, and Corbel; and the monospace Consolas), they're not—at the time of writing—being made freely available, so if you choose to use them, ensure that you fall back to relevant alternatives. The new Microsoft fonts are not used or mentioned again in this book.

Mac vs. Windows: Anti-aliasing

When choosing fonts, it's worth noting that how they look differs on Mac and Windows. By default, Macs anti-alias onscreen text, which affects spacing—in fact, various anti-aliasing algorithms can make text look slightly different in each browser. On Windows, aliased text has historically made for jagged edges, but Internet Explorer 7 smoothes type via the font-smoothing technology ClearType, introduced in Windows XP (disabled by default in XP, but enabled in Vista system-wide).

For body copy, font-smoothing (or not) isn't a major problem—although some prefer aliased text and some prefer anti-aliased, both are fine, as long as the font size is large enough. However, when it comes to rendering large text—such as for headings—aliased text is significantly less visually pleasing.

> *Aliased text is a simplified version of the original font, reduced to a black-and-white bitmap. Anti-aliased text attempts to emulate the soft curves of the original font by introducing gray or colored pixels at the edges.*

Although arguments rage regarding which is the best method of displaying fonts onscreen, this is a moot point for web designers, because you don't control the end user's setup and therefore must be aware of each possibility.

Using images for text

Limitations imposed by web-safe fonts lead some designers to seek out alternative methods of creating online type. It's common to use graphics (mostly GIFs, but sometimes Flash, due to its vector-based, scalable nature) for text. If you have to follow a corporate design style under pain of death, the ability to use graphics can be a lifesaver—after all, most browsers happily render images, and they can be marked up within heading elements, so you can control things like margins via CSS and also retain the structural integrity of your document.

However, graphical text has its share of problems:

- Some browsers do not enable you to resize graphical text in a browser.
- Because the Web is low-resolution, when a page is printed out, graphical text looks pixilated and of poor quality.
- Although GIF-based text tends to be small in terms of file size, it's still larger than HTML-based text.
- People using alternate browsers, such as screen readers, cannot "see" graphical text (although you can use the `alt` attribute to compensate).
- Graphical text cannot be copied and pasted.
- Graphical text cannot be read by search engines.
- Graphical text is a pain to update. To change a word, you must rework the original image, export and upload it, and, if the image size has changed, you must edit the appropriate HTML documents and upload those, too.

In my opinion, graphics should be used as a last resort. A company's style can be made apparent by the use of a corporate logo and other imagery rather than by the use of a font. Also, *never, ever render body copy as an image.* There are many sites out there with body copy rendered as images, and quite frankly, every one of them makes me want to scream. Such sites are often full of typos (perhaps because amending them requires the entire graphic to be reworked, re-exported, and uploaded again), cannot be printed at quality, and cannot be copied to a text editor. Some suggest this means the site's text is "secure." But this goes against one of the fundamental benefits of the Web: that people can share information, and that it can be easily copied and sent on to others. Sure, this presents copyright implications, but everything online is subject to copyright anyway. Also, plenty of sites commit the cardinal sin of rendering things like contact details as a graphic—I'm sure their customers very much appreciate having to type such things out by hand rather than just being able to copy them into their digital address books.

Image-replacement techniques

If you need a greater degree of typographical control over a portion of text, such as the site's main heading, there is an option that enables you to include an image and also enable the text to remain in place, which is useful for users surfing the Web with screen readers. This is generally known as **image replacement**. Note that the technique should be used with care and sparingly—even from a basic practical standpoint, it doesn't make a great deal of sense to set all of your headings as images, simply because it takes time to create and export each one.

Of the techniques available for replacing images, the most common is to assign the relevant piece of text (usually a heading) a class value in HTML, and also add a dummy span element before its content:

```
<h1 class="aFancyHeading"><span></span>A fancy heading</h1>
```

In an image editor, an image-based version of the heading is created and saved, and its dimensions measured. Example files for this are a-fancy-heading.gif, image-replacement. css, and image-replacement.html, located in the chapter 3 folder. In the CSS file, you'll see rules created to define the dimensions of the heading (.aFancyHeading) and span (.aFancyHeading span). The heading's position value is set to relative, and the span element is then positioned in an absolute fashion, which ensures that it sits over the text-based heading's content. The width and height values ensure that the span (and therefore its background image) expands to fill its container. (Note that when used in conjunction with links, it's useful to also set display: block within the CSS rule so that the entire area becomes clickable and the cursor becomes a pointer—this is because some versions of Internet Explorer use the arrow pointer instead of the usual finger pointer. Alternatively, set cursor to pointer in CSS.) The overflow: hidden property/value pair ensures text doesn't peek out from behind the image—an issue that sometimes occurs in Internet Explorer or when text is resized. To deal with zoomed text in IE 7, it may also be necessary to set a pixel font-size value for the heading that's smaller than the height of the image.

> Setting overflow to hidden *can be an issue when this technique is used in conjunction with linked replaced elements, such as linked mastheads and logos. When tabbing through links, replaced elements that have an* overflow *setting of* hidden *will become displaced on receiving the focus, revealing the underlying text as well as the image overlaying it. Caution needs to be used here.*

The following image shows a page using this technique with and without CSS.

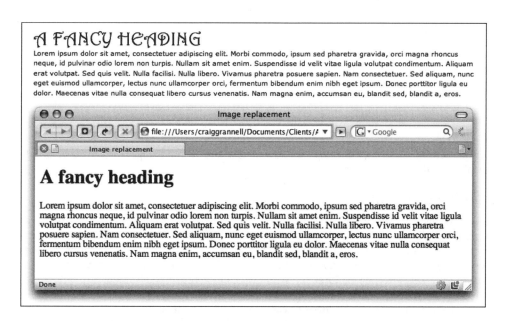

Some methods focus on hiding the text by setting display to none in CSS, but that can cause problems for screen readers, so avoid doing this. Others use text-indent to shift the text off of the page, although using absolute positioning with negative top and left coordinates is better—this prevents vertical space being taken up by the offset text, which is quite often noticeable, especially if margins haven't been controlled.

Scalable Inman Flash Replacement (sIFR) is an alternative to replacing text with GIF images. Instead, is uses a combination of CSS, Flash, and JavaScript to switch out a block of text. Note that although this provides a great deal of typographic flexibility, it should still be used sparingly—pages where too much text is switched out using sIFR tend to be extremely sluggish. See sIFR Beauty (www.alvit.de/sifrbeauty/ sifr-resources.php) for resources and Mike Davidson's site (www.mikeindustries. com/sifr/) for further information.

Defining font size and line height

In theory, defining font sizes should be easy enough. You use the font-size property, and then you can set the value to an absolute size, a relative size, a length, or a percentage. For instance, you might set the following:

```
h1 {
   font-size: 20px;
}
p {
   font-size: 12px;
}
```

Alternatively, you might go for something like this:

```
h1 {
  font-size: 150%;
}
p {
  font-size: 90%;
}
```

Each method of sizing fonts has its advantages and disadvantages, which we'll briefly explore in this section of the book.

Setting text in pixels

Many designers specify font sizes in pixels, largely because pixels are the only measurement that allows you to be relatively certain that your text will look pretty much identical across various browsers and platforms (in the same way that sizing page sections in pixels enables you to keep output consistent). Unfortunately, unlike every other major browser on the market, Internet Explorer for Windows cannot resize pixel-based text, which creates an accessibility problem (although a user can choose to ignore font sizes via the little-known accessibility controls). Internet Explorer's Text Size menu only allows resizing of text sized using legacy methods, keywords, or relative units other than pixels. (Note that Internet Explorer 7 can zoom the entire page, but not the text alone.)

Therefore, if you decide to size text in pixels, ensure that your text is *very* readable. Test it on various people and listen to feedback. If complaints come your way regarding the fact that someone "had trouble reading the words," or rooted around for a microscope before giving up and playing solitaire, you need to increase your pixel size settings. The resulting page might not look quite as "designery," but at least people will be able to read it.

Setting text using keywords and percentages

A combination of keywords and percentages became fairly popular for a while on the Web. Available keyword values are xx-small, x-small, small, medium, large, x-large, and xx-large. A keyword is used to set the base value, using a body selector in CSS, and percentages are then used to set sizes for specific elements, such as headings, paragraphs, and lists. Here's an example:

```
body {
  font-size: small;
}
p {
  font-size: 93%;
}
```

Keyword values don't compound, and most modern browsers set a lower limit, even on xx-small, so text tends never to enter the realm of the illegible.

Although Internet Explorer for Windows can resize text set with keywords (as can all other browsers), this method has several disadvantages. The most problematic from a design perspective is that percentage values aren't particularly consistent across browsers and platforms. Scaling tends to "jump" at fairly arbitrary percentage sizes, so while 93% may look the same in all browsers (using default font-size settings, at least), 94% may look like 100% in one and 93% in another. Also, it's often tricky to equate percentages with the pixel (or point) sizes typically used in mock-ups.

Also, browsers have historically dealt with keywords badly. Early versions of Netscape 4 ignored keywords entirely, and later releases followed the original specification to the letter, which was updated accordingly when it was discovered that anything smaller than medium looked like an ink-footed ant had taken a stroll across your monitor. Not to be outdone, Internet Explorer 4 and 5 welded CSS keywords to Netscape font size tags, resulting in the browser displaying everything at the next size down. (You can use conditional comments to set a different font-size value for Internet Explorer 5—see Chapter 9 for more on this method.)

In more modern versions of Internet Explorer, fonts that are set to Small in the View ➤ Text Size menu can make keyword-set CSS text hard to read, but users can increase the text size by using a more sensible setting. Also, it's worth noting that this is up to user choice, and having a tiny minority of users screwing up their own settings and potentially ending up with unreadable text is better than the vast majority not being able to resize the text because its size is defined in pixels. Still, there's a better method for achieving this, as we shall see.

Setting text using percentages and ems

As mentioned, the problem with sizing text in pixels is that the text is not resizable in Internet Explorer. The main problem with using keywords and percentages is that the text size isn't consistent across platforms or that easy to define—at least in terms of hitting a specific target size. This third method—and the one I typically use for websites I design—enables you to create font sizes that are targeted at a pixel size, but are also resizable in Internet Explorer, since the measurements are relative units.

The system works by first setting a base font size of 62.5% using a body selector:

```
body {
   font-size: 62.5%;
}
```

Since most browsers have a default font size of 16 pixels, the previous rule then sets the default size to 62.5% of that value—in other words, 10 pixels. From here, ems can be used to define font sizes of specific elements, using values that are one-tenth of the target pixel size:

```
h1 {
   font-size: 2.0em; /* will be the equivalent of 20px */
}
p {
   font-size: 1.2em; /* will be the equivalent of 12px */
}
```

The system isn't perfect—relative values defined in ems can be inherited, so if a list item is within another list item, the size of the nested item(s) may increase or decrease, depending on the value assigned to the parent. However, override rules can easily get around this problem (see "Dealing with font-size inheritance" in the "Working with lists" section later in the chapter), and the method generally leads to more satisfactory results from a design, control, and user point of view than either of the other two methods mentioned. It is worth noting, however, that this method is somewhat reliant on the user—if someone has changed the default font size in their browser, your design may not look as intended on their browser, since the value defined for body may be 62.5% of something other than 16 pixels. Still, few people muck around with their browser settings, and the general consensus in the industry is that the 62.5% method is the one to go for.

> *If using this method, ensure that the* font-size *setting of all text-oriented elements you use on the site is adjusted, otherwise you'll end up with some illegible text set at 62.5% of the default font size. Also ensure you test your work at a range of text sizes in various browsers, to ensure things still look OK if the text is zoomed in or out.*

There is one other thing to bear in mind, though: Internet Explorer (again). Although the majority of browser-specific issues are left until Chapter 9 of this book, we'll make an exception now. Internet Explorer has problems with text-zooming when the font size is set below 100%, so an additional rule is required:

```css
html {
   font-size: 100%;
}
```

This doesn't adversely affect other browsers, so you'll find this rule in the boilerplate documents from the download files, even thought it should *technically* be in the conditional comments documents.

Setting line height

Graphic designers will be familiar with leading, and the CSS line-height property enables you to set this. Generally speaking, it's a good idea to be fairly generous with leading for web pages, because text is harder to read onscreen than in print; by placing larger gaps between each line, the eye can more easily scan through large blocks of text.

When setting line-height, you have various options, and can use a number, length, or percentage:

```css
h1 {
   font-size: 14px;
   line-height: 20px;
}
h2 {
   font-size: 1.3em;
   line-height: 1.6em;
}
```

```
p {
  font-size: 1.1em;
  line-height: 1.5;
}
```

The difference between the font-size and line-height measurements is the leading value. Half the value is applied above the text and half below. Should you use a number alone, rather than a length or percentage, that value is multiplied by the font-size setting to define the line height. For example, if font-size is set to 10px and line-height is set to 1.5, the line-height value becomes 15px.

Many web designers who have no graphic design experience ignore the line-height property, but, as mentioned earlier, it's essential for improving the legibility of a web page. In the following screenshots, the left images shows the default spacing and the right one shows increased line height, resulting in increased legibility.

Defining font-style, font-weight, and font-variant

These three properties are straightforward. The first, font-style, enables you to set italic or oblique text. The former is often a defined face within the font itself, whereas the latter is usually computed. Typically, web browsers treat both the same, and only the italic value is in general use (except for the occasional use of normal—the default value—in order to override something set elsewhere).

An element's font-style is set like this:

```
h2 {
  font-style: italic;
}
```

The font-weight property is intended to make a font heavier or lighter, and despite the various available values, only bold and normal are in general use. This is detailed in full in the font-weight entry of Appendix D (CSS Reference).

```
.introParagraph {
  font-weight: bold;
}
```

The font-variant property has two available values: normal (the default) and small-caps. Small caps are often used to de-emphasize uppercase letters in abbreviations and acronyms, and are similar in size to a typeface's lowercase characters. This property only affects lowercase letters, and display of small caps varies across browsers and platforms—for example, older versions of Internet Explorer simply render such text entirely in normal caps (i.e., in standard uppercase letters).

CSS shorthand for font properties

The CSS properties discussed so far can be written in shorthand, enabling you to cut down on space and manage your CSS font settings with greater ease. Like some other shorthand properties, some rules apply:

- Some browsers are more forgiving than others regarding required and optional values, but you should always specify the font-size and font-family values, in that order.
- Omitted values revert to default settings.
- The font-style, font-weight, and font-variant values, if included, should be placed at the start of the rule (in any order), prior to the font-size value.
- The font-size and line-height values can be combined using the syntax font-size/line-height (e.g., 12px/16px for 12px font-size and 16px line-height).

A complete font declaration in shorthand could therefore look like this:

```
p {
  font: italic small-caps bold 100%/1.3em Arial, Helvetica,
  ➥ sans-serif;
}
```

The equivalent in longhand is the following:

```
p {
  font-style: italic;
  font-variant: small-caps;
  font-weight: bold;
  font-size: 100%;
  line-height: 1.3em;
  font-family: Arial, Helvetica, sans-serif;
}
```

As you can see, this is rather weightier!

An *invalid* font declaration is shown in the following code block. Here, the `font-weight` value (bold) is incorrectly placed after the `font-family` value, and the `font-size` value is missing.

```
p.invalid {
   font: Arial, Helvetica, sans-serif bold;
}
```

Controlling text element margins

By default, browsers place margins around block-level text-based elements (such as headings and paragraphs), which can be overridden by CSS. However, many designers get confused when dealing with margins, so a good rule of thumb is to first remove all element margins via the universal selector (see the "Zeroing margins and padding on all elements" section in Chapter 2 for more information).

```
* {
  margin: 0;
  padding: 0;
}
```

Once you've done this, you should primarily control spacing between text elements via the bottom margins:

```
h1, h2 {
  margin-bottom: 10px;
}
p {
  margin-bottom: 1em;
}
```

In the previous example, the margins below headings are small, enabling the eye to rapidly travel from the heading to the related body copy. The margin at the bottom of each paragraph is one character high.

Should you decide, after applying styles, that more room is required between paragraphs and subsequent headings, apply a top margin to the relevant level (or levels) of heading, but be aware that vertical margins collapse.

Later in the chapter, a few exercises will show how margins (along with various other settings) can affect the way a page looks and feels. Certainly, margin definitions shouldn't be throwaway—like in music, where the gaps are almost as important as the notes, the whitespace in typography is almost as important as the content.

Using text-indent for print-like paragraphs

Because of people's familiarity with non-indented paragraphs on the Web, the W3C recommends staying away from indented ones. However, there are times when designers yearn for a more print-based design, as in the following image.

> Lorem ipsum dolor sit amet, consectetuer adipiscing elit. Morbi commodo, ipsum sed pharetra gravida, orci magna rhoncus neque, id pulvinar odio lorem non turpis. Nullam sit amet enim. Suspendisse id velit vitae ligula volutpat condimentum. Aliquam erat volutpat. Sed quis velit.
>
> Nulla facilisi. Nulla libero. Vivamus pharetra posuere sapien. Nam consectetuer. Sed aliquam, nunc eget euismod ullamcorper, lectus nunc ullamcorper orci, fermentum bibendum enim nibh eget ipsum. Donec porttitor ligula eu dolor. Maecenas vitae nulla consequat libero cursus venenatis. Nam magna enim, accumsan eu, blandit sed, blandit a, eros.
>
> Quisque facilisis erat a dui. Nam malesuada ornare dolor. Cras gravida, diam sit amet rhoncus ornare, erat elit consectetuer erat, id egestas pede nibh eget odio. Proin tincidunt, velit vel porta elementum, magna diam molestie sapien, non aliquet massa pede eu

For this effect, two things not previously discussed in this book are required: the `text-indent` CSS property and an **adjacent sibling selector**. This type of selector uses the syntax A+B, where B is the subject of the selector. For paragraph indentation, the CSS rule would look something like the following code block:

```
p+p {
   text-indent: 1.5em;
}
```

In plain English, this is saying, "If a paragraph follows another paragraph, indent the text by 1.5 ems". Therefore, paragraphs preceded by a different element, such as a heading, won't be indented, as is traditional in print.

> *Note that prior to version 7, Internet Explorer didn't support adjacent sibling selectors, and so this effect won't work in version 6 or below of Microsoft's browser. A workaround would be to use a style sheet linked via a conditional comment to indent all paragraphs for Internet Explorer 6 and below. See the "Dealing with Internet Explorer bugs" section in Chapter 9 for more on conditional comments.*

Setting letter-spacing and word-spacing

The `letter-spacing` and `word-spacing` properties work in the same way, taking length values or a default of normal. For `letter-spacing`, the value increases whitespace between characters, and for `word-spacing`, the defined value increases whitespace between words. Negative values are permitted, which cause characters or words to bunch together (or **kern**, if you're a graphic designer). A certain amount of experimentation is recommended if you decide to use these properties. Because the Web's resolution is low, subtle kerning changes are hard to achieve online, and the results often end up looking clunky. Also, spacing varies from platform to platform. One occasion when `letter-spacing` is worth experimenting with, however, is when styling headings for web pages: a small increase in the `letter-spacing` value can help further distinguish headings from body copy.

Examples of these properties in use are shown in the following code block:

```
h1 {
  letter-spacing: 3px;
}
h2 {
  word-spacing: 2px;
}
```

Controlling case with text-transform

The text-transform property enables you to change the case of letters within an element. Available values are capitalize, uppercase, lowercase, and none (the default). The uppercase and lowercase values force the text of the applied element into the relevant case regardless of the original content (e.g., enabling you to override the case of the original content for ensuring that headings are consistent site-wide), whereas capitalize sets the first letter of each word in uppercase.

In the following example, the first heading is styled as uppercase, the second as lowercase, and the third as capitalize. Note that I wouldn't recommend such a mix of styles in a website—these rules are just examples of the properties in use.

Here's the HTML:

```
<h1>A heading</h1>
<h2>Another heading</h2>
<h3>A third heading</h3>
```

Here's the CSS:

```
h1 {
  text-transform: uppercase;
}
h2 {
  text-transform: lowercase;
}
h3 {
  text-transform: capitalize;
}
```

> **A HEADING**
>
> **another heading**
>
> **A Third Heading**

Creating alternatives with classes and spans

It's common in web design to define alternatives to the rules set for tag selectors (h1, h2, p, etc.). This tends to happen most often in one of two situations. The first is when creating alternate styles for a portion of a web page (as in print, it's often beneficial to use different text for sidebars and boxouts—standalone boxes on a magazine page, either housing supplementary information to the main article, or an entirely independent piece that needs to be visually distinct from other content on the page—and sidebars to ensure that each area of content is easy to distinguish from another). In this situation, it's sensible to define a default rule for each element using an element selector, and then create an override for the portion of the page that requires different text by using a contextual selector.

For example, imagine a typical web page that has a sidebar that's marked up as a div with an id value of sidebar. You might use a different paragraph font in the sidebar, to differentiate the text, like so:

```
p {
  font: 1.2em/1.5 Verdana, Arial, sans-serif;
  margin-bottom: 1em;
}
#sidebar p {
  font: 1.2em/1.5 Arial, sans-serif;
}
```

The other occasion where alternatives are required is when creating one-off styles to override an existing style. In such cases, you can define a class in the CSS and then use a class attribute to apply it to an element. Should you only want a portion of some text to take on the style, you can surround the selection with a span element and apply the class to that instead.

For example, if you wanted to create some "warning" text, you could use the following CSS:

```
.warningText {
  color: #ff0000;
  font-size: 120%;
}
```

This can then be applied as follows:

```
<p class="warningText">This paragraph takes on the styles defined in
➥ the warningText class</p>
<p>Only <span class="warningText">this portion</span> of this
➥ paragraph takes on the warningText class styles.</p>
```

Avoid overusing span elements, though. Text works best when it's consistent across the page.

> Note that the preceding CSS style has a capital letter halfway through it—this case is known as **lowerCamelCase**, and is a method of writing multiple-word style names, because underscores and spaces must be avoided in CSS. Take care if you do this, because styles are case sensitive. If you set a class attribute value to warningtext instead of warningText, many browsers fail to display the style, reverting to the default style for the relevant element.

Styling semantic markup

The exercises in this section will combine the elements discussed so far in this chapter, showing how to use the knowledge gained to style some semantic markup. Three different examples are on offer, showing how rapidly you can create great-looking text when working with CSS, and also how you can easily restyle a page of text without touching the markup. The markup that you'll use is as per that in the next code block; and the default web page, without any CSS applied, is shown to its right.

```
<div id="wrapper">
  <h1>Article heading</h1>
  <p>Lorem ipsum dolor sit amet,
consectetuer adipiscing elit. Sed
➥ aliquet elementum erat. Integer
➥ diam mi, venenatis non, cursus
➥ a, hendrerit at, mi. Morbi risus
➥ mi, tincidunt ornare, tempus
➥  ut, eleifend nec, risus.</p>
  <p>Quisque faucibus lorem eget sapien.
➥ In urna sem, vehicula ut,
➥ mattis et, venenatis at, velit.
➥ Ut sodales lacus sed eros.
➥ Pellentesque tristique senectus et
➥ netus et malesuada fames
➥ ac turpis egestas.</p>
  <h2>Curabitur sit amet risus</h2>
  <p>Lorem ipsum dolor sit amet,
➥ consectetuer adipiscing elit. Sed
➥ aliquet elementum erat. Integer
➥ diam mi, venenatis non, cursus
➥ a, hendrerit at, mi. Morbi risus mi, tincidunt ornare, tempus
➥ ut, eleifend nec, risus.</p>
  <p>Quisque faucibus lorem eget sapien. In urna sem, vehicula ut,
➥ mattis et, venenatis at, velit. Ut sodales lacus sed eros.
➥ Pellentesque tristique senectus et netus et malesuada fames
➥ ac turpis egestas.</p>
  <h3>Praesent rutrum</h3>
  <p>Nam scelerisque dignissim quam. Ut bibendum enim in orci. Vivamus
➥ ligula nunc, dictum a, tincidunt in, dignissim ac, odio.</p>
  <h3>Habitant morbid</h3>
  <p>Nam scelerisque dignissim quam. Ut bibendum enim in orci. Vivamus
➥ ligula nunc, dictum a, tincidunt in, dignissim ac, odio.</p>
</div>
```

Article heading

Lorem ipsum dolor sit amet, consectetuer adipiscing elit. Sed aliquet elementum erat. Integer diam mi, venenatis non, cursus a, hendrerit at, mi. Morbi risus mi, tincidunt ornare, tempus ut, eleifend nec, risus.

Quisque faucibus lorem eget sapien. In urna sem, vehicula ut, mattis et, venenatis at, velit. Ut sodales lacus sed eros. Pellentesque tristique senectus et netus et malesuada fames ac turpis egestas.

Curabitur sit amet risus

Lorem ipsum dolor sit amet, consectetuer adipiscing elit. Sed aliquet elementum erat. Integer diam mi, venenatis non, cursus a, hendrerit at, mi. Morbi risus mi, tincidunt ornare, tempus ut, eleifend nec, risus.

Quisque faucibus lorem eget sapien. In urna sem, vehicula ut, mattis et, venenatis at, velit. Ut sodales lacus sed eros. Pellentesque tristique senectus et netus et malesuada fames ac turpis egestas.

Praesent rutrum

Nam scelerisque dignissim quam. Ut bibendum enim in orci. Vivamus ligula nunc, dictum a, tincidunt in, dignissim ac, odio.

Habitant morbid

Nam scelerisque dignissim quam. Ut bibendum enim in orci. Vivamus ligula nunc, dictum a, tincidunt in, dignissim ac, odio.

The code block is simple. The text has three levels of headings, with paragraphs between them. Everything's enclosed in a div element, which will be styled to restrict the width of its content. This makes it simpler to see how the leading—defined via line-height—is working out. If you were surfing at full-screen on a large monitor, the paragraphs might only be shown on a single line.

The default CSS document for these exercises has some rules common to all three examples. These are shown in the following code block:

```
* {
  margin: 0;
  padding: 0;
}

html {
  font-size: 100%;
}

body {
  padding: 20px;
  font-size: 62.5%;
}

#wrapper {
  margin: 0 auto;
  width: 400px;
}
```

The first rule, *, removes margins and padding from all elements, as discussed previously. The html and body rules set the default size of the text on the web page to 62.5%, as explained in the "Setting text using percentages and ems" section earlier in this chapter. Finally, the #wrapper rule defines a width for the wrapper div, and therefore for its content.

Styling semantic markup: A basic example with proportional line heights

Required files	styling-semantic-text-starting-point.html and styling-semantic-text-starting-point.css from the chapter 3 folder.
What you'll learn	How to style headings and paragraphs using sans-serif fonts (Verdana for body copy and Arial for headings) and proportional, unitless line-height settings.
Completed files	styling-semantic-text-1.html and styling-semantic-text-1.css from the chapter 3 folder.

1. Define the font defaults. Using a body selector, define a default font for the web page, along with a default line-height value. As this is a basic example, Verdana is used as the primary font, falling back to Arial and Helvetica. The unitless line-height value means that elements will have proportional line heights based on their font-size values, unless otherwise stated.

```
body {
  font-family: Verdana, Arial, Helvetica, sans-serif;
  line-height: 1.5;
}
```

In the CSS, you'll end up with two body selectors if you follow this to the letter—one for dealing with padding and setting the default font size to 62.5%, and the other for defining the default font-family *value for the page, along with the* line-height. *This enables these exercises to remain modular; in a real site, although it's acceptable to use selectors more than once, you should ensure property values and rules are correctly housed in the relevant section of your boilerplates—see Chapter 10 and Appendix D (CSS Reference) for more information on CSS management.*

2. Define common settings for headings. In this example, the top two levels of headings will have the same font-family value. Therefore, it makes sense to use a grouped selector to define this property:

```
h1, h2 {
   font-family: Arial, Helvetica, sans-serif;
}
```

3. Define specific values for headings. How you style headings will depend on their purpose. For these exercises, h1 is the page heading, h2 is a subheading, and h3 is a crosshead to introduce a section of copy. With that in mind, the crosshead needs to be of similar size to the paragraphs, the main heading needs to be most prominent, and the subheading needs to be somewhere in between. Therefore, in the CSS, the h1 element has a font-size value of 2.5em, the h3 has a much smaller 1.2em, and the h2 has an in-between 2em.

```
h1 {
   font-size: 2.5em;
}
h2 {
   font-size: 2em;
}
h3 {
   font-size: 1.2em;
}
```

4. Style the paragraphs, using the following rule. Whereas the space around headings is taken care of with the line-height setting defined in the body selector, that doesn't work for paragraphs, which must have distinct space between them. Therefore, along with a font-size property/value pair, a margin-bottom value sets the space between each paragraph to slightly more than the height of one character.

```
p {
   font-size: 1.1em;
   margin-bottom: 1.1em;
}
```

5. Refine the element spacing. At this point, the spacing is still a little suspect—the crossheads don't stand out enough. Therefore, add a margin-top value to the h3 rule; this provides a little extra space between paragraphs and level-three headings. (As mentioned earlier, vertical margins collapse, so the space between a paragraph with a bottom margin of 1.1em and a level-three heading with a top margin of 1.65em is 1.65em, *not* the sum of the two margins, which would be 2.75em.)

```
h3 {
  font-size: 1.2em;
  margin-top: 1.65em;
}

h3, p {
  margin-left: 1em;
}
```

The following image shows what your completed page should look like.

Article heading

Lorem ipsum dolor sit amet, consectetuer adipiscing elit. Sed
aliquet elementum erat. Integer diam mi, venenatis non, cursus a,
hendrerit at, mi. Morbi risus mi, tincidunt ornare, tempus ut,
eleifend nec, risus.

Quisque faucibus lorem eget sapien. In urna sem, vehicula ut,
mattis et, venenatis at, velit. Ut sodales lacus sed eros.
Pellentesque tristique senectus et netus et malesuada fames ac
turpis egestas.

Curabitur sit amet risus

Lorem ipsum dolor sit amet, consectetuer adipiscing elit. Sed
aliquet elementum erat. Integer diam mi, venenatis non, cursus a,
hendrerit at, mi. Morbi risus mi, tincidunt ornare, tempus ut,
eleifend nec, risus.

Quisque faucibus lorem eget sapien. In urna sem, vehicula ut,
mattis et, venenatis at, velit. Ut sodales lacus sed eros.
Pellentesque tristique senectus et netus et malesuada fames ac
turpis egestas.

Praesent rutrum
Nam scelerisque dignissim quam. Ut bibendum enim in orci.
Vivamus ligula nunc, dictum a, tincidunt in, dignissim ac, odio.

Habitant morbid
Nam scelerisque dignissim quam. Ut bibendum enim in orci.
Vivamus ligula nunc, dictum a, tincidunt in, dignissim ac, odio.

Styling semantic markup: A modern example with sans-serif fonts

Required files	styling-semantic-text-starting-point.html and styling-semantic-text-starting-point.css from the chapter 3 folder.
What you'll learn	How to create a contemporary-looking page of text using Lucida fonts, as per the text on Apple's website.
Completed files	styling-semantic-text-2.html and styling-semantic-text-2.css from the chapter 3 folder.

1. Set the font defaults. As in the previous exercise, use a body rule to define the default font for the page, the first couple of choices of which are Lucida variants that are installed on Mac OS and Windows. Other fonts are provided for legacy or alternate systems.

```
body {
   font-family: "Lucida Grande", "Lucida Sans Unicode", Lucida, Arial,
   ➥ Helvetica, sans-serif;
   line-height: 1.5;
}
```

2. Style the main heading. An h1 rule is used to style the main heading. The restrictive value for line-height makes the leading value the height of one character of the heading, meaning there's no space underneath it. This means you can define an explicit padding-bottom value can be defined, followed by a border-bottom (here, 1 pixel, solid, and very light gray), followed by a margin-bottom value. The padding-bottom and margin-bottom values are the same, creating a very tight, clean feel for the heading. Elsewhere, the color setting knocks it back slightly so that it doesn't overpower the other content, and the font-weight value removes the default bold setting that browsers apply to headings. This helps the block of text appear light and clean.

```
h1 {
   font-size: 1.8em;
   line-height: 1em;
   padding-bottom: 7px;
   border-bottom: 1px solid #cccccc;
   margin-bottom: 7px;
   color: #666666;
   font-weight: normal;
}
```

> When removing the default bold style from headings, check them across platforms—on some Windows systems, non-bold headings can look a bit spindly, depending on the settings.

3. Style the other headings. For the next two heading levels, font-size values are assigned. In keeping with the modern style, the crossheads are the same size as the paragraph text (styled in the next step)—just displayed in bold; the subheading (h2) is slightly larger, making it a little more prominent. Again, the headings are colored to make them blend in a little more, and not distract from the paragraph text.

```
h2, h3 {
   color: #333333;
}
h2 {
   font-size: 1.3em;
}
h3 {
```

```
    font-size: 1.2em;
    margin-top: 1.65em;
}
```

4. Style the paragraphs. The `font-size` setting is larger than that used on many websites (which typically tend toward 11 pixels, which would require a 1.1em value in this example), but this ensures clarity, and again, enhances the clean nature of the design.

```
p {
    font-size: 1.2em;
    margin-bottom: 1.2em;
}
```

The final rule—an adjacent sibling selector—styles the paragraph following the main heading, making the intro paragraph bold. It's colored a dark gray, rather than black, which would be overpowering and wreck the balance of the page.

```
h1+p {
    font-weight: bold;
    color: #222222;
}
```

The following image shows what your completed page should look like.

Article heading

Lorem ipsum dolor sit amet, consectetuer adipiscing elit. Sed aliquet elementum erat. Integer diam mi, venenatis non, cursus a, hendrerit at, mi. Morbi risus mi, tincidunt ornare, tempus ut, eleifend nec, risus.

Quisque faucibus lorem eget sapien. In urna sem, vehicula ut, mattis et, venenatis at, velit. Ut sodales lacus sed eros. Pellentesque tristique senectus et netus et malesuada fames ac turpis egestas.

Curabitur sit amet risus
Lorem ipsum dolor sit amet, consectetuer adipiscing elit. Sed aliquet elementum erat. Integer diam mi, venenatis non, cursus a, hendrerit at, mi. Morbi risus mi, tincidunt ornare, tempus ut, eleifend nec, risus.

Quisque faucibus lorem eget sapien. In urna sem, vehicula ut, mattis et, venenatis at, velit. Ut sodales lacus sed eros. Pellentesque tristique senectus et netus et malesuada fames ac turpis egestas.

Praesent rutrum
Nam scelerisque dignissim quam. Ut bibendum enim in orci. Vivamus ligula nunc, dictum a, tincidunt in, dignissim ac, odio.

Habitant morbid
Nam scelerisque dignissim quam. Ut bibendum enim in orci. Vivamus ligula nunc, dictum a, tincidunt in, dignissim ac, odio.

Styling semantic markup: A traditional example with serif fonts and a baseline grid

Required files	`styling-semantic-text-starting-point.html`, `styling-semantic-text-starting-point.css`, and `styling-semantic-text-baseline.gif` from the chapter 3 folder.
What you'll learn	How to create a page of traditional-looking text as per a printed book. The text adheres strictly to a baseline grid, maintaining the page's vertical rhythm. This requires some extra calculations when it comes to defining `line-height` values.
Completed files	`styling-semantic-text-3.html` and `styling-semantic-text-3.css` from the chapter 3 folder.

1. Define a default font for the page. Using a body rule, a default font is chosen for the web page. This design primarily uses the Georgia font—a serif—to enhance the traditional feel.

```
body {
    font-family: Georgia, "Times New Roman", Times, serif;
}
```

At this point, it's also important to decide on a target `line-height` value for the page. For this example, it's going to be 18px.

2. Style the main heading. Here's where things get a little tricky. For these examples, we're working with relative units. As mentioned earlier in the chapter, the 62.5% method means that you can define font sizes by setting the `font-size` value to a setting in ems that's one-tenth of the target size in pixels. So, in the following code block, the h1 rule's `font-size` value of `1.8em` means it's effectively displayed at 18 pixels (assuming the user hasn't messed around with their browser's default settings, again as mentioned earlier).

For the `line-height` value to hit the target of 18 pixels, it must therefore be 18 pixels or a multiple of it. However, when using ems, this value is relative to the `font-size` value. One em is equal to the height of one character, and since the `font-size` has been set to `1.8em` (which is equivalent to 18 pixels), we set `line-height` to 1em. This makes the `line-height` of the h1 element the equivalent of 18 pixels.

Similar thinking is used to define the value for `margin-bottom`—this needs to be 18 pixels to keep the vertical rhythm going, so the value is set to 1em.

```
h1 {
    font-size: 1.8em;
    line-height: 1em;
    margin-bottom: 1em;
}
```

3. Style the subheading. For the subheading, the font-size value is set to 1.4em. To keep the line-height vertical rhythm going, you need to find the value that will multiply with the font-size setting to create 1.8 (since 1.8em is the equivalent of 18 pixels). You can get this by dividing 1.8 by the font-size value, which results in a line-height value of 1.2857142em. To keep the rhythm going, this setting can then be used for both the margin-top and margin-bottom values.

```
h2 {
  font-size: 1.4em;
  line-height: 1.2857142em;
  margin-top: 1.2857142em;
  margin-bottom: 1.2857142em;
}
```

However, what this serves to do is isolate the heading on its own line, rather than making it obviously lead to the subsequent paragraph. Two solutions exist for dealing with this. The first is simply to remove the bottom margin; the second is to create asymmetrical margins, making the top margin larger than the bottom one. To keep the entire space the element takes up strictly within the grid and not interrupt the vertical rhythm too much, it's sensible to take half the margin-bottom value and add it to the margin-top value.

```
h2 {
  font-size: 1.4em;
  line-height: 1.2857142em;
  margin-top: 1.9285713em;
  margin-bottom: 0.6428571em;
}
```

4. Style the crossheads and paragraphs. For this example, the crossheads and paragraphs are identical, save for the default styling on the headings that renders them in bold. The font-size value is 1.2em. Again, 1.8 is divided by the font-size figure to arrive at the line-height and margin values, both of which are set to 1.5em. Note that the h3 rule has no margin-bottom value, meaning that each level-three heading hugs the subsequent paragraph.

```
h3 {
  font-size: 1.2em;
  line-height: 1.5em;
  margin-top: 1.5em;
}
p {
  font-size: 1.2em;
  line-height: 1.5em;
  margin-bottom: 1.5em;
}
```

At this point, your page should look like the following image.

Article heading

Lorem ipsum dolor sit amet, consectetuer adipiscing elit. Sed aliquet elementum erat. Integer diam mi, venenatis non, cursus a, hendrerit at, mi. Morbi risus mi, tincidunt ornare, tempus ut, eleifend nec, risus.

Quisque faucibus lorem eget sapien. In urna sem, vehicula ut, mattis et, venenatis at, velit. Ut sodales lacus sed eros. Pellentesque tristique senectus et netus et malesuada fames ac turpis egestas.

Curabitur sit amet risus

Lorem ipsum dolor sit amet, consectetuer adipiscing elit. Sed aliquet elementum erat. Integer diam mi, venenatis non, cursus a, hendrerit at, mi. Morbi risus mi, tincidunt ornare, tempus ut, eleifend nec, risus.

Quisque faucibus lorem eget sapien. In urna sem, vehicula ut, mattis et, venenatis at, velit. Ut sodales lacus sed eros. Pellentesque tristique senectus et netus et malesuada fames ac turpis egestas.

Praesent rutrum
Nam scelerisque dignissim quam. Ut bibendum enim in orci. Vivamus ligula nunc, dictum a, tincidunt in, dignissim ac, odio.

Habitant morbid
Nam scelerisque dignissim quam. Ut bibendum enim in orci. Vivamus ligula nunc, dictum a, tincidunt in, dignissim ac, odio.

5. Add a (temporary) grid. When working on text that adheres to a baseline grid, it can help to create a tiled background image that you can use to check whether your measurements are accurate. The 18-pixel-high image file, `styling-semantic-text-baseline.gif`, has a single-pixel line at the bottom of the image. When applied to the wrapper div's background via the #wrapper rule (see the following code), a ruled background is shown. Although intended as a temporary design aid, you could retain the grid permanently, because it can help readers to rapidly skim text. However, the aid only works when a browser is using default settings—when the text is enlarged, the background image stays as it is, resulting in the grid of the image and the grid of the text being out of sync.

```
#wrapper {
  margin: 0 auto;
  width: 400px;
  background: url(styling-semantic-text-baseline.gif);
}
```

The following image shows how this image works behind the text styled in this exercise—as you can see, the vertical rhythm is maintained right down the page.

Article heading

Lorem ipsum dolor sit amet, consectetuer adipiscing elit. Sed aliquet elementum erat. Integer diam mi, venenatis non, cursus a, hendrerit at, mi. Morbi risus mi, tincidunt ornare, tempus ut, eleifend nec, risus.

Quisque faucibus lorem eget sapien. In urna sem, vehicula ut, mattis et, venenatis at, velit. Ut sodales lacus sed eros. Pellentesque tristique senectus et netus et malesuada fames ac turpis egestas.

Curabitur sit amet risus

Lorem ipsum dolor sit amet, consectetuer adipiscing elit. Sed aliquet elementum erat. Integer diam mi, venenatis non, cursus a, hendrerit at, mi. Morbi risus mi, tincidunt ornare, tempus ut, eleifend nec, risus.

Quisque faucibus lorem eget sapien. In urna sem, vehicula ut, mattis et, venenatis at, velit. Ut sodales lacus sed eros. Pellentesque tristique senectus et netus et malesuada fames ac turpis egestas.

Praesent rutrum

Nam scelerisque dignissim quam. Ut bibendum enim in orci. Vivamus ligula nunc, dictum a, tincidunt in, dignissim ac, odio.

Habitant morbid

Nam scelerisque dignissim quam. Ut bibendum enim in orci. Vivamus ligula nunc, dictum a, tincidunt in, dignissim ac, odio.

Creating drop caps and pull quotes using CSS

The previous exercise showed how something aimed primarily at the world of print design—a baseline grid—can actually work well online, and this section will continue that theme, showing how to use CSS to create drop caps and pull quotes. Drop caps—large letters typically used at the start of a printed article—are rare online, although they can be a useful way of drawing the eye to the beginning of the body copy. Pull quotes are more common, and while part of their use in print—taking a choice quote and making it stand out on the page to draw in the reader—is less effective online, pull quotes are still handy for highlighting a piece of text (such as a quote or idea) or for providing client quotes on a company website.

Creating a drop cap using a CSS pseudo-element

Required files	`styling-semantic-text-2.html` and `styling-semantic-text-2.css` from the chapter 3 folder.
What you'll learn	How to create a drop cap for a website, and how to use the CSS `float` property. Any element can be floated left or right in CSS, and this causes subsequent content to wrap around it.
Completed files	`drop-cap.html` and `drop-cap.css` from the chapter 3 folder.

1. Create a new rule that targets the relevant character. For this, you can use a **pseudo-element**, `first-letter`, and the adjacent sibling selector created earlier in the "Styling semantic markup" section. See Appendix D ("CSS Reference") for more on pseudo-elements.

```
h1+p:first-letter {

}
```

In plain English, this rule is saying, "Apply this rule to the first letter of the paragraph that follows the level-one heading."

2. Float the character and increase its size. Add a `float: left` property/value pair to float the first character in the paragraph to the left, which makes subsequent content wrap around it. Then set a large `font-size` value to increase the size of the character compared to the surrounding text.

```
h1+p:first-letter {
  float: left;
  font-size: 3em;
}
```

3. Finally, tweak the positioning. Define a `line-height` value and `margin-top` value to vertically position the character; you may need to experiment some when working on your own designs outside of this exercise, since the values required are somewhat dependent on the `font-size` setting. The `margin-right` setting provides some spacing between the drop cap and the subsequent text.

```
h1+p:first-letter {
  float: left;
  font-size: 3em;
  line-height: 1.0em;
  margin-top: -3px;
  margin-right: 0.15em;
}
```

> Note that you can use the `first-line` *pseudo-element to target the first line of some text—for example, to make it bold, which is a commonly used design element in magazines.*

Although this technique is the most straightforward one for working with drop caps, the results aren't entirely satisfactory. Due to the way different browsers deal with the `first-letter` pseudo-element, display isn't particularly consistent across browsers and platforms—see the following two images, which show the results in Firefox and Safari. Therefore, if you want to use drop caps with more precision, it's best to fall back on a more old-fashioned but tried-and-tested method: the span element.

Article heading
L orem ipsum dolor sit amet, consectetuer adipiscing Sed aliquet elementum erat. Integer diam mi, venen non, cursus a, hendrerit at, mi. Morbi risus mi, tinci ornare, tempus ut, eleifend nec, risus.

Article heading
L orem ipsum dolor sit amet, consectetuer adipiscing Sed aliquet elementum erat. Integer diam mi, venen non, cursus a, hendrerit at, mi. Morbi risus mi, tincidun tempus ut, eleifend nec, risus.

Creating a drop cap with span elements and CSS

Required files	styling-semantic-text-2.html and styling-semantic-text-2.css from the chapter 3 folder.
What you'll learn	How to create a drop cap for a website, using span elements to aid positioning.
Completed files	drop-cap-with-spans.html and drop-cap-with-spans.css from the chapter 3 folder. The variant with colored backgrounds uses the files drop-cap-with-spans-b.html and drop-cap-with-spans-b.css.

1. Add the span elements. Wrap a span element around the first character of the paragraph and give it a class value of dropCap. Wrap another span element around the initial character, without any class attribute. The additional span makes it easier to fine-tune the positioning of the drop cap.

```
<p><span class="dropCap"><span>L</span></span>orem ipsum dolor […]
```

2. Size the drop cap. Using a contextual selector, define a font-size setting of 4.8em for the content of the span element within the dropCap span. This is the height of three lines of text, from the top of a character in the first line to the bottom of a character in the third.

```
.dropCap span {
  font-size: 4.8em;
  line-height: 1em;
}
```

3. Float the drop cap. In order for subsequent text to flow around the drop cap, it has to be floated. This is done via the float: left property/value pair. The display: block pair sets the dropCap span as a block-level element, enabling you to set edge dimensions for it. By defining a height value that's slightly smaller than the font-size setting, subsequent text won't sit underneath the drop cap once it's correctly positioned.

```
.dropCap {
  float: left;
  height: 4.7em;
}
```

4. Tweak positioning of the drop cap. Use top and left margins (positive and negative) to move the drop cap into position, so that it correctly lines up with the other text on the page. The margin-right setting ensures that text to the right of the drop cap doesn't hug it.

```
.dropCap {
  float: left;
  height: 4.7em;
  margin-top: -0.2em;
  margin-left: -0.4em;
  margin-right: 0.5em;
}
```

The following image shows what your page should look like so far.

5. Review the code and add a colored background. This method also isn't without its problems—the span elements have no semantic value and are therefore "bloated code"; and the values set in steps 2 and 3 require some experimentation for each different font and paragraph setting you use them with. However, it usually doesn't take long to get everything working, and once you have a design, it's easy enough to tweak. For example, amend the rules as follows to change the drop cap to one with a colored background:

```
.dropCap {
  float: left;
  height: 3.9em;
  margin-top: -0.2em;
  margin-left: -0.4em;
  margin-right: 0.5em;
  border: 1px solid #aaaaaa;
  background: #dddddd;
  color: #ffffff;
  padding: 0.2em 0.6em;
}

.dropCap span {
  font-size: 4.0em;
  line-height: 1em;
}
```

Article heading

L orem ipsum dolor sit amet, consectetuer adipiscing elit. Sed aliquet elementum erat. Integer diam mi, venenatis non, cursus a, hendrerit at, mi. Morbi risus mi, tincidunt ornare, tempus ut, eleifend nec, risus.

> *Note that the image-replacement techniques described earlier in the chapter offer another means of adding a drop cap of a more graphical nature, should such a thing be required.*

Creating pull quotes in CSS

Required files	styling-semantic-text-2.html, styling-semantic-text-2.css, quote-open.gif, and quote-close.gif from the chapter 3 folder.
What you'll learn	How to create a magazine-style pull quote, which can draw the user's attention to a quote or highlight a portion of an article.
Completed files	pull-quote.html and pull-quote.css from the chapter 3 folder.

1. Add the HTML. The required markup for a basic pull quote is simple, centering around the blockquote element and nesting a paragraph within. Add the following to the web page, above the code `<h2>Curabitur sit amet risus</h2>`:

```
<blockquote>
  <p>This is the pull quote. It's really very exciting, so read it now!
  ➥ Lorem ipsum dolor sit amet, consectetuer adipiscing elit.</p>
</blockquote>
```

2. Style the blockquote element. Create a blockquote rule and use the background property to add the open quote image as its background. Set vertical margins that are larger than the margins between the paragraphs (to ensure that the pull quote stands out from the surrounding text) and the horizontal margins (to ensure that the pull quote doesn't span the entire column width, which also helps it visually stand out).

```
blockquote {
  background: url(quote-open.gif) 0 0 no-repeat;
  margin: 2.4em 2em;
}
```

3. Style the pull quote paragraph text. Using the contextual selector blockquote p, style the paragraph text within the blockquote element. Making the text bold and larger than the surrounding copy helps it stand out—but to ensure it doesn't become too distracting, knock back its color a little.

```
blockquote p {
  color: #555555;
  font-size: 1.3em;
  font-weight: bold;
  text-align: justify;
}
```

4. Use the background property to add the closing quote mark, which is added to the paragraph, since you can only add one background image to an element in CSS. The background's position is set to 100% 90%—far right and almost at the bottom. Setting it at the absolute bottom would align the closing quote with the bottom of the *leading* under the last line of the paragraph text; setting the vertical position value to 90%, however, lines up the closing quote with the bottom of the text itself.

```
blockquote p {
  color: #555555;
  font-size: 1.3em;
  font-weight: bold;
  text-align: justify;
  background: url(quote-close.gif) 100% 90% no-repeat;
}
```

5. Tweak the positioning. If you test the page now, you'll see the paragraph content appearing over the top of the background images. To avoid this, padding needs to be applied to the quote mark to force its content inward, but still leave the background images in place. Since the quote images are both 23 pixels wide, a horizontal padding value of 33px provides room for the images and adds an additional 10 pixels so that the content of the paragraph doesn't abut the quote marks. Finally, the default margin-bottom value for paragraphs is overridden (via a 0 value), since it's redundant here.

```
blockquote p {
  color: #555555;
  font-size: 1.3em;
  font-weight: bold;
  text-align: justify;
  background: url(quote-close.gif) 100% 90% no-repeat;
  padding: 0 33px;
  margin-bottom: 0;
}
```

The following image shows your pull quote page so far.

> et, venenatis at, velit. Ut sodales lacus sed eros. Pellentesque
> tristique senectus et netus et malesuada fames ac turpis egestas.
>
> **66** This is the pull quote. It's really very
> exciting, so read it now! Lorem ipsum dolor
> sit amet, consectetuer adipiscing elit. **99**
>
> **Curabitur sit amet risus**
> Lorem ipsum dolor sit amet, consectetuer adipiscing elit. Sed aliquet

6. Next, credit the quotation. To add a credit to the quote, add another paragraph, with a nested cite element, inside which is the relevant content.

```
<blockquote>
  <p>This is the pull quote. It's really very exciting, so read it now!
  ➥ Lorem ipsum dolor sit amet, consectetuer adipiscing elit.</p>
  <p><cite>Fred Bloggs</cite></p>
</blockquote>
```

7. In CSS, add the following rule:

```
cite {
  background: none;
  display: block;
  text-align: right;
  font-size: 1.1em;
  font-weight: normal;
  font-style: italic;
}
```

8. Some of the property values in cite are there to override the settings from block-quote p, and to ensure that the second paragraph's text is clearly distinguishable from the quote itself. However, at this point, both paragraphs within the block-quote element have the closing-quote background, so a final rule is required.

```
blockquote>p+p {
  background: none;
}
```

This fairly complex rule uses both a child selector (>) and an adjacent selector (+), and styles the paragraph that comes immediately after the paragraph that's a child element of the blockquote (which is the paragraph with the cite element). The rule overrides the background value defined in step 5 for paragraphs within the block quote). Note that this assumes the quote itself will only be a single paragraph. If you have multi-paragraph quotes, you'll need to apply a class to the final paragraph and set the quote-close.gif image as a background on that, rather than on blockquote p.

> et, venenatis at, velit. Ut sodales lacus sed eros. Pellentesque tristique senectus et netus et malesuada fames ac turpis egestas.
>
> **66** This is the pull quote. It's really very exciting, so read it now! Lorem ipsum dolor sit amet, consectetuer adipiscing elit. **99**
>
> *Fred Bloggs*
>
> **Curabitur sit amet risus**
> Lorem ipsum dolor sit amet, consectetuer adipiscing elit. Sed aliquet

Note that the advanced selector shown isn't understood by versions of Internet Explorer prior to 7. The best workaround for that browser is to use conditional comments (see Chapter 9) to remove the quote graphic backgrounds.

Using classes and CSS overrides to create an alternate pull quote

Required files	pull-quote.html and pull-quote.css from the chapter 3 folder.
What you'll learn	How to use CSS classes to create alternatives to the default pull quote. In this example, you'll create a narrow pull quote that floats to the right of the body copy.
Completed files	pull-quote-2.html and pull-quote-2.css from the chapter 3 folder.

3

1. Amend the HTML. First, add a class to the blockquote element so that it can be targeted in CSS:

```
<blockquote class="floatRight">
```

2. Position the blockquote. Create a new CSS rule that targets the blockquote from the previous step by using the selector blockquote.floatRight. Set float and width values to float the pull quote and define its width.

```
blockquote.floatRight {
    float: right;
    width: 150px;
}
```

3. Remove the quote mark background image by setting background to none. Add the two border property/value pairs shown to visually separate the pull quote from its surroundings, drawing the eye to its content.

```
blockquote.floatRight {
    float: right;
    width: 150px;
    background: none;
    border-top: 5px solid #dddddd;
    border-bottom: 5px solid #dddddd;
}
```

4. Add padding and margins. First, add vertical padding to ensure that the pull quote's contents don't hug the borders added in the previous step. Next, define margin values, overriding those set for the default blockquote from the previous exercise. Because this alternate pull quote is floated right, there's no need for top and right margins, hence them being set to 0; the bottom and left margin values are left intact.

```
blockquote.floatRight {
    float: right;
    width: 150px;
    background: none;
    border-top: 5px solid #dddddd;
    border-bottom: 5px solid #dddddd;
    padding: 10px 0;
```

```
    margin: 0 0 2em 2.4em;
}
```

5. Override the paragraph styles. The background and padding settings for the default blockquote style are no longer needed, so they're set to none and 0, respectively. Finally, text-align is set to center, which is appropriate for a narrow pull quote such as this.

```
blockquote.floatRight p {
    text-align: center;
    background: none;
    padding: 0;
}
```

Curabitur sit amet risus
Lorem ipsum dolor sit amet, consectetuer adipiscing elit. Sed aliquet elementum erat. Integer diam mi, venenatis non, cursus a, hendrerit at, mi. Morbi risus mi, tincidunt ornare, tempus ut, eleifend nec, risus.

Quisque faucibus lorem eget sapien. In urna sem, vehicula ut, mattis et, venenatis at, velit. Ut sodales lacus sed eros. Pellentesque tristique senectus et netus et malesuada fames ac turpis egestas.

This is the pull quote. It's really very exciting, so read it now! Lorem ipsum dolor sit amet, consectetuer adipiscing elit.
Fred Bloggs

Adding reference citations

The blockquote element can have a cite attribute, and the content from this attribute can be displayed by using the following CSS rule. Note, however, that at the time of writing, this doesn't work in Internet Explorer.

```
blockquote[cite]:after {
    display : block;
    margin : 0 0 5px;
    padding : 0 0 2px 0;
    font-weight : bold;
    font-size : 90%;
    content : "[source: "" " attr(cite)"]";
}
```

Working with lists

This chapter concludes with the last of the major type elements: the list. We'll first look at the different types of lists—unordered, ordered, and definition—and also see how to nest them. Then we'll move on to cover how to style lists in CSS, list margins and padding, and inline lists.

Unordered lists

The **unordered list**, commonly referred to as a **bullet point list**, is the most frequently seen type of list online. The list is composed of an unordered list element (<ul></ul>) and any number of list items within, each of which looks like this (prior to content being added): <li></li>. An example of an unordered list follows, and the resulting browser display is shown to the right. As you can see, browsers typically render a single-level unordered list with solid black bullet points.

```
<ul>
  <li>List item one</li>
  <li>List item two</li>
  <li>List item 'n'</li>
</ul>
```

- List item one
- List item two
- List item 'n'

Unlike HTML, XHTML lists require end tags on all list elements. In HTML, the </li> end tag was optional.

Ordered lists

On occasion, list items must be stated in order, whereupon an **ordered list** is used. It works in the same way as an unordered list, the only difference being the containing element, which is <ol></ol>.

```
<ol>
  <li>List item one</li>
  <li>List item two</li>
  <li>List item 'n'</li>
</ol>
```

1. List item one
2. List item two
3. List item 'n'

Web browsers automatically insert the item numbers when you use ordered lists. The only way of controlling numbering directly is via the start *attribute, whose value dictates the first number of the ordered list. Note, though, that this attribute is deprecated—use it and your web page will not validate as XHTML Strict.*

Definition lists

A **definition list** isn't a straightforward list of items. Instead, it's a list of terms and explanations. This type of list isn't common online, but it has its uses. The list itself is enclosed in the definition list element (<dl></dl>), and within the element are placed terms and definitions, marked up with <dt></dt> and <dd></dd>, respectively. Generally speaking, browsers display the definition with an indented left-hand margin, as in the following example.

```
<dl>
  <dt>Cat</dt>
  <dd>Four-legged, hairy animal, with an
  ➥ inflated sense of self-importance</dd>
  <dt>Dog</dt>
  <dd>Four-legged, hairy animal, often with
  ➥ an inferiority complex</dd>
</dl>
```

> Cat
> > Four-legged, hairy animal, with an inflated sense of self-importance
> Dog
> > Four-legged, hairy animal, often with an inferiority complex

Nesting lists

Lists can be nested, but designers often do so incorrectly, screwing up their layouts and rendering web pages invalid. The most common mistake is placing the nested list outside any list items, as shown in the following *incorrect* example:

```
<ul>
  <li>List item one</li>
  <ul>
    <li>Nested list item one</li>
    <li>Nested list item two</li>
  </ul>
  <li>List item two</li>
  <li>List item 'n'</li>
</ul>
```

Nested lists must be placed inside a list item, after the relevant item that leads into the nested list. Here's an example:

```
<ul>
  <li>List item one
    <ul>
      <li>Nested list item one</li>
      <li>Nested list item two</li>
    </ul>
  </li>
  <li>List item two</li>
  <li>List item 'n'</li>
</ul>
```

Always ensure that the list element that contains the nested list is closed with an end tag. Not doing so is another common mistake, and although it's not likely to cause as many problems as the incorrect positioning of the list, it can still affect your layout.

Styling lists with CSS

Lists can be styled with CSS, making it easy to amend item spacing or create custom bullet points. I tend to think bullet points work well for lists. They're simple and—pardon the pun—to the point. However, I know plenty of people would rather have something more visually interesting, which is where the list-style-image property comes in.

list-style-image property

The `list-style-image` property replaces the standard bullet or number from an unordered or ordered list with whatever image you choose. If you set the following in your CSS, the resulting list will look like that shown to the right. (Note that this is the nested list created earlier in this chapter.)

```
ul {
    list-style-image: url(bullet.gif);
}
```

```
☐ List item one
    ☐ Nested list item one
    ☐ Nested list item two
☐ List item two
☐ List item 'n'
```

Contextual selectors were first mentioned in Chapter 1 (see the section "Types of CSS selectors"). These enable you to style things in context, and this is appropriate when working with lists. You can style list items with one type of bullet and nested list items with another. The original rule stays in place but is joined by a second rule:

```
ul {
    list-style-image: url(bullet.gif);
}
ul ul {
    list-style-image: url(bullet-level-two.gif);
}
```

```
☐ List item one
    ⌐ Nested list item one
    ⌐ Nested list item two
☐ List item two
☐ List item 'n'
```

This second rule's selector is `ul ul`, which means that the declaration is applied only to unordered lists within an unordered list (i.e., nested lists). The upshot is that the top-level list items remain with the original custom bullet, but the nested list items now have a different bullet graphic.

With this CSS, each subsequent level would have the nested list bullet point, but it's feasible to change the bullet graphic for each successive level, by using increasingly complex contextual selectors.

> *When using custom bullet images, be wary of making them too large. Some browsers clip the bullet image, and some place the list contents at the foot of the image. In all cases, the results look terrible.*

Dealing with font-size inheritance

Most of the `font-size` definitions in this chapter (and indeed, in this book) use relative units. The problem with using ems, however, is that they compound. For example, if you have a typical nested list like the one just shown, and you define the following CSS, the first level of the list will have text sized at 1.5em; but the second-level list is a list within a list, so its `font-size` value will be compounded (1.5 × 1.5 = 2.25em).

```
html {
    font-size: 100%;
}
body {
    font-size: 62.5%;
    font-family: Verdana, Arial,
    ➥ Helvetica, sans-serif;
}
li {
    font-size: 1.5em;
}
```

```
❑ List item one
      ⏺ Nested list item one
      ⏺ Nested list item two
❑ List item two
❑ List item 'n'
```

The simple workaround for this is to use a contextual selector—li li—to set an explicit font-size value for list items within list items, as shown in the following rule.

```
li li {
    font-size: 1em;
}
```

With this, all nested lists take on the same font-size value as the parent list, which in this case is 1.5em.

list-style-position property

This property has two values: inside and outside. The latter is how list items are usually displayed: the bullet is placed in the list margin, and the left margin of the text is always indented. However, if you use inside, bullets are placed where the first text character would usually go, meaning that the text will wrap underneath the bullet.

list-style-type property

The list-style-type property is used to amend the bullets in an unordered or ordered list, enabling you to change the default bullets to something else (other than a custom image). In an unordered list, this defaults to disc (a black bullet), but other values are available, such as circle (a hollow disc bullet), square (a square bullet), and none, which results in no bullet points. For ordered lists, this defaults to decimal (resulting in a numbered list), but a number of other values are available, including lower-roman (i, ii, iii, etc.) and upper-alpha (A, B, C, etc.) A full list of supported values is in Appendix D (CSS Reference).

Generally speaking, the values noted are the best supported, along with the upper and lower versions of roman and alpha for ordered lists. If a browser doesn't understand the numbering system used for an ordered list, it usually defaults to decimal. The W3C recommends using decimal whenever possible, because it makes web pages easier to navigate. I agree—things like alpha and roman are too esoteric for general use, plus there's nothing in the CSS specifications to tell a browser what to do in an alphabetic system after z is reached (although most browsers are consistent in going on to aa, ab, ac, etc.).

List style shorthand

As elsewhere in CSS, there is a shorthand property for list styles, and this is the aptly named `list-style` property. An example of its use is shown in the following piece of CSS:

```
ul {
  list-style-type: square;
  list-style-position: inside;
  list-style-image: url(bullet.gif);
}
```

which can be rewritten as follows:

```
ul {
  list-style: square inside url(bullet.gif);
}
```

List margins and padding

Browsers don't seem to be able to agree on how much padding and margin to place around lists by default, and also how margin and padding settings affect lists in general. This can be frustrating when developing websites that rely on lists and pixel-perfect element placement. By creating a list and using CSS to apply a background color to the list and a different color to list items, and then removing the page's padding and margins, you can observe how each browser creates lists and indents the bullet points and content.

In Gecko browsers (e.g., Mozilla Firefox), Opera, and Safari, the list background color is displayed behind the bullet points, which suggests that those browsers place bullet points within the list's left-hand padding (because backgrounds extend into an element's padding). Internet Explorer shows no background color there, suggesting it places bullet points within the list's left-hand margin.

This is confirmed if you set the `margin` property to 0 for a `ul` selector in CSS. The list is unaffected in all browsers but Internet Explorer, in which the bullets abut the left edge of the web browser window. Conversely, setting padding to 0 makes the same thing happen in Gecko browsers, Safari, and Opera.

To get all browsers on a level playing field, you must remove margins and padding, which, as mentioned previously in this book, is done in CSS by way of the universal selector:

```
* {
margin: 0;
padding: 0;
}
```

With this in place, all browsers render lists in the same way, and you can set specific values as appropriate. For example, bring back the bullet points (which may be at least partially hidden if margins and padding are both zeroed) by setting either the `margin-left` or `padding-left` value to 1.5em (i.e., set `margin: 0 0 0 1.5em` or `padding: 0 0 0 1.5em`). The difference is that if you set `padding-left`, any background applied to the list will appear behind the bullet points, but if you set `margin-left`, it won't. Note that `1.5em` is a big enough value to enable the bullet points to display (in fact, lower values are usually sufficient, too—although take care not to set values too low, or the bullets will be clipped); setting a higher value places more space to the left of the bullet points.

Inline lists for navigation

Although most people think of lists as being vertically aligned, you can also display list items inline. This is particularly useful when creating navigation bars, as you'll see in Chapter 5. To set a list to display inline, you simply add `display: inline;` to the `li` selector. Adding `list-style-type: none;` to the `ul` selector ensures that the list sits snug to the left of its container (omitting this tends to indent the list items). Adding a `margin-right` value to `li` also ensures that the list items don't sit right next to each other. Here's an example:

```
ul {
   list-style-type: none;
}
li {
   display: inline;
   margin-right: 10px;
}
```

Thinking creatively with lists

The final part of this chapter looks at creating lists with a little panache. Although most lists are perfectly suited to straightforward bullet points, sometimes some added CSS and imagery can go a long way.

Creating better-looking lists

Required files	The HTML and CSS documents from the basic-boilerplates folder as a starting point, along with the images better-list-hollow-square.gif, better-list-shadow.gif, better-list-square.gif, and better-list-star.gif from the chapter 3 folder.
What you'll learn	How to style a three-level list to look great, using background images and overrides.
Completed files	better-looking-lists.html and better-looking-lists.css from the chapter 3 folder.

1. Create the list. Within the HTML document's wrapper div, add the following code:

```
<ul>
  <li>List - 1.1
    <ul>
      <li>List - 2.1</li>
      <li>List - 2.2
        <ul>
          <li>List - 3.1</li>
          <li>List - 3.2</li>
          <li>List - 3.3</li>
        </ul>
      </li>
      <li>List - 2.3</li>
    </ul>
  </li>
</ul>
```

2. Amend the body rule. Add some padding to the body element so that page content doesn't hug the browser window edges during testing:

```
body {
  font: 62.5%/1.5 Verdana, Arial, Helvetica, sans-serif;
  padding: 20px;
}
```

3. Style the list elements. This kind of heavily styled list typically requires you to define specific property values at one level and then override them if they're not required for subsequent levels. This is done by adding the three rules in the following code block. For this example, the top level of the list (styled via ul) has a star background image that doesn't repeat (the 1px vertical value is used to nudge the image into place so it looks better positioned), and the list-style-type value of none removes the default bullet points of all lists on the page.

For the second level of lists (the first level of nesting), styled via ul ul, a horizontally tiling background image is added, giving the impression that the top-level list is casting a soft shadow. The border-left setting creates a soft boundary to the nested list's left, thereby enclosing the content. The padding value ensures that there's space around nested lists.

For the third level of lists (the second level of nesting—that is, a nested list within a nested list), styled via ul ul ul, no specific styles are required, but to deal with inherited styles from ul ul, background is set to none and border-left is set to 0. If this weren't done, third-level lists would also have the shadow background and dotted left-hand border.

```
ul {
  list-style-type: none;
  background: url(better-list-star.gif) 0 1px no-repeat;
}
ul ul {
  background: url(better-list-shadow.gif) repeat-x;
  border-left: 1px dotted #aaaaaa;
```

113

```
  padding: 10px;
}
ul ul ul {
  background: none;
  border-left: 0;
}
```

4. Style the list item elements. For the top-level list items, the li rule styles them in uppercase, adds some padding (to ensure the items don't sit over the background image applied in ul), and makes the text bold and gray. For the nested list items, the li li rule overrides the text-transform property, returning the text to sentence case, and adds a square gray bullet as a background image. The font-weight value is an override, and the color setting is darker than for the parent list's list items so that the non-bold text of the nested list items stand out. Finally, for the third-level list items, styled using the selector li li li, a background override provides a unique bullet point image (a hollow square).

```
li {
  text-transform: uppercase;
  padding-left: 20px;
  font-weight: bold;
  color: #666666;
}
li li {
  text-transform: none;
  background: url(better-list-square.gif) 0 2px no-repeat;
  font-weight: normal;
  color: #333333;
}
li li li {
  background: url(better-list-hollow-square.gif) 0 2px no-repeat;
}
```

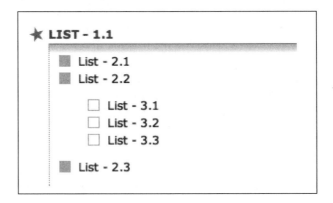

When creating lists such as this, don't overcomplicate things, and try to avoid going to many levels of nesting, or combining ordered and unordered lists; otherwise, the selectors required for overrides become extremely complicated.

Displaying blocks of code online

Required files	The HTML and CSS documents from the basic-boilerplates folder as a starting point.
What you'll learn	How to style a list for displaying code online (complete with exercise headings and line numbers).
Completed files	display-code-online.html and display-code-online.css from the chapter 3 folder.

1. Create the list. Code blocks require terminology and descriptions, meaning that a definition list can be used to mark them up. For this example, the code block from the preceding "List style shorthand" section will be used. Within the wrapper div, create a definition list and give it a class value of codeList. For the term, add a description of the code, and for the definition, add an ordered list, with each line of code within its own list item. Each line of code should also be nested within a code element.

```
<dl class="codeList">
  <dt>Writing out list styles in full</dt>
  <dd>
    <ol>
      <li><code>ul {</code></li>
      <li><code>list-style-type: square;</code></li>
      <li><code>list-style-position: inside;</code></li>
      <li><code>list-style-image: url(bullet.gif);</code></li>
      <li><code>}</code></li>
    </ol>
  </dd>
</dl>
```

2. Amend the body and #wrapper CSS rules, adding some padding to the former (so the content doesn't hug the browser window edges during testing) and a shorthand font definition to the latter (in place of existing content).

```
body {
  font: 62.5%/1.5 Verdana, Arial, Helvetica, sans-serif;
  padding: 20px;
}
#wrapper {
  font: 1.2em/1.5em 'Lucida Grande', 'Lucida Sans Unicode', Lucida,
  ➥ Arial, Helvetica,   sans-serif;
}
```

115

3. Style the list. Add the following rule, which adds a solid border around the definition list that has a codeList class value:

```
.codeList {
  border: 1px solid #aaaaaa;
}
```

4. Style the definition term element. Add the following rule, which styles the dt element. The rule colors the background of dt elements within any element with a class value of codeList, and also adds some padding so the content of the dt elements doesn't hug their borders. The font-weight value of bold ensures the content stands out, while the border-bottom value will be used as a device throughout the other rules, separating components of the design with a fairly thin white line.

```
.codeList dt {
  background: #dddddd;
  padding: 7px;
  font-weight: bold;
  border-bottom: 2px solid #ffffff;
}
```

5. Style the list items within the ordered list by adding the following rule. The margin-left value places the bullets within the definition list, rather than outside of it.

```
.codeList li {
  background: #ffffff;
  margin-left: 2.5em;
}
```

> *Note that in Internet Explorer, the bullets typically display further to the left than in other browsers. This behavior can be dealt with by overriding the* margin-left *value of* .codeList li *in an IE-specific style sheet attached using a conditional comment— see Chapter 9 for more on this technique.*

6. Finally, style the code elements. The background value is slightly lighter than that used for the dt element, ensuring that each element is distinct. By setting display to block, the code elements stretch to fill their container (meaning that the background color also does this). The borders ensure that each line of code is visibly distinct, and the border-right setting essentially provides a border all the way around the code lines, seeing as the border-bottom setting in .codeList dt defines one at the top of the first line of code. The font is set to a monospace font, and the padding values place some space around the code, making it easier to read.

```
.codeList code {
  background: #eaeaea;
  display: block;
  border-bottom: 2px solid #ffffff;
  border-right: 2px solid #ffffff;
  font : 1.2em "Courier New", Courier, monospace;
  padding: 2px 10px;
}
```

Writing out list styles in full

```
1.  ul {
2.      list-style-type: square;
3.      list-style-position: inside;
4.      list-style-image: url(bullet.gif);
5.  }
```

That just about wraps things up for online type. After all that text, it's time to change track. In Chapter 4, you'll look at working with images on the Web, and in Chapter 5, you'll combine what you've learned so far and add anchors into the mix to create web navigation.

In this chapter:

- Understanding color theory
- Choosing the best image format
- Avoiding common mistakes
- Working with images in XHTML
- Using alt text to improve accessibility
- Using CSS when working with images
- Displaying a random image from a selection

Introduction

Although text makes up the bulk of the Web's content, it's inevitable that you'll end up working with images at some point—that is, unless you favor terribly basic websites akin to those last seen in 1995. Images are rife online, comprising the bulk of interfaces, the navigation of millions of sites, and a considerable amount of actual content, too. As the Web continues to barge its way into every facet of life, this trend can only continue; visitors to sites now expect a certain amount of visual interest, just as readers of a magazine expect illustrations or photographs.

Like anything else, use and misuse of images can make or break a website—so, like elsewhere in this book, this chapter covers more than the essentials of working with HTML and CSS. Along with providing an overview of color theory, I've compiled a brief list of common mistakes that people make when working with images for the Web—after all, even the most dedicated web designers pick up bad habits without realizing it. Finally, at the end of the chapter, I'll introduce your first piece of JavaScript, providing you with a handy cut-out-and-keep script to randomize images on a web page.

Color theory

Color plays a massively important role in any field of design, and web design is no exception. Therefore, it seems appropriate to include in this chapter a brief primer on color theory and working with colors on the Web.

Color wheels

Circular color diagrams—commonly referred to as **color wheels**—were invented by Newton and remain a common starting point for creative types wanting to understand the relationship between colors and also for creating color schemes. On any standard color wheel, the three **primary colors** are each placed one-third of the way around the wheel, with **secondary colors** equally spaced between them—secondary colors being a mix of two primary colors. Between secondary and primary colors are **tertiary colors**, the result of mixing primary and secondary colors. Some color wheels blend the colors together, creating a continuous shift from one color to another, while others have rather more defined blocks of color; however, in all cases, the positioning is the same.

Additive and subtractive color systems

Onscreen colors use what's referred to as an **additive system**, which is the color system used by light—where black is the absence of color, and colored light is added together to create color mixes. The additive primaries are red, green, and blue (hence the commonly heard **RGB** when referring to definition of screen colors). Mix equal amounts of red, green, and blue light and you end up with white; mix secondaries from the primaries and you end up with magenta, yellow, and cyan.

In print, a **subtractive system** is used, similar to that used in the natural world. This works by absorbing colors before they reach the eye—if an object reflects all light it appears white, and if it absorbs all light, it appears black. Inks for print are transparent, acting as filters to enable light to pass through, reflect off the print base (such as paper), and produce unabsorbed light. Typically, the print process uses cyan, magenta, and yellow as primaries, along with a key color—black—since equal combination of three print inks tends to produce a muddy color rather than the black that it should produce in theory.

Although the technology within computers works via an additive system to display colors, digital-based designers still tend to work with subtractive palettes when working on designs (using red, yellow, and blue primaries), because that results in natural color combinations and palettes.

Creating a color scheme using a color wheel

Even if you have a great eye for color and can instinctively create great schemes for websites, it pays to have a color wheel handy. These days, you don't have to rely on reproductions in books or hastily created painted paper wheels. There are now digital color wheels that enable you to experiment with schemes, including Color Consultant Pro for the Mac (www.code-line.com/software/colorconsultantpro.html), shown in the following screenshot, and Color Wheel Pro (www.color-wheel-pro.com) and ColorImpact (www.tigercolor.com/Default.htm), both for Windows.

When working on color schemes and creating a palette for a website, there are various schemes available for you. The simplest is a **monochromatic** scheme, which involves variations in the saturation (effectively the intensity or strength) of a single hue. Such schemes can be soothing—notably when based on green or blue—but also have a tendency to be bland, unless used with striking design and black and white. A slightly richer scheme can be created by using colors adjacent on the color wheel—this is referred to as an **analogous scheme**, and is also typically considered harmonious and pleasing to the eye.

For more impact, a **complementary scheme** can be used, which uses colors on opposite sides of the color wheel (such as red/green, orange/blue, and yellow/purple); this scheme is often seen in art, such as a pointillist using orange dots in areas of blue to add depth. Complementary schemes work well due to a subconscious desire for visual harmony—an equal mix of complementary colors results in a neutral gray. Such effects are apparent in human color vision: if you look at a solid plane of color, you'll see its complementary color when you close your eyes.

A problem with a straight complementary scheme is that overuse of its colors can result in garish, tense design. A subtler but still attention-grabbing scheme can be created by using a color and the hues adjacent to the complementary color. This kind of scheme (which happens to be the one shown in the previous screenshot) is referred to as **split-complementary**.

Another scheme that offers impact—and one often favored by artists—is the **triadic scheme**, which essentially works with primary colors or shifted primaries—that is, colors equally spaced around the color wheel. The scheme provides plenty of visual contrast and, when used with care, can result in a balanced, harmonious result.

How colors "feel" also plays a part in how someone reacts to them—for example, people often talk of "warm" and "cool" colors. Traditionally, cooler colors are said to be passive, blending into backgrounds, while warmer colors are cheerier and welcoming. However, complexity is added by color intensity—a strong blue will appear more prominent than a pale orange. A color's temperature is also relative, largely defined by what is placed around it. On its own, green is cool, yet it becomes warm when surrounded by blues and purples.

Against black and white, a color's appearance can also vary. Against white, yellow appears warm, but against black, yellow has an aggressive brilliance. However, blue appears dark on white, but luminescent on black.

The human condition also adds a further wrench in the works. Many colors have cultural significance, whether from language (*cowardly* yellow) or advertising and branding. One person may consider a color one thing (green equals fresh), and another may have different ideas entirely (green equals moldy). There's also the problem of color blindness, which affects a significant (although primarily male) portion of the population, meaning you should never rely entirely on color to get a message across. Ultimately, stick to the following rules, and you'll likely have some luck when working on color schemes:

- Work with a color wheel, and be mindful of how different schemes work.
- Use tints and shades of a hue, but generally avoid entirely monochromatic schemes—inject an adjacent color for added interest.
- Create contrast by adding a complementary color.
- Keep saturation levels and value levels the same throughout the scheme (a color's **value** increases the closer it is to white).
- Keep things simple—using too many colors results in garish schemes.
- Don't rely on color to get a message across—if in doubt about the effects of color blindness, test your design with a color blindness simulator application such as Color Oracle (http://coloracle.cartography.ch/).
- Go with your gut reaction—feelings play an important part when creating color schemes. What feels right is often a good starting point.

Working with hex

The CSS specifications support just 17 color names: aqua, black, blue, fuchsia, gray, green, lime, maroon, navy, olive, orange, purple, red, silver, teal, white, and yellow. All other colors must be written in another format, such as RGB numbers or percentages—rgb(255,0,0) or rgb(100%,0%,0%)—or hexadecimal format, which tends to be most popular in online design. Note that to keep things consistent, it actually makes sense to write all colors—even the 17 with supported names—in hex. Colors written in hex comprise a hash sign followed by six digits. The six digits are comprised of pairs, representing the red, green, and blue color values, respectively:

- **#XXxxxx**: Red color value
- **#xxXXxx**: Green color value
- **#xxxxXX**: Blue color value

Because the hexadecimal system is used, the digits can range in value from 0 to f, with 0 being the lowest value (nothing) and f being the highest. Therefore, if we set the first two digits to full (ff) and the others to 0, we get #ff0000, which is the hex color value for red. Likewise, #00ff00 is green and #0000ff is blue.

Of course, there are plenty of potential combinations—16.7 million of them, in fact. Luckily, any half-decent graphics application will do the calculations for you, so you won't have to work out for yourself that black is #000000 and white is #ffffff—just use an application's color picker/eyedropper tool, and it should provide you with the relevant hex value.

> *When a hex value is made up of three pairs, the values can be abbreviated. For example, the value #ffaa77 can be written #fa7. Some designers swear by this abbreviated form. I tend to use the full six-figure hex value because it keeps things consistent.*

Web-safe colors

Modern PCs and Macs come with some reasonable graphics clout, but this wasn't always the case. In fact, many computers still in common use cannot display millions of colors. Back in the 1990s, palette restrictions were even more ferocious, with many computers limited to a paltry 256 colors (8-bit). Microsoft and Apple couldn't agree on which colors to use, hence the creation of the web-safe palette, which comprises just 216 colors that are supposed to work accurately on both platforms without dithering. (For more information about dithering, see the "GIF" section later in this chapter.) Applications such as Photoshop have built-in web-safe palettes, and variations on the palette can be seen at www.visibone.com.

Colors in the web-safe palette are made up of combinations of RGB in 20% increments, and as you might expect, the palette is limited. Also discouraging, in the article "Death of the Websafe Color Palette?" on Webmonkey (www.webmonkey.com/00/37/index2a.html; posted September 6, 2000), David Lehn and Hadley Stern reported that all but 22 of these colors were incorrectly shifted in some way when tested on a variety of platforms and color displays—in other words, only 22 of the web-safe colors are actually totally web-safe.

While the rise of PDAs means that the web-safe palette may make a comeback in specialist circles (although PDAs and even cell phones are increasingly powerful when it comes to graphics), most designers these days ignore it. The majority of people using the Web have displays capable of millions of colors, and almost everyone else can view at least thousands of colors. Unless you're designing for a very specific audience with known restricted hardware, stick with sRGB (the default color space of the Web—see www.w3.org/Graphics/Color/sRGB) and design in millions of colors. And consider yourself lucky that it's not 1995.

Choosing formats for images

In order to present images online in the best possible way, it's essential to choose the best file format when exporting and saving them. Although the save dialogs in most graphics editors present a bewildering list of possible formats, the Web typically uses just two: JPEG and GIF (along with the GIF89, or transparent GIF, variant), although a third, PNG, is finally gaining popularity, largely due to Internet Explorer 7 finally offering full support for it.

JPEG

The JPEG (Joint Photographic Experts Group) format is used primarily for images that require smooth color transitions and continuous tones, such as photographs. JPEG supports millions of colors, and relatively little image detail is lost—at least when compression settings aren't too high. This is because the format uses **lossy compression**, which removes information that the eye doesn't need. As the compression level increases, this information loss becomes increasingly obvious, as shown in the following images. As you can see from the image on the right, which is much more compressed than the one on the left, nasty artifacts become increasingly dominant as the compression level increases. At extreme levels of compression, an image will appear to be composed of linked blocks (see the following two images, the originals of which are in the chapter 4 folder as tree.jpg and tree-compressed.jpg).

Although it's tricky to define a cutoff point, it's safe to say that for photographic work where it's important to retain quality and detail, 50 to 60% compression (40 to 50% quality) is the highest you should go for. Higher compression is sometimes OK in specific circumstances, such as for very small image thumbnails, but even then, it's best not to go over 70% compression.

If the download time for an image is unacceptably high, you could always try reducing the dimensions rather than the quality—a small, detailed image usually looks better than a large, heavily compressed image. Also, bear in mind that common elements—that is, images that appear on every page of a website, perhaps as part of the interface—will be cached and therefore only need to be downloaded once. Because of this, you can get away with less compression and higher file sizes.

> *Be aware that applications have different means of referring to compression levels. Some, such as Adobe applications, use a quality scale, in which 100 is uncompressed and 0 is completely compressed. Others, such as Paint Shop Pro, use compression values, in which higher numbers indicate increased compression. Always be sure you know which scale you're using.*

Some applications have the option to save progressive JPEGs. Typically, this format results in larger file sizes, but it's useful because it enables your image to download in multiple passes. This means that a low-resolution version will display rapidly and gradually progress to the quality you saved it at, allowing viewers to get a look at a simplified version of the image without having to wait for it to load completely.

GIF

GIF (Graphics Interchange Format) is in many ways the polar opposite of JPEG—it's **lossless**, meaning that there's no color degradation when images are compressed. However, the format is restricted to a maximum of 256 colors, thereby rendering it ineffective for color photographic images. Using GIF for such images tends to produce banding, in which colors are reduced to the nearest equivalent. A fairly extreme example of this is shown in the following illustration.

GIF is useful for displaying images with large areas of flat color, such as logos, line art, and type. As I mentioned in the previous chapter, you should generally avoid using graphics for text on your web pages, but if you do, GIF is the best choice of format.

Although GIF is restricted to 256 colors, it's worth noting that you don't have to use the *same* 256 colors every time. Most graphics applications provide a number of palette options, such as **perceptual**, **selective**, and **Web**. The first of those, perceptual, tends to prioritize colors that the human eye is most sensitive to, thereby providing the best color integrity. Selective works in a similar fashion, but balances its color choices with web-safe colors, thereby creating results more likely to be safe across platforms. Web refers to the 216-color web-safe palette discussed earlier. Additionally, you often have the option to lock colors, which forces your graphics application to use only the colors within the palette you choose.

Images can also be dithered, which prevents continuous tones from becoming bands of color. Dithering simulates continuous tones, using the available (restricted) palette. Most graphics editors allow for three different types of dithering: **diffusion**, **pattern**, and **noise**—all of which have markedly different effects on an image. Diffusion applies a random pattern across adjacent pixels, whereas pattern applies a half-tone pattern rather like that seen in low-quality print publications. Noise works rather like diffusion, but without diffusing the pattern across adjacent pixels. Following are four examples of the effects of dithering on an image that began life as a smooth gradient. The first image (1) has no dither, and the gradient has been turned into a series of solid, vertical stripes. The second image (2) shows the effects of diffusion dithering; the third (3), pattern; and the fourth (4), noise.

127

| 1 | 2 | 3 | 4 |

GIF89: The transparent GIF

The GIF89 file format is identical to GIF, with one important exception: you can remove colors, which provides a very basic means of transparency and enables the background to show through. Because this is not alpha transparency (a type of transparency that enables a smooth transition from solid to transparent, allowing for many levels of opacity), it doesn't work in the way many graphic designers expect. You cannot, for instance, fade an image's background from color to transparent and expect the web page's background to show through—instead, GIF89's transparency is akin to cutting a hole with a pair of scissors: the background shows through the removed colors only. This is fine when the "hole" has flat horizontal or vertical edges. But if you try this with irregular shapes—such as in the following image of the cloud with drop shadow—you'll end up with ragged edges. In the example, the idea was to have the cloud casting a shadow onto the gray background. However, because GIFs can't deal with alpha transparency, we instead end up with an unwanted white outline. (One way around this is to export the image with the same background color as that of the web page, but this is only possible if the web page's background is a plain, flat color.)

Because of these restrictions, GIF89s are not used all that much these days. They do cling on in one area of web design, though: as spacers for stretching table cells, in order to lay out a page. However, in these enlightened times, that type of technique should be avoided, since you can lay out precisely spaced pages much more easily using CSS.

PNG

For years, PNG (pronounced *ping*, and short for Portable Network Graphics) lurked in the wilderness as a capable yet unloved and unused format for web design. Designed primarily as a replacement for GIF, the format has plenty to offer, including a far more flexible palette than GIF and true alpha transparency. Some have mooted PNG as a JPEG replacement, too, but this isn't recommended—PNGs tend to be much larger than JPEGs for photographic images. For imagery with sharp lines, areas of flat color, or where alpha transparency is required, it is, however, a good choice.

The reason PNG is still less common than GIF or JPEG primarily has to do with Internet Explorer. Prior to version 7, Microsoft's browser didn't offer support for PNG alpha transparency, instead replacing transparent areas with white or gray. Although a proprietary workaround exists (see Chapter 9's "Dealing with Internet Explorer bugs" section), it isn't intuitive, and it requires extra code. With post–version 6 releases of Internet Explorer finally supporting alpha transparency (and Internet Explorer's share of the market decreasing somewhat, primarily due to competition from Firefox), it's worth looking into PNG when creating layouts.

The three adjacent images highlight the benefit of PNG over GIF, as shown in a web browser. The first illustration shows two PNGs on a white background. The second illustration shows this background replaced by a grid. Note how the button's drop shadow is partially see-through, while the circle's center is revealed as being partially transparent, increasing in opacity toward its edge. The third illustration shows the closest equivalent when using GIFs—the drop shadow is surrounded by an ugly cutout, and the circle's central area loses its transparency. Upon closer inspection, the circle is also surrounded by a jagged edge, and the colors are far less smooth than those of the PNG.

> For more information about this format, check out the PNG website at www.libpng.org/pub/png.

Other image formats

You may have worked on pages in the past and added the odd BMP or TIFF file, or seen another site do the same. These are not standard formats for the Web, though, and while they may work fine in some cases, they require additional software in order to render in some browsers (in many cases, they won't render at all, or they'll render inconsistently across browsers). Furthermore, JPEG, GIF, and PNG are well-suited to web design because they enable you to present a lot of visual information in a fairly small file. Presenting the same in a TIFF or BMP won't massively increase the image's quality (when taking into account the low resolution of the Web), but it will almost certainly increase download times. Therefore, quite simply, don't use any formats other than JPEG, GIF, or PNG for your web images (and if you decide to use PNG transparency, be sure that your target audience will be able to see the images).

Common web image gaffes

The same mistakes tend to crop up again and again when designers start working with images. In order to avoid making them, read on to find out about some common ones (and how to avoid them).

Using graphics for body copy

Some sites out there use graphics for body copy on web pages, in order to get more typographical control than CSS allows. However, using graphics for body copy causes text to print poorly—much worse than HTML-based text. Additionally, it means the text can't be read by search engines, can't be copied and pasted, and can't be enlarged, unless you're using a browser (or operating system) that can zoom—and even then it will be pixilated. If graphical text needs to be updated, it means reworking the original image (which could include messing with line wraps, if words need to be added or removed), re-exporting it, and reuploading it.

As mentioned in the "Image-replacement techniques" section of Chapter 3, the argument is a little less clear-cut for headings (although I recommend using styled HTML-based text for those, too), but for body copy, you should always avoid using images.

Not working from original images

If it turns out an image on a website is too large or needs editing in some way, the original should be sourced to make any changes if the online version has been in any way compressed. This is because continually saving a compressed image reduces its quality each time. Also, under no circumstances should you increase the dimensions of a compressed JPEG. Doing so leads to abysmal results every time.

Overwriting original documents

The previous problem gets worse if you've deleted your originals. Therefore, be sure that you never overwrite the original files you're using. If resampling JPEGs from a digital camera for the Web, work with copies so you don't accidentally overwrite your only copy of that great photo you've taken with a much smaller, heavily compressed version. More important, if you're using an application that enables layers, save copies of the layered documents prior to flattening them for export—otherwise you'll regret it when having to make that all-important change and having to start from scratch.

Busy backgrounds

When used well, backgrounds can improve a website, adding visual interest and atmosphere—see the following image, showing the top of a version of the Snub Communications homepage. However, if backgrounds are too busy, in terms of complicated artwork and color, they'll distract from the page's content. If placed under text, they may even make your site's text-based content impossible to read. With that in mind, keep any backgrounds behind content subtle—near-transparent single-color watermarks tend to work best.

For backgrounds outside of the content area (as per the "Watermarks" section in Chapter 2), you must take care, too. Find a balance in your design and ensure that the background doesn't distract from the content, which is the most important aspect of the site.

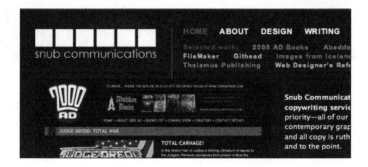

Lack of contrast

It's common to see websites that don't provide enough contrast between text content and the background—for example, (very) light gray text on a white background, or pale text on an only slightly darker background. Sometimes this lack of contrast finds its way into other elements of the site, such as imagery comprising interface elements. This isn't always a major problem—in some cases, designs look stylish if a subtle scheme is used with care. You should, however, ensure that usability isn't affected—it's all very well to have a subtle color scheme, but not if it stops visitors from being able to easily find things like navigation elements, or from being able to read the text.

Using the wrong image format

Exporting photographs as GIFs, using BMPs or TIFFs online, rendering soft and blotchy line art and text as a result of using the JPEG format—these are all things to avoid in the world of creating images for websites. See the section "Choosing formats for images" earlier in this chapter for an in-depth discussion of formats.

Resizing in HTML

When designers work in WYSIWYG editing tools, relying on a drag-and-drop interface, it's sometimes tempting to resize all elements in this manner (and this can sometimes also be done by accident), thereby compromising the underlying code of a web page. Where images are concerned, this has a detrimental effect, because the pixel dimensions of the image no longer tally with its width and height values. In some cases, this may lead to distorted imagery (as shown in the rather extreme example that follows); it may also lead to visually small images that have ridiculously large files sizes by comparison. In most cases, distortion of detail will still occur, even when proportion is maintained.

There are exceptions to this rule, however, although they are rare. For instance, if you work with pixel art saved as a GIF, you can proportionately enlarge an image, making it large on the screen. Despite the image being large, the file size will be tiny.

Not balancing quality and file size

Bandwidth can be a problem in image-heavy sites—both in terms of the host getting hammered when visitor numbers increase, and in terms of the visitors—many of whom may be stuck with slower connections than you—having to download the images. Therefore, you should always be sure that your images are highly optimized, in order to save on hosting costs and ensure that your website's visitors don't have to suffer massive downloads. (In fact, they probably won't—they'll more than likely go elsewhere.)

But this doesn't mean that you should compress every image on your website into a slushy mess (and I've seen plenty of sites where the creator has exported JPEGs at what looks like 90% compression—"just in case").

Err on the side of caution, but remember: common interface elements are cached, so you can afford to save them at a slightly higher quality. Any image that someone requests (such as via a thumbnail on a portfolio site) is something they *want* to see, so these too can be saved at a higher quality because the person is likely to wait. Also, there is no such thing as an optimum size for web images. If you've read in the past that no web image should ever be larger than 50 KB, it's hogwash. The size of your images depends entirely on context, the type of site you're creating, and the audience you're creating it for.

Text overlays and splitting images

Some designers use various means to stop people from stealing images from their site and reusing them. The most common are including a copyright statement on the image itself, splitting the image into a number of separate images to make it harder to download, and adding an invisible transparent GIF overlay.

The main problem with copyright statements is that they are often poorly realized (see the following example), ruining the image with a garish text overlay. Ultimately, while anyone can download images from your website to their hard drive, you need to remember that if someone uses your images, they're infringing your copyright, and you can deal with them accordingly (and, if they link directly to images on your server, try changing the affected images to something text-based, like "The scumbag whose site you're visiting stole images from me").

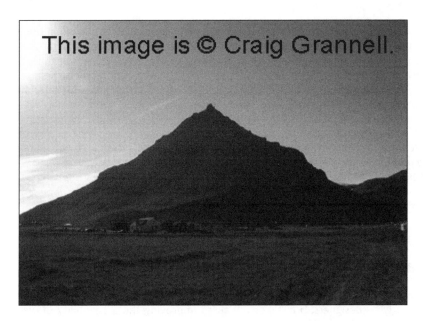

As for splitting images into several separate files or placing invisible GIFs over images to try to stop people from downloading them, don't do this—there are simple workarounds in either case, and you just end up making things harder for yourself when updating your site. Sometimes you even risk compromising the structural integrity of your site when using such methods.

Stealing images and designs

Too many people appear to think that the Internet is a free-for-all, outside of the usual copyright restrictions, but this isn't the case: copyright exists on the Web just like everywhere else. Unless you have permission to reuse an image you've found online, you shouldn't do so. If discovered, you may get the digital equivalent of a slap on the wrist, but you could also be sued for copyright infringement.

Although it's all right to be influenced by someone else's design, you should also ensure you don't simply rip off a creation found on the Web—otherwise you could end up in legal trouble, or the subject of ridicule as a feature on Tim Murtaugh's Pirated Sites forum (see www.pirated-sites.com/vanilla/).

Working with images in XHTML

The img element is used to add images to a web page. It's an empty tag, so it takes the combined start and end tag form with a trailing slash, as outlined in Chapter 1. The following code block shows an example of an image element, complete with relevant attributes:

```
<img src="sunset.jpg" height="200" width="400" alt="Sunset in
➥ Reykjavík" />
```

Perhaps surprisingly, the height and width attributes are actually optional, although I recommend including them because they assist the browser in determining the size of the image before it downloads (thereby speeding up the process of laying out the page). The only two image element attributes required in XHTML are src and alt. The first, src, is the path to the image file to be displayed; and the second, alt, provides some **alternative text** for when the image is not displayed.

> Note that this chapter's section on images largely concerns itself with inline images— the addition of images to the content of a web page. For an overview of using images as backgrounds, see the "Web page backgrounds" section of Chapter 2; for an overview of working with images within web navigation and with links in general, see much of Chapter 5.

Using alt text for accessibility benefits

Alternate text—usually referred to as "alt text," after its attribute—is often ignored or used poorly by designers, but it's essential for improving the accessibility of web pages. Visitors using screen readers rely on the alt attribute's value to determine what an image shows. Therefore, always include a *succinct* description of the image's content and avoid using the image's file name, because that's often of little help. Ignoring the alt attribute not only renders your page invalid according to the W3C recommendations, but it also means that screen readers (and browsers that cannot display images) end up with something like this for output: [IMAGE][IMAGE][IMAGE]—not very helpful, to say the least.

Descriptive alt text for link-based images

Images often take on dual roles, being used for navigation purposes as well as additional visual impact. In such cases, the fact that the image is a navigation aid is likely to be of more significance than its visual appearance. For instance, many companies use logos as links to a homepage—in such cases, some designers would suggest using "Company X homepage" for the alt text, as it's more useful than "Company X."

Alternatively, stick with using the alt attribute for describing the image, and add a title attribute to the link, using that to describe the target. Depending on user settings, the link's title attribute will be read out in the absence of any link text.

> *If you don't have access to screen-reading software for testing* alt *text and various other accessibility aspects of a website, either install the text-based browser Lynx, or run Opera in User mode, which can emulate a text browser.*

4

Null alt attributes for interface images

In some cases, images have no meaning at all (e.g., if they're a part of an interface), and there is some debate regarding the best course of action with regard to such images' alt values. Definitely never type something like spacer or interface element, otherwise screen readers and text browsers will drive their users crazy relaying these values back to them. Instead, it's recommended that you use a **null** alt **attribute**, which takes the form alt="".

Null alt attributes are unfortunately not interpreted correctly by all screen readers; some, upon discovering a null alt attribute, go on to read the image's src value. A common workaround is to use empty alt attributes, which just have blank space for the value (alt=" "). However, the null alt attribute has valid semantics, so it should be used despite some screen readers not being able to deal with it correctly.

Alternatively, try reworking your design so that images without meaning are applied as background images to div elements, rather than placed inline.

Using alt and title text for tooltips

Although the W3C specifically states that alt text shouldn't be visible if the image can been seen, Internet Explorer ignores this, displaying alt text as a tooltip when the mouse cursor hovers over an image, as shown in the adjacent example.

Internet Explorer users are most likely accustomed to this by now, and, indeed, you may have used alt text to create tooltips in your own work. If so, it's time to stop. This behavior is not recommended by the W3C and it's also not common across all browsers and platforms.

If an image requires a tooltip, most browsers display the value of a title attribute as one. In spite of this, if the text you're intending for a pop-up is important, you should instead place it within the standard text of your web page, rather than hiding it where most users won't see it. This is especially important when you consider that Firefox crops the values after around 80 characters, unlike some browsers, which happily show multiline tooltips.

> *Another alternative for extended descriptions for images is the* longdesc *attribute. It's not fully supported, but Firefox, SeaMonkey, and Netscape display the attribute's contents as a description field when you view image properties. It's also fully supported in the JAWS screen reader, thereby warranting its use should your image descriptions be lengthy.*

Using CSS when working with images

In the following section, we're going to look at relevant CSS for web page images. You'll see how best to apply borders to images and wrap text around them, as well as define spacing between images and other page elements.

Applying CSS borders to images

You may have noticed earlier that I didn't mention the border attribute when working through the img element. This is because the border attribute is deprecated; adding borders to images is best achieved and controlled by using CSS. (Also, because of the flexibility of CSS, this means that if you only want a simple surrounding border composed of flat color, you no longer have to add borders directly to your image files.) Should you want to add a border to every image on your website, you could do so with the following CSS:

```
img {
  border: 1px solid #000000;
}
```

In this case, a 1-pixel solid border, colored black (#000000 in hex), would surround every image on the site. Using contextual selectors, this can be further refined. For instance, should you only want the images within a content area (marked up as a div with an id value of content) to be displayed with a border, you could write the following CSS:

```
div#content img {
  border: 1px solid #000000;
}
```

Alternatively, you could set borders to be on by default, and override them in specific areas of the website via a rule using grouped contextual selectors:

```css
img {
  border: 1px solid #000000;
}

#masthead img, #footer img, #sidebar img {
  border: 0;
}
```

Finally, you could override a global border setting by creating a noBorder class and then assigning it to relevant images. In CSS, you'd write the following:

```css
.noBorder {
  border: 0;
}
```

And in HTML, you'd add the noBorder class to any image that you didn't want to have a border:

```html
<img class="noBorder" src="sunset.jpg" height="200" width="400"
➥ alt="A photo of a sunset" />
```

Clearly, this could be reversed (turning off borders by default and overriding this with, say, an addBorder style that could be used to add borders to specific images). Obviously, you should go for whichever system provides you with the greatest flexibility when it comes to rapidly updating styles across the site and keeping things consistent when any changes occur. Generally, the contextual method is superior for achieving this.

Although it's most common to apply borders using the shorthand shown earlier, it's possible to define borders on a per-side basis, as demonstrated in the "Using classes and CSS overrides to create an alternate pull quote" exercise in Chapter 3. If you wanted to style a specific image to resemble a Polaroid photograph, you could set equal borders on the top, left, and right, and a larger one on the bottom. In HTML, you would add a class attribute to the relevant image:

```html
<img class="photo" src="sunset.jpg" height="300" width="300"
➥ alt="Sunset photo" />
```

In CSS, you would write the following:

```css
.photo {
  border-width: 8px 8px 20px;
  border-style: solid;
  border-color: #ffffff;
}
```

The results of this are shown in the image to the right. (Obviously, the white border only shows if you have a contrasting background—you wouldn't see a white border on a white background!)

Should you want to, you can also reduce the declaration's size by amalgamating the border-style and border-color definitions:

```
.photo {
   border: solid #ffffff;
   border-width : 8px 8px 20px;
}
```

Note that when you've used a contextual selector with an id value to style a bunch of elements in context, overriding this often requires the contextual selector to again be included in the override rule. In other words, a class value of .override would not necessarily override values set in #box img, even if applied to an image in the box div. In such cases, you'd need to add the id to the selector: #box .override.

There are other border-style values that can be used with images, as well. Examples include dashed and dotted—see the border-style entry in Appendix D (CSS Reference) for a full list. However, overdone decoration can distract from the image, so always ensure that your borders don't overpower your imagery.

Using CSS to wrap text around images

You can use the float and margin properties to enable body copy to wrap around an image. The method is similar to the pull quote example in the previous chapter, so we won't dwell too much on this. Suffice to say that images can be floated left or right, and margins can be set around edges facing body copy in order to provide some whitespace. For example, expanding on the previous example, you could add the following rules to ensure that the surrounding body copy doesn't hug the image:

```
.photo {
   border-width: 8px 8px 20px 8px;
   border-style: solid;
   border-color: #ffffff;
   float: right;
   margin-left: 20px;
   margin-bottom: 20px;
}
```

This results in the following effect shown in the following image.

See `using-css-to-wrap-around-images.html`, `using-css-to-wrap-around-images.css`, and `sunset.jpg` in the chapter 4 folder for a working example of this page.

Displaying random images

This final section of the chapter looks at creating a simple system for displaying a random image from a selection. This has several potential uses, such as randomizing banners on a commercial website, or giving the impression that a site is updated more often than it is by showing visitors some new content each time they arrive. Also, for portfolios, it's useful to present a random piece of work from a selection.

Prior to starting work, you need to prepare your images. Unless you're prepared for subsequent layout elements to shift upon each visit to the page, aim to export all your images with equal dimensions. Should this not be an option, try to keep the same height setting. Note, however, that you can use different file formats for the various images. It's good housekeeping to keep these images in their own folder, too; for this exercise, the images are placed within `assets/random-images`.

Creating a JavaScript-based image randomizer

Required files	The image-randomizer-starting-point folder from the chapter 4 folder.
What you'll learn	How to create an image randomizer using JavaScript.
Completed files	The image-randomizer-javascript folder in the chapter 4 folder.

1. Edit the HTML. Open randomizer.html. In the body of the web page, add the following img element. The src value is for the default image, and this is what's shown if JavaScript is unavailable. The id value is important—this is a hook for both the JavaScript function written in steps 4 through 6 and a CSS rule to add a border to the image.

```
<img src="assets/random-images/road.jpg" id="randomImage"
➥ name="randomImage" height="300" width="300" />
```

Next, add an onload attribute to the body start tag, as shown in the following code block. Note that the value of this attribute will be the name of the JavaScript function.

```
<body onload="randomImage()">
```

2. In randomizer.js, create arrays for image file names and alt attribute values. For the former, only the image file names are needed—not the path to them (that will be added later). Note that the order of the items in the arrays must match—in other words, the text in the first item of the chosenAltCopy array should be for the first image in the chosenImage array.

```
var chosenImage=new Array();
chosenImage[0]="stream.jpg";
chosenImage[1]="river.jpg";
chosenImage[2]="road.jpg";

var chosenAltCopy=new Array();
chosenAltCopy[0]="A stream in Iceland";
chosenAltCopy[1]="A river in Skaftafell, Iceland";
chosenAltCopy[2]="A near-deserted road in Iceland";
```

3. Create a random value. The following JavaScript provides a random value:

```
var getRan=Math.floor(Math.random()*chosenImage.length);
```

4. Create a function. Add the following text to start writing the JavaScript function, which was earlier dubbed randomImage (see step 1's onload value). If you're not familiar with JavaScript, then note that content from subsequent steps must be inserted into the space between the curly brackets.

```
function randomImage()
{
}
```

5. Add JavaScript to set the image. By manipulating the **Document Object Model (DOM)**, we can assign values to an element via its id value. Here, the line states to set the src attribute value of the element with the id value randomImage (i.e., the image added in step 1) to the stated path value plus a random item from the chosenImage array (as defined via getRan, a variable created in step 3).

```
document.getElementById('randomImage').setAttribute
➥('src','assets/random-images/'+chosenImage[getRan]);
```

6. Add JavaScript to set the alt text. Setting the alt text works in a similar way to step 5, but the line is slightly simpler, due to the lack of a path value for the alt text:

```
document.getElementById('randomImage').setAttribute
➥('alt',chosenAltCopy[getRan]);
```

7. Style the image. In CSS, add the following two rules. The first removes borders by default from images that are links. The second defines a border for the image added in step 1, which has an id value of randomImage.

```
a img {
  border: 0;
}
#randomImage {
  border: solid 1px #000000;
}
```

Upon testing the completed files in a browser, each refresh should show a random image from the selection, as shown in the following screenshot. (Note that in this image, the padding value for body was set to 20px 0 0 20px, to avoid the random image hugging the top left of the browser window.)

There are a couple of things to note regarding the script. To add further images/alt text, copy the previous items in each array, increment the number in square brackets by one and then amend the values—for example:

```
var chosenImage=new Array();
chosenImage[0]="stream.jpg";
chosenImage[1]="river.jpg";
chosenImage[2]="road.jpg";
chosenImage[3]="harbor.jpg";

var chosenAltCopy=new Array();
chosenAltCopy[0]="A stream in Iceland";
chosenAltCopy[1]="A river in Skaftafell, Iceland";
chosenAltCopy[2]="A near-deserted road in Iceland";
chosenAltCopy[3]="The harbor in Reykjavík ";
```

You'll also note that in this example, the height and widths of the images is identical. However, these can also be changed by editing the script. For example, to set a separate height for each image, you'd first add the following array:

```
var chosenHeight=new Array();
chosenHeight[0]="200";
chosenHeight[1]="500";
chosenHeight[2]="400";
```

And you'd next add the following line to the function:

```
document.getElementById('randomImage').setAttribute
➥('height',chosenHeight[getRan]);
```

Remember, however, the advice earlier about the page reflowing if the image dimensions vary—if you have images of differing sizes, your design will need to take this into account.

Creating a PHP-based image randomizer

Required files	The image-randomizer-starting-point folder from the chapter 4 folder.
What you'll learn	How to create an image randomizer using PHP.
Completed files	The image-randomizer-php folder in the chapter 4 folder.

If you have access to web space that enables you to work with PHP, it's simple to create an equivalent to the JavaScript exercise using PHP. The main benefit is that users who disable JavaScript will still see a random image, rather than just the default. Note that you need some method of running PHP files to work on this exercise, such as a local install of Apache. Note also that prior to working through the steps, you should remove the HTML document's script element, and you should also amend the title element's value, changing it to something more appropriate.

1. Define the CSS rules. In CSS, define a border style, as per step 7 of the previous exercise, but also edit the existing paragraph rule with a font property/value pair, because in this example, you're going to add a caption based on the alt text value.

```
a img {
  border: 0;
}
#randomImage {
  border: solid 1px #000000;
}
p {
  font: 1.2em/1.5em Verdana, sans-serif;
  margin-bottom: 1.5em;
}
```

2. Set up the PHP tag. Change the file name of randomizer.html to randomizer.php to make it a PHP document. Then, place the following on the page, in the location where you want the randomized image to go. Subsequent code should be placed within the PHP tags.

```
<?php
?>
```

3. Define the array. One array can be used to hold the information for the file names and alt text. In each case, the alt text should follow its associated image.

```
$picarray = array("stream" => "A photo of a stream", "river" => "A
➥ photo of a river", "road" => "A photo of a road");
$randomkey = array_rand($picarray);
```

4. Print information to the web page. Add the following lines to write the img and p elements to the web page, using a random item set from the array for the relevant attributes. Note that the paragraph content is as per the alt text. Aside from the caption, the resulting web page looks identical to the JavaScript example.

```
echo '<img src="assets/random-images/'.$randomkey.'.jpg"
➥ alt="'.$picarray[$randomkey].'" width="300" height="300"
➥ class="addBorder" />';

echo '<p>'.$picarray[$randomkey].'</p>';
```

5. Use an include. This is an extra step of sorts. If you want to make your PHP more modular, you can copy everything within the PHP tags to an external document, save it (e.g., as random-image.php) and then cut it into the web page as an include:

```
<?php
@include($_SERVER['DOCUMENT_ROOT'] . "/random-image.php");
?>
```

> *For more on working with PHP, see* PHP Solutions: Dynamic Web Design Made Easy, *by David Powers.*

Hopefully you've found this chapter of interest and now feel you have a good grounding in working with images on the Web. It's amazing to think how devoid of visual interest the Web used to be in contrast to today, now that images are essential to the vast majority of sites. As I've mentioned before, the importance of images on the Web lies not only in content, but in interface elements as well, such as navigation—a topic we're covering in the next chapter.

5 USING LINKS AND CREATING NAVIGATION

In this chapter:

- Introducing web navigation
- Creating links
- Controlling CSS link states
- Mastering the cascade
- Looking at links and accessibility
- Examining a JavaScript alternative to pop-ups
- Creating navigation bars
- Working with CSS-based rollovers

Introduction to web navigation

The primary concern of most websites is the provision of information. The ability to enable nonlinear navigation via the use of links is one of the main things that sets the Web apart from other media. But without organized, coherent, and usable navigation, even a site with the most amazing content will fail.

During this chapter, we'll work through how to create various types of navigation. Instead of relying on large numbers of graphics and clunky JavaScript, we'll create rollovers that are composed of nothing more than simple HTML lists and a little CSS. And rather than using pop-up windows to display large graphics when a thumbnail image is clicked, we'll cover how to do everything on a single page.

Navigation types

There are essentially three types of navigation online:

- **Inline navigation**: General links within web page content areas
- **Site navigation**: The primary navigation area of a website, commonly referred to as a navigation bar
- **Search-based navigation**: A search box that enables you to search a site via terms you input yourself

Although I've separated navigation into these three distinct categories, lines blur, and not every site includes all the different types of navigation. Also, various designers call each navigation type something different, and there's no official name in each case, so in the following sections, I'll expand a little on each type.

Inline navigation

Inline navigation used to be the primary way of navigating the Web, which, many moons ago, largely consisted of technical documentation. Oddly, inline navigation—links within a web page's body copy—is less popular than it once was. Perhaps this is due to the increasing popularity of visually oriented web design tools, leading designers to concentrate more on visuals than usability. Maybe it's because designers have collectively forgotten that links can be made anywhere and not just in navigation bars. In any case, links—inline links in particular—are the main thing that differentiates the Web from other media, making it unique. For instance, you can make specific words within a document link directly to related content. A great example of this is Wikipedia (`www.wikipedia.org`), the free encyclopedia.

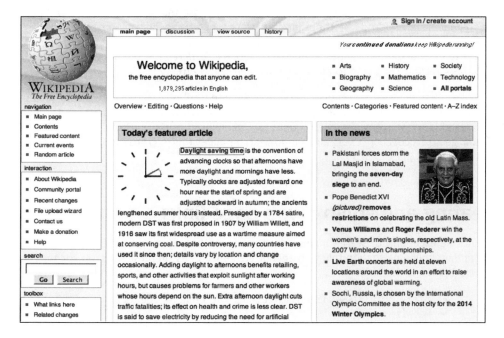

Site navigation

Wikipedia showcases navigation types other than inline. To the left, underneath the logo, is a navigation bar that is present on every page of the site, allowing users to quickly access each section. This kind of thing is essential for most websites—long gone are the days when users often expected to have to keep returning to a homepage to navigate to new content.

As Wikipedia proves, just because you have a global navigation bar, that doesn't mean you should skimp on inline navigation. In recent times, I've seen a rash of sites that say things like, "Thank you for visiting our website. If you have any questions, you can contact us by clicking the contact details link on our navigation bar." Quite frankly, this is bizarre. A better solution is to say, "Thank you for visiting our website. If you have any questions, please contact us," and to turn "contact us" into a link to the contact details page. This might seem like common sense, but not every web designer thinks in this way.

Search-based navigation

Wikipedia has a search box within its navigation sidebar. It's said there are two types of web users: those who eschew search boxes and those who head straight for them. The thing is, search boxes are not always needed, despite the claims of middle managers the world over. Indeed, most sites get by with well-structured and coherent navigation.

However, sites sometimes grow very large (typically those that are heavy on information and that have hundreds or thousands of pages, such as technical repositories, review archives, or large online stores, such as Amazon and eBay). In such cases, it's often not feasible to use standard navigation elements to access information. Attempting to do so leads to users getting lost trying to navigate a huge navigation tree.

Unlike other types of navigation, search boxes aren't entirely straightforward to set up, requiring server-side scripting for their functionality. However, a quick trawl through a search engine provides many options, including Google Custom Search Engine (www.google.com/coop/cse/) and Yahoo Search Builder (http://builder.search.yahoo.com/m/promo).

Creating and styling web page links

With the exception of search boxes, which are forms based on and driven by server-side scripting, online navigation relies on anchor elements. In its simplest form, an anchor element looks like this:

```
<a href="http://www.friendsofed.com/">A link to the friends of ED
➥ website</a>
```

By placing a trailing slash in this type of URL, you make only one call to the server instead of two. Also, some incorrectly configured Apache servers generate a "File not found" error if the trailing slash is omitted.

The href attribute value is the URL of the destination document, which is often another web page, but can in fact be any file type (MP3, PDF, JPEG, and so on). If the browser can display the document type (either directly or via a plug-in), it does so; otherwise, it downloads the file (or brings up some kind of download prompt).

Never omit end tags when working with links. Omitting </a> *is not only shoddy and invalid XHTML, but most browsers then turn all subsequent content on the page into a link.*

There are three ways of linking to a file: **absolute links**, **relative links**, and **root-relative links**. We'll cover these in the sections that follow, and you'll see how to create internal page links, style link states in CSS, and work with links and images. We'll also discuss enhanced link accessibility and usability, and link targeting.

Absolute links

The preceding example shows an absolute link, sometimes called a full URL, which is typically used when linking to external files (i.e., those on other websites). This type of link provides the entire path to a destination file, including the file transfer protocol, domain name, any directory names, and the file name itself. A longer example is

```
<a href="http://www.wireviews.com/lyrics/instar.html">Instar lyrics</a>
```

In this case, the file transfer protocol is http://, the domain is wireviews.com, the directory is lyrics, and the file name is instar.html.

Depending on how the target site's web server has been set up, you may or may not have to include www *prior to the domain name when creating this kind of link. Usually it's best to include it, to be on the safe side. An exception is if you're linking to a subdomain, such as* http://browsers.evolt.org.

If you're linking to a website's homepage, you can usually leave off the file name, as in the earlier link to the friends of ED site, and the server will automatically pick up the default document—assuming one exists—which can be index.html, default.htm, index.php, index.asp, or some other name, depending on the server type. However, adding a trailing slash after the domain is beneficial (such as http://www.wireviews.com/). If no default document exists, you'll be returned a directory listing or an error message, depending on whether the server's permissions settings enable users to browse directories.

Relative links

A relative link is one that locates a file in relation to the current document. Taking the Wireviews example, if you were on the instar.html page, located inside the lyrics directory, and you wanted to link back to the homepage via a relative link, you would use the following code:

```
<a href="../index.html">Wireviews homepage</a>
```

5

The index.html file name is preceded by ../, which tells the web browser to move up one directory prior to looking for index.html. Moving in the other direction is done in the same way as with absolute links: by preceding the file name with the path. Therefore, to get from the homepage back to the instar.html page, you would write the following:

```
<a href="lyrics/instar.html">Instar lyrics</a>
```

In some cases, you need to combine both methods. For instance, this website has HTML documents in both the lyrics and reviews folders. To get from the instar.html lyrics page to a review, you have to go up one level, and then down into the relevant directory to locate the file:

```
<a href="../reviews/alloy.html">Alloy review</a>
```

Root-relative links

Root-relative links work in a similar way to absolute links, but from the root of the website. These links begin with a forward slash, which tells the browser to start the path to the file from the root of the current website. Therefore, regardless of how many directories deep you are in the Wireviews website, a root-relative link to the homepage always looks like this:

```
<a href="/index.html">Homepage</a>
```

And a link to the instar.html page within the lyrics directory always looks like this:

```
<a href="/lyrics/instar.html">Instar lyrics</a>
```

This type of link therefore ensures you point to the relevant document without your having to type an absolute link or mess around with relative links, and is, in my opinion, the safest type of link to use for linking to documents elsewhere on a website. Should a page be moved from one directory to one higher or lower in the hierarchy, none of the links (including links to style sheets and script documents) would require changing. Relative links, on the other hand, would require changing; and although absolute links wouldn't require changing, they take up more space and are less modular from a testing standpoint; if you're testing a site, you don't want to be restricted to the domain in question—you may wish to host the site locally or on a temporary domain online so that clients can access the work-in-progress creation.

> All paths in href attributes must contain forward slashes only. Some software—notably older releases from Microsoft—creates and permits backward slashes (e.g., lyrics\wire\154.html), but this is nonstandard and does not work in non-Microsoft web browsers.

Internal page links

Along with linking to other documents, it's possible to link to another point in the same web page. This is handy for things like a FAQ (frequently asked questions) list, enabling the visitor to jump directly to an answer and then back to the list of questions; or for top-of-page links, enabling a user single-click access to return to the likely location of a page's masthead and navigation, if they've scrolled to the bottom of a long document.

When linking to other elements on a web page, you start by providing an id value for any element you want to be able to jump to. To link to that, you use a standard anchor element (<a>) with an href value equal to that of your defined id value, preceded by a hash symbol (#).

For a list of questions, you can have something like this:

```
<ul id="questions">
  <li><a href="#answer1">Question one</a></li>
  <li><a href="#answer2">Question two</a></li>
  <li><a href="#answer3">Question three</a></li>
</ul>
```

Later on in the document, the first two answers might look like this:

```
<p id="answer1">The answer to question 1!</p>
<p><a href="#questions">Back to questions</a></p>
<p id="answer2">The answer to question 2!</p>
<p><a href="#questions">Back to questions</a></p>
```

As you can see, each link's href value is prefixed by a hash sign. When the link is clicked, the web page jumps to the element with the relevant id value. Therefore, clicking the Question one link, which has an href value of #answer1, jumps to the paragraph with the id value of answer1. Clicking the Back to questions link, which has an id value of #questions, jumps back to the list, because the unordered list element has an id of questions.

> It's worth bearing in mind that the page only jumps directly to the linked element if there's enough room underneath it. If the target element is at the bottom of the web page, you'll see it plus a browser window height of content above.

Backward compatibility with fragment identifiers

In older websites, you may see a slightly different system for accessing content within a web page, and this largely involves obsolete browsers such as Netscape 4 not understanding how to deal with links that solely use the id attribute. Instead, you'll see a fragment identifier, which is an anchor tag with a name attribute, but no href attribute. For instance, a fragment identifier for the first answer is as follows:

```
<p><a id="answer1" name="answer1">Answer 1!</a></p>
```

The reason for the doubling up, here—using both the name and id attributes, is because the former is on borrowed time in web specifications, and it should therefore only be used for backward compatibility.

Top-of-page links

Internal page links are sometimes used to create a top-of-page/back-to-top link. This is particularly handy for websites that have lengthy pages—when a user has scrolled to the bottom of the page, they can click the link to return to the top of the document, which usually houses the navigation. The problem here is that the most common internal linking method—targeting a link at #top—fails in many browsers, including Firefox and Opera.

```
<a href="#top">Back to top</a>
```

You've likely seen the previous sort of link countless times, but unless you're using Internet Explorer or Safari, it's as dead as a dodo. There are various workarounds, though, one of which is to include a fragment identifier at the top of the document. At the foot of the web page is the Back to top link shown previously, and the fragment identifier is placed at the top of the web page:

```
<a id="top" name="top"></a>
```

This technique isn't without its problems, though. Some browsers ignore empty elements such as this (some web designers therefore populate the element with a single space); it's tricky to get the element right at the top of the page and not to interfere with subsequent content; and, if you're working with XHTML Strict, it's not valid to have an inline element on its own, outside of a block element, such as p or div.

Two potential solutions are on offer. The simplest is to link the top-of-page link to your containing div—the one within which your web page's content is housed. For sites I create—as you'll see in Chapter 7—I typically house all content within a div that has an id value of wrapper. This enables me to easily control the width of the layout, among other things. In the context of this section of this chapter, the wrapper div also provides something for a top-of-page link to jump to. Clicking the link in the following code block would enable a user to jump to the top of the wrapper div, at (or very near to) the top of the web page.

```
<a href="#wrapper">Top of page</a>
```

Note that since standalone inline elements aren't valid in XHTML Strict, the preceding would either be housed within a paragraph or a footer div, depending on the site.

Another solution is to nest a fragment identifier within a div and then style the div to sit at the top left of the web page. The HTML for this is the following:

```
<div id="topOfPageAnchor">
  <a id="top" name="top">  </a>
</div>
```

In CSS, you would then add the following:

```
div#topOfPageAnchor {
  position: absolute;
  top: 0;
  left: 0;
  height: 0;
}
```

Setting the div's height to 0 means it takes up no space and is therefore not displayed; setting its positioning to absolute means it's outside the normal flow of the document, so it doesn't affect subsequent page content. You can test this by setting the background color of a following element to something vivid—it should sit tight to the edge of the browser window edges.

Link states

By default, links are displayed underlined and in blue when viewed in a web browser. However, links have five states, and their visual appearance varies depending on the current state of the link. The states are as follows:

- link: The link's standard state, before any action has taken place
- visited: The link's state after having been clicked
- hover: The link's state while the mouse cursor is over it
- focus: The link's state while focused
- active: The link's state while being clicked

The visited and active states also have a default appearance. The former is displayed in purple and the latter in red. Both are underlined.

If every site adhered to this default scheme, it would be easier to find where you've been and where you haven't on the Web. However, most designers prefer to dictate their own color schemes rather than having blue and purple links peppering their designs. In my view, this is fine. Despite what some usability gurus claim, most web users these days probably don't even know what the default link colors are, and so hardly miss them.

In HTML, you may have seen custom link colors being set for the link, active, and visited states via the link, alink, and vlink attributes of the body element. These attributes are deprecated, though, and should be avoided. This is a good thing, because you need to define them in the body element of every page of your site, which is a tiresome process—even more so if they later need changing; as you might have guessed, it's easier to define link states in CSS.

5

Defining link states with CSS

CSS has advantages over the obsolete HTML method of defining link states. You gain control over the hover and focus states and can do far more than just edit the state colors—although that's what we're going to do first.

Anchors can be styled by using a tag selector:

```
a {
  color: #3366cc;
}
```

In this example, all anchors on the page—including links—are turned to a medium blue. However, individual states can be defined by using **pseudo-class selectors** (so called because they have the same effect as applying a class, even though no class is applied to the element):

```
a:link {
  color: #3366cc;
}
a:visited {
  color: #666699;
}
a:hover {
  color: #0066ff;
}
a:focus {
  background-color: #ffff00;
}
a:active {
  color: #cc00ff;
}
```

Correctly ordering link states

The various states have been defined in a specific order in the previous example: link, visited, hover, focus, active. This is because certain states override others, and those "closest" to the link on the web page take precedence.

There is debate regarding which order the various states should be in, so I can only provide my reasoning for this particular example. It makes sense for the link to be a certain color when you hover over it, and then a different color on the active state (when clicked), to confirm the click action. However, if you put the hover and active states in the other order (active, hover), you may not see the active one when the link is clicked. This is because you're still hovering over the link when you click it.

The focus state is probably primarily use keyboard users, and so they won't typically see hover anyway. However, for mouse users, it makes logical sense to place focus after hover, because it's a more direct action—in other words, the link is selected, ready for activation during the focus state; but if you ordered the states focus, hover, a link the cursor is hovering over would not change appearance when focused, which from a user standpoint is unhelpful.

> *A simple way of remembering the basic state order (the five states minus focus) is to think of the words **lo**ve, **ha**te: link, visited, hover, active. If focus is included and my order is used, there's the slightly awkward (but equally memorable) **lo**ve **h**er **f**or **a**lways/**lo**ve **h**im **f**or **a**lways: link, visited, hover, focus, active.*

However, there is a counter argument that recommends putting focus before hover, so that when an already focused link (or potentially any other focused element for non-IE browsers) is hovered over, it will change from the focused state to indicate that it is now being hovered over. Ultimately, this is a chicken-and-egg scenario—do you want a hovered link to change from hover to focus to active? The focus will get lost somewhere in there until the link is depressed (and the active state removed), by which time the link will be in the process of being followed.

In the end, the decision should perhaps rest with how you're styling states and what information you want to present to the user, and often the focus state is a duplication of hover anyway, for the benefit of keyboard users. And on some occasions, it doesn't matter too much where it's put, if the styling method is much different from that for other states—for example, when a border is applied to focus, but a change of color or removal of underlines is used for the other states. However, if you decide on LVFHA or some other order, you'll have to make your own way of remembering the state order!

The difference between a and a:link

Many designers don't realize the difference between the selectors a and a:link in CSS. Essentially, the a selector styles all anchors, but a:link styles only those that are clickable links (i.e., those that include an href attribute) that have not yet been visited. This means that, should you have a site with a number of fragment identifiers, you can use the a:link selector to style clickable links only, avoiding styling fragment identifiers, too. (This prevents the problem of fragment identifiers taking on underlines, and also prevents the potential problem of user-defined style sheets overriding the a rule.) However, if you define a:link instead of a, you then must define the visited, hover, and active states, otherwise they will be displayed in their default appearances. This is particularly important when it comes to visited, because that state is mutually exclusive to link, and doesn't take on any of its styling. Therefore, if you set font-weight to bold via a:link alone, visited links will not appear bold (although the hover and active states will for unvisited links—upon the links being visited, they will become hover and active states for visited links and will be displayed accordingly).

Editing link styles using CSS

Along with changing link colors, CSS enables you to style links just like any other piece of text. You can define specific fonts; edit padding, margins, and borders; change the font weight and style; and also amend the standard link underline, removing it entirely if you wish (by setting the `text-decoration` property to none).

```
a:link {
  color: #3366cc;
  font-weight: bold;
  text-decoration: none;
}
```

Removing the standard underline is somewhat controversial, even in these enlightened times, and causes endless (and rather tedious) arguments among web designers. My view is that it can be OK to do so, but with some caveats.

If you remove the standard underline, ensure your links stand out from the surrounding copy in some other way. Having your links in the same style and color as other words and not underlined is a very bad idea. The only exception is if you don't want users to easily find the links and click them (perhaps for a children's game or educational site).

A common device used by web designers is to recolor links, in order to distinguish them from body copy. However, this may not be enough (depending on the chosen colors), because a significant proportion of the population has some form of color blindness. A commonly quoted figure for color blindness in Western countries is 8%, with the largest affected group being white males (the worldwide figure is lower, at approximately 4%). Therefore, a change of color (to something fairly obvious) *and* a change of font weight to bold often does the trick.

Whatever your choice, be consistent—don't have links change style on different pages of the site. Also, it's useful to reinforce the fact that links are links by bringing back the underline on the hover state. An example of this is shown to the right (see editing-link-styles-using-css.html and editing-link-styles-using-css.html in the chapter 5 folder of the completed files).

> Lorem ipsum dolor sit amet, consectetuer adipiscing elit. Morbi commodo, ipsum sed pharetra gravida, orci magna rhoncus neque, id pulvinar odio lorem non turpis. Nullam sit amet enim. **Suspendisse id velit** vitae ligula volutpat condimentum. Aliquam erat volutpat. Sed quis velit. **Nulla facilisi**. Nulla libero. Vivamus pharetra posuere sapien. Nam consectetuer. Sed aliquam, nunc eget euismod ullamcorper, lectus nunc ullamcorper orci, fermentum bibendum enim nibh eget ipsum. Donec porttitor ligula eu dolor. Maecenas vitae nulla consequat libero cursus venenatis.

Links are bold and orange, making them stand out from surrounding text. On the hover state, the link darkens to red and the standard underline returns. The second of those things is achieved by setting `text-decoration` to underline in the a:hover declaration. Note that even when presented in grayscale, such as in this book, these two states can be distinguished from surrounding text.

You can also combine pseudo-classes. For example, if you add the rules shown following to a style sheet (these are from the editing-link-styles-using-css documents), you'd have links going gray when visited, but turning red on the hover state (along with showing the underline). Note that because the link and visited states are exclusive, the bold value for font-weight is assigned using the grouped selector. It could also be applied to individual rules, but this is neater.

```
a:link, a:visited {
  font-weight: bold;
}
a:link {
  color: #f26522;
  text-decoration: none;
}
a:visited {
  color: #8a8a8a;
}
a:hover {
  color: #f22222;
  text-decoration: underline;
}
a:active {
  color: #000000;
  text-decoration: underline;
}
```

If you decided that you wanted visited links to retain their visited color on the hover state, you could add the following rule:

```
a:visited:hover {
  color: #8a8a8a;
}
```

The :focus pseudo-class

Rarely used due to a lack of browser support, the :focus pseudo-class is worth being mindful of. It enables you to define the link state of a focused link. Focusing usually occurs when tabbing to a link, and so the :focus pseudo-class can be a handy usability aid. At the time of writing, it works in Firefox and Safari, but is ignored in Opera and Internet Explorer, although Microsoft's browser does at least surround any focused links with a dotted line. (Note that Firefox and Safari also surround focused links with a dotted line and aqua border, respectively.)

The following example, used in editing-link-styles-using-css.css, turns the background of focused links yellow in compliant browsers:

```
a:focus {
  background: yellow;
}
```

5

Multiple link states: The cascade

A common problem web designers come up against is multiple link styles within a document. While you should be consistent when it comes to styling site links, there are specific exceptions, one of which is site navigation. Web users are quite happy with navigation bar links differing from standard inline links. Elsewhere, links may differ slightly in web page footers, where links are often displayed in a smaller font than that used for other web page copy; also, if a background color makes the standard link color hard to distinguish, it might be useful to change it (although in such situations it would perhaps be best to amend either the background or your default link colors).

A widespread error is applying a class to every link for which you want a style other than the default—you end up with loads of inline junk that can't be easily amended at a later date. Instead, with the careful use of divs (with unique ids) on the web page and contextual selectors in CSS, you can rapidly style links for each section of a web page.

Styling multiple link states

Required files	XHTML-basic.html and CSS-default.css from the basic-boilerplates folder as a starting point.
What you'll learn	How to use the cascade to set styles for links housed in specific areas of a web page.
Completed files	multiple-links-the-cascade.html and multiple-links-the-cascade.css from the chapter 5 folder.

1. Add the basic page content structure shown following, placing it within the existing wrapper div of the boilerplate. This has three divs, which have id values of navigation, content, and footer, respectively. The first houses an unordered list that forms the basis of a navigation bar. The second is the content area, which has an inline link within a paragraph. The third is the footer, which is sometimes used to repeat the navigation bar links, albeit in a simplified manner.

```
<div id="navigation">
  <ul>
    <li><a href="index.html">Homepage</a></li>
    <li><a href="products.html">Products</a></li>
    <li><a href="contact-details.html">Contact details</a></li>
  </ul>
</div>
<div id="content">
  <p>Hello there. Our new product is a <a href="banjo.html">fantastic
  ➥ banjo</a>!</p>
</div>
<div id="footer">
```

```
    <a href="index.html">Homepage</a> | <a href="products.html">
    ➥Products</a> | <a href="contact-details.html">Contact
    ➥ details</a>
</div>
```

> Note that the code block could be simplified, such as by dispensing with the navigation div and instead applying the relevant id value directly to the unordered list. However, this exercise aims to show how to create links in context, using a simplified web page layout that has specific areas for certain content types. See Chapters 7 and 10 for more on layout.

2. Add some padding to the existing body rule in the CSS to add some spacing around the page content:

```
body {
    font: 62.5%/1.5 Verdana, Arial, Helvetica, sans-serif;
    padding: 30px;
}
```

```
• Homepage
• Products
• Contact details
  Hello there. Our new product is a fantastic banjo!

  Homepage | Products | Contact details
```

3. Add some rules to define the main states for links on the web page. The following rules color links orange, change them to red on the hover state, make them gray on the visited state, and make them black on the active state.

```
a:link {
    color: #f26522;
}
a:visited {
    color: #8a8a8a;
}
a:hover {
    color: #f22222;
}
a:active {
    color: #000000;
}
```

4. Next, style the navigation links. Contextual selectors are used to style the links within the navigation div.

```
#navigation a, #navigation a:visited {
  text-decoration: none;
  font-weight: bold;
  color: #666666;
  text-transform: uppercase;
}
#navigation a:hover {
  text-decoration: underline;
}
```

The first rule removes the underline from all links within the navigation div, renders them in bold and uppercase, and colors them a medium gray. The second rule brings back the underline on the hover state.

> You'll note that the visited state is the same as the standard state in the previous code block. While I don't recommend doing this for links in a page's general content area, or for pages that have a lot of navigation links, I feel it's acceptable for sites that have a small number of navigation links, where it's not likely a visitor will need notification regarding which pages or sections have been accessed.

5. Style the footer links. Add another contextual selector to style the footer links, making them smaller than links elsewhere on the page:

```
#footer a:link, #footer a:visited {
  font-size: 0.8em;
}
```

- **HOMEPAGE**
- **PRODUCTS**
- **CONTACT DETAILS**
  Hello there. Our new product is a fantastic banjo!

  Homepage | Products | Contact details

And there we have it: three different link styles on the same page, without messing around with classes.

Enhanced link accessibility and usability

We've already touched on accessibility and usability concerns during this chapter, so we'll now briefly run through a few attributes that can be used with anchors (and some with area elements—see the "Image Maps" section later in the chapter) to enhance your web page links.

The title attribute

Regular users of Internet Explorer for Windows may be familiar with its habit of popping up alt text as a tooltip. This has encouraged web designers to wrongly fill alt text with explanatory copy for those links that require an explanation, rather than using the alt text for a succinct overview of the image's content. Should you require a pop-up, add a title attribute to your surrounding a element to explain what will happen when the link is clicked. The majority of web browsers display its value when the link is hovered over for a couple of seconds (see right), although some older browsers, such as Netscape 4, don't provide this functionality.

```
<a href="large-image.html" title="Click to view a larger image">
➡<img src="image.jpg" alt="This is some text that explains what
➡ the image is" width="400" height="300" /></a>
```

There are a few things to be mindful of when using title attributes. The first is that behavior varies slightly between browsers, and the positioning and style of the tooltip cannot be controlled. Internet Explorer exhibits some particularly quirky behavior. In addition to displaying alt text as a tooltip, alt text defined within an img element will override (and therefore be displayed instead of) title text for a surrounding a element. However, if the title and alt attributes are both placed within the img element, the title attribute wins out. Therefore, some technically unnecessary duplication of content is required to ensure compliance from Internet Explorer. Also, Microsoft's browser does not display title text when you mouse over area elements within image maps.

> *Firefox tends to crop tooltips after 80 characters or so. Therefore, keep your* title *text fairly succinct. If you need a much longer piece of text, implement the technique described in the "Adding pop-ups to images" section later in this chapter.*

Using accesskey and tabindex

I've bundled the accesskey and tabindex attributes because they have similar functions—that is, enabling keyboard access to various areas of the web page. Most browsers enable you to use the Tab key to cycle through links, although if you end up on a web page with dozens of links, this can be a soul-destroying experience. (And before you say "So what?" you should be aware that many web users cannot use a mouse. You don't have to be severely disabled or elderly to be in such a position either—something as common as repetitive strain injury affects plenty of people's ability to use a mouse.)

The accesskey attribute can be added to anchor and area elements. It assigns an access key to the link, whose value must be a single character. In tandem with your platform's assigned modifier key (Alt for Windows and Ctrl for Mac), you press the key to highlight or activate the link, depending on how the browser you're using works.

```
<a href="index.html" accesskey="/">Home page</a>
```

An ongoing problem with access keys is that the shortcuts used to activate them are mostly claimed by various technologies, leaving scant few characters. In fact, research conducted by WATS.ca (www.wats.ca/show.php?contentid=32) concluded that just three characters were available that didn't clash with anything at all: /, \ and]. This, combined with a total lack of standard access key assignments/bindings, has led to many accessibility gurus conceding defeat, admitting that while there's a definite need for the technology, it's just not there yet.

The tabindex attribute has proved more successful. This is used to define the attribute's value as anything from 0 (which excludes the element from the tabbing order, which can be useful) to 32767, thereby setting its place in the tab order, although if you have 32,767 tabbable elements on your web page, you really do need to go back and reread the earlier advice on information architecture (see Chapter 1). Note that tab orders needn't be consecutive, so it's wise to use tabindex in steps of ten, so you can later insert extra ones without renumbering everything.

Not all browsers enable tabbing to links, and others require that you amend some preferences to activate this function, and so tabindex ultimately only really comes in handy when working with forms, as you'll see in Chapter 8. When used for too many other elements, you also run the risk of tabindex values hijacking the mouse cursor, meaning that instead of the Tab key moving the user from the first form field to the second, it might end up highlighting something totally different, elsewhere on the page. What's logical to some people—in terms of tab order—may not be to others, so always ensure you test your websites thoroughly, responding to feedback.

Skip navigation links

Designers who work with CSS layouts tend to focus on information structure, rather than blindly putting together layouts in a visual editor. This is good from an accessibility standpoint, because you can ensure information is ordered in a logical manner by checking its location in the code. However, when considering alternate browsers, it's clear that some of the information on the page will be potentially redundant. For example, while a user surfing with a standard browser can ignore the masthead and navigation in a split second, rapidly focusing on the information they want to look at, someone using a screen reader will have to sit through the navigation links being read out each time, which can prove extremely tedious if there are quite a few links.

Various solutions exist to help deal with this problem, and although you can use CSS to reorder the page information (most commonly by placing the code for the masthead at the end of the HTML document and then using absolute positioning to display it at the top when the page is viewed in a browser), it's more common to use what's typically referred to as **skip navigation**.

Creating a skip navigation link

Required files	skip-navigation-starting-point.html and skip-navigation-starting-point.css from the chapter 5 folder as a starting point.
What you'll learn	How to create some basic skip navigation.
Completed files	skip-navigation-completed.html and skip-navigation-completed.css from the chapter 5 folder.

1. Examine the web page. Successful skip navigation relies in part on semantic and logical document structure. Open skip-navigation-starting-point.html and you'll see it's a basic web page, with all of the page's content—title, navigation, and main content—contained within a wrapper div; next is a masthead div, containing a heading and a few links. Under the masthead div is a content div, which, suitably enough, houses the page's main content. The beginning of the content is immediately visible, even on monitors with low resolutions, but for users of screen readers, the site's name and navigation links will be read out every single time a page is accessed—a tedious process for the user.

A VERY SIMPLE WEBSITE
Home page   About us   Contact details

Lorem ipsum dolor sit amet, consectetuer adipiscing elit. Morbi commodo, ipsum sed pharetra gravida, orci magna rhoncus neque, id pulvinar odio lorem non turpis. Nullam sit amet enim. Suspendisse id velit vitae ligula volutpat condimentum. Aliquam erat volutpat. Sed quis velit. Nulla facilisi. Nulla libero. Vivamus pharetra posuere sapien. Nam consectetuer. Sed aliquam, nunc eget euismod ullamcorper, lectus nunc ullamcorper orci, fermentum bibendum enim nibh eget ipsum. Donec porttitor ligula eu dolor. Maecenas vitae nulla consequat libero cursus venenatis. Nam magna enim, accumsan eu, blandit sed, blandit a, eros.

2. Immediately after the body element start tag, add a div with an id value of skipLink, which is a hook to later style the div and its link using CSS. The href value for the anchor is set to #content. As you will remember from earlier in the chapter, this will make the page jump to the element with an id value of content when the link is clicked (i.e., the content div in this example's case).

```
<div id="skipLink">
  <a href="#content">Skip to content</a>
</div>
```

3. Test the web page. Already, the benefits of this are apparent. You can use Opera's User mode or CSS ➤ Disable Styles ➤ All Styles in the Firefox Web Developer toolbar to temporarily remove the CSS and emulate a text browser (roughly equating to the content available to screen readers)—see the following left-hand image. Click the skip to content link and the page will jump to the web page's content—see the right-hand image. Even with three links, this proves useful, but if the site has a couple of dozen links, this improves usability for screen reader users no end.

Styling a skip navigation link

Required files	skip-navigation-completed.html and skip-navigation-completed.css from the chapter 5 folder as a starting point.
What you'll learn	How to style skip navigation.
Completed files	skip-navigation-styled.html and skip-navigation-styled.css from the chapter 5 folder.

When skip navigation is styled, it's common to set the containing div (in this case, the skipLink one) to display: none, thereby making it invisible. This is all well and good in theory, but some screen readers render CSS, meaning that your cunning skip navigation won't be accessible. Therefore, this exercise will show how to hide the skip navigation within the existing page design. (Note that, depending on your site and target audience, you may wish to leave the skip navigation visible to aid users whose sight is fine, but who have difficulty with motor tasks. That said, the exercise still shows how to style skip navigation in general, and should therefore prove useful regardless.)

1. Style the `skipLink` div. Remove the `skipLink` div from the document flow (thereby meaning it won't affect the positioning of any other element) by setting position to absolute in a CSS rule targeting the element (see the following code snippet); Chapter 7 has more information on positioning div elements. The `top` and `right` values define the div's position in relation to its parent element (which in this case is body—effectively the entire browser window view area). The settings place the div inside the masthead.

```
#skipLink {
position: absolute;
top: 30px;
right: 30px;
}
```

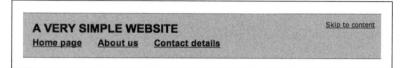

2. Make the link invisible—via the use of contextual selectors you can set the link's color to blend with that of the web page element it's positioned over. You can also use the `:hover` and `:focus` pseudo-classes mentioned earlier in this chapter to make the link visible on the hover and focus states.

```
#skipLink a:link, #skipLink a:visited {
  color: #cecece;
}
#skipLink a:hover, #skipLink a:focus {
  color: #000000;
}
```

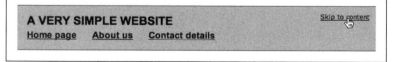

Enhancing skip navigation with a background image

Required files	`skip-navigation-completed.html`, `skip-navigation-completed.css`, and `skip-navigation-down-arrow.gif` from the chapter 5 folder.
What you'll learn	How to create skip navigation that sits centrally at the top of the web page and is invisible, but that displays a rollover effect during the hover and focus states.
Completed files	`skip-navigation-background-image.html`, `skip-navigation-background-image.css`, and `skip-navigation-down-arrow.gif` (unchanged during the tutorial) from the chapter 5 folder.

1. Position the skipNav div. Add the following link to remove the skipNav div from the document flow and position it at the top of the web page. The width and text-align property values stretch the div to the full width of the browser window and center the text horizontally, respectively.

```
#skipLink {
  position: absolute;
  top: 0;
  left: 0;
  width: 100%;
  text-align: center;
}
```

2. Style the skip navigation link. Add the following rule to style the link within the skipLink div. By setting display to block, the active area of the link stretches to fill its container, thereby effectively making the entire containing div clickable. The padding-bottom setting is important, because this provides space at the bottom of the div for displaying the background image used for the hover state, added in the next step. The color value is black (#000000) at this point, which ensures that the text fits happily within the space available above the page content. (This may change for users with non-default settings, but for the default and first zoom setting, it'll be fine.)

```
#skipLink a:link, #skipLink a:visited {
  display: block;
  color: #000000;
  font: 1.0em Arial, Helvetica, sans-serif;
  padding-top: 5px;
  padding-bottom: 20px;
}
```

Skip to content

A VERY SIMPLE WEBSITE
Home page   About us   Contact details

3. Recolor the skip navigation link. Change the color property so that the link blends into the background.

```
#skipLink a:link, #skipLink a:visited {
  display: block;
  color: #fefefe;
  font: 1.0em Arial, Helvetica, sans-serif;
  padding-top: 5px;
  padding-bottom: 20px;
}
```

4. Define the hover and focus states. Add the following rule to set the style for the hover and focus states. This essentially makes the text visible (via the color setting) and defines a background image—a wide GIF89 image with a downward-facing arrow at its center now appears when the user places their mouse cursor over the top of the web page.

```
#skipLink a:hover, #skipLink a:focus {
  color: #000000;
  background: url(skip-navigation-down-arrow.gif) 50% 100% no-repeat;
}
```

Link targeting

Although a fairly common practice online, link targeting—using the target attribute on a and area elements (see the following code for an example), typically to open a link in a new window—is not without its problems and should be avoided.

```
<a href="a-web-page.html" target="_blank">Open in a new window</a>
```

While some argue that this practice is beneficial, enabling users to look at external content and return to your site, what it actually does is take control of the browser *away* from users. After all, if someone actually wants to open content in a new window, they can do so using keyboard commands and/or contextual menus. More important, opening documents in new windows breaks the history path. For many, this might not be a huge issue, but for those navigating the Web via a screen reader, pop-ups are a menace. New content opens up, is deemed to not be of interest, and the back function is invoked. But this is a new window, with its own blank history. Gnashing of teeth ensues. There's also the problem that you can't guarantee what will happen when this attribute is used anyway—many users configure browsers to suppress new windows, either forcing them to open in a new tab or over the top of the current page.

There's also the issue that target is deprecated. Although it remains valid when working with XHTML Transitional (and XHTML Frameset), it's not when using XHTML Strict.

There is, however, a JavaScript alternative for those very rare occasions where you need to use a link to open a new window (this is explored on Bruce Lawson's website, at www.brucelawson.co.uk/2005/opening-links-in-new-windows-in-xhtml-strict-2/); essentially, you attach the script to your web pages and then add rel="external" to the a start tag for external links. Complying with the W3C's Web Content Accessibility Guidelines (WCAG), the script also warns when new windows are about to be opened. Ultimately, though, you should avoid new windows whenever possible. For occasions when you want to provide a temporary new window (such as for a terms-and-conditions box during a checkout process), use a JavaScript pop-up, or place the terms inline by using a scrollable content area (see Chapter 7 for more on those).

Links and images

Although links are primarily text-based, it's possible to wrap anchor tags around an image, thereby turning it into a link:

```
<a href="a-link.html"><img src="linked-image.gif" width="40"
➥ height="40" /></a>
```

Some browsers border linked images with whatever link colors have been stated in CSS (or the default colors, if no custom ones have been defined), which looks nasty and can displace other layout elements. Historically, designers have gotten around this by setting the border attribute within an img element to 0, but this has been deprecated. Therefore, it's best to use a CSS contextual selector to define images within links as having no border.

```
a img {
  border: 0;
}
```

Clearly, this can be overridden for specific links. Alternatively, you could set an "invisible" border (one that matches the site's background color) on one or more sides, and then set its color to that of your standard hover color when the user hovers over the image. This would then provide visual feedback to the user, confirming that the image is a link.

```
a img {
  border: 0;
  border-bottom: 1px solid #ffffff;
}

a:hover img {
  border-bottom: 1px solid #f22222;
}
```

In any case, you must always have usability and accessibility at the back of your mind when working with image-based links. With regard to usability, is the image's function obvious? Plenty of websites use icons instead of straightforward text-based navigation, resulting in frustrated users if the function of each image isn't obvious. People don't want to learn what each icon is for, and they'll soon move on to competing sites. With regard to accessibility, remember that not all browsers can zoom images, and so if an image-based link has text within it, ensure it's big enough to read easily. Whenever possible, offer a text-based alternative to image-based links, and never omit `alt` and `title` attributes (discussed earlier in this chapter). The former can describe the image content and the latter can describe the link target (i.e., what will happen when the link is clicked).

Therefore, the example from earlier becomes the following:

```
<a href="a-link.html"><img title="Visit our shop"
➥ src="linked-image.gif"width="40" height="40"
➥ alt="Shopping trolley" /></a>
```

Adding pop-ups to images

On occasion, when a user hovers their mouse cursor over an image, you might like to add a pop-up that's a little more flamboyant than what a `title` attribute can provide. Using CSS, you can add a fully stylable pop-up to an image, when the user moves their cursor over it. Note, however, that this technique should be used sparingly, and you should *never* rely on users accessing this information, unless you make it clear that the pop-up exists—for example, you could use it for a game, showing the answer to a question when the user mouses over an image. (However, if something is extremely important for your users to see immediately, don't hide it away in a pop-up—display it in plain sight.) The following walkthrough shows you how to use pop-ups in such a way.

Adding a pop-up to an image

Required files	XHTML-basic.html and CSS-default.css from the basic-boilerplates folder as a starting point, along with the two image files add-a-pop-up-image.jpg and add-a-pop-up-pop-up.jpg from the chapter 5 folder.
What you'll learn	How to create a totally CSS-based pop-up that can be applied to an image.
Completed files	add-a-pop-up.html and add-a-pop-up.css in the chapter 5 folder, along with the two images, which remain unchanged.

1. Create a container for the pop-up. Add the div shown following to the web page, within the wrapper; the div will act as a container for the pop-up.

```
<div id="popupContainer">
</div>
```

2. Add the main image in the usual fashion, placing it inside the div created in step 1.

```
<img src="add-a-pop-up-image.jpg" alt="Landscape" width="500"
➥ height="375" />
```

5

3. Add a link and pop-up content. Surround the image with a dummy link, and then add a span element immediately after the image. Within this, place the pop-up content, which can contain text and even other images. Text can be styled within inline elements (strong, em, and anchors, for example). In this example, the span contains an image, which will be floated right, and some text (which is truncated for space reasons—the completed version in the download files is longer). To ensure that the floated image is "cleared," making the span's background appear behind it once styled, a clearFix class is added to the span start tag, and an associated CSS rule created (in step 10). More on this float-clearing technique, along with floats and clears in general, is given in Chapter 7.

```
<a href="#"><img src="add-a-pop-up-to-an-image.jpg" alt="Landscape"
➥ width="500" height="375" /><span class="clearFix"><img
➥ src="add-a-pop-up-pop-up.jpg" alt="Winter shot" width="126"
➥ height="215" />
The text for the pop-up goes here…</span></a>
```

> Because you can't place paragraphs within a span element, you need to stick to a single block of text, or split paragraphs with double line breaks (

), despite the iffy semantics of doing that.

4. Set defaults. At this stage, the page content is displayed in a linear fashion—large image followed by small image followed by text—so some CSS is now needed. In the CSS document, add some padding to the existing body element, ensuring the page content doesn't hug the browser window edges when you're testing the page.

```
body {
  font: 62.5%/1.5 Verdana, Arial, Helvetica, sans-serif;
  padding: 20px;
}
```

5. Give the images a border. Add the following rule to apply a thin gray border to the images on the page.

```
img {
  border: 1px solid #666666;
}
```

6. Define the pop-up area size. Add the following rule to define the size of the pop-up area (the width setting defines its width and display: block stretches the active area of the link to the size of its container—the image). The other settings override link defaults, making the text within the div and anchor black and not underlined.

```
#popupContainer a:link, #popupContainer a:visited {
  position: relative;
  display: block;
  width: 500px;
  text-decoration: none;
  color: #000000;
}
```

7. Make the pop-up invisible. Add the following rule to make the pop-up initially not display onscreen (i.e., outside of the viewing area of the browser).

```
#popupContainer a span {
  position: absolute;
  left: -10000px;
  top: -10000px;
}
```

8. Style the span element. The following rule styles the span element during the hover state. The `display` property value of `block` defines the pop-up as a block-level element, rather than an inline one, while the `position` setting of `relative` overrides that set in the previous step (as do the `left` and `top` values). The `width` setting defines a width for the pop-up. The negative `margin-top` setting pulls the pop-up upward, so it no longer sits under the main image. The value is the same as the height of the main image minus the vertical offset required. (If it were set to the height of the main image, the pop-up would sit flush to the top of the image during the hover state, which looks cluttered.) The `margin-left` value provides a horizontal offset, while the `padding` value places some padding within the span, so its contents don't hug its borders. The other settings style colors and fonts.

```
#popupContainer a:hover span, #popupContainer a:focus span,
➥ #popupContainer a:active span {
  display: block;
  position: relative;
  left: 0;
  top: 0;
  width: 360px;
  color: #000000;
  font: 1.1em/1.5 Arial, Helvetica, sans-serif;
  margin-top: -335px;
  margin-left: 50px;
  padding: 20px;
  background-color: #e0e4ef;
  border: 1px solid #666666;
}
```

The selector for step 8's code block offers three alternate routes for users to access the pop-up: the hover *state (for mouse users), the* focus *state (for keyboard users), and the* active *state (for Internet Explorer keyboard users, since that browser doesn't yet support* :focus*).*

9. Next, a rule is needed to float the image within the span. The margin settings ensure that the image doesn't hug the text-based content.

```
#popupContainer a:hover span img, #popupContainer a:focus span img,
➥ #popupContainer a:active span img {
  border: 1px solid #666666;
  float: right;
```

```
    margin-left: 15px;
    margin-bottom: 5px;
}
```

10. Apply the `clearFix` rule. Floated elements are outside the standard document flow. Therefore, if there's little text, the image appears to stick out of the span box, as shown in the following example.

This can be fixed by adding the following rule (this technique is fully explained in Chapter 7):

```
.clearFix:after {
    content: ".";
    display: block;
    height: 0;
    clear: both;
    visibility: hidden;
}
```

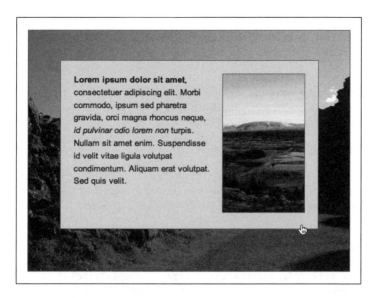

5

Because of a bug in Internet Explorer pre-version 7, you need to add the following rule to make the pop-up work in Internet Explorer 6 or 5.5: #popupContainer a:hover {text-indent: 0;}. Ideally, this should be added in a style sheet linked via a conditional comment—see Chapter 9 for more on hacks for old browsers.

Image maps

Image maps enable you to define multiple links within a single image; for example, if you have a weather map, you could use an image map to link to each region's weather forecast; or if you had a picture of your office, you could use an image map to make each of the objects clickable, leading to pages explaining more about each of them. Clickable regions within image maps can be fairly basic—rectangles or circles—or complex polygonal shapes. Note that there are both server-side and client-side versions of image maps— server-side image maps are now considered obsolete and pose accessibility problems, and even client-side image maps tend to be avoided by most designers, although use of alt text can help them become reasonably accessible.

Regardless of the complexity of the image and the defined regions, the method of creating an image map remains the same. To the right is the image used in this section to show how a basic image map is created. It contains three geometric shapes that will be turned into clickable hot-spots.

The image is added to the web page in the usual way (and within a block element, since img is an inline element), but with the addition of a usemap attribute, whose value must be preceded by a hash sign (#).

```
<div id="wrapper">
  <img src="image-map-image.gif" alt="Shapes" width="398" height="398"
➥ usemap="#shapes" />
</div>
```

The value of the usemap attribute must correlate with the name and id values of the associated map element. Note that the name attribute is required for backward compatibility, whereas the id attribute is mandatory.

```
<map id="shapes" name="shapes">
</map>
```

The map element acts as a container for specifications regarding the map's active areas, which are added as area elements.

```
<map id="shapes" name="shapes">
  <area title="Access the squares page." shape="rect"
➥ coords="29,27,173,171" href="square.html" alt="A square" />
  <area title="Access the circles page" shape="circle"
➥ coords="295,175,81" href="circle.html" alt="A circle" />
  <area title="Access the triangles page" shape="poly"
➥ coords="177,231,269,369,84,369" href="triangle.html"
➥ alt="A triangle" />
</map>
```

Each of the preceding area elements has a shape attribute that corresponds to the intended active link area:

- rect defines a rectangular area; the coords (coordinates) attribute contains two pairs that define the top-left and bottom-right corners of the rectangle in terms of pixel values (which you either take from your original image or guess, should you have amazing pixel-perfect vision).

- circle is used to define a circular area; of the three values within the coords attribute, the first two define the horizontal and vertical position of the circle's center, and the third defines the radius.

- poly enables you to define as many coordinate pairs as you wish, which allows you to define active areas for complex and irregular shapes—in the previous code block, there are three pairs, each of which defines a corner of the triangle.

Creating image maps is a notoriously tedious process, and it's one of the few occasions when I advise using a visual web design tool, if you have one handy, which can be used to drag out hot-spots. However, take care not to overlap defined regions—this is easy to do, and it can cause problems with regard to each link's active area. If you don't have such a tool handy, you'll have to measure out the coordinates in a graphics package.

Note that some browsers will place a border around the image used for an image map. This can be removed by using CSS to set the image's border to 0 (either via applying a class to the image, or via a contextual selector).

Faking images maps using CSS

Although there's no direct equivalent to image maps in CSS, you can fashion a similar effect by creating block-level anchors (rather like the one in the pop-up example). The most common way of structuring this "fake" image map is by using an unordered list, placing links within each list item, and using absolute positioning to set the locations of the links. Further CSS trickery can be used to make all hot-spots visible when the mouse cursor is placed over the image, and to change the image on the rollover state.

In the following exercise, a picture of three sheep minding their own business is going to be used for the fake image map. When you mouse over the image, all three hot-spots will be shown (as a 1-pixel, black border). Placing the cursor over a hot-spot will then turn that portion of the grayscale image into color (by way of placing a second image as a background on the hot-spot), along with showing a caption.

As you might imagine, with CSS being based around boxes, the technique tends to work best with highly regular, box-shaped rollover areas.

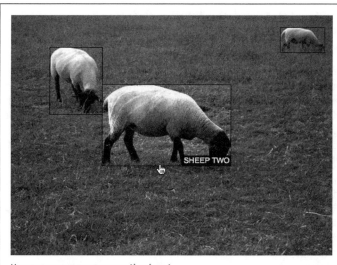

Hover your mouse cursor over the sheep!

Using CSS to create a fake image map with rollovers

Required files	XHTML-basic.html and CSS-default.css from the basic-boilerplates folder, along with image files fake-image-map-color.jpg and fake-image-map-gray.jpg from the chapter 5 folder.
What you'll learn	How to fake an image map using CSS, which will enable two levels of rollover.
Completed files	fake-image-map.html and fake-image-map.css in the chapter 5 folder, along with the image files, which are unchanged.

1. Add the structure for the fake image map. In the body of the HTML document, add the following code, which structures the content for the fake image map. Note how the unordered list has a unique class value and how each of the list items has a class value referring to the hot-spot relating to a specific item on the image.

```
<ul class="sheepImageMap">
  <li class="sheepOne"><a href="#"><span>Sheep one</span></a></li>
  <li class="sheepTwo"><a href="#"><span>Sheep two</span></a></li>
  <li class="sheepThree"><a href="#"><span>Sheep three</span></a></li>
</ul>
<p>Hover your mouse cursor over the sheep!</p>
```

2. Set page defaults. Add some padding to the existing body rule:

```
body {
  font: 62.5%/1.5 Verdana, Arial, Helvetica, sans-serif;
  padding: 20px;
}
```

3. Add the following rule to style the unordered list. The font and text-transform property values define the font styles for the captions. The background value defines the grayscale image as the background for the list, and the width and height values ensure the list's dimensions are the same as that of the background image. The position property is set to relative because this enables the list item positioning to then be set from the top left of the unordered list, rather than from the top left of the browser window.

```
.sheepImageMap {
  font: 1.0em/1 Arial, Helvetica, sans-serif;
  text-transform: uppercase;
  background: url(fake-image-map-gray.jpg);
  width: 500px;
  height: 375px;
  position: relative;
  margin-bottom: 10px;
}
```

Hover your mouse cursor over the sheep!

4. Style the links. By setting `display` to block, the links stretch to fit their container (the list items). The `text-indent` setting is used to massively offset the indent of the text within the links, effectively making the text invisible by default, but keeping the element itself visible and clickable. The `text-decoration` value of none turns off the default underline for the links.

```
.sheepImageMap a {
  display: block;
  text-indent: -100000px;
  text-decoration: none;
}
```

> *In some circumstances, offsetting using* `text-indent` *can lead to minor layout issues. This wouldn't be a problem in the layout being created here; but with more finely tuned layouts, it could—due to some browsers keeping the space taken up by the element's height available to it, and thus forcing subsequent content to appear below where it's meant to be by an equivalent amount. In cases like those, absolute positioning and offsetting both vertically and horizontally works well.*

5. Set hot-spot borders. Utilizing the `:hover` pseudo-class, the following rule makes it so that when the list is hovered over, the three hot-spots show a 1-pixel border:

```
.sheepImageMap:hover .sheepOne, .sheepImageMap:hover .sheepTwo,
➥ .sheepImageMap:hover .sheepThree {
  border: 1px solid #000000;
}
```

6. Add the following rule to style the list items, removing the default bullet point (via the list-style value of none) and defining them to be positioned in an absolute manner and displayed as block elements.

```
.sheepImageMap li {
  list-style: none;
  position: absolute;
  display: block;
}
```

7. Create the first hot-spot. In a graphics package, four values are required for each hot-spot: its width, its height, and the distance from the top and left corners. These are then translated, respectively, into the width, height, left, and top values in a rule applied to the relevant hot-spot:

```
.sheepOne {
  width: 80px;
  height: 104px;
  left: 60px;
  top: 50px;
}
```

Two more rules complete the effect. The first ensures the relevant anchor has the correct height (note how the height value is the same as in the previous rule):

```
.sheepOne a {
  height: 104px;
}
```

The second rule sets the color version of the image to be displayed as a background on the hover state (as in, when the user mouses over the hot-spot area, the relevant area is displayed in color). By default, the top left of the image will be shown, and so negative positioning values are used to pull it into place. Note how these are the negatives of the values defined for left and top in the .sheepOne rule, minus 1 further pixel. The reason for the extra pixel is to take into account the 1-pixel border defined in step 5. If the borders weren't used (although they are handy, since they show all the hot-spots), the positioning values would just be the direct negatives of the left and top values from .sheepOne.

```
.sheepOne a:hover {
  background: url(fake-image-map-color.jpg) -61px -51px;
}
```

Hover your mouse cursor over the sheep!

5

Note that the a *selector is used in this exercise rather than* a:link. *Because the rules are strictly based on context—anchors within the defined areas of the fake image map—this is acceptable, and it saves having to use both* :link *and* :visited *selectors.*

8. Create the other hot-spots. The other two hot-spots are created in the same way as the first one in step 7. Again, the positioning values in the hover states are negative values minus 1 of the left and top values in the rules that defined the dimensions and positions of the hot-spots.

```
.sheepTwo {
  width: 200px;
  height: 126px;
  left: 141px;
  top: 108px;
}
.sheepTwo a {
  height: 126px;
}
.sheepTwo a:hover {
  background: url(fake-image-map-color.jpg) -142px -109px;
}
.sheepThree {
  width: 68px;
  height: 38px;
  left: 418px;
  top: 19px;
}
```

```
.sheepThree a {
  height: 38px;
}
.sheepThree a:hover {
  background: url(fake-image-map-color.jpg) -419px -20px;
}
```

9. Add styles for the captions. In step 4, the `text-indent` property was set to a huge negative value, which made the text effectively disappear. To bring it back on the hover state, add the following rule to your CSS, which also colors the text in white:

```
.sheepImageMap a:hover {
  text-indent: 0;
  color: #ffffff;
}
```

At this stage, the text still doesn't stand out enough. Therefore, add the following rule, which styles the span elements wrapped around the text in each list item, setting a background color and adding some padding around the content:

```
.sheepImageMap a:hover span {
  padding: 2px;
  background-color: #000000;
}
```

This looks fine, but with some further absolute positioning, these captions can be positioned elsewhere within the hot-spot. By adding the bolded rules shown following, the captions are positioned at the bottom right of the hot-spots, as shown in the original example screenshot before the start of the exercise.

```
.sheepImageMap a:hover span {
  padding: 2px;
  background-color: #000000;
  position: absolute;
  bottom: 0;
  right: 0;
}
```

> Pre-version 7, Internet Explorer didn't respond to `:hover` unless it was used on a link. Because of this, the borders will not appear in that browser, causing a 1-pixel "jog" up and left when you mouse over a hot-spot. You can get around this by applying the border to the following rules (via a conditional style sheet): `.sheepOne a:hover`, `.sheepTwo a:hover`, and `.sheepThree a:hover`.

Enhancing links with JavaScript

In this section, we're going to use a little JavaScript, showing some methods of providing enhanced interactivity and functionality to links. Note that in all cases, a non-JavaScript backup (or fallback) to essential content is required for those who choose to surf the Web with JavaScript disabled. In all cases, JavaScript can be added either to external JavaScript files attached to your HTML documents (which is the preferred method; see the section "Attaching favicons and JavaScript" in Chapter 2) or in a `script` element within the head of the HTML page:

```
<script type="text/javascript">
// <![CDATA[
  (script goes here)
// ]]>
</script>
```

Specifically, we'll look at pop-up windows, swapping images using JavaScript, and toggling `div` visibility with JavaScript.

Creating a pop-up window

Pop-up windows are mostly an annoyance, especially when automated and when they remove browser controls. However, they are occasionally useful, such as for providing a user with brief access to terms and conditions without interrupting a checkout process. Some portfolio sites also use pop-up windows to display larger versions of images (although we'll later see a better method of creating an online gallery).

Should you require a pop-up window of your very own, the JavaScript is simple:

```
function newWindow()
{
  window.open("location.html");
}
```

And this HTML calls the script using the onclick attribute:

```
<a href="location.html" onclick="newWindow(); return false;">Open a
➥ new window!</a>
```

Note how the `href` attribute still has a value, which caters to users with JavaScript disabled (loading the document into the current window). The `return false` part of the `onclick` value ensures the `href` value is ignored for browsers with JavaScript activated (otherwise both the original and pop-up window would display with the new web page).

Creating a system to open windows with varied URLs requires only slight changes to both script and HTML. The script changes to this:

```
function newWindow(webURL)
{
  window.open(webURL);
}
```

183

The HTML changes to this:

```
<a href="location-one.html" onclick="newWindow('location-one.html');
➥ return false;">Open location one in a new window!</a>
<a href="location-two.html" onclick="newWindow('location-two.html');
➥ return false;">Open location two in a new window!</a>
```

Note how the target location is now within the single quotes of the onclick value. This could be any file name, and the link type can be absolute, relative, or root-relative. To provide a warning when a pop-up is opened (as recommended by WCAG—Web Content Accessibility Guidelines), you can add a single line to the JavaScript:

```
function newWindow(webURL)
{
  alert("You are about to open a new window.");
  window.open(webURL);
}
```

It's also possible to control the settings of a pop-up window. To do so, the script needs to be amended as follows:

```
function newWindow(webURL)
{
  alert("You are about to open a new window.");
  var newWin = window.open(webURL,"new_window",
  ➥"toolbar,location,directories,
  ➥status,menubar,scrollbars,resizable,
  ➥copyhistory,width=300,height=300");
  newWin.focus();
}
```

The values within the set of quotes that begin "toolbar, location... enable you to set the pop-up window's dimensions and appearance. There must be no whitespace in the features list, and it must all be on one line. Most of the items are self-explanatory, but some that may not be are location, which defines whether the browser's address bar is visible, and directories, which defines whether secondary toolbars such as the links bar are visible. Note that if you specify one or more of these, any you don't specify will be turned off—therefore, you must specify all the features you want in the pop-up window.

Now, a word of warning: as alluded to earlier, having control of the web browser wrenched away from them makes some users want to kick a puppy. Therefore:

- *Never* use JavaScript to pop up windows without the user knowing that it's going to happen. (The integrated alert mentioned earlier is one thing, but you should *always* also mention next to the relevant link that a pop-up will be created if the link is clicked.)

- *Never* create a site that automatically pops up a window and removes the window controls.

- *Never* use a pop-up window unless it's absolutely necessary.

Some designers might argue about aesthetics and for the clean nature of a browser window at full-screen, devoid of its controls, but there are no real reasons for using pop-up windows in this manner other than that; there are, however, counterarguments, such as taking control from the user, the general annoyance factor, a full-screen window suddenly covering everything else, and so on. Ultimately, pop-ups and nonrequested new windows are a *very bad thing*, so avoid using them.

Creating an online gallery

As mentioned earlier, there's a better way of creating an online gallery than using pop-up windows when thumbnails are clicked. Instead, JavaScript can be used to swap out an image that's on a web page, replacing it with another, as shown in the following exercise.

Switching images using JavaScript

Required files	gallery-starting-point folder in the chapter 5 folder.
What you'll learn	How to create a basic online gallery that enables you to easily switch the main image by clicking on thumbnails.
Completed files	gallery-completed folder in the chapter 5 folder.

1. Add the script. Create a new text document and save it as gallery.js in the same folder as the files from the gallery-starting-point folder. Add the following to it:

```
function swapPhoto(photoSRC) {
  document.images.imgPhoto.src = "assets/" + photoSRC;
}
```

Be aware of the case-sensitive nature of JavaScript and also the path to the images, which is set here as assets/.

2. Add the main image. This requires an id attribute that correlates with the one provided in step 1 (imgPhoto). Leave off the height and/or width attributes if your images have varied dimensions. If your images have one identical dimension (such as the same widths), include that, but omit the other. (The img is placed within a div so that the document conforms to XHTML Strict. This also enables the gallery width to be defined later in CSS.)

```
<div id="wrapper">
  <img src="assets/image-1.jpg" width="500" height="375" id="imgPhoto"
  ➥ alt="Main photo" />
</div>
```

3. Add thumbnails. In each case, the swapPhoto value is the file name of the image to be loaded. Remember that the path to the images was defined in step 1, so it's not needed here. The href value links directly to the full-size image to accommodate users who have disabled JavaScript.

```
<a href="assets/image-1.jpg" onclick="javascript:swapPhoto
➥('image-1.jpg'); return false;"><img src="assets/image-1-t.jpg"
➥ alt="sheep" width="100" height="75" /></a>
<a href="assets/image-2.jpg" onclick="javascript:swapPhoto
➥('image-2.jpg'); return false;"><img src="assets/image-2-t.jpg"
➥ alt="hillside" width="100" height="75" /></a>
```

4. Add some CSS. To the gallery.css file, add the following rules, the first of which sets a width value for the wrapper div, and the second of which removes the default border from image-based links.

```
#wrapper {
  width: 500px;
}
a img {
border: 0;
}
```

And that's all there is to it. The solution is elegant and doesn't require pop-up windows. Instead, users can see thumbnails on the same page as the main image, making navigation through the portfolio that much easier. For those users who don't have JavaScript, the values in the href attributes ensure they still get access to the full-size images, too.

Adding captions to your image gallery

Required files	The gallery-completed folder from the chapter 5 folder.
What you'll learn	Without context, some pictures are meaningless, so this exercise shows how to take the gallery created in the previous exercise and add a caption to each image.
Completed files	The gallery-captions folder in the chapter 5 folder.

1. Edit the script. Add the elements shown in bold to your script (in gallery.js). These will enable you to target an element on the page with an id value of caption, loading new text into it when a thumbnail is clicked.

```
function swapPhoto(photoSRC,theCaption) {
  var displayedCaption = document.getElementById("caption");
  displayedCaption.firstChild.nodeValue = theCaption;
  document.images.imgPhoto.src = "assets/" + photoSRC;
}
```

2. Add a caption. Under the main image in the gallery.html file, add a paragraph with an id value of caption, along with the caption text for the default image.

```
<img src="assets/image-1.jpg" width="500" height="375" id="imgPhoto"
➥ alt="Main photo" />
<p id="caption">Some sheep, grazing.</p>
```

3. Edit the thumbnails. For each thumbnail, add some caption text, as shown following. Ensure that there's a comma between the two swapPhoto values you now have.

```
<a href="assets/image-1.jpg" onclick="javascript:swapPhoto
➥('image-1.jpg','Some sheep, grazing.'); return false;"><img
➥ src="assets/image-1-t.jpg" alt="sheep" width="100"
➥ height="75" /></a>
```

> *Some characters are invalid for captions, because they terminate the script early. If you want to add a single quote mark (often used as an apostrophe online, when "smart" quotes aren't being used), you must escape the character first, using a back-slash, like so: \\'. If you wish to add a double quote mark, you need to define it as an HTML entity: ".*

5

The hillside at Uffington.

Automated gallery scripts

The kind of script mentioned in the previous exercise is great for creating a gallery fine-tuned to your specific website: you can control the styles and positioning with ease. However, there are a number of ready-made scripts online, one of the best of which is Lightbox2 (www.huddletogether.com/projects/lightbox2/), by Lokesh Dhakar. The script is highly automated, darkening the screen and providing next/previous buttons, along with the capability to rapidly add captions.

In terms of setup, you attach the various scripts and the CSS file from the download files, and check the paths to the included images (which can be replaced, if you don't like the defaults). You then simply add rel="lightbox" to any link or thumbnail that's to be used to activate the lightbox script. The optional title element enables you to add a caption.

```
<a href="assets/image-1.jpg" rel="lightbox" title="The caption"><img
➥ src="assets/image-1-t.jpg" alt="thumbnail" width="100"
➥ height="75" /></a>
```

It's also possible to add more complex captions, including links, by using character entities to encode the <, >, and " characters when adding HTML. (See Appendix C—"Entities Reference"—for more on entities.)

```
<a href="assets/image-1.jpg" rel="lightbox" title="The caption - &lt;
➥a href=&quot;http://www.a-website.com&quot;&gt;Link content
➥&lt;/a&gt;"><img src="assets/image-1-t.jpg" alt="thumbnail"
➥ width="100" height="75" /></a>
```

Usefully, groups of images can be defined just by adding square brackets and a group name, directly after lightbox in the rel value. This automates the inclusion of prev and next buttons, along with providing an image count (such as "Image 4 of 10") for the current group.

```
<a href="assets/image-1.jpg" rel="lightbox[groupName]" title="The
➥ caption"><img src="assets/image-1-t.jpg" alt="thumbnail"
➥ width="100" height="75" /></a>
<a href="assets/image-2.jpg" rel="lightbox[groupName]" title="The
➥ second caption"><img src="assets/image-2-t.jpg" alt="thumbnail"
➥ width="100" height="75" /></a>
<a href="assets/image-3.jpg" rel="lightbox[groupName]" title="The
➥ third caption"><img src="assets/image-3-t.jpg" alt="thumbnail"
➥ width="100" height="75" /></a>
```

The following image shows how the site looks (this example is from Pinkflag.com's gallery in the look section). If you're fine with the look of the gallery (although some of its elements can be restyled and tweaked in CSS) and its popularity (it's used on a lot of sites these days), it can save a bit of time, and it's also very easy for clients to update themselves. For a more unique take, you'll need to get your hands dirty with your own code.

5

Note that some may consider the behavior of Lightbox2 at odds with user expectation, because the browser back button returns you to the previous page you visited, rather than closing the lightbox. In my opinion, this is logical—after all, Lightbox2 is internal page content, not a separate page. However, if you'd like to override the default behavior and have the back button on the browser close the lightbox, instructions are available from www.cloversignsblog.com/2007/06/fixing-the-back-button-in-lightbox/.

Collapsible page content

The DOM enables you to access and dynamically control various aspects of a web page, and this allows you to use a nifty little trick to toggle the visibility of divs. This has numerous uses, from providing a method of hiding "spoiler" content unless someone wants to see it, to various navigation-oriented uses, which will be more fully explored later in the chapter.

Setting up a collapsible div

Required files	The collapsible-div-starting-point folder from the chapter 5 folder.
What you'll learn	How to create a collapsible div.
Completed files	The collapsible-div-completed folder from the chapter 5 folder.

1. Examine the script. Open collapsible-div.js. The code enables you to target any div with a unique id value. Each time the script is run, it determines whether the display value of the div is set to block (which makes it visible). If it is, the value is set to none, thereby making it invisible. If it isn't set to block (which means it's set to none), the script sets the value to block.

```
function swap(targetId){
  if (document.getElementById)
  {
    target = document.getElementById(targetId);
    if (target.style.display == "block")
    {
      target.style.display = "none";
    }
    else
    {
      target.style.display = "block";
    }
  }
}
```

2. Add a link. Add the code block shown following—when clicked, the link will toggle the hidden content. The value within the onclick attribute (hiddenDiv, in this case) is the id value of the div that this link will toggle.

```
<p><a href="#" title="Toggle section" onclick="toggleDiv('hiddenDiv');
➥ return false;">Toggle div!</o>
```

3. Add a div, and give it an id value equal to the onclick value from the previous step. Within the div, add whatever content you want. The style attribute makes the div initially hidden.

```
<p><a href="#" title="Toggle section" onclick="toggleDiv('hiddenDiv');
➥ return false;">Toggle div!</a></p>
<div id="hiddenDiv" style="display: none;">
<p>Initially hidden content goes here.</p>
</div>
```

A combination of the previous two exercises can be seen in action in a previous version of my Images from Iceland website—see www.snubcommunications.com/iceland/iceland-old.html. This site expands on the div toggler by also toggling the arrow images when a section is toggled, and it shows what you can do with some straightforward JavaScript, some decent photographs, and a bit of imagination.

Enhancing accessibility for collapsible content

Although the old version of the Images from Iceland site looks good, it has a problem in common with the previous exercise: when JavaScript is disabled, the initially hidden content is inaccessible. The Iceland site was quickly knocked together a number of years back and has been superseded with a new site, but for any site developed today, there should be no excuses.

In the previous exercise, the hidden content is set to be hidden by default and the display property is toggled via the JavaScript function. What therefore needs to be done is to make the content visible by default and then override this, making it invisible, but only if the user has JavaScript. The first thing to do is remove the style attribute from the following line of code:

```
<div id="hiddenDiv" style="display: none;">
```

Next, a style sheet is created (named javascript-overrides.css for this example), with a rule that targets the relevant div and sets display to none.

```
#hiddenDiv {
  display: none;
}
```

Finally, amendments are made to the JavaScript file, adding some lines that attach the new JavaScript document to the web page:

```
var cssNode = document.createElement('link');
cssNode.setAttribute('rel', 'stylesheet');
cssNode.setAttribute('type', 'text/css');
cssNode.setAttribute('href', 'javascript-overrides.css');
document.getElementsByTagName('head')[0].appendChild(cssNode);
```

The results of this are the following:

- If a user has JavaScript enabled, javascript-overrides.css is loaded, applying the display value of none to the togglable div.
- If a user has JavaScript disabled, javascript-overrides.css is not loaded, meaning the togglable div contents are visible.

See the collapsible-div-accessible folder within the chapter 5 folder for reference files.

Modularizing the collapsible content script

Although the previous script works perfectly well for a single div, it's awkward if you want to use several divs over the course of a page. That's how the old Images from Iceland site works, and I had to keep track of id names and values while constructing it. However, it is possible to make a toggler strip more modular, although this relies on keeping document structure *very* strict as far as the collapsible sections go. The files for this section are in the collapsible-div-modular folder within the chapter 5 folder.

The JavaScript is similar to that in the previous example.

```
function toggle(toggler) {
  if(document.getElementById) {
    targetElement = toggler.parentNode.nextSibling;

    if(targetElement.className == undefined) {
      targetElement = toggler.parentNode.nextSibling.nextSibling;
    }
```

```
      if (targetElement.style.display == "block") {
        targetElement.style.display = "none";
      }
      else {
        targetElement.style.display = "block";
      }
    }
  }
```

The main change is that instead of targeting a div with a specific id value, the script targets an element in relation to the one being used as a toggler, by way of the parentNode/nextSibling JavaScript properties.

If you look at the HTML document, you'll see that the parent of the anchor element is the p element. What the next sibling element is depends on the browser—Internet Explorer just looks for the next element in the document (div), but other browsers count white-space as the next sibling.

```
<p><a href="#" title="Toggle section" onclick="toggle(this); return
➥ false;">Toggle div 1!</a></p>
<div class="expandable">
  <p>Initially hidden content (div 1) goes here.</p>
</div>
```

It would be possible to get around this by stripping whitespace. However, a line in the JavaScript makes this unnecessary.

```
if(document.getElementById) {
  targetElement = toggler.parentNode.nextSibling;

if(targetElement.className == undefined) {
  targetElement = toggler.parentNode.nextSibling.nextSibling;
}
```

The first line of the previous code block sets the target to the next sibling of the parent element of the link. In Internet Explorer this works, but other browsers find only white-space. Therefore, the second line essentially says, "If you find whitespace (undefined), then set the target to the next sibling on." It's a bit of a workaround, but it's only one line of JavaScript.

The JavaScript also includes the method used in the preceding "Enhancing accessibility for collapsible content" section, to make the togglable sections initially invisible in JavaScript-enabled browsers only. Note that the related CSS is slightly different to that shown in the previous section—instead of hidden content being in a div with an id value of hiddenDiv, it's now in multiple divs, all of which have a class value of expandable. Therefore, the selector in the CSS rule has been updated accordingly:

```
.expandable {
  display: none;
}
```

Toggle div 1!	Toggle div 1!
Initially hidden content (div 1) goes here.	Initially hidden content (div 1) goes here.
Toggle div 2!	Toggle div 2!
	Initially hidden content (div 2) goes here.

This system enables you to use as many collapsible divs as you like on the page, and you don't have to set id values—the toggling is essentially automated. However, as mentioned earlier, you must ensure that your structure remains the same for each area that can be toggled, otherwise the script won't find the correct element to make visible or invisible when the links are clicked.

How to find targets for collapsible content scripts

If you want to change your document structure when using the script from the previous section in this chapter, you need to find the parent/sibling path, in Internet Explorer and in other browsers. If you've a good grasp of JavaScript, this should be simple; however, if you don't—or you just want to sanity-check your values—it's simple to find out what an element's parent is, what it's next sibling is, and various combinations thereof.

First, give your clickable element a unique id value:

```
<p><a id="linkToggler" href="#" title="Toggle section"
➥ onclick="toggle(this); return false;">Toggle div 1!</a></p>
```

Elsewhere within the web page, add the following script:

```
<script type="text/javascript">
 //<![CDATA[
   alert(document.getElementById("linkToggler").nodeName);
 //]]>
</script>
```

Before .nodeName, add whatever combination of .parentNode and .nextSibling you like—here's an example:

```
<script type="text/javascript">
 //<![CDATA[
   alert(document.getElementById("linkToggler").parentNode.
     ➥nextSibling.nextSibling.nodeName);
 //]]>
</script>
```

When you load the web page in a browser, an alert message will be displayed. This will detail what the target element is, based on the path defined in the previous code block.

In this section, you've seen a bare-bones, unstyled version of how to work with collapsible content. Later in the chapter, this method will be used to create collapsible sections for a navigation bar.

Creating navigation bars

The chapter has so far largely concentrated on inline navigation, so we'll now turn our attention to navigation bars. Before getting immersed in the technology, you need to decide what names you're going to use for your navigation bar's items. When designing the basic structure of the site, content should be grouped into categories, and this is often defined by what the user can do with it. It therefore follows that navigation bar links tend to be one of the following:

- **Action-based** (buy now, contact us, read our history)
- **Site audience–based** (end users, resellers, employees)
- **Topic-based** (news, services, contact details)

Whenever possible, keep to one of the preceding categories rather than mixing topics and actions. This sits easier with readers. Navigation links should also be succinct, to the point, and appropriate to the brand and tone of the website.

In this section, we'll cover using lists for navigation, styling list-based navigation bars, working with inline lists, and creating graphical navigation bars with rollover graphics.

Using lists for navigation bars

Think back to what we've covered to this point about semantic markup. Of the HTML elements that exist, which is the most appropriate for a navigation bar? If you said, "a table," go to the back of the class. Using tables for navigation bars might be a rapid way of getting them up and running, but it's not structurally sound. When looked at objectively, navigation bars are essentially a list of links to various pages on the website. It therefore follows that HTML lists are a logical choice to mark up navigation bars.

When creating the initial pass of the website, just create the list as it is, along with all the associated pages, and let people play around with the bare-bones site. This enables users to get a feel for its structure, without getting distracted by content, colors, and design. However, sooner or later, you're going to want to make that list look a little fancier.

Much of the remainder of this chapter is concerned with CSS and how it can be used to style lists. From a plain HTML list, you can rapidly create exciting visual designs—and ones that are easy to update, both in terms of content and design. After all, adding another navigation link is usually just a matter of adding another list item.

Using HTML lists and CSS to create a button-like vertical navigation bar

Required files	`XHTML-basic.html` and `CSS-default.css` from the basic-boilerplates folder.
What you'll learn	How to create a vertically aligned navigation bar, and how to style it with CSS to create a 3D-like effect for each of the list items.
Completed files	The `vertical-navigation-bar` folder in the chapter 5 folder.

1. Create the list structure. Add the following code block to create the structure of the navigation bar. By using nested lists, you can provide the navigation bar with a hierarchical structure (and you can style each level in CSS). In this example, the list has two levels. (Refer to Chapter 3 for an overview of correctly formatting lists.) This list is nested within a div with an id value of navigation, which we'll later take advantage of by using contextual selectors. (For this example, dummy href values of # are being used, but in a live site, always check that your links lead somewhere!)

```
<div id="navigation">
  <ul>
    <li>
      <a href="#">Section one</a>
      <ul>
        <li><a href="#">A link to a page</a></li>
        <li><a href="#">A link to a page</a></li>
        <li><a href="#">A link to a page</a></li>
        <li><a href="#">A link to a page</a></li>
      </ul>
    </li>
    <li>
      <a href="#">Section two</a>
      <ul>
        <li><a href="#">A link to a page</a></li>
        <li><a href="#">A link to a page</a></li>
        <li><a href="#">A link to a page</a></li>
        <li><a href="#">A link to a page</a></li>
      </ul>
    </li>
```

```
      <li>
        <a href="#">Section three</a>
        <ul>
          <li><a href="#">A link to a page</a></li>
          <li><a href="#">A link to a page</a></li>
          <li><a href="#">A link to a page</a></li>
          <li><a href="#">A link to a page</a></li>
        </ul>
      </li>
    </ul>
</div>
```

2. Add some padding to the body element, so page content doesn't hug the browser window edges. Also, add the background-color pair shown following:

```
body {
font: 62.5%/1.5 Verdana, Arial, Helvetica, sans-serif;
padding: 20px;
background-color: #aaaaaa;
}
```

3. Style the list. Add the following rule to remove the default bullet points from unordered lists within the navigation div, define a width for the lists, and also set the default font style.

```
#navigation ul {
  list-style-type: none;
  width: 140px;
  font: 1.2em/1 Arial, Helvetica, sans-serif;
}
```

4. Set an override for nested lists. As you can see from the previous image, the nested links have much larger text. This is because font sizes in ems are inherited, and therefore the font size within the nested lists ends up at 1.2ems multiplied by 1.2ems. By adding the following rule, the font size of nested lists is reset to 1em, making nested lists look the same as top-level lists.

```
#navigation ul ul {
  font-size: 1em;
}
```

5. Style the buttons. Use a contextual selector to style links within the navigation div (i.e., the links within this list). These styles initially affect the entire list, but you'll later override them for level-two links. Therefore, the styles you're working on now are intended only for level-one links (which are for sections or categories). This first set of property/value pairs turns off the default link underline, sets the list items to uppercase, and defines the font weight as bold.

```
#navigation a:link, #navigation a:visited {
  text-decoration: none;
  text-transform: uppercase;
  font-weight: bold;
}
```

6. Set button display and padding. Still within the same rule, set the buttons to display as block, thereby making the entire container an active link (rather than just the link text). Add some padding so the links don't hug the edge of the container.

```
#navigation a:link, #navigation a:visited {
  text-decoration: none;
  text-transform: uppercase;
  font-weight: bold;
  display: block;
  padding: 3px 12px 3px 8px;
}
```

7. Define colors and borders. Define the button background and foreground colors, setting the former to gray and the latter to white. Then add borders to create a 3D effect. Borders can be styled individually. By setting the left and top borders to a lighter shade than the background, and the right and bottom borders to a darker shade, a 3D effect is achieved. (Don't use black and white, because it will make the result is too harsh.)

```
#navigation a:link, #navigation a:visited {
  text-decoration: none;
  text-transform: uppercase;
  font-weight: bold;
  display: block;
  padding: 3px 12px 3px 8px;
  background-color: #666666;
  color: #ffffff;
  border-top: 1px solid #dddddd;
  border-right: 1px solid #333333;
  border-bottom: 1px solid #333333;
  border-left: 1px solid #dddddd;
}
```

8. Define other link states. The hover state is defined by just changing the background color, making it slightly lighter.

```
#navigation a:hover {
  background-color: #777777;
}
```

The active state enables you to build on the 3D effect: the padding settings are changed to move the text up and left by 1 pixel, the background and foreground colors are made slightly darker, and the border colors are reversed.

```
#navigation a:active {
  padding: 2px 13px 4px 7px;
  background-color: #444444;
  color: #eeeeee;
  border-top: 1px solid #333333;
  border-right: 1px solid #dddddd;
  border-bottom: 1px solid #dddddd;
  border-left: 1px solid #333333;
}
```

9. Style nested list item links. The selector #navigation li li a enables you to style links within a list item that are themselves within a list item (which happen to be in the navigation div). In other words, you can create a declaration for level-two links. These need to be differentiated from the section links, hence the following rule setting them to lowercase and normal font weight (instead of bold). The padding settings indent these links more than the section links, and the background and foreground colors are different, being very dark gray (almost black) on light gray rather than white on a darker gray.

```
#navigation li li a:link, #navigation li li a:visited {
  text-decoration: none;
  text-transform: lowercase;
  font-weight: normal;
  padding: 3px 3px 3px 17px;
  background-color: #999999;
  color: #111111;
}
```

10. Style nested item hover and active states. This is done in the same way as per the section links, changing colors as appropriate and again reversing the border colors on the active state.

```
#navigation li li a:hover {
  background-color: #aaaaaa;
}
#navigation li li a:active {
  padding: 2px 4px 4px 16px;
  background-color: #888888;
  color: #000000;
  border-top: 1px solid #333333;
  border-right: 1px solid #dddddd;
  border-bottom: 1px solid #dddddd;
  border-left: 1px solid #333333;
}
```

The navigation bar is now complete and, as you can see from the following images (which depict, from left to right, the default, hover, and active states), the buttons have a tactile feel to them. Should this not be to your liking, it's easy to change the look of the navigation bar because everything's styled in CSS. To expand on this design, you could introduce background images for each state, thereby making the navigation bar even more graphical. However, because you didn't simply chop up a GIF, you can easily add and remove items from the navigation bar, just by amending the list created in step 1. Any added items will be styled automatically by the style sheet rules.

Creating a vertical navigation bar with collapsible sections

Required files	The files from vertical-navigation-bar in the chapter 5 folder.
What you'll learn	How to take the navigation bar created in the previous exercise and make its sections collapsible.
Completed files	vertical-navigation-bar-collapsible in the chapter 5 folder.

1. Set up the JavaScript. Create a new JavaScript document and attach it to the HTML file via a script element in the head of the document. (In the example files, this document has been named vertical-navigation-bar.js.) First, add the JavaScript lines first shown in the "Enhancing accessibility for collapsible content" section:

```
var cssNode = document.createElement('link');
cssNode.setAttribute('rel', 'stylesheet');
cssNode.setAttribute('type', 'text/css');
cssNode.setAttribute('href', 'javascript-overrides.css');
document.getElementsByTagName('head')[0].appendChild(cssNode);
```

Next, add the toggler script shown in the "Modularizing the collapsible content script" section, but amend the target element as shown:

```
function toggle(toggler) {
  if(document.getElementById) {
  targetElement = toggler.nextSibling;
```

```
      if(targetElement.className == undefined) {
      targetElement = toggler.nextSibling.nextSibling;
      }

  if (targetElement.style.display == "block")
    {
    targetElement.style.display = "none";
    }
    else
    {
    targetElement.style.display = "block";
    }
    }
  }
```

> *Note that if you wanted to toggle different kinds of elements on your page, the two scripts shown so far in this chapter would clash. Therefore, you would need to create two different functions, with different names; for example, you could change all instances of* toggle(toggler) *in this exercise to* toggleNav(toggler).

2. Amend the list. To each top-level navigation link, add the onclick attribute, as shown following. And to each second-level list that you initially want to be invisible, add the class attribute shown. For any list you want to be visible, instead add style="display: block;".

```
<li>
  <a href="#" onclick="toggle(this); return false;">Section one</a>
  <ul class="collapsibleList">
    <li><a href="#">A link to a page</a></li>
    <li><a href="#">A link to a page</a></li>
    <li><a href="#">A link to a page</a></li>
    <li><a href="#">A link to a page</a></li>
  </ul>
</li>
```

3. Add a style sheet. Create and save the style sheet document javascript-overrides.css, and add the following rule to initially hide any lists with the collapsibleList class value in JavaScript-enabled browsers.

```
#navigation ul.collapsibleList {
  display: none;
}
```

The following images show the results (which depict, from left to right, the default, hover, and active states).

Working with inline lists

By default, list items are displayed in a vertical fashion, one under the other. However, this behavior can be overridden in CSS, enabling you to create inline lists. This is handy for website navigation, since many navigation bars are horizontally oriented. Some designers mark up horizontal navigation up by using strings of links separated by vertical bars or spaces:

```
<a href="link.html">A link</a> | <a href="link.html">A link</a> |
➡ <a href="link.html">A link</a>
```

However, a horizontal navigation bar is still a list of links, and so semantically should be marked up in the same way as the vertical navigation bar in the previous exercise. In this section, you'll find out how to work with inline lists, discovering how to create breadcrumb navigation, CSS-only "tabbed" navigation, and various graphical navigation bars, complete with rollover effects—all without relying on JavaScript.

Creating breadcrumb navigation

Required files	XHTML-basic.html and CSS-default.css from the basic-boilerplates folder, along with double-arrow.gif from navigation-images within the chapter 5 folder.
What you'll learn	How to create breadcrumb navigation by using a list styled in CSS. Breadcrumb links show the path you've taken to the current document.
Completed files	The breadcrumb-navigation folder in the chapter 5 folder.

1. Add the list. In the HTML document, add the following code for the breadcrumbs. Note that the last item signifies the current page—this is why it's not a link.

```
<ul id="breadcrumbs">
  <li><a href="#">Home page</a></li>
  <li><a href="#">Reviews</a></li>
  <li><a href="#">Live gigs</a></li>
  <li>London, 2008</li>
</ul>
```

2. Add some body padding. Add a padding value to the existing body rule.

```
body {
    font: 62.5%/1.5 Verdana, Arial, Helvetica, sans-serif;
    padding: 20px;
}
```

3. Style the list by adding the following rule. The font-size setting specifies the font size for the list items, and the margin-bottom setting adds a margin under the list.

```
ul#breadcrumbs {
    font-size: 1.2em;
    margin-bottom: 1em;
}
```

4. Add the following rule to style the list items. By setting display to inline, list items are stacked horizontally. The background value sets double-arrow.gif as the background to each list item (ensure it's in the same directory as the CSS document, or modify the path accordingly); the positioning values ensure the background is set at 0 horizontally and 50% vertically, thereby vertically centering it at the left—at least once no-repeat is set, which stops the background tiling. Finally, the padding value sets padding at the right of each list item to 10px, ensuring items don't touch the subsequent background image; the left padding value of 15px provides room for the background image, ensuring the list item text doesn't sit on top of it.

```
#breadcrumbs li {
    display: inline;
    background: url(double-arrow.gif) 0 50% no-repeat;
    padding: 0 10px 0 15px;
}
```

> *Note that when list items are displayed inline, the default bullet points are not displayed. This is one reason why the bullets in this example are background images, although we also wanted something more visually relevant, right-facing arrows showing the path direction.*

```
>> Home page   >> Reviews   >> Live gigs   >> London, 2008
```

5. Remove the first bullet. As the trail is leading from the first item, it shouldn't have a bullet. This can be dealt with via a simple, standards-compliant rule that removes the background from only the list item that is the first child of the unordered list (i.e., the first list item in the list):

```
ul#breadcrumbs li:first-child {
  background: none;
}
```

> Note that prior to Internet Explorer 7, first-child *was not implemented correctly. If you want to create the same effect in Internet Explorer 6 and before, you must instead apply a class to the first list item and then style it to have no background using CSS.*

Creating a simple horizontal navigation bar

Required files	The graphical-navigation-starting-point folder from the chapter 5 folder.
What you'll learn	How to create a good-looking navigation bar, entirely based on HTML text and styled using CSS.
Completed files	The simple-horizontal-navigation-bar folder in the chapter 5 folder.

1. Examine the web page. The web page for this exercise—graphical-navigation. html—is designed for flexibility when it comes to styling elements on the page, making it easy to change elements without touching the markup (this page is used with a few modifications in subsequent exercises, too).

The page's contents are placed within a wrapper div, within which are the masthead and content divs. The latter contains some paragraphs, and the former includes a navContainer div, which houses a navigation div, which in turn houses the unordered list shown in the following code block. (This nesting of divs isn't required for all sites—often you can get away with a single div around the navigation list—or, indeed, none at all, applying the id value of navigation to the list itself; however, having an additional wrapper or two is often useful for more complex layouts.)

The list is an unordered list. The main difference to previous lists is the inclusion of an id value for each list item. For horizontal lists, especially those that will be highly styled, this is worth doing, because it enables you to work all manner of CSS trickery later on, which can benefit the web page. (In fact, some of the techniques can be applied to vertical lists, too.)

```
<ul>
  <li id="homePageLink"><a href="#">Home page</a></li>
  <li id="servicesPageLink"><a href="#">Services</a></li>
```

```
    <li id="customerSupportPageLink"><a href="#">Customer support</a>
    ➥</li>
    <li id="contactDetailsPageLink"><a href="#">Contact details</a></li>
</ul>
```

2. Edit the body and p rules. This design is going to have a classic feel, so in the CSS file, edit the body rule to amend the font set, add a light gray background, and amend the p rule to change the font size.

```
body {
font: 62.5%/1.5 Georgia, "Times New Roman", Times, serif;
background: #dddddd;
}
p {
  font-size: 1.3em;
  margin-bottom: 1em;
}
```

3. Style the structural divs. First, add a rule to style the wrapper div, as shown in the following code block. This sets a fixed width for the div, centers it horizontally, and applies borders on all edges except the top one. The background value provides a white background for the page's content. (Note that there's plenty of explanation about page layout in Chapter 7.) For the content area, add some horizontal padding by adding the #content rule shown in the following code block.

```
#wrapper {
  width: 700px;
  margin: 0 auto;
  border-right: 1px solid #898989;
  border-bottom: 1px solid #898989;
  border-left: 1px solid #898989;
  background: #ffffff;
}
#content {
  padding: 0 15px;
}
```

4. Style the navigation container by adding the following rule to style the navContainer div. In this rule, the font style for the navigation bar's links is set, and the text-align value centers the content horizontally. The padding value applies some padding at the top and bottom of the navContainer div, ensuring its content doesn't hug its edges—in design, the space is often as important as the content, so don't cram things in.

```
#navContainer {
  font: 1.1em/1 Georgia, "Times New Roman", Times, serif;
  background: #d7d7d7;
  text-align: center;
  padding: 7px 0px;
  border-top: 1px solid #898989;
  border-bottom: 1px solid #898989;
  margin-bottom: 10px;
}
```

```
                        • Home page
                        • Services
                     • Customer support
                      • Contact details
   Lorem ipsum dolor sit amet, consectetuer adipiscing elit. Morbi commodo, ipsum sed pharetra gravida, orci magna
   rhoncus neque, id pulvinar odio lorem non turpis. Nullam sit amet enim.

   Suspendisse id velit vitae ligula volutpat condimentum. Aliquam erat volutpat. Sed quis velit. Nulla facilisi. Nulla
   libero. Vivamus pharetra posuere sapien. Nam consectetuer. Sed aliquam, nunc eget euismod ullamcorper, lectus
   nunc ullamcorper orci, fermentum bibendum enim nibh eget ipsum.
```

5. Style the list items. Now that the structure's styled, it's time to get cracking on the list. First, add a rule to remove the default bullets from the unordered list within the navigation div.

```
#navigation ul {
  list-style: none;
}
```

Next, set the list items to display inline, as with the breadcrumbs. Add some horizontal padding, and also, as shown, add a border to each item's right-hand edge, which will act as a visual separator, making each link more distinct.

```
#navigation li {
  display: inline;
  padding: 0px 9px;
  border-right: 1px solid #aaaaaa;
}
```

If you test the page at this point, you'll see that all the links have a right-edge border—not a terrible crime—but from a design standpoint, the one at the far right shouldn't have one (after all, separators are only needed between pairs of links). Luckily, because of the id values applied to the list items earlier, each one can be individually styled, which also means an override can be applied to a specific link. In this case, add the following rule, which removes the border from the list item with an id value of contactDetailsPageLink:

```
#navigation #contactDetailsPageLink {
  border-right: none;
}
```

6. The last thing to do is style the links. The following rules set the link text to uppercase, removing the default underline and coloring them black by default. The links are then gray on the visited state, have an underline on the hover state, and are red on the active state.

```
#navigation a:link, #navigation a:visited {
  text-transform: uppercase;
  text-decoration: none;
}
#navigation a:link {
  color: #000000;
}
#navigation a:visited {
```

```
    color: #222222;
  }
  #navigation a:hover {
    text-decoration: underline;
  }
  #navigation a:active {
    color: #ff0000;
  }
```

| HOME PAGE | SERVICES | CUSTOMER SUPPORT | CONTACT DETAILS |

Lorem ipsum dolor sit amet, consectetuer adipiscing elit. Morbi commodo, ipsum sed pharetra gravida, orci magna rhoncus neque, id pulvinar odio lorem non turpis. Nullam sit amet enim.

Suspendisse id velit vitae ligula volutpat condimentum. Aliquam erat volutpat. Sed quis velit. Nulla facilisi. Nulla libero. Vivamus pharetra posuere sapien. Nam consectetuer. Sed aliquam, nunc eget euismod ullamcorper, lectus nunc ullamcorper orci, fermentum bibendum enim nibh eget ipsum.

Donec porttitor ligula eu dolor. Maecenas vitae nulla consequat libero cursus venenatis. Nam magna enim, accumsan eu, blandit sed, blandit a, eros. Quisque facilisis erat a dui. Nam malesuada ornare dolor. Cras gravida, diam sit amet

In this example, the color of the navigation links—which have no underline—is the same as the body copy. While this would be a very bad idea for inline links, it's fine for the navigation links, because they're obviously distinct from the text elsewhere on the page, due to the background color and horizontal line that separates the navigation area from the content area.

Creating a CSS-only tab bar that automates the active page

Required files	The graphical-navigation-starting-point folder from the chapter 5 folder.
What you'll learn	How to create a tab-style navigation bar, using only CSS for styling (no images).
Completed files	The css-only-tab-bar folder in the chapter 5 folder.

1. Edit the body element—in the HTML page, edit the body start tag, adding the class value shown. Its significance will be explained later.

```
<body id="homePage">
```

2. Edit the body rule. In the CSS document, amend the body rule as shown to add a light gray background:

```
body {
  font: 62.5%/1.5 Verdana, Arial, Helvetica, sans-serif;
  background: #dddddd;
}
```

3. Style structural divs. Add the following #wrapper rule, which defines a set width for the page, centers it, and sets the background color to white.

```
#wrapper {
  width: 700px;
  margin: 0 auto;
  background: #ffffff;
}
```

Next, style the content div by adding the following rule, which adds a border to all edges but the top one, and defines internal padding:

```
#content {
  padding: 15px 15px 0;
  border-right: 1px solid #898989;
  border-bottom: 1px solid #898989;
  border-left: 1px solid #898989;
}
```

These rules work slightly differently from those in the previous exercise. We want the content borders to start right under the navigation, hence the padding being applied to the top of the content div, rather than a margin below the navContainer div.

4. Style the navContainer div. Add the following rule to style the navContainer div. The font settings define a size and family. Avoid setting a line-height value, because that makes it much harder to line up the tabs with the borders later. The padding value applies some padding above the soon-to-be-created tabs, and the border-bottom value finally surrounds all edges of the content div with a border. Because the wrapper div has a white background, this currently shows through the navContainer div, and so a background setting is applied, using the same background color value as applied to the body element.

```
#navContainer {
  font: 1.1em Arial, Helvetica, sans-serif;
  text-align: center;
  padding: 20px 0 0;
  border-bottom: 1px solid #909090;
  background: #dddddd;
}
```

5. Style the list. Add the following rule to style the list. The bottom padding value (5px here) adds padding to the bottom of the list, and needs to be equivalent to the padding value you want to be under the text in each tab.

```
#navigation ul {
  padding: 0 0 5px;
}
```

Next, style the list items to make them display inline.

```
#navigation li {
  display: inline;
}
```

6. Add the following rule to style the links. Most of the property values should be familiar by now. Note how the border value applies a border to each link; this, in tandem with the background value, gives all the links the appearance of background tabs. The padding setting provides space around the link contents (and note how the vertical padding value is the same as the bottom padding value in step 5), and the margin-right setting adds some space between each tab.

```
#navigation a:link, #navigation a:visited {
  text-transform: uppercase;
  text-decoration: none;
  color: #000000;
  background: #bbbbbb;
  border: 1px solid #898989;
  padding: 5px 10px;
  position: relative;
  margin-right: 5px;
}
```

As per the previous exercise, the unwanted right-hand value for the rightmost tab (in this case, the margin-right setting) can be overridden by using a contextual selector that takes advantage of the id values defined in the HTML document's unordered list items.

```
#navigation #contactDetailsPageLink a:link, #navigation
➥ #contactDetailsPageLink a:visited {
  margin-right: 0;
}
```

7. Style other link states. Add the following two rules to define the other link states. The first makes the text slightly lighter when a link has been visited. The second brings back the default underline on the hover state, along with making the link's background slightly lighter.

```
#navigation a:visited {
  color: #222222;
}
#navigation a:hover {
  text-decoration: underline;
  background: #cccccc;
}
```

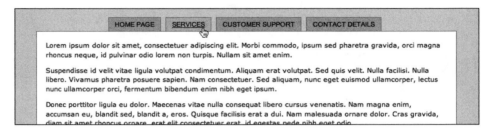

8. Create page-specific overrides. Remember back in step 1, when you defined an id value for the body element? This can now be used to automate the active tab via the following rule:

```
#homePage #homePageLink a:link, #homePage #homePageLink a:visited,
➥ #servicesPage #servicesPageLink a:link, #servicesPage
➥ #servicesPageLink a:visited, #customerSupportPage
➥ #customerSupportPageLink a:link, #customerSupportPage
➥ #customerSupportPageLink a:visited, #contactDetailsPage
➥ #contactDetailsPageLink a:link, #contactDetailsPage
➥ #contactDetailsPageLink a:visited {
  background: #ffffff;
  border-bottom-color: #ffffff;
}
```

The declaration is simple: a white background is applied and the bottom border color is changed to white. The grouped selector is more complex, so I'll start by explaining the first contextual selector, which is #homePage #homePageLink a:link. What this means is, "Apply the declaration to the link within an element with an id of homePageLink that's in an element with an id of homePage." In the page you've been working on, the body element has an id of homePage, and the first list element in the unordered list has an id of homePageLink. Therefore, the link within this list item is automatically given the style, making it look like the active tab (since the background blends directly into the content area).

The other selectors in the grouped selector behave in the same way (in each case for the link and visited styles); so if, for example, you change the id value of the body start tag in the HTML document to customerSupportPage and then refresh the web page, you'll see the third link become the active tab.

Graphical navigation with rollover effects

Working with text and CSS alone is fine, but designers are creative types and tend to like working with graphics. Many enjoy creating more visually arresting navigation bars, which make use of imagery and rollovers. Historically, such systems have required a number of images (three or more per tab) and the use of JavaScript. However, it's possible to use CSS, the same unordered list as used for the previous two exercises, and just a single image to create a graphical navigation bar, as shown in the next exercise.

Using CSS backgrounds to create a navigation bar

Required files	The graphical-navigation-starting-point folder and css-tab-rollover-image.gif from the navigation-images folder in the chapter 5 folder.
What you'll learn	How to create a graphical navigation bar with four different states, driven by CSS, without using any JavaScript.
Completed files	The graphical-navigation-bar folder in the chapter 5 folder.

For this exercise, graphical tabs will be created, using a single GIF image that contains four variations on the graphic: three are for link states for which styles will be defined (active, hover, and then link and visited, which share an image); the other is to flag the current page. By applying this image as a background to links, and then amending its vertical positioning on each state, only the relevant portion of the image will be shown. This is great for updating a site (you only need to amend a single image), and also from a bandwidth standpoint (one image deals with every tab and every state—no need for preloading anything), and it's easy to implement.

1. Edit the body element. Like in the previous exercise, edit the body start tag, adding the id value shown.

```
<body id="homePage">
```

211

2. Style the structural divs. This page's structure is simple, as are the CSS rules required to style it. The #wrapper rule sets a fixed width (which is four times the width of one of the tabs) and centers the design in the browser window. The #masthead rule adds some padding at the top of the masthead, so the tabs won't hug the top of the browser window.

The #navContainer rule has a bottom border (to firmly separate the navigation from the other page content) and a defined height, which is the height of a tab. The height setting is useful, because these tabs will be floated, meaning they're outside of the standard document flow. By giving the container a fixed height, the border is shown in the right place; without the height definition, the border would be displayed at the top of the navContainer div, because as far as browsers are concerned, floated elements technically don't take up any height within the standard document flow.

Finally, the #content rule gives that area a background color and some padding.

```css
#wrapper {
  width: 740px;
  margin: 0 auto;
}
#masthead {
  padding-top: 20px;
}
#navContainer {
  height: 30px;
  border-bottom: 5px solid #ad3514;
}
#content {
  padding: 10px;
  background-color: #eeeeee;
}
```

3. Style list items. Items within the list are styled to float left. The background value includes the location of the rollover image, with additional settings being no-repeat (to stop it from tiling), and then 0 and 0, to ensure the relevant portion of the rollover image is seen by default. The width and height values are the same as that of the image: 185px and 30px, respectively.

```css
#navigation li {
  float: left;
  background: url(css-tab-rollover-image.gif) no-repeat 0 0;
  width: 185px;
  height: 30px;
}
```

4. Next, style the links. The text is rendered in white, uppercase, and in Arial, and the default underlines are removed. Setting display to block makes the entire link container into an active link, thereby making the navigation bar work in the traditional manner (rather than just the text being active). Finally, the padding settings position the text correctly over the background images. The height setting, combined with the padding top setting of 9px, adds up to the height of the container—30px. Without this, the space underneath the text would not be active.

```
#navigation a:link, #navigation a:visited {
    font: bold 1.1em Arial, Helvetica, sans-serif;
    text-transform: uppercase;
    color: #ffffff;
    text-decoration: none;
    display: block;
    height: 21px;
    padding: 9px 0px 0px 30px;
}
```

5. Style other link states. For the hover and active states, you define which portion of the rollover graphic is supposed to be visible. This is done via background position values. The first of these remains 0, because you always want to see the image from its far left. The vertical reading depends on where the relevant portion of the image appears in the rollover graphic.

If you check css-tab-rollover-image.gif in an image editor, you'll see the hover state graphic is 40 pixels from the top and the active state graphic is 80 pixels from the top. This means the image needs to be vertically moved –40 pixels and –80 pixels for the hover and active states, respectively. Therefore, the rules for these states are as follows:

```
#navigation a:hover {
    background: url(css-tab-rollover-image.gif) 0 -40px;
}
#navigation a:active {
    background: url(css-tab-rollover-image.gif) 0 -80px;
}
```

6. Define the active section state. As per step 8 of the previous exercise, the active state graphic can be set. In this case, this is done by displaying the fourth state in the rollover image via the following rule:

```
#homePage #homePageLink a:link, #homePage #homePageLink a:visited,
➥ #servicesPage #servicesPageLink a:link, #servicesPage
➥ #servicesPageLink a:visited, #customerSupportPage
➥ #customerSupportPageLink a:link, #customerSupportPage
➥ #customerSupportPageLink a:visited, #contactDetailsPage
➥ #contactDetailsPageLink a:link, #contactDetailsPage
➥ #contactDetailsPageLink a:visited {
    background: url(css-tab-rollover-image.gif) 0 -120px;
}
```

Again, you can change the id value of the body element to one of the other list item id values to change the active section link.

Using a grid image for multiple link styles and colors

Required files	The files from the graphical-navigation-bar folder and css-rollover-grid.gif from the navigation-images folder in the chapter 5 folder.
What you'll learn	How to amend the previous exercise, in order to create a different tab for each link—still by using a single image.
Completed files	The graphical-navigation-bar-grid folder in the chapter 5 folder.

Taking the previous exercise's completed files as a starting point, along with css-rollover-grid.gif, which will be used as the rollover image, you're now going to have a different tab for each link. This will be done via more background positioning and by making use of the list item id values to create rules with contextual selectors specific to each item. Naturally, the rollover image contains all of the states for the rollover images.

1. Amend the list item style. To apply the new background to the list items, amend the #navigation li rule:

```
#navigation li {
  float: left;
  display: inline;
  width: 185px;
  height: 30px;
  background: url(css-rollover-grid.gif) no-repeat 0 0;
}
```

2. Amend the navContainer div border. Because the tabs are now multicolored, the orange border at the bottom of the navContainer div won't look good, so change it to dark gray.

```
#navContainer {
  height: 30px;
  border-bottom: 5px solid #333333;
}
```

3. Set specific background positions. Each tab now requires a separate background position to show the relevant portion of the background image for each tab. Again, negative margins are used to pull the image into place in each case. (Because the different colors aren't obvious in grayscale, the tabs also have unique icons at the far left.) These rules should be placed after the #navigation a:link, #navigation a:visited rule.

```
#navigation #homePageLink {
  background-position: 0 0;
}
#navigation #servicesPageLink {
  background-position: -185px 0;
}
```

```
#navigation #customerSupportPageLink {
   background-position: -370px 0;
}
#navigation #contactDetailsPageLink {
   background-position: -555px 0;
}
```

4. Edit the active-page state for each tab. The correct portion of the image needs to show when a tab is the active page, and this is done by replacing the rule from step 6 of the previous exercise with the following four rules, which should be placed after the rules added in the previous step.

```
#homePage #homePageLink a:link, #homePage #homePageLink a:visited {
   background: url(css-rollover-grid.gif) 0 -120px;
}
#servicesPage #servicesPageLink a:link, #servicesPage
➡ #servicesPageLink a:visited {
   background: url(css-rollover-grid.gif) -185px -120px;
}
#customerSupportPage #customerSupportPageLink a:link,
➡ #customerSupportPage #customerSupportPageLink a:visited  {
   background: url(css-rollover-grid.gif) -370px -120px;
}
#contactDetailsPage #contactDetailsPageLink a:link,
➡ #contactDetailsPage #contactDetailsPageLink a:visited {
   background: url(css-rollover-grid.gif) -555px -120px;
}
```

5. Finally, the two rules for the hover and active states need to be replaced by four rules each—one for each tab. Again, negative margin values are used to display the relevant portion of the background image for each state for each image. Add these rules after those from the previous step.

```
#navigation li#homePageLink a:hover {
   background: url(css-rollover-grid.gif) 0 -40px;
}
#navigation li#servicesPageLink a:hover {
   background: url(css-rollover-grid.gif) -185px -40px;
}
#navigation li#customerSupportPageLink a:hover {
   background: url(css-rollover-grid.gif) -370px -40px;
}
#navigation li#contactDetailsPageLink a:hover {
   background: url(css-rollover-grid.gif) -555px -40px;
}

#navigation li#homePageLink a:active {
   background: url(css-rollover-grid.gif) 0 -80px;
}
#navigation li#servicesPageLink a:active {
   background: url(css-rollover-grid.gif) -185px -80px;
}
```

```
}
#navigation li#customerSupportPageLink a:active {
   background: url(css-rollover-grid.gif) -370px -80px;
}
#navigation li#contactDetailsPageLink a:active {
   background: url(css-rollover-grid.gif) -555px -80px;
}
```

Once again, change the `id` value of the body element to amend the active section link.

Creating graphical tabs that expand with resized text

Required files	The files from the graphical-navigation-bar folder, and the images css-tab-rollover-image-left.gif and css-tab-rollover-image-right.gif from the navigation-images folder from the chapter 5 folder.
What you'll learn	How to amend the result from the "Using CSS backgrounds to create a navigation bar" exercise, enabling the tabs to expand, resizing with their content.
Completed files	graphical-navigation-bar-sliding-doors in the chapter 5 folder.

With both of the graphical tab exercises so far, there is a problem: when the text is resized, the tabs don't resize with it.

This can be dealt with using a technique typically referred to as "sliding doors." This requires two images in place of the original background image tab—one for its left-hand part and one for the right-hand part, with enough vertical repetition to expand horizontally. With wider links, more of the right-hand image will be displayed.

Note that the increase in flexibility in this method is only horizontal. If you need more flexibility vertically, increase the height of each "state" in the graphical tabs, remove the height *values from both* #navigation li *and* #navigation a:link, #navigation a:visited, *and add a* padding-bottom *value to the latter of those two rules.*

1. Amend the list. To the list items, apply the css-tab-rollover-image-left.gif background image, and add a padding-left value that's the same width as the image. This provides the left-hand side of each tab. The reason for the padding value is so that the right-hand side of the tab (applied to the link) doesn't overlap the left-hand image.

```
#navigation li {
  float: left;
  background: url(css-tab-rollover-image-left.gif) no-repeat 0 0;
  padding-left: 30px;
  height: 30px;
}
```

2. Amend the link style. Because the padding at the left of the link is now dealt with by the previous rule, there's no need for a padding-left value in #navigation a:link, #navigation a:visited. However, because the link now stretches with the content, a padding-right value is required, to stop the tab content in each case from hugging the edge of the tab. This explains the amended values for the padding property. For the background property, the image file name is amended, along with its horizontal position, which is now at the far right (100%).

```
#navigation a:link, #navigation a:visited {
    font: bold 1.1em Arial, Helvetica, sans-serif;
    text-transform: uppercase;
    color: #ffffff;
    text-decoration: none;
    display: block;
    height: 21px;
    padding: 9px 30px 0px 0px;
    background: url(css-tab-rollover-image-right.gif) no-repeat 100% 0;
}
```

3. With this technique, the left-hand portion of the tab is no longer an active link. It's therefore usually recommended to keep the left-hand image as narrow as possible. In this example, the left-hand image is 30 pixels wide, but this was used to show how to convert a standard graphical navigation bar into one where the tabs can expand—it's not recommended for the graphical design of such a system. However, this means the hover and current page states need amending; otherwise, there's no feedback. Therefore, for #navigation a:hover, set text-decoration to underline, and delete everything else within the rule; and for the large, complex rule at the end, set color: #fff200; as the sole property/value pair in the declaration.

Creating a two-tier navigation menu

Required files	The files from the graphical-navigation-bar folder and the images active-section-tab-background.gif and sub-navigation-background-tile.gif from the navigation-images folder from the chapter 5 folder.
What you'll learn	How to create a two-tier navigation system, with different backgrounds and styles for each tier. This is another method for dealing with navigation text resizing, and it's also useful for larger websites, providing a place for subnavigation.
Completed files	two-tier-navigation in the chapter 5 folder.

1. Edit the body element. In the HTML page, give the body start tag an id value of homePage.

```
<body id="homePage">
```

2. Add some subnavigation. Open the HTML document and add another list for sub-navigation, directly after the navigation div.

```
<div id="subNavigation">
  <ul>
    <li><a href="#">Sub-nav one</a></li>
    <li><a href="#">Sub-nav two</a></li>
    <li><a href="#">Sub-nav three</a></li>
    <li><a href="#">Sub-nav four</a></li>
    <li><a href="#">Sub-nav five</a></li>
    <li><a href="#">Sub-nav six</a></li>
    <li><a href="#">Sub-nav seven</a></li>
  </ul>
</div>
```

3. Amend the body rule. In the CSS document, edit the body rule to add a dark gray background color and some padding at the top of the document.

```
body {
  font: 62.5%/1.5 Verdana, Arial, Helvetica, sans-serif;
  background: #333333;
  padding-top: 20px;
}
```

4. Style the structural divs—add the following three rules to style the three main structural divs. Adding a light gray bottom border to the masthead makes the transition between the vibrant navigation to the black-text-on-white-background content area less harsh.

```
#wrapper {
  width: 750px;
  margin: 0 auto;
  background-color: #ffffff;
```

```
  border: 1px solid #555555;
}
#masthead {
  border-bottom: 8px solid #cccccc;
}
#content {
  background: #ffffff;
  padding: 10px;
}
```

5. Add the following two rules to remove list defaults, center list content, and display list items inline.

```
#navContainer ul {
  text-align: center;
}
#navContainer li {
  display: inline;
}
```

Home page Services Customer support Contact details
Sub-nav one Sub-nav two Sub-nav three Sub-nav four Sub-nav five Sub-nav six Sub-nav seven

Lorem ipsum dolor sit amet, consectetuer adipiscing elit. Morbi commodo, ipsum sed pharetra gravida, orci magna rhoncus neque, id pulvinar odio lorem non turpis. Nullam sit amet enim.

Suspendisse id velit vitae ligula volutpat condimentum. Aliquam erat volutpat. Sed quis velit. Nulla facilisi. Nulla libero. Vivamus pharetra posuere sapien. Nam consectetuer. Sed aliquam, nunc eget euismod ullamcorper, lectus nunc ullamcorper orci, fermentum bibendum enim nibh eget ipsum.

Donec porttitor ligula eu dolor. Maecenas vitae nulla consequat libero cursus venenatis. Nam magna enim, accumsan eu, blandit sed, blandit a, eros. Quisque facilisis erat a dui. Nam malesuada ornare dolor. Cras gravida, diam sit amet rhoncus ornare, erat elit consectetuer erat, id egestas pede nibh eget odio.

6. Style the navigation div and its links. Add the following three rules to style the navigation div and the links within. The padding settings work as per the earlier exercises in this chapter: again, the vertical padding must be kept constant between the container and the links, hence the vertical padding being set to 6px in both cases. Note the hover color—a bright yellow, designed to stand out against both the black background of the main navigation bar and the orange background of the subnavigation and highlighted tab.

```
#navigation {
  background: #111111;
  padding: 6px 0;
}
#navigation a:link, #navigation a:visited {
  font: bold 1.2em Arial, Helvetica, sans-serif;
  color: #ffffff;
  text-decoration: none;
  padding: 6px 10px;
}
#navigation a:hover {
  color: #ffd800;
}
```

7. Style the active page link. Using one of those grouped contextual selectors we seem to like so much in this chapter, set a rule to style the active page link. In this case, a background image is tiled horizontally and set to sit at the bottom of the links. A background color is also defined, which is handy for if the text is zoomed—if no background color were defined, the image might run out, leaving the navigation div's background color to show through instead. This rule, however, ensures that the background will always have some color, regardless of the font size. The color setting itself was taken from the top pixel of the background image, so it blends seamlessly with said image.

```
#homePage #homePageLink a:link, #homePage #homePageLink a:visited,
➥ #servicesPage #servicesPageLink a:link, #servicesPage
➥ #servicesPageLink a:visited, #customerSupportPage
➥ #customerSupportPageLink a:link, #customerSupportPage
➥ #customerSupportPageLink a:visited, #contactDetailsPage
➥ #contactDetailsPageLink a:link, #contactDetailsPage
➥ #contactDetailsPageLink a:visited {
  background: #28b767 url(active-section-tab-background.gif)
  ➥ 0 100% repeat-x;
  border-top: 1px solid #ca8d5c;
}
```

8. Add the following three rules to style the subnavigation. Here, a background image is tiled horizontally behind the entire subNavigation div, and it works in a similar way to the one used in step 7, blending into a background color if the text is zoomed, dramatically changing the div's height. The border-bottom setting provides a darker base to the navigation, which works better than having the light gray masthead border directly beneath it. The margin-top setting pulls the entire subNavigation div up two pixels, which stops the layout from splitting at some levels of text zoom.

```
#subNavigation {
  margin-top: -2px;
  background: #b76628 url(sub-navigation-background-tile.gif) 0 100%
  ➥ repeat-x;
```

```
    border-bottom: 1px solid #6b6b6b;
    padding: 6px 0;
}
#subNavigation a:link, #subNavigation a:visited
    font: bold 1.1em Arial, Helvetica, sans-serif;
    color: #ffffff;
    text-decoration: none;
    padding: 6px 10px;
}
#subNavigation a:hover {
    color: #ffd800;
}
```

As you can see from the following images, this navigation bar deals really well with increased text sizes—only when the text is absolutely massive does it not work entirely as expected, although, crucially, it still remains usable.

The subNavigation div *in this technique sometimes suffers from the* hasLayout *bug in Internet Explorer 6. See Chapter 9 for a method of dealing with* hasLayout.

Creating a drop-down menu

Required files	Files from the graphical-navigation-bar folder and drop-down-menu-background.gif (which is a crop of the list item background image) from the navigation-images folder in the chapter 5 folder.
What you'll learn	How to work with an existing CSS-based navigation menu and convert it into a drop-down menu.
Completed files	The drop-down-menu folder in the chapter 5 folder.

The next type of navigation we're going to explore in this chapter is the drop-down menu. In part popularized by operating systems such as Windows and Mac OS, drop-down menus are convenient for storing plenty of links in a relatively small space. However, use them with caution, because the second tier of navigation is initially hidden from view, unlike in the previous exercise's system, where it was visible. However, with drop-downs, all second-tier navigation is available from the menu.

1. Edit the web page. For any link you want to have a drop-down menu spawn from, nest an unordered list in its parent list item, as per the example in the following code block.

```
<li id="servicesPageLink">
  <a href="#">Services</a>
  <ul>
    <li><a href="#">Drop-down link one</a></li>
    <li><a href="#">Drop-down link two</a></li>
    <li><a href="#">Drop-down link three</a></li>
    <li><a href="#">Drop-down link four</a></li>
  </ul>
</li>
```

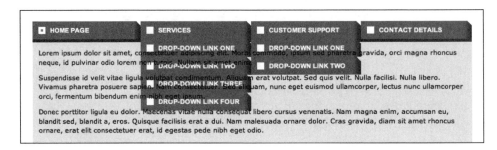

2. Create the drop-downs. Test your page now, and it will look odd because nested list items pick up the styles for the standard list items. To start dealing with this, add position: relative; to the #navigation li rule, which will enable nested absolute-positioned elements to take their top and left values from their containers

rather than the page as a whole. Then, after the existing rules in the CSS, add the #navigation li ul rule shown in the following code block. By setting position to absolute and left to a large negative value, the nested lists (i.e., the drop-down menus) are placed offscreen by default, but are still accessible to screen readers. Adding the top border helps visually separate the nested list from its parent button.

```
#navigation li ul {
  border-top: 1px solid #ad3514;
  width: 185px;
  position: absolute;
  left: -10000px
}
```

Next, add the following rule to bring the nested lists back when you hover the cursor over the parent list item. Upon doing so, the list item's descendant list's display value is set to block, and it's displayed directly underneath the parent item.

```
#navigation li:hover ul  {
  display: block;
  left: 0;
}
```

3. Style nested list items and links. Add the following rule to replace the default background for list items with one specifically for the drop-down menus. The border-bottom value visually separates each of the list items.

```
#navigation li li {
  background: url(drop-down-menu-background.gif) repeat-y;
  border-bottom: 1px solid #ad3514;
}
```

Next, add the following rule to style nested list item links, overriding the text-transform and padding values of top-level list items.

```
#navigation li li a:link, #navigation li li a:visited {
  text-transform: none;
  padding-left: 10px;
}
```

4. The final step is to override the hover and active states. For this example, the background value for top-level lists is overridden and the background image removed (meaning the hover state for nested list links has no unique background). To make the hover state stand out, the links are given a vibrant left border. This also moves the text inward by the width of the border.

```
#navigation li li a:hover, #navigation li li a:active {
  background: none;
  border-left: 5px solid #f7bc1d;
}
```

5

These property values are common to both states, apart from the border color (orange for the hover state and red for the active state, roughly matching the colors applied to the top-level tab icons in the same states, although the orange is brighter for the drop-downs so that they stand out more); therefore, add the following rule to change only the left border's color on the active state:

```
#navigation li li a:active {
  border-left-color: #ed1c24;
}
```

If you decide to create drop-down menu–based navigation, avoid copying an operating system's menu style, because this may confuse visitors using that operating system and irritate visitors using a rival system. The exception to this rule is if you're creating a site that centers around nostalgia for the days where operating systems used to come on floppy disks. One such site—an amusing Mac OS System 7 look-alike—can be found at http://myoldmac.net/.

Creating a multicolumn drop-down menu

Required files	The drop-down-menu folder from the chapter 5 folder.
What you'll learn	How to create a multicolumn drop-down menu, based on the code from the previous exercise.
Completed files	The drop-down-menu-multi-column folder in the chapter 5 folder.

The final example in this chapter is a multicolumn drop-down menu. These are increasingly common, enabling sites to provide a lot of links in a drop-down that simply wouldn't fit on the screen if they were listed vertically. For an example of such a drop-down in action (although one that uses a different method), visit www.2000adonline.com/books/ and hover over the Books List link.

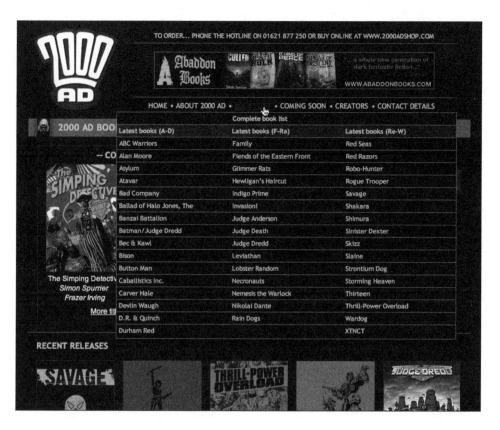

1. Edit the HTML to remove the existing nested lists. Then, for the multicolumn drop-down, decide which link you want it to spawn from and place an unordered link in its parent list item, with a single list item of its own. Within *that* list item, place the unordered lists for the columns in the drop-down, one after the other. Note that if some columns have fewer items, they must still have the same number of list items. However, list items can be left empty, despite this technically being a presentational hack. (Note that HTML Tidy might have problems with this and trim the empty list items. If you use that tool, add a nonbreaking space as the list's content.)

```
<li id="servicesPage">
  <a href="#">Services</a>
  <ul>
    <li>
      <ul>
        <li><a href="#">Drop-down link 1.1</a></li>
        <li><a href="#">Drop-down link 1.2</a></li>
        <li><a href="#">Drop-down link 1.3</a></li>
        <li><a href="#">Drop-down link 1.4</a></li>
      </ul>
      <ul>
        <li><a href="#">Drop-down link 2.1</a></li>
        <li><a href="#">Drop-down link 2.2</a></li>
```

5

```
          <li></li>
          <li></li>
        </ul>
        <ul>
          <li><a href="#">Drop-down link 3.1</a></li>
          <li><a href="#">Drop-down link 3.2</a></li>
          <li><a href="#">Drop-down link 3.3</a></li>
          <li></li>
        </ul>
      </li>
    </ul>
</li>
```

2. Next, edit the nested list. The list that contains the three lists that form the columns of the drop-down needs styling. Having larger borders on multicolumn drop-downs is a good idea, because it enables users to focus on the contents more easily, hence the amended border setting in the following code block. The other change is to the width setting, which must be a multiple of three (here, it's set to 465px, meaning that each column will be 155 pixels wide). With multicolumn drop-downs, it's best to avoid making each column the same width as a tab, otherwise the result will look strange.

```
#navigation li ul {
  border: 2px solid #ad3514;
  width: 465px;
  position: absolute;
  left: -10000px
}
```

3. Now, the list item within the nested list needs amending. For the previous exercise, the #navigation li li rule dealt with the list items in the drop-down, but here it's primarily for the container of the three columns. Therefore, the height and width settings need to be set to auto to enable the list item to stretch to fit its nested items. The background image is superfluous, so it's replaced by a flat color, and the border-bottom pair is removed—the borders will be moved to list items within the columns.

```
#navigation li li {
  background: #d27448;
  height: auto;
  width: auto;
}
```

4. The link rules should be styled next. Since the links are now one level deeper in the list, instances of li li in the selectors are changed to li li li. In this example, this change isn't technically necessary, but it always pays to keep your selectors as precise and accurate as possible. For the link and visited states, padding settings for the top-level links are overridden, as are width and height settings. For the other states, the border used for the hover and active effects is replaced by a change in background color. Note that the rule that originally had both the hover and active states in the selector (#navigation li li a:hover, #navigation li

li a:active) now only requires the hover state (#navigation li li li a:hover), because the rules have nothing in common.

```
#navigation li li li a:link, #navigation li li li a:visited {
  text-transform: none;
  padding: 10px;
  width: 135px;
  height: auto;
}
#navigation li li li a:hover {
  background: #ad3514;
}
#navigation li li li a:active {
  background: #ed1c24;
}
```

5. Style the column list items. Add a rule to define a width and height for the column list items, along with a bottom border. The last of those things makes it easier to scan the rows within the list, while the width and height settings ensure that the layout isn't affected if the list items have no links within. (If the width and height settings were omitted, the list items within the columns would show their bottom borders only underneath their content's width—and not at all if they were empty.) The height setting is defined in ems rather than pixels, because this makes it possible for the list items to stretch vertically if the web page's text is resized.

```
#navigation li li li {
width: 155px;
height: 3em;
border-bottom: 1px solid #ad3514;
}
```

6. Finally, add a rule to float and define a width for the lists that comprise the containers for the list items styled in the previous step.

```
#navigation ul ul ul {
  border: 0;
  width: 155px;
  float: left;
  position: relative;
}
```

> *Although the drop-down examples work in currently shipping browsers, neither works as is in Internet Explorer 6, because that browser doesn't enable you to do anything with the hover state unless it's on a link. To cater for that browser, JavaScript must be used as a backup.*

The dos and don'ts of web navigation

So, that's the end of our navigation chapter. Before we move on to working with layout, here are a few succinct tips regarding designing web navigation.

Do

- Use appropriate types of navigation.
- Provide alternate means of accessing information.
- Ensure links stand out.
- Take advantage of link states to provide feedback for users.
- Get the link state order right (link, visited, hover, active).
- Use styled lists for navigation.
- Use CSS and as few images as possible (preferably one) for rollovers.

Don't

- Add search boxes just for the sake of it.
- Use deprecated body attributes.
- Style navigation links like normal body copy.
- Use image maps unless absolutely necessary.
- Open new windows from links or use pop-ups.
- Use clunky JavaScript for rollovers.

6 TABLES: HOW NATURE (AND THE W3C) INTENDED

A playlist of great music	
Time	**Artist**
3:34	Wire
3:18	Worm Is Green
6:07	Silo
4:48	Fischerspooner
3:21	Bloc Party
3:58	Cansei De Ser Sexy (CSS)
3:45	Tom Vek
5:05	Björk
4:21	Charlotte Hatherley
4:04	The Delgados

Templates	6:07
Emerge	4:48
Banquet	3:21
Alala	3:58
I Ain't Saying My Goodbyes	3:45
Jóga	5:05
Kim Wilde	4:21
Witness	4:04
Feel Good Inc.	3:41
Returning Wheel	3:26
P.E.T.R.O.L.	6:21
Pweization	3:08

Banquet	3:21
Alala	3:58
I Ain't Saying My Goodbyes	3:45
Jóga	5:05
Kim Wilde	4:21
Witness	4:04
Feel Good Inc.	3:41
Returning Wheel	3:26
P.E.T.R.O.L.	6:21
Pweization	3:08
Betrayed	3:05
When The Sun Hits	4:47
Little Eyes	4:20

In this chapter:

- Introducing how tables work
- Using borders, padding, and spacing
- Creating accessible tables
- Enhancing tables with CSS
- Designing tables for web page layout

The great table debate

Tables were initially intended as a means of displaying tabular data online, enabling web designers to rapidly mark up things like price lists, statistical comparisons, specification lists, spreadsheets, charts, forms, and so on (the following example shows a simple table, taken from www.macuser.co.uk).

PRODUCT	SUPPLIER	PRICE	RATING
Canon Bubble Jet i9950	Pixmania.com	£446.00	5✳
Canon Bubble Jet i6500	Canon	£291.00	4
Epson Stylus Photo 2100	ebuyer.com	£434.00	4
Epson Stylus Photo 1290	Simply	£273.00	3
HP Designjet 30	Dabs.com	£532.00	3
HP Deskjet 9650	Savastore.com	£329.00	3

It wasn't long, however, before web designers realized that you could place any web content within table cells, and this rapidly led to web designers chopping up Photoshop layouts and piecing them back together in table-based web pages, often by using automated tools. CSS should have put an end to that, but many web designers continue to use tables for layout because they're simple to set up—even though they cause problems (see the "Tables for layout" section later in the chapter).

The strong will of CSS advocates, who typically shout that tables are evil, sometimes leads designers to believe that tables should be ditched entirely—however, that's not the case at all. As mentioned, tables have a specific purpose in HTML, and one that's still valid. Therefore, the bulk of this chapter is going to look at tables in the context for which they're intended: the formatting of tabular data. Web page layout will be looked at in the next chapter, which concentrates on CSS layout.

How tables work

In this section, we're going to look at how tables are structured, and some of the table element's attributes, which enable you to define the table's dimensions and borders, along with the spacing, padding, and alignment of its cells.

Tabular data works via a system of rows and columns, and HTML tables work in the same way. The table element defines the beginning and end of a table. Within the table element are table row elements (<tr></tr>), and nested within those are table cell elements (<td></td>). The actual content is placed inside the td elements. Therefore, a simple table with two rows containing two cells each is created like this:

```
<table>
  <tr><td>Cell one</td><td>Cell two</td></tr>
  <tr><td>Cell three</td><td>Cell four</td></tr>
</table>
```

> *Always ensure that you include all end tags when working with tables. If you began working with HTML in the mid-1990s, you may have learned that it's OK to omit the odd end tag from tables or table cells. However, not only does this result in invalid XHTML, but some browsers won't render tables accurately (or at all) when end tags are omitted. Furthermore, there's evidence to suggest some search engines can't properly spider pages that contain broken tables.*

6

Adding a border

You can place a border around table cells by using the border attribute and setting its value to 1 or greater. The adjacent example shows how this looks in a web browser.

HTML borders for tables have a kind of 3D effect and tend to look clunky and old-fashioned. If you want to add a border to a table, this is best done in CSS.

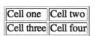

Cell spacing and cell padding

In addition to amending the border size, it's possible to change the amount of padding within a table's cells, as well as the spacing between all the cells in a table. This is done with the cellpadding and cellspacing attributes, respectively. In the rather extreme example that follows, cellpadding is set to 20, cellspacing to 40, and border to 5, so that each can be differentiated with ease (see the subsequent screenshot). As you can see, cellspacing not only affects the spacing between the cells, but also the distance between the cells and the table's edges. (The CSS property border-spacing is intended to do the same thing as cellspacing, but Internet Explorer to version 7 doesn't support it.)

```
<table cellpadding="20" cellspacing="40" border="5">
  <tr><td>Cell one</td><td>Cell two</td></tr>
  <tr><td>Cell three</td><td>Cell four</td></tr>
</table>
```

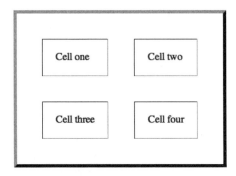

You might be thinking that design-wise, this example sucks, and you'd be right. The chunk-o-vision 3D border isn't particularly tasteful. However, you can omit the border attribute and use CSS to style borders instead—see the "Styling a table" section later on in this chapter. That section also details how to set padding in CSS, which provides you with site-wide control over cell padding. CSS also gives you much finer control over the individual elements in a table—whereas the inline HTML attributes impose a one-style-fits-all straightjacket.

Spanning rows and cells

It's sometimes necessary for data to span multiple rows or columns. This is achieved via the rowspan and colspan attributes, respectively. In the following table, the first row has three cells. However, in the second row, the first cell spans two rows and the second cell spans two columns. This means the second row lacks a third cell, and the third row also only has two cells (whose contents align with the second and third cells of the top row). See the following screenshot of the table to help make sense of this.

```
<table border="1" cellpadding="2">
  <tr>
    <td>A cell</td>
    <td>Another cell</td>
    <td>Yet another cell!</td>
  </tr>
  <tr>
    <td rowspan="2">A cell that spans two rows</td>
    <td colspan="2">A cell that spans two columns</td>
  </tr>
  <tr>
```

```
      <td>Another cell</td>
      <td>The last cell</td>
    </tr>
  </table>
```

A cell		Another cell	Yet another cell!
A cell that spans two rows		A cell that spans two columns	
		Another cell	The last cell

> In the preceding HTML, the cell elements are indented to make it easier for you to make them out. This wasn't done earlier in the chapter. Either method of writing markup is fine—it's up to you. Note, however, that if you use images within table cells, this extra whitespace in the HTML sometimes causes layouts to break, and must therefore be deleted.

Take care when spanning rows or columns with a cell, because it's easy to add extra cells accidentally. For instance, in the preceding example, it would be easy to absentmindedly add a third cell to both the second and third rows—however, doing so appends the extra cells to the end of the table (see the following example), which looks bad, and—more important—makes little structural sense. Also, some screen readers have difficulty handling such data, often assigning the wrong headers to various pieces of data (see the "Creating accessible tables" section later in the chapter for information on table headers).

A cell		Another cell	Yet another cell!	
A cell that spans two rows		A cell that spans two columns	This shouldn't be here	
		Another cell	The last cell	A wrongly added cell

Setting dimensions and alignment

As you can see from the examples so far, browsers by default set cell sizes to the smallest possible values that are large enough to accommodate the contents and any cell padding settings defined. Although this is suitable for the majority of purposes, designers tend to want more visual control over layouts.

Long-time designers may be well-versed in the practice of using height and width attributes to control table and cell dimensions, but beware. The width attribute is fine to use on table start tags (the possible values of which are a number denoting the width in pixels of the table, and a percentage, which is a percentage of the parent element's size). However, the height attribute is nonstandard and fails in the majority of web browsers (in fact, if using an XHTML DTD, it fails in every currently shipping mainstream browser), which might come as something of a shock to those people who enjoy centering content in a browser window by using a table.

As for setting widths and heights within table cells, that's something that should be avoided altogether—height and width attributes within table cells are deprecated. You might argue that this is irrelevant—after all, all major browsers support these attributes. Although this is true, deprecated attributes are not guaranteed to be supported in the future. Also, table cells always expand to accommodate the widest or tallest element in a row or column. As a result of this, defining heights and widths is often a futile attempt to control the uncontrollable.

> Take care when using visual web design applications: many of them add deprecated elements to tables if you manually drag the cells around. Use your favored application's preferences to turn off this feature, otherwise you'll end up with obsolete and redundant markup.

Vertical alignment of table cell content

If you set your table's width to a small value, or if you have a lot of content in one cell and relatively little in an adjacent one, something else becomes apparent: web browsers vertically align content in the middle of cells. (Generally, horizontal alignment is, as with other text, to the left.) See the image on the right for an example.

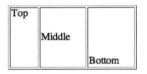

Historically, designers have used the valign attribute to override this vertical-centering behavior—the attribute can be added to a row or cell start tag, and set to top: valign="top". Other values are middle (the default) and bottom, the results of which are shown in the adjacent screenshot.

The problem with valign is that it's presentational markup and shouldn't really be used; in fact, because it's a deprecated attribute—which means it can't be used if you're creating valid XHTML Strict documents—you should instead work with the CSS alternative, the vertical-align property, which provides practically identical results.

As an example of vertical-align in use, say you wanted all cells within a table that had a class value of priceList to be vertically aligned to the top; you could add the following rule to your CSS:

```
table.priceList td {
  vertical-align: top;
}
```

This results in the same effect as valign="top", as discussed earlier. Likewise, you can set the vertical-align property to middle, bottom, and various other values, as outlined in Appendix D, "CSS Reference."

That's pretty much where many web designers leave tables; however, there are other elements and attributes that should be used when creating tables, which will be covered in the following sections.

Creating accessible tables

Many web designers ignore all but the most basic elements when working with tables, and in doing so they end up with output that causes problems for screen readers. By correctly and carefully structuring and formatting a table, not only will users of screen readers benefit, but you as a designer will also have far more control over its visual appearance. Additionally, extendable browsers like Firefox can also enable you to use the table data in other ways, including outside of the browser. For example, the TableTools plug-in (https://addons.mozilla.org/en-US/firefox/addon/2637) enables sorting, filtering, and exporting of tabular data from a web page. A properly formatted table will enhance this, making the table even more useful. Adding a few extra elements and attributes to your table is a win-win situation, and it's surprising to note how few designers bother with anything other than rows and cells in their tables.

6

Captions and summaries

Two seldom-used table additions that enable you to provide explanations of a table's contents are the caption element and the summary attribute. The former is usually placed directly after the table start tag, and enables you to provide a means of associating the table's title with the table itself. Obviously, this also helps users—particularly those with screen readers. After reading the caption, the screen reader will go on to read the table headers (see the "Using table headers" section later in this chapter). Without the caption, the table's contents might be relatively meaningless.

By default, most browsers center captions horizontally, and some set their contents in bold type, but these default styles can be overridden with CSS.

The summary attribute, which is invisible in browsers, is used by screen readers to give the user an overview of the table's contents prior to accessing the content. The contents of the summary attribute should be kept succinct, highlighting the most important aspects of the table contents, letting the user know what to anticipate.

Many suggest that summaries should be included on all tables, but this isn't necessarily the case. A summary should be used only when it performs the task for which it's designed: to make available a succinct summary of data within a table. Should you be using tables for layout (which I don't recommend), there's little point including summaries within each layout table—after all, someone using a screen reader is hardly going to jump for joy upon hearing, for the umpteenth time, "This table is used for laying out the web page." Summaries should save time, not waste it.

Using table headers

Only a fraction of data tables on the Web make use of table headers, even though the majority of tables include cell data that would be better placed within headers. The table header cell element (<th></th>) performs a similar function to the standard table cell, but is useful with regard to accessibility. Imagine a long data table comprised solely of standard cells. The first row likely contains the headers, but because they're not differentiated, a screen reader might treat them as normal cells, read them once, and then continue reading the remainder of the data. (If it doesn't do this, it still has to *assume* which cells are headers, and it might guess wrong.) When using table headers, the data is usually read in context (header/data, header/data, and so on), enabling the user to make sense of everything. Things can be sped up slightly by using the abbr attribute—long table headers can be cut down, reducing what needs to be repeated when a table's data is being read out. An example of table header cells and a row of data cells follows:

```
<th>Country</th><th abbr="Capital">Capital city</th>
<td>France</td><td>Paris</td>
```

In this case, a screen reader should read the headers and then provide them with the data of each cell (Country: France, Capital: Paris, etc.). But even with screen-based browsers, the inclusion of headers proves beneficial for users, because table header cell content by default is styled differently from data cell content, meaning the two cell types can be easily differentiated.

Although headers are often at the top of a table, they may also be aligned down the left-hand side. Therefore, you also need to specify whether the header provides header information for the remainder of the row, column, row group, or column group that contains it. This can be done with the scope attribute, which is added to the table header start tag and given the relevant value (row, col, rowgroup, or colgroup). It's also possible to use the headers attribute in conjunction with id values. See the following "Scope and headers" section for more information.

Row groups

Row group elements are almost never used, the main reason being a supposed lack of browser support. The three possible row group elements—<thead></thead>, <tbody></tbody>, and <tfoot></tfoot>—enable browsers to support the scrolling of the body area of long tables, with the head and foot of the table remaining fixed. Furthermore, when tables are printed, the aforementioned elements enable the table head and foot to be printed on each page.

Although browser support comes up short in some areas, I still recommend using row groups, because they encourage you as a designer to think about the structure of the tables you're creating. Also, although browsers don't do all they might with the elements, they still recognize them, which means they can be used as selectors in CSS, enabling you to set separate styles for the head, body, and foot data.

When using row groups, you can have one or more tbody elements and zero or one thead and tfoot elements. They should be ordered with the head first, foot second, and body/bodies third, thereby enabling the browser to render the foot prior to receiving all of the data. Note, however, that despite this order in HTML, browsers visually render the row groups in the order you'd expect: head, body, and foot.

Scope and headers

Although table header cells provide a means of differentiating headers and other data, a direct means of associating one with the other can be added via the use of various attributes. For simple data tables, the scope attribute, added to table headers, provides an indication of which data a heading refers to. For example, in the previous code block, the table is oriented in columns—the headers are above their associated data. Therefore, adding a scope attribute to the header cells, with a value of col, clearly defines this relationship—and this is something that comes in handy for screen readers.

```
<th scope="col">Country</th><th scope="col">Capital city</th>
<td>France</td><td>Paris</td>
```

If the alignment of the table were changed, with the headers at the left, the row value would instead be used.

```
<th scope="row">Country</th><td>France</td>
<th scope="row">Capital city</th><td>Paris</td>
```

Note that if a table header contains colspan or rowspan attributes—for example, if a header, such as food, spanned two columns (thereby having the attribute/value pair colspan="2") and had underneath two further headings, such as fruit and vegetables—you could set scope="colgroup" in the table header start tag. The equivalent is true for headers with a rowspan attribute, whereupon the scope value changes to rowgroup. In such cases, you also need to use the colgroup/rowgroup elements.

These are positioned between the caption and thead of the table (see the following code, and see the following section for an overview of the various structural elements of tables combined).

```
<colgroup span="2">
<colgroup span="2">
<thead>
  <tr>
    <th scope="colgroup" colspan="2">Fruit</th>
    <th scope="colgroup" colspan="2">Vegetable</th>
  </tr>
  <tr>
    <th scope="col">Citrus</th>
    <th scope="col">Berry</th>
    <th scope="col">Root</th>
    <th scope="col">Legume</th>
  </tr>
</thead>
```

For more complex tables that have intricate structures, using many colspans or rowspans, where it wouldn't be immediately obvious where the relationship lies between a data cell and a header, you can use id values and the headers element. Each table header cell should be assigned a unique id value. Each table data cell that refers to one or more headers requires a headers element. The value of the headers element is the id or ids that the cell data refers to. Even for simpler data tables, this method can work well—see the following code block for how our fruit and vegetables table snippet works with id and headers.

```
<thead>
  <tr>
    <th id="fruit" colspan="2">Fruit</th>
    <th id="vegetables" colspan="2">Vegetable</th>
  </tr>
  <tr>
    <th id="citrus">Citrus</th>
    <th id="berry" >Berry</th>
    <th id="root" >Root</th>
    <th id="legume" >Legume</th>
  </tr>
</thead>

<tbody>
  <tr>
    <td headers="fruit citrus">Lemon</td>
    <td headers="fruit berry">Blueberry</td>
    <td headers="vegetable root">Potato</td>
    <td headers="vegetable legume">Pea</td>
  </tr>
</tbody>
```

Note that the code blocks in this section are here to highlight the attributes and elements being discussed—they should not be seen as examples of complete tables.

You can instead use the axis *attribute to categorize groups of header cells (or data cells), using code such as* <th id="citrus" axis="fruit">. *This helps imply the relationship between groups of headers via the markup, further benefiting screen reader users. This can be particularly useful when an extra header row defining those categories hasn't been used as it is in the previous code block (i.e., if the* fruit *and vegetable headings were omitted).*

Building a table

You're now going to build a table, taking into account all of the information mentioned so far. This will be based on an iTunes playlist.

▲	Name	Time	Artist	Album	Play Count
1	☑ In The Art Of Stopping	3:34	Wire	Send	5
2	☑ Electron John	3:18	Worm Is Green	Push Play	43
3	☑ Templates	6:07	Silo	Instar	11
4	☑ Emerge	4:48	Fischerspooner	Fischerspooner #1	24
5	☑ Banquet	3:21	Bloc Party	Silent Alarm	25
6	☑ Alala	3:58	Cansei De Ser Se...	Cansei De Ser Sexy	10
7	☑ I Ain't Saying My Goodbyes	3:45	Tom Vek	We Have Sound	42
8	☑ Jóga	5:05	Björk	Homogenic	26
9	☑ Kim Wilde	4:21	Charlotte Hatherley	Grey Will Fade	18
10	☑ Witness	4:04	The Delgados	The Great Eastern	10
11	☑ Feel Good Inc.	3:41	Gorillaz	Demon Days	21
12	☑ Returning Wheel	3:26	Malka Spigel	Hide	14
13	☑ P.E.T.R.O.L.	6:21	Orbital	Pi (OST)	10
14	☑ Pweization	3:08	Pop Will Eat Itself...	Karmadrome	12
15	☑ Betrayed	3:05	Project Noise	Listen to me	31
16	☑ When The Sun Hits	4:47	Slowdive	Souvlaki	2
17	☑ Little Eyes	4:20	Yo La Tengo	Summer Sun	29

As you can see from the screenshot, the playlist lends itself well to being converted to an HTML table. At the top is the table head, which details each column's data type (song name, time, etc.). And although there's no table foot, you can simply add some information regarding whose choice of music this is—something of a signature—although the table foot can also be used to provide a succinct summary of the table's contents, akin to the value of the summary attribute discussed earlier.

Building the table

Required files	XHTML-basic.html from the basic-boilerplates folder as a starting point, along with building-the-table-body.txt from the chapter 6 folder.
What you'll learn	How to create a table.
Completed files	building-the-table.html in the chapter 6 folder.

1. Structure the table element. In order to emulate the structure of the iTunes playlist, set the table's width to a percentage value. This means the table will stretch with the browser window. As explained earlier, you should also use the summary attribute to succinctly detail what the table's all about.

```
<table width="90%" border="1" cellspacing="0"
➥ summary="Music selected by Craig Grannell, with details of song,
➥ playing time, artist, album and play count.">
</table>
```

Strictly speaking, the border *attribute should be omitted. However, prior to adding CSS rules, it's a handy way to more prominently show the table's structure in a browser. Note also the use of* cellspacing—*without this, most browsers place gaps between the table cells of unstyled tables.*

2. Add a caption. Immediately after the table start tag, add a caption element to provide the table with a title.

```
<caption>A playlist of great music</caption>
```

3. Add the basic table structure. Use row groups to provide the table with its basic structure.

```
<thead>
</thead>
<tfoot>
</tfoot>
<tbody>
</tbody>
```

> Remember that row groups must be added in the order outlined in the previous "Row groups" section.

4. Using table header cell elements, add the content for the table head (the column headers) as in the following code block, remembering to include relevant scope attribute/value pairs:

```
<thead>
  <tr>
    <th scope="col">Song Name</th>
    <th scope="col">Time</th>
    <th scope="col">Artist</th>
    <th scope="col">Album</th>
    <th scope="col">Play Count</th>
  </tr>
</thead>
```

There's no need to add any styling—not even strong tags. By default, most browsers display table header cell content in bold (and centered) to differentiate it from table data; also, in the following section, you'll be using CSS to style everything, anyway.

> It's always best to keep your HTML as simple as possible, and do any styling in CSS. This reduces page load times, and means that you have a greater degree of control. It also means that people without the ability to view CSS see the browser defaults, which are sensible and clear.

5. Add table foot content. As mentioned, the footer for this table is to essentially be a signature, stating who's at fault for this selection of music. Because this is a single line of text that could potentially span the entire table width, simply include a single table cell, set to span five rows (using the `colspan` attribute).

```
<tfoot>
  <tr><td colspan="5">Music selection by:
  ➡ www.snubcommunications.com</td></tr>
</tfoot>
```

6. Add table body content. Finally, add the table's body content via the usual method, using table row and table cell elements. This table will have nearly 20 rows, so to save on trees, only the first two rows are detailed in the following printed code block—you can add all the others in the same way, or just copy across the content of `building-the-table-body.txt` from the download files, to save inputting the data yourself.

```
<tbody>
  <tr>
    <td>In The Art Of Stopping</td>
    <td>3:34</td>
    <td>Wire</td>
    <td>Send</td>
    <td>3</td>
  </tr>
  <tr>
    <td>Electron John</td>
    <td>3:18</td>
    <td>Worm Is Green</td>
    <td>Push Play</td>
    <td>42</td>
  </tr>
</tbody>
```

6

> *Take care that your table body content aligns correctly with your table headers. Badly formed tables are one thing, but when the headers and data don't correlate, the table is useless.*

The following image shows the table so far.

A playlist of great music				
Song Name	**Time**	**Artist**	**Album**	**Play Count**
In The Art Of Stopping	3:34	Wire	Send	3
Electron John	3:18	Worm Is Green	Push Play	42
Templates	6:07	Silo	Instar	9
Emerge	4:48	Fischerspooner	Fischerspooner #1	23
Banquet	3:21	Bloc Party	Silent Alarm	23
Alala	3:58	Cansei De Ser Sexy (CSS)	Cansei De Ser Sexy	6
I Ain't Saying My Goodbyes	3:45	Tom Vek	We Have Sound	40
Jóga	5:05	Björk	Homogenic	24
Kim Wilde	4:21	Charlotte Hatherley	Grey Will Fade	16
Witness	4:04	The Delgados	The Great Eastern	9
Feel Good Inc.	3:41	Gorillaz	Demon Days	20
Returning Wheel	3:26	Malka Spigel	Hide	13
P.E.T.R.O.L.	6:21	Orbital	Pi (OST)	8
Pweization	3:08	Pop Will Eat Itself (PWEI)	Karmadrome	11
Betrayed	3:05	Project Noise	Listen to me	31
When The Sun Hits	4:47	Slowdive	Souvlaki	1
Little Eyes	4:20	Yo La Tengo	Summer Sun	28
Music selection by: www.snubcommunications.com				

This table's not pretty, but it's structurally sound, and it includes all the relevant elements to at least help make it accessible. As you can see, the addition of the caption and table header cells also makes a difference. If you're unsure of this, look at the following screenshot of the same table, with plain table data cells throughout and no caption.

Song Name	Time	Artist	Album	Play Count
In The Art Of Stopping	3:34	Wire	Send	3
Electron John	3:18	Worm Is Green	Push Play	42
Templates	6:07	Silo	Instar	9
Emerge	4:48	Fischerspooner	Fischerspooner #1	23
Banquet	3:21	Bloc Party	Silent Alarm	23
Alala	3:58	Cansei De Ser Sexy (CSS)	Cansei De Ser Sexy	6
I Ain't Saying My Goodbyes	3:45	Tom Vek	We Have Sound	40
Jóga	5:05	Björk	Homogenic	24
Kim Wilde	4:21	Charlotte Hatherley	Grey Will Fade	16
Witness	4:04	The Delgados	The Great Eastern	9
Feel Good Inc.	3:41	Gorillaz	Demon Days	20
Returning Wheel	3:26	Malka Spigel	Hide	13
P.E.T.R.O.L.	6:21	Orbital	Pi (OST)	8
Pweization	3:08	Pop Will Eat Itself (PWEI)	Karmadrome	11
Betrayed	3:05	Project Noise	Listen to me	31
When The Sun Hits	4:47	Slowdive	Souvlaki	1
Little Eyes	4:20	Yo La Tengo	Summer Sun	28
Music selection by: www.snubcommunications.com				

All the information might be there, but it's harder to pick out the headers, and users will have to rely on body copy elsewhere to discover what the data in the table represents.

Styling a table

Flip back over the past few pages and you might notice that the table doesn't exactly bear a striking resemblance to the iTunes playlist as yet. But then, we're only halfway through building the table. Now it's time to start styling it using CSS.

Adding borders to tables

As mentioned earlier, it's a good policy to avoid using the default HTML table border. It looks ugly and old-fashioned, and it's a far cry from a clean, flat, 1-pixel border. You might think it's a straightforward process to add CSS borders to a table—logically, it makes sense to simply add a border property/value pair to a grouped selector that takes care of both the table headers and table data cells.

```
th, td {
  border: 1px solid #c9c9c9;
}
```

But this doesn't work. As the screenshot to the right shows, this method results in the correct single-pixel border around the edge of the table, but creates double-thick borders everywhere else. This is because the borders don't collapse by default, meaning that the right-hand border of one cell sits next to the left-hand border of an adjacent cell, and so on.

Designers have historically gotten around this by using a rule to define a style for the top and left borders of the table, and another to define a style for the right and bottom borders of table cells. However, there's a perfectly good property that deals with the double-border syndrome: border-collapse. When this property, with a value of collapse, is applied to the table element via an element selector, borders collapse to a single border wherever possible. The other available border-collapse property value, which reverts borders back to their "standard" state, is separate.

```
table {
  border-collapse: collapse;
}
```

With this brief explanation of table borders completed, we'll now move into exercise mode and style the table.

Styling the playlist table

Required files	styling-the-playlist-table-starting-point.html, styling-the-playlist-table-starting-point.css, and table-header-stripe.gif from the chapter 6 folder.
What you'll learn	How to style a table.
Completed files	styling-the-playlist-table.html and styling-the-playlist-table.css in the chapter 6 folder (along with the GIF image, which isn't amended).

1. Set things up. If they still exist, remove the border, cellpadding, and cellspacing attributes within the table start tag. Add the universal selector rule (*) to remove margins and padding, as shown a bunch of times already in this book. Also, set the default font by using the html and body rules, as detailed in Chapter 3 of this book. Because we're creating a playlist based on the iTunes interface, it may as well be a little more Apple-like, hence the use of Lucida variants as the primary fonts. Note that the padding value in the body rule is there to ensure that the table doesn't hug the browser window when you're previewing the page.

```
* {
  padding: 0;
  margin: 0;
}
html {
  font-size: 100%;
}
body {
  font: 62.5%/1.5 "Lucida Grande", "Lucida Sans Unicode", Arial,
  ➥ Helvetica, sans-serif;
  padding: 20px;
}
```

2. Style the table borders. As per the "Adding borders to tables" section, style the table borders.

```
table {
  border-collapse: collapse;
}
th, td {
  border: 1px solid #c9c9c9;
}
```

3. Style the caption. The borders have been dealt with already, so the next step is to style the caption, which currently lacks impact. The caption is effectively a title, and titles should stand out. Therefore, place some padding underneath it, set font-weight to bold, font-size to 1.3em, and text-transform to uppercase.

Note that, in the following code block, CSS shorthand is used for three values for setting padding; as you may remember from Chapter 2, the three values set the top, horizontal (left and right), and bottom values, respectively; meaning the caption will have 0px padding everywhere except at the bottom, where the padding will be 5px.

> Note that Internet Explorer exhibits slightly quirky behavior when it comes to styling caption elements, so be sure to thoroughly test any styles you define for this element.

```
caption {
  font-weight: bold;
  font-size: 1.3em;
  text-transform: uppercase;
  padding: 0 0 5px;
}
```

6

A PLAYLIST OF GREAT MUSIC				
Song Name	Time	Artist	Album	Play Count
In The Art Of Stopping	3:34	Wire	Send	3
Electron John	3:18	Worm Is Green	Push Play	42
Templates	6:07	Silo	Instar	0

4. Style the header cells. To make the header cells stand out more, apply the CSS rule outlined in the following code block. The url value set in the background property adds a background image to the table headers, which mimics the subtle metallic image shown in the same portion of the iTunes interface; the 0 50% values vertically center the graphic; and the repeat-x setting tiles the image horizontally. From a design standpoint, the default centered table heading text looks iffy, hence the addition of a text-align property set to left. These settings ensure that the table header contents stand out from the standard data cell content.

```
th {
  background: url(table-header-stripe.gif) 0 50% repeat-x;
  text-align: left;
}
```

5. Set the font and pad the cells. At the moment, the table cell text hugs the borders, so it needs some padding; the text is also too small to comfortably read, so its size needs increasing. This is dealt with by adding font-size and padding pairs to the th, td rule, as shown:

```
th, td {
  border: 1px solid #c9c9c9;
  font-size: 1.1em;
  padding: 1px 4px;
}
```

6. Style the footer. The footer content needs to be easy to differentiate from the other data cells; you can achieve this by setting a background color for the entire row within the tfoot element, and then by making the color of the text have less contrast. Also, centering the text and making it smaller than text within the other data cells ensures it doesn't distract from the main content in the table. Centering it also provides some balance, because the caption is also centered.

```css
tfoot {
  background-color: #dddddd;
  color: #555555;
}
  tfoot td {
  font-size: 1.0em;
  text-align: center;
}
```

A PLAYLIST OF GREAT MUSIC				
Song Name	**Time**	**Artist**	**Album**	**Play Count**
In The Art Of Stopping	3:34	Wire	Send	3
Electron John	3:18	Worm Is Green	Push Play	42
Templates	6:07	Silo	Instar	9
Emerge	4:48	Fischerspooner	Fischerspooner #1	23
Banquet	3:21	Bloc Party	Silent Alarm	23
Alala	3:58	Cansei De Ser Sexy (CSS)	Cansei De Ser Sexy	6
I Ain't Saying My Goodbyes	3:45	Tom Vek	We Have Sound	40
Jóga	5:05	Björk	Homogenic	24
Kim Wilde	4:21	Charlotte Hatherley	Grey Will Fade	16
Witness	4:04	The Delgados	The Great Eastern	9
Feel Good Inc.	3:41	Gorillaz	Demon Days	20
Returning Wheel	3:26	Malka Spigel	Hide	13
P.E.T.R.O.L.	6:21	Orbital	Pi (OST)	8
Pweization	3:08	Pop Will Eat Itself (PWEI)	Karmadrome	11
Betrayed	3:05	Project Noise	Listen to me	31
When The Sun Hits	4:47	Slowdive	Souvlaki	1
Little Eyes	4:20	Yo La Tengo	Summer Sun	28
Music selection by: www.snubcommunications.com				

In Chapter 3, we warned against using text with low contrast against a background graphic. In the case of the table's footer in this exercise, the contrast is lower than for other text, but it's still readable; also, the content is not a huge chunk of body copy— it's only a single line of text.

Adding separator stripes

One of iTunes's best visual features (and something seen in usable tables all over the Internet, but more often in print and in applications) is missing from the completed table: colored separator stripes, which assist you in rapidly scanning rows of data. Although you could conceivably add a class (setting a background color) to alternating rows, such a solution is poor when creating a static site—if you had to add a row in the middle of the table, you'd need to update every subsequent table row start tag, which is hardly efficient.

David Miller's article, "Zebra Tables," on A List Apart (see www.alistapart.com/articles/zebratables/), offers a far more elegant solution. This was later reworked by Matthew Pennell (www.thewatchmakerproject.com), whose article "Stripe Your Tables the OO Way" (www.thewatchmakerproject.com/journal/309/stripe-your-tables-the-oo-way) offers the lowdown on his technique, including an improved version of his script at www.thewatchmakerproject.com/zebra.html.

Applying separator stripes

Required files	styling-the-playlist-table.html, styling-the-playlist-table.css, table-header-stripe.gif, and styling-the-playlist-table-stripes.js from the chapter 6 folder.
What you'll learn	How to add separator stripes to a table.
Completed files	styling-the-playlist-table-stripes.html and styling-the-playlist-table-stripes.css in the chapter 6 folder (along with the GIF image and JavaScript document, neither of which are amended).

6

1. Link to the JavaScript document. Taking things up from the completed table from the previous exercise (also available in the download files as styling-the-playlist-table.html and styling-the-playlist-table.css), add a script element in the HTML document's head section to link to the JavaScript file styling-the-playlist-table.js. Note that the JavaScript document is also available in the download files.

```
<script src="styling-the-playlist-table-stripes.js"
➥ type="text/javascript"></script>
```

2. Give the table a unique id. For the script to do its work, the table start tag must be given a unique id value. This must match the value given in styling-the-playlist-table.js in the onload function. Therefore, add the id attribute and value shown in the following code block:

```
<table id="playlist1" width="90%" border="0" summary="A playlist of
➥ great music, selected by www.snubcommunications.com.">
```

In the JavaScript, the relevant code that matches this is already defined, as shown in the following code block:

```
window.onload = function() {
  zebraTable.stripe('playlist1');
}
```

3. Assign a separator stripe style. The script creates alternating table rows, which are given a class value of alt. This can then be styled in CSS by using a rule with the selector tbody tr.alt td:

```
tbody tr.alt td {
   background: #e7edf6;
}
```

The previous code block styles the background of alternate rows in a light blue.

4. Define a table row hover state. The script also provides a hover state, making it easy for users to highlight entire table rows by placing the mouse cursor over one of the row's cells. This is styled using the rule shown in the following code block. Note that both background and color settings are defined, which pretty much reverse the standard colors (white on blue, rather than black on a light color). This makes the highlighted row stand out more, and is the same device applications tend to use. Also note that there are two selectors here. The first is for compliant browsers, which apply :hover rules to more than just anchors. The second is a fall-back for older versions of Internet Explorer (before version 7), which didn't do this.

```
tbody tr:hover td, tbody tr.over td {
   background: #5389d7;
   color: #ffffff;
}
```

5. Remove some horizontal borders. With the stripes in place, the top and bottom borders of table cells in the tbody area are now redundant. Therefore, remove them by adding the following rule:

```
tbody td {
   border-top: 0;
   border-bottom: 0;
}
```

Your table should now look like the following image.

A PLAYLIST OF GREAT MUSIC

Song Name	Time	Artist	Album	Play Count
In The Art Of Stopping	3:34	Wire	Send	3
Electron John	3:18	Worm Is Green	Push Play	42
Templates	6:07	Silo	Instar	9
Emerge	4:48	Fischerspooner	Fischerspooner #1	23
Banquet	3:21	Bloc Party	Silent Alarm	23
Alala	3:58	Cansei De Ser Sexy (CSS)	Cansei De Ser Sexy	6
I Ain't Saying My Goodbyes	3:45	Tom Vek	We Have Sound	40
Jóga	5:05	Björk	Homogenic	24
Kim Wilde	4:21	Charlotte Hatherley	Grey Will Fade	16
Witness	4:04	The Delgados	The Great Eastern	9
Feel Good Inc.	3:41	Gorillaz	Demon Days	20
Returning Wheel	3:26	Malka Spigel	Hide	13
P.E.T.R.O.L.	6:21	Orbital	Pi (OST)	8
Pweization	3:08	Pop Will Eat Itself (PWEI)	Karmadrome	11
Betrayed	3:05	Project Noise	Listen to me	31
When The Sun Hits	4:47	Slowdive	Souvlaki	1
Little Eyes	4:20	Yo La Tengo	Summer Sun	28

Music selection by: www.snubcommunications.com

> *To add stripes to more tables, just assign each one a unique* id *value and then add another line to the* window.onload *function in the JavaScript document, as per the instructions in this exercise. For example, if you added a table with an* id *value of* playlist2, *the line of JavaScript to add to the function would be* ZebraTable.stripe('playlist2');.

Adding separator stripes with PHP

If you're creating a table from data stored in a database, automating separator stripes is a relatively simple process. After the PHP for retrieving data and the opening table markup (including headers), you add the following:

```php
$alternate = TRUE;
while ($row = mysql_fetch_object($sqlresult)) :
  if($alternate) :
    $class = ' class="alt"';
    $alternate = FALSE;
  else :
    $class = "";
    $alternate = TRUE;
  endif;

  echo '<tr'.$class.'>';
  echo '<td>' . $row->field1 . '</td>';
  echo '<td>' . $row->field2 . '</td>';
  echo '</tr>';
endwhile;
```

This is then followed by the markup to close the table. Note that in this example, the alt class value is applied to alternate table rows, so the CSS from the previous exercise should still work fine.

Tables for layout

This section is going to be brief, because you should avoid using tables for layout, or even components of a layout (excepting tabular data, obviously). There are exceptions—for instance, some web designers consider tables acceptable for laying out forms. However, generally speaking, tables are less accessible than CSS, harder to maintain and update, slow to render in browsers, and don't print particularly well. More importantly, once you know how to create CSS-based layouts, you'll mostly find working with tables for layout frustrating and clunky.

A common way of creating tabular layouts is to chop up a Photoshop layout and use images to stretch table cells to the correct size. (As mentioned earlier, table cells expand to the dimensions of their content.) Many designers then use a 1-pixel invisible GIF89 (often referred to as a spacer or shim) to force content into position or stretch table cells to a certain size. Because the 1-pixel GIF is a tiny file that's cached, it can be used hundreds of times without impacting download times. However, spacer and table layout usage pretty much destroys the idea of a semantic Web. Because so much of the layout is defined via inline HTML, updating it requires amendments to every page on the site (which must also be uploaded and tested in each case), rather than the simple editing and uploading of an external CSS file.

It is possible to combine CSS and tables—something that's usually referred to as a transitional layout, although one might argue that the "transition" from tables to CSS layouts should now be considered an historic event. Such layouts are usually created to ensure layout-based backward compatibility with obsolete devices. This direction should only be taken when the target audience is known to definitely include a *significant* number of users of very obsolete browsers, and also when the layout is paramount to the working of the site (rather than just the content). When working on such a layout, there are a few golden rules:

- **Avoid nesting tables whenever possible**: Although tables can be nested like any other HTML element, doing so makes for a web page that is slow to render and nightmarish to navigate for a screen reader. (Obviously, there are exceptions, such as if you need to present a table of tabular data within your layout table.)

- **Structure the information on the page logically**: When designers use tables (particularly those exported from a graphics package), they have a tendency to think solely about how the page looks rather than its underlying code. However, it's important to look at how the information appears in the HTML, because that's how a screen reader will see it. The content should still make sense with regard to its flow and order even if the table is removed entirely. If it doesn't, you need to rework your table. (You can use Opera's User mode to temporarily disable tables to find out how your information is ordered without them. Chris Pederick's Web Developer toolbar for Firefox [www.chrispederick.com/work/web-developer/] offers similar functionality via Miscellaneous ➤ Linearize Page.) Ensure that content is immediately available; if it isn't, provide a link that skips past extraneous content, such as the masthead and navigation—otherwise, people using screen readers will be driven bonkers. (See www.w3.org/TR/WAI-WEBCONTENT/ for more on web content accessibility guidelines.)

- **Avoid deprecated attributes**: For instance, there's little point in setting the table's height to 100% when many web browsers ignore that rule (or need to be in quirks mode to support it).

- **Use CSS whenever possible to position elements**: To give an example—if you're working with a 3-cell table and want the middle cell's content to begin 100 pixels from the top of the cell, don't use a spacer GIF. Instead, provide the cell with a class or unique ID, and use CSS padding.

The last two of these rules are primarily concerned with ensuring that if you design for legacy browsers, you don't compromise your work for more modern efforts.

As I keep hammering home, CSS is the way to go for high-quality, modern web page layouts, and tables should be left for the purpose for which they were designed—formatting data. The arguments that rumbled on for a few years after the 1990s came to a close—that browsers didn't support enough CSS to make CSS layouts possible, and that visual design tools such as Dreamweaver couldn't cope with CSS layouts—are now pretty much moot. Even the *previous major release* of the worst offender (yes, I'm talking about Internet Explorer 6) has more than adequate support for the vast majority of CSS layouts, and anything shipping today is more than capable of dealing with CSS.

In my experience, the main reason designers avoid CSS involves their not knowing how to work with it. Suitably, then, the next chapter deals with this very issue—showing how to create page layout elements using CSS.

6

7 PAGE LAYOUTS WITH CSS

— COMING SOON —

The Simping Detective
Simon Spurrier

Judge Dredd: Mandr
John Wagner

elit. Morbi
rhoncus
amet enim.

um. Aliquam
o. Vivamus
quam, nunc
orci,

consequat
an eu,
ui. Nam

BOXOUT TITLE

Phasellus aliquam enim et t
Quisque aliquet, quam elem
condimentum feugiat, tellus
consectetuer wisi, vel nonun
sem neque in elit. Curabitur
eleifend wisi iaculis ipsum.
Pellentesque habitant morbi
tristique senectus et netus e
malesuada fames ac turpis
egestas. In non velit non lig
laoreet ultrices. Praesent ult

m guitarist and main tunesmith. In
'emier back-room boy,
nd authoring all Wire releases. He
es new and archive Wire material,

lin has worked on many other
ums, he's produced, arranged
Compact, French megastar Alain
Silo.

SELECTED WORKS
Being Sucked In Again

"There's something
wholly inexplicable about
this song. Each verse is
in a separate key and the
lyric, inspired by the
legend of the succubus,
has a nightmarish
quality. Yet despite this,
the piece has a timeless quality. I love the
beginning, the way the synth chords ping in like
child miming a bullet (the result of a poor
drop-in), the bass pedal and heavily 'mutronne'
guitar crashes that prefigure the arrival of the
guitar riff and drums, when the whole thing shi
up a gear. One of the best Wire intros ever!"

Madman's Honey (Alternate Mix)

"This has always been my
preferred version of this
song, done for a single
that never got released.
The main synth line was
based on the guitar line
the song was written
around, and during

Wire's 'retrospective' period in 2000 we did an
all-guitar version—a stage highlight! Like most
1980s Wire, which in my view is cast in an

In this chapter:

- Explaining CSS workflow
- Positioning web page elements with CSS
- Creating boxouts and sidebars
- Creating column-based layouts
- Amending layouts, depending on body class settings
- Creating scrollable content areas

Layout for the Web

Although recent years have seen various institutions offer web-oriented courses, the fact remains that many web designers out there are not "qualified," per se. What I mean by this is that plenty of them have come from some sort of design or technology background related to—but not necessarily a part of—the Web. Therefore, we often see print designers moving over to the Web through curiosity or sheer necessity and technologists dipping their toes into the field of design.

This accounts for the most common issues seen in web layouts: many designers coming from print try to shoehorn their knowledge into their website designs, despite the Web being a very different medium from print. Conversely, those with no design knowledge lack the basic foundations and often omit design staples. Even those of us who've worked with the Web almost from the beginning and who also come from a design or arts background sometimes forget that the best sites tend to be those that borrow the best ideas from a range of media, and then tailor the results to the desired output medium.

In this section, we'll take a brief look at a few layout techniques: grids and boxes, columns, and fixed vs. liquid design.

Grids and boxes

Like print-oriented design, the basis of web page design tends to be formed from grids and boxes. Regardless of the underlying layout technology (previously, tables; more recently, CSS), web pages are formed of rectangular areas that are then populated with content. However, unlike print design, web design tends to be horizontally and vertically oriented, with few, if any, curves. This is largely because of the limitations of technology; although text on a curve is a relatively simple thing to achieve in a desktop publishing application, doing the same thing on the Web is extremely difficult, unless you're rendering text as a graphic, or using XML (SVG), which isn't well supported across browsers. Similarly, although areas of rectangular color can easily be defined in CSS (by creating a div of certain dimensions and then setting its background color), you currently need to use graphics to have curved background areas and shapes (although rounded corners on rectangular boxes can be dynamically added using JavaScript—see Nifty Corners Cube at www.html.it/articoli/niftycube/).

A good rule of thumb for web design is to keep things relatively simple. Plan the layout on paper prior to going near any design applications, and simplify the structure as much as possible. A typical web page may end up with as few as three or four structural areas (such as masthead, navigation, content, and footer areas), which can then be styled to define their relationship with each other and the page as a whole.

Working with columns

The vast majority of print media makes heavy use of columns. The main reason for this is that the eye generally finds it easier to read narrow columns of text than paragraphs that span the width of an entire page. However, when working with print, you have a finite and predefined area within which to work, and by and large, the "user" can see the entire page at once. Therefore, relationships between page elements can be created over the entire page, and the eye can rapidly scan columns of text.

On the Web, things aren't so easy. Web pages may span more than the screen height, meaning that only the top portion of the page is initially visible. Should a print page be translated directly to the Web, you may find that some elements essential for understanding the page's content are low down the page and not initially visible. Furthermore, if using columns for text and content, you may end up forcing the user to scroll down and up the page several times. Finally, it's almost impossible—due to the variations in output from various browsers and platforms—to ensure that text columns are the same length anyway. (CSS should eventually enable designers to more easily deal with these problems, but it will be some time before such solutions are supported.)

Therefore, web designers tend to eschew columns—but let's not be too hasty. It's worth bearing in mind something mentioned earlier: the eye finds it tricky to read wide columns of text. Therefore, it's often good practice to limit the width of body copy on a website to a comfortable reading width. Also, if you have multiple pieces of content that you want the user to be able to access at the same time, columns can come in handy. This can be seen in the following screenshots from the Thalamus Publishing website (www.thalamus-books.com).

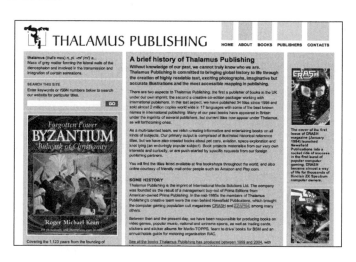

As you can see, the main, central column of the About page provides an overview of the company. To the left is the site-wide search and an advertisement for one of the company's publications; and to the right is a sidebar that provides ancillary information to support the main text. This provides text columns that are a comfortable, readable width, and enables faster access to information than if the page content were placed in a linear, vertical fashion.

Fixed vs. liquid design

As already mentioned in this book, the Web is a unique medium in that end users have numerous different systems for viewing the web page. When designing for print, the dimensions of each design are fixed, and although television resolutions are varied (PAL, NTSC, HDTV), those designing for the screen work within a fixed frame—and regardless of the size of the screen, the picture content is always the same.

In a similar fashion, it's possible to design fixed-width sites for the Web. The earlier shot of the Thalamus Books site is an example of this. Fixed-width sites are beneficial in that they enable you to position elements exactly on a web page. However, because they don't expand with the browser window, fixed-width sites restrict you to designing for the lowest common screen size for your intended audience, meaning that people using larger resolutions see an area of blank space (or a background pattern).

You can get around this limitation by creating a **liquid** web design—one that stretches with the web browser window. The benefit of a liquid design is that it's irrelevant what resolution the end user's machine has—the design stretches to fit. The drawback is that you have to be mindful when designing that web page elements move, depending on each end user's monitor resolution and/or browser window size. You therefore cannot place elements with pixel-perfect precision.

Generally speaking, largely text-based sites tend to work best with liquid layouts, although you have to take care to ensure the content area is always readable. (I've seen numerous liquid sites where the text spans the entire web page width, which is tricky enough to read at 800×600, let alone on larger monitor resolutions.) Sites that are largely image-based in nature (such as portfolios and many online magazines) tend to work better as fixed websites. For instance, for any site with fixed-width images at the top of text columns (common for online magazines), the images would not sit snugly within the columns if the layout were liquid, and could instead end up lost among large areas of whitespace.

Overall, though, there are no hard-and-fast rules and, despite what some designers might claim, neither fixed nor liquid design is better than the alternative. You should use whatever technique is suitable for each project you work on. Later in the chapter, you'll see various methods for creating strict, fixed layout skeletons, liquid designs, and combinations of the two. Some of these will then be turned into full page designs in Chapter 10.

Layout technology: Tables vs. CSS

Unless you're the sort of person who favors very basic web pages, with most elements sitting underneath each other, you'll need to employ some kind of layout technology when designing your web pages. Historically, web designers tended to use tables for doing this, combined with invisible GIFs (sometimes called spacers or shims) to stretch table cells to the required size. In the early 2000s, CSS layouts gained a foothold, and now more and more designers are moving toward CSS as a means of page layout.

With few exceptions, pretty much everything you can do with a table can be done faster, better, and with a greater emphasis on accessibility when using CSS. With content and design separated, it's much easier to tweak or rework a website, because you're editing an external document that controls spacing and positioning, rather than messing around with complex tables. We discuss one of CSS's major benefits in this regard, how it encourages logical element placement, in the next section. Tables should really be reserved for their original purpose: formatting tabular data.

Logical element placement

Besides the ability to rapidly edit CSS-based layouts, the greatest benefit when using CSS is the emphasis on accessibility, partly because it encourages the designer to think about the structure of the document, and therefore logically place the elements within the web page (first comes the masthead, then the navigation, then the content, etc.). Each element is then styled to suit.

Using CSS for layout instead of tables is one way of working toward this ideal. The logical placement of each element in the web page's structure results in improved document flow. And if you're scratching your head, wondering what on earth I'm talking about, let me explain. A web page should still make sense if you remove all formatting and design elements. This is how a screen reader sees the page—it simply reads from the top of the HTML page downward. Because of the way table-based layouts are created, most designers aren't concerned with how the document is structured—merely how it looks. Therefore, although one element may follow another *visually* onscreen, that may not be the case when you look at the document's code. (Also, tables tend to encourage superfluous markup, which can also hamper accessibility.) When working with CSS, the structure of the web page isn't compromised.

Workflow for CSS layouts

Many designers use CSS for styling fonts, but few venture further. This section—and, indeed, much of this chapter—shows how straightforward creating CSS layouts can be, so long as you carefully plan what you're going to do. Upon working through the chapter, the benefits of a CSS-based system will become obvious, including the following: rapidly editing a website's entire visual appearance from a single, external file; fine-tuning the placement of elements; and creating flowing, accessible pages.

Before we begin, it is worth mentioning that some browsers have problems with CSS, and this is often given as a reason to not proceed with CSS-based layouts. Of those browsers still in widespread use, Internet Explorer 6 (and the increasingly rare 5.x) for Windows causes the most frustration; however, that browser's usage is in terminal decline. And although Safari, Opera, Firefox, and Internet Explorer 7 don't always see eye to eye, their

7

differences are generally slight. For supporting earlier browsers and dealing with bugs, there are usually simple workarounds anyway (see Chapter 9), leading me to believe that many naysayers of CSS are negative because they don't know how to create such layouts.

Anatomy of a layout: Tables vs. CSS

To use a fine art analogy, working with tables is like painting by numbers: you create a skeleton layout and then fill in the gaps with the content of choice. And, like painting by numbers, a lot of work is required to change the layout after it's completed. Working with CSS is more akin to sculpting with clay: you begin with something simple and then gradually fashion your layout. Making changes, tweaks, and even additions at a later date is simpler, and the whole process feels more organic.

Long-time web designers may feel intimidated by CSS because they don't initially have the skeleton layout of table borders to work with. In some ways, CSS sits at the extremes of web technologies, being both very graphic and design-like (in its flexibility), but also quite technical (in how it's created). Tables tend to sit in the middle of these two extremes. However, once you get the hang of CSS workflow, it soon becomes second nature. Now, we'll look at how to create a web page structure, and we'll then recap the CSS box model.

Creating a page structure

We've covered semantic markup—that is, using HTML elements for the purpose for which they were created. This theme continues when working with CSS-based layouts. With tables, cells are used to lay out a design and are merged, split, chopped, and changed until everything works visually. But when working with CSS, you need to be aware of the structure of your web page from the start. That way, you can create structural elements with id values that relate to their purpose, and then style them to suit.

For basic page structure, you mostly work with the div element. This element has been around for some time, but used to be used for aligning text left, right, or centrally. However, its real purpose is as a divider element, used to divide a document into block-level groups or divisions. Therefore, in CSS-based layouts, the div element's role is pivotal: a number of divs are added to the web page in logical order, creating the basic structure; each is provided with a unique id relating to its purpose; and the divs are then styled to provide spacing, padding, backgrounds, and so on.

> *Just as tables can be abused, so too can div elements. Some websites seemingly suffer from "divitis," in which designers use too many divs, nesting many inside each other or adding superfluous divs around elements that don't need them. In all cases, you should hone down your structure, using as few div elements as possible.*

Box formatting

The box model is mentioned elsewhere in this book (see Chapter 2 and again in Appendix D—CSS Reference), and this is a timely place for a recap, because the box model is something that confuses some web designers.

In CSS, every element is considered to be within its own box, and you can define the dimensions of the content and then add padding, a border, and a margin to each edge as required, as shown in the following image.

THE CSS BOX MODEL HIERARCHY

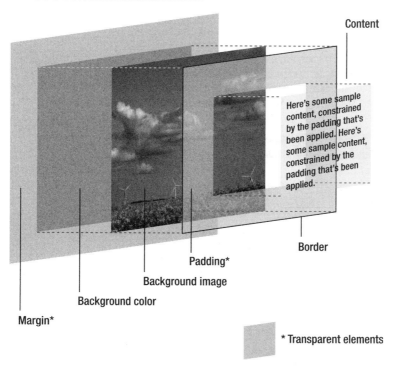

Content

Here's some sample content, constrained by the padding that's been applied. Here's some sample content, constrained by the padding that's been applied.

Border

Padding*

Background image

Background color

Margin*

* Transparent elements

© Jon Hicks (www.hicksdesign.co.uk)

This is one of the trickiest things to understand about the CSS box model: padding, borders, and margins are added to the set dimensions of the content, and so the sum of these elements is the overall space that they take up. In other words, a 100-pixel-wide element with 20 pixels of padding will take up an overall width of 140 pixels, not 100 pixels with 20 pixels of padding within.

Note that the top and bottom margins on adjacent elements collapse, meaning that the overall box dimensions aren't necessarily fixed, depending on your design. For instance, if you set the bottom margin to 50px on an element, and you have a top margin of 100px on the element below it, the effective margin between the two elements will be 100 pixels, not 150 pixels.

> Internet Explorer 5.x for Windows gets the box model wrong, placing padding and borders inside the defined dimensions of an element. The bug is explained in full in Chapter 9, which also offers workarounds to fix layouts that get broken in aging versions of Microsoft's browser.

CSS layouts: A single box

In the remainder of this chapter, we'll walk through a number of common CSS layout techniques, which can be combined to form countless layouts. In Chapter 10, these skeleton layouts will form the basis of various full web page layouts, which will also integrate techniques shown elsewhere in the book (such as navigation bars).

The starting point for any layout is a single box, which this section concentrates on. I typically refer to these as "wrappers" (and accordingly provide said divs with an id value of wrapper); and you can think of them as site containers, used to define a width for the site, or set a fixed-size design in the center of the browser window.

Creating a fixed-width wrapper

Required files	Files from the basic-boilerplates folder as a starting point.
What you'll learn	How to create a fixed-width div.
Completed files	create-a-fixed-width-wrapper in the chapter 7 folder.

1. Set things up. Rename the boilerplate documents to create-a-fixed-width-wrapper.html and create-a-fixed-width-wrapper.css. Link the CSS document to the web page by amending the url value of the style element.

   @import url(**create-a-fixed-width-wrapper**.css);

2. Add some content. The web page already has a div element with an id of wrapper. Within it, add a bunch of paragraphs and test the web page. You'll see that the content stretches with the browser window and goes right up to its edges—this is a basic liquid design. If the browser window is very wide, this makes the content all but unreadable.

Lorem ipsum dolor sit amet, consectetuer adipiscing elit. Morbi commodo, ipsum sed pharetra gravida, orci magna rhoncus neque, id pulvinar odio lorem non turpis. Nullam sit amet enim.

Suspendisse id velit vitae ligula volutpat condimentum. Aliquam erat volutpat. Sed quis velit. Nulla facilisi. Nulla libero. Vivamus pharetra posuere sapien. Nam consectetuer. Sed aliquam, nunc eget euismod ullamcorper, lectus nunc ullamcorper orci, fermentum bibendum enim nibh eget ipsum.

Donec porttitor ligula eu dolor. Maecenas vitae nulla consequat libero cursus venenatis. Nam magna enim, accumsan eu, blandit sed, blandit a, eros. Quisque facilisis erat a dui. Nam malesuada ornare dolor. Cras gravida, diam sit amet rhoncus ornare, erat elit consectetuer erat, id egestas pede nibh eget odio.

Proin tincidunt, velit vel porta elementum, magna diam molestie sapien, non aliquet massa pede eu diam. Aliquam iaculis. Fusce et ipsum et nulla tristique facilisis. Donec eget sem sit amet ligula viverra gravida. Etiam vehicula urna vel turpis. Suspendisse sagittis ante a urna.

Morbi a est quis orci consequat rutrum. Nullam egestas feugiat felis. Integer adipiscing semper ligula. Nunc molestie, nisl sit amet cursus convallis, sapien lectus pretium metus, vitae pretium enim wisi id lectus. Donec vestibulum. Etiam vel nibh. Nulla facilisi. Mauris pharetra. Donec augue. Fusce ultrices, neque id dignissim ultrices, tellus mauris dictum elit, vel lacinia enim metus eu nunc.

Proin at eros non eros adipiscing mollis. Donec semper turpis sed diam. Sed consequat ligula nec tortor. Integer eget sem. Ut vitae enim eu est vehicula gravida. Morbi ipsum ipsum, porta nec, tempor id, auctor vitae, purus. Pellentesque neque. Nulla luctus erat vitae libero. Integer nec enim.

3. Restrict the wrapper's width. In CSS, add the following rule:

```
#wrapper {
  width: 600px;
  margin: 0 auto;
}
```

The `width` setting defines a width in pixels for the wrapper div. The `margin` setting provides automatic margins to the left and right of the div, which has the effect of centering the layout in the browser window, as shown in the following screenshot.

Lorem ipsum dolor sit amet, consectetuer adipiscing elit. Morbi commodo, ipsum sed pharetra gravida, orci magna rhoncus neque, id pulvinar odio lorem non turpis. Nullam sit amet enim.

Suspendisse id velit vitae ligula volutpat condimentum. Aliquam erat volutpat. Sed quis velit. Nulla facilisi. Nulla libero. Vivamus pharetra posuere sapien. Nam consectetuer. Sed aliquam, nunc eget euismod ullamcorper, lectus nunc ullamcorper orci, fermentum bibendum enim nibh eget ipsum.

Donec porttitor ligula eu dolor. Maecenas vitae nulla consequat libero cursus venenatis. Nam magna enim, accumsan eu, blandit sed, blandit a, eros. Quisque facilisis erat a dui. Nam malesuada ornare dolor. Cras gravida, diam sit amet rhoncus ornare, erat elit consectetuer erat, id egestas pede nibh eget odio.

Proin tincidunt, velit vel porta elementum, magna diam molestie sapien, non aliquet massa pede eu diam. Aliquam iaculis. Fusce et ipsum et nulla tristique facilisis. Donec eget sem sit amet ligula viverra gravida. Etiam vehicula urna vel turpis. Suspendisse sagittis ante a urna.

Morbi a est quis orci consequat rutrum. Nullam egestas feugiat felis. Integer adipiscing semper ligula. Nunc molestie, nisl sit amet cursus convallis, sapien lectus pretium metus, vitae pretium enim wisi id lectus. Donec vestibulum. Etiam vel nibh. Nulla facilisi. Mauris pharetra. Donec augue. Fusce ultrices, neque id dignissim ultrices, tellus mauris dictum elit, vel lacinia enim metus eu nunc.

Proin at eros non eros adipiscing mollis. Donec semper turpis sed diam. Sed consequat ligula nec tortor. Integer eget sem. Ut vitae enim eu est vehicula gravida. Morbi ipsum ipsum, porta nec, tempor id, auctor vitae, purus. Pellentesque neque. Nulla luctus erat vitae libero. Integer nec enim.

7

Adding padding, margins, and backgrounds to a layout

Required files	Files from add-starting-point in the chapter 7 folder as a starting point.
What you'll learn	How to add style to a fixed-width div.
Completed files	add-completed in the chapter 7 folder.

1. Add a page background. In the add-starting-point folder, there are two images, both of which are gradients. One is a black gradient, fading toward gray at its bottom edge; this is intended for a page background. Add this by adding the following rule to the style sheet (after the `add your code below` comment):

```
body {
  background: #4d4d4d url(page-background.gif) repeat-x;
}
```

The `repeat-x` value ensures that the background tiles horizontally only; the color value #4d4d4d is the color of the bottom pixel of the gradient image, ensuring the gradient seamlessly blends with the web page background.

Note that in some examples in this book, selectors are used multiple times, such as body here. This is perfectly acceptable, although if you want to merge rules, you can—just be mindful of the cascade if you do so.

2. Add a border to the wrapper. Amend the #wrapper rule to add a border around the wrapper. Note that the wrapper in this example sits flush with the top edge of the browser window view area, and so no top border is needed. That's why the border-top pair is added, overriding the previous rule for the top border only.

```
#wrapper {
  width: 600px;
  margin: 0 auto;
  border: 2px solid #777777;
  border-top: 0;
}
```

3. Add a wrapper background. If you test the page now, the background shows behind all of the page's content, thereby making it unreadable. Therefore, add the background pair to the rule, which sets a background color for the wrapper div, and also sets the second image in the add-starting-point folder (a white-to-light-gray vertical gradient) to tile horizontally at the bottom of the div:

```
#wrapper {
  width: 600px;
  margin: 0 auto;
  border: 2px solid #777777;
  border-top: 0;
  background: #ffffff url(wrapper-background.gif) 0 100% repeat-x;
}
```

Lorem ipsum dolor sit amet, consectetuer adipiscing elit. Morbi commodo, ipsum sed pharetra gravida, orci magna rhoncus neque, id pulvinar odio lorem non turpis. Nullam sit amet enim.

Suspendisse id velit vitae ligula volutpat condimentum. Aliquam erat volutpat. Sed quis velit. Nulla facilisi. Nulla libero. Vivamus pharetra posuere sapien. Nam consectetuer. Sed aliquam, nunc eget euismod ullamcorper, lectus nunc ullamcorper orci, fermentum bibendum enim nibh eget ipsum.

Donec porttitor ligula eu dolor. Maecenas vitae nulla consequat libero cursus venenatis. Nam magna enim, accumsan eu, blandit sed, blandit a, eros. Quisque facilisis erat a dui. Nam malesuada ornare dolor. Cras gravida, diam sit amet rhoncus ornare, erat elit consectetuer erat, id egestas pede nibh eget odio.

Proin tincidunt, velit vel porta elementum, magna diam molestie sapien, non aliquet massa pede eu diam. Aliquam iaculis. Fusce et ipsum et nulla tristique facilisis. Donec eget sem sit amet ligula viverra gravida. Etiam vehicula urna vel turpis. Suspendisse sagittis ante a urna.

Morbi a est quis orci consequat rutrum. Nullam egestas feugiat felis. Integer adipiscing semper ligula. Nunc molestie, nisl sit amet cursus convallis, sapien lectus pretium metus, vitae pretium enim wisi id lectus. Donec vestibulum. Etiam vel nibh. Nulla facilisi. Mauris pharetra. Donec augue. Fusce ultrices, neque id dignissim ultrices, tellus mauris dictum elit, vel lacinia enim metus eu nunc.

Proin at eros non eros adipiscing mollis. Donec semper turpis sed diam. Sed consequat ligula nec tortor. Integer eget sem. Ut vitae enim eu est vehicula gravida. Morbi ipsum ipsum, porta nec, tempor id, auctor vitae, purus. Pellentesque neque. Nulla luctus erat vitae libero. Integer nec enim.

7

4. Add some padding. Test the page now and you'll see two major layout errors commonly seen on the Web. First, the content hugs the edges of the div, which makes it hard to read and also looks cluttered, despite the div being 600 pixels wide. Secondly, the text at the bottom of the div is displayed over the gradient—it's still readable, but it looks a little messy. By adding padding (more to the bottom edge, to account for the gradient), these issues are dealt with:

```
#wrapper {
  width: 600px;
  margin: 0 auto;
  border: 2px solid #777777;
  border-top: 0;
  background: #ffffff url(wrapper-background.gif) 0 100% repeat-x;
  padding: 20px 20px 50px;
}
```

Lorem ipsum dolor sit amet, consectetuer adipiscing elit. Morbi commodo, ipsum sed pharetra gravida, orci magna rhoncus neque, id pulvinar odio lorem non turpis. Nullam sit amet enim.

Suspendisse id velit vitae ligula volutpat condimentum. Aliquam erat volutpat. Sed quis velit. Nulla facilisi. Nulla libero. Vivamus pharetra posuere sapien. Nam consectetuer. Sed aliquam, nunc eget euismod ullamcorper, lectus nunc ullamcorper orci, fermentum bibendum enim nibh eget ipsum.

Donec porttitor ligula eu dolor. Maecenas vitae nulla consequat libero cursus venenatis. Nam magna enim, accumsan eu, blandit sed, blandit a, eros. Quisque facilisis erat a dui. Nam malesuada ornare dolor. Cras gravida, diam sit amet rhoncus ornare, erat elit consectetuer erat, id egestas pede nibh eget odio.

Proin tincidunt, velit vel porta elementum, magna diam molestie sapien, non aliquet massa pede eu diam. Aliquam iaculis. Fusce et ipsum et nulla tristique facilisis. Donec eget sem sit amet ligula viverra gravida. Etiam vehicula urna vel turpis. Suspendisse sagittis ante a urna.

Morbi a est quis orci consequat rutrum. Nullam egestas feugiat felis. Integer adipiscing semper ligula. Nunc molestie, nisl sit amet cursus convallis, sapien lectus pretium metus, vitae pretium enim wisi id lectus. Donec vestibulum. Etiam vel nibh. Nulla facilisi. Mauris pharetra. Donec augue. Fusce ultrices, neque id dignissim ultrices, tellus mauris dictum elit, vel lacinia enim metus eu nunc.

Proin at eros non eros adipiscing mollis. Donec semper turpis sed diam. Sed consequat ligula nec tortor. Integer eget sem. Ut vitae enim eu est vehicula gravida. Morbi ipsum ipsum, porta nec, tempor id, auctor vitae, purus. Pellentesque neque. Nulla luctus erat vitae libero. Integer nec enim.

Note that due to the padding and borders added to this div, *it now takes up 644 pixels of horizontal space, due to the 20-pixel horizontal padding values and the 2-pixel borders. To return the overall width to 600 pixels, subtract the 44 pixels from the* width *setting, reducing it to* 556px.

Creating a maximum-width layout

Required files	Files from add-completed in the chapter 7 folder as a starting point.
What you'll learn	How to create a div with a maximum width.
Completed files	max-width-example in the chapter 7 folder.

1. Amend a rule. Replace the width pair in the #wrapper rule with the max-width pair shown following. This works much like you'd expect: the design works in a liquid manner, up until the point at which the content area's width (this does *not* include the padding and borders) is the value defined for max-width, whereupon the layout becomes fixed.

```
#wrapper {
  max-width: 800px;
  margin: 0 auto;
  border: 2px solid #777777;
  border-top: 0;
  background: #ffffff url(wrapper-background.gif) 0 100% repeat-x;
  padding: 20px 20px 50px;
}
```

2. Amend the body rule. At small browser widths, the design fills the browser window. If you still want some space around the wrapper, even when the browser window is narrow, all you need do is amend the body rule, adding some horizontal padding.

```
body {
  background: #4d4d4d url(page-background.gif) repeat-x;
  padding: 0 30px;
}
```

> *Note that it's possible to use the* min-width *property to set the minimum width of a div. In all cases when using* max-width *and* min-width, *be sure to test the usability of your design at a wide range of browser window sizes. Also, these properties are not understood by Internet Explorer 6; see Chapter 9 for workarounds.*

7

Using absolute positioning to center a box onscreen

Required files	Files from basic-boilerplates in the chapter 7 folder as a starting point.
What you'll learn	How to center a div within the browser window.
Completed files	center-a-box-on-screen in the chapter 7 folder.

The final exercise in this section shows how to center a box within the browser window, horizontally and vertically. Note that this kind of layout isn't particularly flexible, because it needs the containing wrapper to have a fixed width and height. Therefore, take care when using this device, because if your page has plenty of content, your users may be forced to scroll a lot.

1. Add a few paragraphs of text to the web page, placing them inside the wrapper div.

2. Add some backgrounds and style the wrapper div.

```
body {
  background: #666666;
}
#wrapper {
```

```
    background: #ffffff;
    border: 4px solid #000000;
    padding: 20px;
    width: 400px;
    height: 300px;
}
```

Lorem ipsum dolor sit amet, consectetuer adipiscing elit. Morbi commodo, ipsum sed pharetra gravida, orci magna rhoncus neque, id pulvinar odio lorem non turpis. Nullam sit amet enim.

Suspendisse id velit vitae ligula volutpat condimentum. Aliquam erat volutpat. Sed quis velit. Nulla facilisi. Nulla libero. Vivamus pharetra posuere sapien. Nam consectetuer. Sed aliquam, nunc eget euismod ullamcorper, lectus nunc ullamcorper orci, fermentum bibendum enim nibh eget ipsum.

Donec porttitor ligula eu dolor. Maecenas vitae nulla consequat libero cursus venenatis. Nam magna enim, accumsan eu, blandit sed, blandit a, eros. Quisque facilisis erat a dui. Nam malesuada ornare dolor. Cras gravida, diam sit amet rhoncus ornare, erat elit consectetuer erat, id egestas pede nibh eget odio.

3. Position the div. Set the wrapper div's position value to absolute, and the top and left values to 50%. This sets the top-left position of the div to the center of the browser window.

```
#wrapper {
    background: #ffffff;
    border: 4px solid #000000;
    padding: 20px;
    width: 400px;
    height: 300px;
    position: absolute;
    top: 50%;
    left: 50%;
}
```

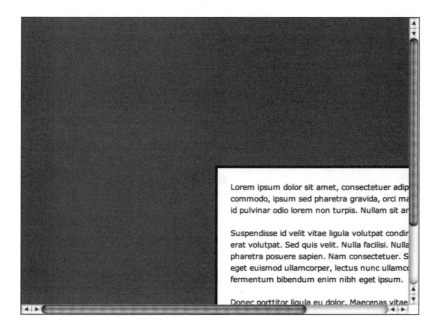

Lorem ipsum dolor sit amet, consectetuer adip
commodo, ipsum sed pharetra gravida, orci ma
id pulvinar odio lorem non turpis. Nullam sit an

Suspendisse id velit vitae ligula volutpat condir
erat volutpat. Sed quis velit. Nulla facilisi. Nulla
pharetra posuere sapien. Nam consectetuer. S
eget euismod ullamcorper, lectus nunc ullamcc
fermentum bibendum enim nibh eget ipsum.

Donec porttitor ligula eu dolor. Maecenas vitae

4. Use negative margins. Clearly, the div is not positioned correctly as yet, and that's—as mentioned in the previous step—because absolute positioning and the top and left values specify the position of the top left of the element they're applied to. In order to place the div centrally, negative top and left margins are used to pull it into place, the values of which are half the width or height, depending on the margin in question. For the margin-left value, you need the negative of half the horizontal space the div takes up, which is found by adding its width, horizontal padding, and horizontal margin values (4 + 20 + 400 + 20 + 4 = 444), dividing by two (222), and making the number negative (–222). Similarly, the margin-top value is the sum of the vertical dimensions (300px height, two lots of 20px padding and two lots of 4px borders, which comes to 344px) divided by 2 and made negative.

```
#wrapper {
  background: #ffffff;
  border: 4px solid #000000;
  padding: 20px;
  width: 400px;
  height: 300px;
  position: absolute;
  top: 50%;
  left: 50%;
  margin-left: -222px;
  margin-top: -172px;
}
```

Lorem ipsum dolor sit amet, consectetuer adipiscing elit. Morbi commodo, ipsum sed pharetra gravida, orci magna rhoncus neque, id pulvinar odio lorem non turpis. Nullam sit amet enim.

Suspendisse id velit vitae ligula volutpat condimentum. Aliquam erat volutpat. Sed quis velit. Nulla facilisi. Nulla libero. Vivamus pharetra posuere sapien. Nam consectetuer. Sed aliquam, nunc eget euismod ullamcorper, lectus nunc ullamcorper orci, fermentum bibendum enim nibh eget ipsum.

Donec porttitor ligula eu dolor. Maecenas vitae nulla consequat libero cursus venenatis. Nam magna enim, accumsan eu, blandit sed, blandit a, eros. Quisque facilisis erat a dui. Nam malesuada ornare dolor. Cras gravida, diam sit amet rhoncus ornare, erat elit consectetuer erat, id egestas pede nibh eget odio.

> *Note that if you use this kind of layout and have too much content for your wrapper, it will spill out of it. See later in the chapter for dealing with this issue by creating scrollable areas for page content.*

Nesting boxes: Boxouts

Boxouts are design elements commonly used in magazines, but they can, in principle, also be used on the Web. A boxout is a box separate from other page content that is often used to house images, captions, and other ancillary information. In magazines, these may be used for supporting text, alternate features, or magazine mastheads (with contributor information). Online, this enables you to immediately present content that's complementary to the main text.

In the following screenshot of the 2000 AD Books website (www.2000adonline.com/books), a boxout is used to house thumbnails of upcoming books, with a link to a page with further titles that are coming soon.

Creating a boxout in CSS is mostly done by floating a div.

The float property

Mastering the float property is key to creating CSS-based web page layouts. It enables you to float an element to the left or right of other web page content, which then wraps around it. This enables you to do away with ugly hacks such as fixed-width tables aligned right to create a boxout.

The benefit of using the float property over older methods is the ability to control a styled boxout's appearance site-wide from an external CSS file (and to control the cascade, in order to amend the appearance of elements within it). Structurally, the page is also more logical.

Creating a boxout

Required files	Files from boxout-starting-point in the chapter 7 folder as a starting point.
What you'll learn	How to create and style a boxout in CSS.
Completed files	boxout-complete in the chapter 7 folder.

As mentioned earlier, boxouts can be handy on web pages for displaying ancillary content simultaneously with the main text (rather than having supporting text following the main content). Like any other div, a boxout can also be styled, which is what this exercise will show how to do. Steps 1 through 3 show you how to create a basic, plain boxout, and step 4 onward shows how to style it. The final boxout will look like that shown in the image to the right: the corners are rounded; the plain background of the content area darkens slightly at its base; and the heading is on a colored background with a gradient (not obvious in a grayscale book, but if you check out the completed files, you'll see it's orange) and a white stripe beneath it to help make the boxout's heading and content distinct.

BOXOUT TITLE

Phasellus aliquam enim et tortor. Quisque aliquet, quam elementum condimentum feugiat, tellus odio consectetuer wisi, vel nonummy sem neque in elit. Curabitur eleifend wisi iaculis ipsum. Pellentesque habitant morbi tristique senectus et netus et malesuada fames ac turpis egestas. In non velit non ligula laoreet ultrices. Praesent ultricies facilisis nisl.

1. Examine the web page. Open boxout.html and look at the page's body content. The content of the web page is within a wrapper div. The bulk of the page content is a bunch of paragraphs. The boxout comprises a div with a class value of boxout, and this is placed *before* the content the boxout is supposed to float right of. (In other words, by placing the boxout before the other content, the other content will wrap around it once the boxout is floated.)

2. Style the wrapper and body. The boxout-starting-point folder contains the images from the "Adding padding, margins, and backgrounds to a layout" exercise earlier in this chapter, so add the body and #wrapper rules from that exercise to style the page's general layout.

```
body {
  background: #4d4d4d url(page-background.gif) repeat-x;
}
#wrapper {
  width: 600px;
  margin: 0 auto;
  border: 2px solid #777777;
  border-top: 0;
  background: #ffffff url(wrapper-background.gif) 0 100% repeat-x;
  padding: 20px 20px 50px;
}
```

3. Position the boxout. To do so, you need to float it right and assign it a fixed width—if no width is set, the boxout will span the width of its container, which in this case would be the width of the wrapper div. Margin values at the bottom and left ensure that the boxout doesn't hug content that wraps around it.

```
.boxout {
  float: right;
  width: 180px;
  margin: 0 0 20px 20px;
}
```

Lorem ipsum dolor sit amet, consectetuer adipiscing elit. Morbi commodo, ipsum sed pharetra gravida, orci magna rhoncus neque, id pulvinar odio lorem non turpis. Nullam sit amet enim.

Suspendisse id velit vitae ligula volutpat condimentum. Aliquam erat volutpat. Sed quis velit. Nulla facilisi. Nulla libero. Vivamus pharetra posuere sapien. Nam consectetuer. Sed aliquam, nunc eget euismod ullamcorper, lectus nunc ullamcorper orci, fermentum bibendum enim nibh eget ipsum.

Donec porttitor ligula eu dolor. Maecenas vitae nulla consequat libero cursus venenatis. Nam magna enim, accumsan eu, blandit sed, blandit a, eros. Quisque facilisis erat a dui. Nam malesuada ornare dolor. Cras gravida, diam sit amet rhoncus ornare, erat elit consectetuer erat, id egestas pede nibh eget odio.

Boxout title
Phasellus aliquam enim et tortor. Quisque aliquet, quam elementum condimentum feugiat, tellus odio consectetuer wisi, vel nonummy sem neque in elit. Curabitur eleifend wisi iaculis ipsum. Pellentesque habitant morbi tristique senectus et netus et malesuada fames ac turpis egestas. In non velit non ligula laoreet ultrices. Praesent ultricies facilisis nisl.

Proin tincidunt, velit vel porta elementum, magna diam molestie sapien, non aliquet massa pede eu diam. Aliquam iaculis. Fusce et ipsum et nulla tristique facilisis. Donec eget sem sit amet ligula viverra gravida. Etiam vehicula urna vel turpis. Suspendisse sagittis ante a urna.

4. Add a background. As shown earlier, the boxout has a background, and this is added by applying a background image to the boxout that blends into a solid background color. The background pair in the following code block does this—#e1e1e1 is a color value taken from the top of the image; 0 100% positions the image at the bottom left of the boxout div; and no-repeat ensures that it doesn't tile. Finally, padding values are added. The background image is 200 pixels wide, and the assigned width of the div is 180px. Therefore, horizontal padding of 10px is required. This ensures that the entire image is shown and that the boxout content doesn't go right up to the edge of the background.

Boxout title
Phasellus aliquam enim et tortor. Quisque aliquet, quam elementum condimentum feugiat, tellus odio consectetuer wisi, vel nonummy sem neque in elit. Curabitur eleifend wisi iaculis ipsum. Pellentesque habitant morbi tristique senectus et netus et malesuada fames ac turpis egestas. In non velit non ligula laoreet ultrices. Praesent ultricies facilisis nisl.

```
.boxout {
  float: right;
  width: 180px;
  margin: 0 0 20px 20px;
  background: #e1e1e1 url(boxout-bottom.gif) 0 100% no-repeat;
  padding: 0 10px;
}
```

5. The boxout header now needs styling, which will add the second part of the background. A contextual selector is used for this, ensuring that the style only applies to level-two headings within an element with a class value of boxout. The first three pairs in the rule style the header font (see Chapter 3 for more on styling type); the background pair works as per the one in step 4, except that the solid background color was taken from the bottom pixel of the background image. Also, as this image is applied at the top left, no positioning values are required.

```
.boxout h2 {
  font: bold 1.2em Arial, Helvetica, sans-serif;
  text-transform: uppercase;
  color: #ffffff;
  background: #d7932a url(boxout-top-orange.gif) no-repeat;
}
```

6. Position the header. If you test the page, you'll see that the header has a gap at its left and right. This is because the header is within the boxout div, which has 10 pixels of padding on its left and right edges. By applying negative margins of the same value to the header, the horizontal space it takes up is increased to span the entire width of the boxout. Some padding is then added to ensure that the heading text doesn't hug its container's edges. Next, the bottom-border setting shown following adds a single-pixel white line under the header.

```
.boxout h2 {
  font: bold 1.2em Arial, Helvetica, sans-serif;
  text-transform: uppercase;
  color: #ffffff;
  background: #d7932a url(boxout-top-orange.gif) no-repeat;
  margin: 0 -10px 10px;
  padding: 5px 10px;
  border-bottom: 1px solid #ffffff;
}
```

A final rule styles paragraphs within the boxout, differentiating them from other text.

```
.boxout p {
  font-size: 0.9em;
}
```

Lorem ipsum dolor sit amet, consectetuer adipiscing elit. Morbi commodo, ipsum sed pharetra gravida, orci magna rhoncus neque, id pulvinar odio lorem non turpis. Nullam sit amet enim.

Suspendisse id velit vitae ligula volutpat condimentum. Aliquam erat volutpat. Sed quis velit. Nulla facilisi. Nulla libero. Vivamus pharetra posuere sapien. Nam consectetuer. Sed aliquam, nunc eget euismod ullamcorper, lectus nunc ullamcorper orci, fermentum bibendum enim nibh eget ipsum.

Donec porttitor ligula eu dolor. Maecenas vitae nulla consequat libero cursus venenatis. Nam magna enim, accumsan eu, blandit sed, blandit a, eros. Quisque facilisis erat a dui. Nam malesuada ornare dolor. Cras gravida, diam sit amet rhoncus ornare, erat elit consectetuer erat, id egestas pede nibh eget odio.

Proin tincidunt, velit vel porta elementum, magna diam molestie sapien, non aliquet massa pede eu diam. Aliquam iaculis. Fusce et ipsum et nulla tristique facilisis. Donec eget sem sit amet ligula viverra gravida. Etiam vehicula urna vel turpis. Suspendisse sagittis ante a urna.

BOXOUT TITLE

Phasellus aliquam enim et tortor. Quisque aliquet, quam elementum condimentum feugiat, tellus odio consectetuer wisi, vel nonummy sem neque in elit. Curabitur eleifend wisi iaculis ipsum. Pellentesque habitant morbi tristique senectus et netus et malesuada fames ac turpis egestas. In non velit non ligula laoreet ultrices. Praesent ultricies facilisis nisl.

Note that because of the way the header's background is styled, using an image that blends into a solid color, there's no chance of the background running out, even if the page's text is massively zoomed (see the following image). Although the vast majority of users will never use such settings, it always pays to see how well your sites fare when very atypical settings are used in the browser. While some problems will be tricky to get around, others just require a little lateral thinking, as shown here.

7

Lorem ipsum dolor sit amet, consectetuer adipiscing elit. Morbi commodo, ipsum sed pharetra gravida, orci magna rhoncus neque, id pulvinar odio lorem non turpis. Nullam sit amet enim.

Suspendisse id velit vitae ligula volutpat condimentum.

BOXOUT TITLE

Phasellus aliquam enim et tortor. Quisque aliquet, quam elementum condimentum feugiat, tellus odio

Advanced layouts with multiple boxes and columns

The layouts so far in this chapter have laid the foundation, showing you how to get to grips with creating a wrapper for site content and then nesting a div within the wrapper, providing a little added scope for layout. In this section, you're going to find out how to fashion the basic building blocks of more complex layouts, working with two and then three or more structural divs, finding out how they can be styled using CSS. In all cases, try to think in a modular fashion, because the methods for creating the basic building blocks shown can be combined in many different ways to create all sorts of layouts.

One of the main reasons for working with two structural divs is to create columns on a web page. Although columns of the sort found in newspapers and magazines should be avoided online, columns can be useful when you're working with various types of content. For instance, you may offer current news in one column and an introduction to an organization in another. Using columns makes both sets of information immediately available. If a linear layout is instead used, you'll need to decide which information you want the user to see first and which information will initially be out of sight. The general principle of columns is about more than written site content, though. For example, you could use one column to house a vertical navigation bar and another to contain thumbnail images relating to an article.

Working with two structural divs

In previous exercises, you've worked with two divs, but one has been nested within the other. In the following exercise, you'll work with two structural divs, seeing how seemingly small changes to CSS rules can make a major difference to the layout of the web page. This will highlight the flexibility of web layouts, showing how quickly you can build pages, and also how easy it is to experiment with designs and make edits and rapid changes should they be required.

Manipulating two structural divs for fixed-width layouts

Required files	Files from `two-divs-starting-point` in the chapter 7 folder as a starting point.
What you'll learn	How to use two structural divs to create various types of fixed-width layouts, including two-column designs.
Completed files	`two-divs-fixed-complete` in the chapter 7 folder.

1. **Examine the code.** Open up `two-divs.html` and you'll see a simple page layout. A level-one heading is followed by the first div, with an id value of divOne. This is then followed by a second div, which has an id value of divTwo. Both divs have a level-two heading and some paragraphs within. Some initial styles are also in the style sheet, defining the fonts and placing 20 pixels of padding around the page's content (via the padding pair in the body rule) so the page content doesn't hug the browser window edge.

Working with two divs

Div one

Lorem ipsum dolor sit amet, consectetuer adipiscing elit. Morbi commodo, ipsum sed pharetra gravida, orci magna rhoncus neque, id pulvinar odio lorem non turpis. Nullam sit amet enim.

Suspendisse id velit vitae ligula volutpat condimentum. Aliquam erat volutpat. Sed quis velit. Nulla facilisi. Nulla libero. Vivamus pharetra posuere sapien. Nam consectetuer. Sed aliquam, nunc eget euismod ullamcorper, lectus nunc ullamcorper orci, fermentum bibendum enim nibh eget ipsum.

Donec porttitor ligula eu dolor. Maecenas vitae nulla consequat libero cursus venenatis. Nam magna enim, accumsan eu, blandit sed, blandit a, eros. Quisque facilisis erat a dui. Nam malesuada ornare dolor. Cras gravida, diam sit amet rhoncus ornare, erat elit consectetuer erat, id egestas pede nibh eget odio.

Div two

Proin tincidunt, velit vel porta elementum, magna diam molestie sapien, non aliquet massa pede eu diam. Aliquam iaculis. Fusce et ipsum et nulla tristique facilisis. Donec eget sem sit amet ligula viverra gravida. Etiam vehicula urna vel turpis. Suspendisse sagittis ante a urna.

Morbi a est quis orci consequat rutrum. Nullam egestas feugiat felis. Integer adipiscing semper ligula. Nunc molestie, nisl sit amet cursus convallis, sapien lectus pretium metus, vitae pretium enim wisi id lectus. Donec vestibulum. Etiam vel nibh. Nulla facilisi. Mauris pharetra. Donec augue. Fusce ultrices, neque id dignissim ultrices, tellus mauris dictum elit, vel lacinia enim metus eu nunc.

Proin at eros non eros adipiscing mollis. Donec semper turpis sed diam. Sed consequat ligula nec tortor. Integer eget sem. Ut vitae enim eu est vehicula gravida. Morbi ipsum ipsum, porta nec, tempor id, auctor vitae, purus. Pellentesque neque. Nulla luctus erat vitae libero. Integer nec enim.

---

2. **Add the background colors.** When initially working on CSS layouts and hand-coding, it's often useful to apply background colors to your main structural divs. This enables you to more easily see their edges and how they interact. Therefore, add the following rules to your CSS:

```
#divOne {
  background: #dddddd;
}
#divTwo {
  background: #aaaaaa;
}
```

If you test the web page at this point, you'll see the divs are positioned in a basic linear fashion. The gap between the two occurs because the paragraphs have margins assigned on their bottom edges—therefore, the gap is from the margin of the top div's last paragraphs.

Working with two divs

Div one

Lorem ipsum dolor sit amet, consectetuer adipiscing elit. Morbi commodo, ipsum sed pharetra gravida, orci magna rhoncus neque, id pulvinar odio lorem non turpis. Nullam sit amet enim.

Suspendisse id velit vitae ligula volutpat condimentum. Aliquam erat volutpat. Sed quis velit. Nulla facilisi. Nulla libero. Vivamus pharetra posuere sapien. Nam consectetuer. Sed aliquam, nunc eget euismod ullamcorper, lectus nunc ullamcorper orci, fermentum bibendum enim nibh eget ipsum.

Donec porttitor ligula eu dolor. Maecenas vitae nulla consequat libero cursus venenatis. Nam magna enim, accumsan eu, blandit sed, blandit a, eros. Quisque facilisis erat a dui. Nam malesuada ornare dolor. Cras gravida, diam sit amet rhoncus ornare, erat elit consectetuer erat, id egestas pede nibh eget odio.

Div two

Proin tincidunt, velit vel porta elementum, magna diam molestie sapien, non aliquet massa pede eu diam. Aliquam iaculis. Fusce et ipsum et nulla tristique facilisis. Donec eget sem sit amet ligula viverra gravida. Etiam vehicula urna vel turpis. Suspendisse sagittis ante a urna.

Morbi a est quis orci consequat rutrum. Nullam egestas feugiat felis. Integer adipiscing semper ligula. Nunc molestie, nisl sit amet cursus convallis, sapien lectus pretium metus, vitae pretium enim wisi id lectus. Donec vestibulum. Etiam vel nibh. Nulla facilisi. Mauris pharetra. Donec augue. Fusce ultrices, neque id dignissim ultrices, tellus mauris dictum elit, vel lacinia enim metus eu nunc.

Proin at eros non eros adipiscing mollis. Donec semper turpis sed diam. Sed consequat ligula nec tortor. Integer eget sem. Ut vitae enim eu est vehicula gravida. Morbi ipsum ipsum, porta nec, tempor id, auctor vitae, purus. Pellentesque neque. Nulla luctus erat vitae libero. Integer nec enim.

Note that for an actual website, you should use id *(and* class*) values relevant and appropriate to the content within them, as evidenced by* wrapper *and* boxout *earlier in this chapter. The values of* divOne *and* divTwo *are used in this exercise to enable you to easily keep track of each one.*

---

3. Make the divs flush to each other. By adding padding-bottom values equal to the margin-bottom value for paragraphs, you can make the div backgrounds flush to subsequent content.

```
#divOne {
  background: #dddddd;
  padding-bottom: 1.5em;
}
#divTwo {
  background: #aaaaaa;
  padding-bottom: 1.5em;
}
```

Working with two divs

Div one

Lorem ipsum dolor sit amet, consectetuer adipiscing elit. Morbi commodo, ipsum sed pharetra gravida, orci magna rhoncus neque, id pulvinar odio lorem non turpis. Nullam sit amet enim.

Suspendisse id velit vitae ligula volutpat condimentum. Aliquam erat volutpat. Sed quis velit. Nulla facilisi. Nulla libero. Vivamus pharetra posuere sapien. Nam consectetuer. Sed aliquam, nunc eget euismod ullamcorper, lectus nunc ullamcorper orci, fermentum bibendum enim nibh eget ipsum.

Donec porttitor ligula eu dolor. Maecenas vitae nulla consequat libero cursus venenatis. Nam magna enim, accumsan eu, blandit sed, blandit a, eros. Quisque facilisis erat a dui. Nam malesuada ornare dolor. Cras gravida, diam sit amet rhoncus ornare, erat elit consectetuer erat, id egestas pede nibh eget odio.

Div two

Proin tincidunt, velit vel porta elementum, magna diam molestie sapien, non aliquet massa pede eu diam. Aliquam iaculis. Fusce et ipsum et nulla tristique facilisis. Donec eget sem sit amet ligula viverra gravida. Etiam vehicula urna vel turpis. Suspendisse sagittis ante a urna.

Morbi a est quis orci consequat rutrum. Nullam egestas feugiat felis. Integer adipiscing semper ligula. Nunc molestie, nisl sit amet cursus convallis, sapien lectus pretium metus, vitae pretium enim wisi id lectus. Donec vestibulum. Etiam vel nibh. Nulla facilisi. Mauris pharetra. Donec augue. Fusce ultrices, neque id dignissim ultrices, tellus mauris dictum elit, vel lacinia enim metus eu nunc.

Proin at eros non eros adipiscing mollis. Donec semper turpis sed diam. Sed consequat ligula nec tortor. Integer eget sem. Ut vitae enim eu est vehicula gravida. Morbi ipsum ipsum, porta nec, tempor id, auctor vitae, purus. Pellentesque neque. Nulla luctus erat vitae libero. Integer nec enim.

7

4. Float the divs to make columns. By adding width values and floating both divs in the same direction, the divs stack horizontally, thereby creating columns.

```
#divOne {
   background: #dddddd;
   padding-bottom: 1.5em;
   float: left;
   width: 350px;
}
#divTwo {
   background: #aaaaaa;
   padding-bottom: 1.5em;
   float: left;
   width: 250px;
}
```

Working with two divs

Div one

Lorem ipsum dolor sit amet, consectetuer adipiscing elit. Morbi commodo, ipsum sed pharetra gravida, orci magna rhoncus neque, id pulvinar odio lorem non turpis. Nullam sit amet enim.

Suspendisse id velit vitae ligula volutpat condimentum. Aliquam erat volutpat. Sed quis velit. Nulla facilisi. Nulla libero. Vivamus pharetra posuere sapien. Nam consectetuer. Sed aliquam, nunc eget euismod ullamcorper, lectus nunc ullamcorper orci, fermentum bibendum enim nibh eget ipsum.

Donec porttitor ligula eu dolor. Maecenas vitae nulla consequat libero cursus venenatis. Nam magna enim, accumsan eu, blandit sed, blandit a, eros. Quisque facilisis erat a dui. Nam malesuada ornare dolor. Cras gravida, diam sit amet rhoncus ornare, erat elit consectetuer erat, id egestas pede nibh eget odio.

Div two

Proin tincidunt, velit vel porta elementum, magna diam molestie sapien, non aliquet massa pede eu diam. Aliquam iaculis. Fusce et ipsum et nulla tristique facilisis. Donec eget sem sit amet ligula viverra gravida. Etiam vehicula urna vel turpis. Suspendisse sagittis ante a urna.

Morbi a est quis orci consequat rutrum. Nullam egestas feugiat felis. Integer adipiscing semper ligula. Nunc molestie, nisl sit amet cursus convallis, sapien lectus pretium metus, vitae pretium enim wisi id lectus. Donec vestibulum. Etiam vel nibh. Nulla facilisi. Mauris pharetra. Donec augue. Fusce ultrices, neque id dignissim ultrices, tellus mauris dictum elit, vel lacinia enim metus eu nunc.

Proin at eros non eros adipiscing mollis. Donec semper turpis sed diam. Sed consequat ligula nec tortor. Integer eget sem. Ut vitae enim eu est vehicula gravida. Morbi ipsum ipsum, porta nec, tempor id, auctor vitae, purus. Pellentesque neque. Nulla luctus erat vitae libero. Integer nec enim.

Note how with CSS layouts, each div *only stretches to fill its content. This is in marked contrast to an equivalent table-based layout, where cells (and therefore their backgrounds) stretch to the overall height of the table. Later, you'll find out how to mimic full-height columns by using a background image (creating what are known as faux columns).*

5. Switch the column order. You can switch the stack direction by amending the float values, changing left to right. This can be useful for when you want information to be displayed in a certain order onscreen, but in a different order in code. For example, your main content might be on the right and a sidebar on the left onscreen, but screen readers would go through the main content before the sidebar.

Note that floats start stacking from the edge of their container, which in this case is 20 pixels in from the browser window edge. For more control over the overall layout, columns can be placed in a wrapper, which will be discussed later in the chapter.

```
#divOne {
  background: #dddddd;
  padding-bottom: 1.5em;
  float: right;
  width: 350px;
}
#divTwo {
  background: #aaaaaa;
  padding-bottom: 1.5em;
  float: right;
  width: 250px;
}
```

Working with two divs

Div two

Proin tincidunt, velit vel porta elementum, magna diam molestie sapien, non aliquet massa pede eu diam. Aliquam iaculis. Fusce et ipsum et nulla tristique facilisis. Donec eget sem sit amet ligula viverra gravida. Etiam vehicula urna vel turpis. Suspendisse sagittis ante a urna.

Morbi a est quis orci consequat rutrum. Nullam egestas feugiat felis. Integer adipiscing semper ligula. Nunc molestie, nisl sit amet cursus convallis, sapien lectus pretium metus, vitae pretium enim wisi id lectus. Donec vestibulum. Etiam vel nibh. Nulla facilisi. Mauris pharetra. Donec augue. Fusce ultrices, neque id dignissim ultrices, tellus mauris dictum elit, vel lacinia enim metus eu nunc.

Proin at eros non eros adipiscing mollis. Donec semper turpis sed diam. Sed consequat ligula nec tortor. Integer eget sem. Ut vitae enim eu est vehicula gravida. Morbi ipsum ipsum, porta nec, tempor id, auctor vitae, purus. Pellentesque neque. Nulla luctus erat vitae libero. Integer nec enim.

Div one

Lorem ipsum dolor sit amet, consectetuer adipiscing elit. Morbi commodo, ipsum sed pharetra gravida, orci magna rhoncus neque, id pulvinar odio lorem non turpis. Nullam sit amet enim.

Suspendisse id velit vitae ligula volutpat condimentum. Aliquam erat volutpat. Sed quis velit. Nulla facilisi. Nulla libero. Vivamus pharetra posuere sapien. Nam consectetuer. Sed aliquam, nunc eget euismod ullamcorper, lectus nunc ullamcorper orci, fermentum bibendum enim nibh eget ipsum.

Donec porttitor ligula eu dolor. Maecenas vitae nulla consequat libero cursus venenatis. Nam magna enim, accumsan eu, blandit sed, blandit a, eros. Quisque facilisis erat a dui. Nam malesuada ornare dolor. Cras gravida, diam sit amet rhoncus ornare, erat elit consectetuer erat, id egestas pede nibh eget odio.

7

6. Add padding and margins. Switch the `right` values for `float` back to `left`, and then change the `padding-bottom` properties to `padding`, adding values for the top and horizontal edges. A `margin-right` setting for `#divOne` provides a gap between the two divs.

```
#divOne {
  background: #dddddd;
  padding: 10px 10px 1.5em;
  float: left;
  width: 350px;
  margin-right: 10px;
}
#divTwo {
  background: #aaaaaa;
  padding: 10px 10px 1.5em;
  float: left;
  width: 250px;
}
```

Working with two divs

Div one

Lorem ipsum dolor sit amet, consectetuer adipiscing elit.
Morbi commodo, ipsum sed pharetra gravida, orci magna
rhoncus neque, id pulvinar odio lorem non turpis. Nullam
sit amet enim.

Suspendisse id velit vitae ligula volutpat condimentum.
Aliquam erat volutpat. Sed quis velit. Nulla facilisi. Nulla
libero. Vivamus pharetra posuere sapien. Nam
consectetuer. Sed aliquam, nunc eget euismod
ullamcorper, lectus nunc ullamcorper orci, fermentum
bibendum enim nibh eget ipsum.

Donec porttitor ligula eu dolor. Maecenas vitae nulla
consequat libero cursus venenatis. Nam magna enim,
accumsan eu, blandit sed, blandit a, eros. Quisque facilisis
erat a dui. Nam malesuada ornare dolor. Cras gravida,
diam sit amet rhoncus ornare, erat elit consectetuer erat,
id egestas pede nibh eget odio.

Div two

Proin tincidunt, velit vel porta
elementum, magna diam molestie
sapien, non aliquet massa pede eu diam.
Aliquam iaculis. Fusce et ipsum et nulla
tristique facilisis. Donec eget sem sit
amet ligula viverra gravida. Etiam
vehicula urna vel turpis. Suspendisse
sagittis ante a urna.

Morbi a est quis orci consequat rutrum.
Nullam egestas feugiat felis. Integer
adipiscing semper ligula. Nunc molestie,
nisl sit amet cursus convallis, sapien
lectus pretium metus, vitae pretium enim
wisi id lectus. Donec vestibulum. Etiam
vel nibh. Nulla facilisi. Mauris pharetra.
Donec augue. Fusce ultrices, neque id
dignissim ultrices, tellus mauris dictum
elit, vel lacinia enim metus eu nunc.

Proin at eros non eros adipiscing mollis.
Donec semper turpis sed diam. Sed
consequat ligula nec tortor. Integer eget
sem. Ut vitae enim eu est vehicula
gravida. Morbi ipsum ipsum, porta nec,
tempor id, auctor vitae, purus.
Pellentesque neque. Nulla luctus erat
vitae libero. Integer nec enim.

Manipulating two structural divs for liquid layouts

Required files	Files from two-divs-starting-point in the chapter 7 folder as a starting point.
What you'll learn	How to use two structural divs to create various types of liquid layouts, including two-column designs.
Completed files	two-divs-liquid-complete in the chapter 7 folder.

This exercise looks at working with liquid rather than fixed layouts. Because of the nature of liquid layouts, there are some very important differences in method that must be taken into account, as you'll see.

1. Add backgrounds and padding. As per the previous exercise, add background colors to the two divs to make it easy to see their boundaries.

```
#divOne {
   background: #dddddd;
}
#divTwo {
   background: #aaaaaa;
}
```

2. Float the divs and set widths. As explained in the previous exercise, setting a width for the two divs and then floating them both in the same direction enables you to stack them horizontally, thereby providing columns. Note that in this exercise, we'll only be floating divs left, but you can float them right, too. Regarding width values, you must ensure that their sum doesn't exceed 100%, because otherwise the divs will be wider in total than their container and will display in a linear fashion, one under the other.

```
#divOne {
   background: #dddddd;
   float: left;
   width: 40%;
}
#divTwo {
   background: #aaaaaa;
   float: left;
   width: 60%;
}
```

7

Working with two divs

Div one

Lorem ipsum dolor sit amet, consectetuer adipiscing elit. Morbi commodo, ipsum sed pharetra gravida, orci magna rhoncus neque, id pulvinar odio lorem non turpis. Nullam sit amet enim.

Suspendisse id velit vitae ligula volutpat condimentum. Aliquam erat volutpat. Sed quis velit. Nulla facilisi. Nulla libero. Vivamus pharetra posuere sapien. Nam consectetuer. Sed aliquam, nunc eget euismod ullamcorper, lectus nunc ullamcorper orci, fermentum bibendum enim nibh eget ipsum.

Donec porttitor ligula eu dolor. Maecenas vitae nulla consequat libero cursus venenatis. Nam magna enim, accumsan eu, blandit sed, blandit a, eros. Quisque facilisis erat a dui. Nam malesuada ornare dolor. Cras gravida, diam sit amet rhoncus ornare, erat elit consectetuer erat, id egestas pede nibh eget odio.

Div two

Proin tincidunt, velit vel porta elementum, magna diam molestie sapien, non aliquet massa pede eu diam. Aliquam iaculis. Fusce et ipsum et nulla tristique facilisis. Donec eget sem sit amet ligula viverra gravida. Etiam vehicula urna vel turpis. Suspendisse sagittis ante a urna.

Morbi a est quis orci consequat rutrum. Nullam egestas feugiat felis. Integer adipiscing semper ligula. Nunc molestie, nisl sit amet cursus convallis, sapien lectus pretium metus, vitae pretium enim wisi id lectus. Donec vestibulum. Etiam vel nibh. Nulla facilisi. Mauris pharetra. Donec augue. Fusce ultrices, neque id dignissim ultrices, tellus mauris dictum elit, vel lacinia enim metus eu nunc.

Proin at eros non eros adipiscing mollis. Donec semper turpis sed diam. Sed consequat ligula nec tortor. Integer eget sem. Ut vitae enim eu est vehicula gravida. Morbi ipsum ipsum, porta nec, tempor id, auctor vitae, purus. Pellentesque neque. Nulla luctus erat vitae libero. Integer nec enim.

3. Add a margin. In the previous exercise, a margin was included to separate the two divs. This can be done here, again by adding a `margin-right` value to #divOne. However, you need to ensure the overall width of the width *and* margin values doesn't exceed 100%. In this example, the margin is set to 2%, and 1% is removed from each of the two width values to cater for this.

```
#divOne {
  background: #dddddd;
  float: left;
  width: 39%;
  margin-right: 2%;
}
#divTwo {
  background: #aaaaaa;
  float: left;
  width: 59%;
}
```

Working with two divs

Div one

Lorem ipsum dolor sit amet, consectetuer adipiscing elit. Morbi commodo, ipsum sed pharetra gravida, orci magna rhoncus neque, id pulvinar odio lorem non turpis. Nullam sit amet enim.

Suspendisse id velit vitae ligula volutpat condimentum. Aliquam erat volutpat. Sed quis velit. Nulla facilisi. Nulla libero. Vivamus pharetra posuere sapien. Nam consectetuer. Sed aliquam, nunc eget euismod ullamcorper, lectus nunc ullamcorper orci, fermentum bibendum enim nibh eget ipsum.

Donec porttitor ligula eu dolor. Maecenas vitae nulla consequat libero cursus venenatis. Nam magna enim, accumsan eu, blandit sed, blandit a, eros. Quisque facilisis erat a dui. Nam malesuada ornare dolor. Cras gravida, diam sit amet rhoncus ornare, erat elit consectetuer erat, id egestas pede nibh eget odio.

Div two

Proin tincidunt, velit vel porta elementum, magna diam molestie sapien, non aliquet massa pede eu diam. Aliquam iaculis. Fusce et ipsum et nulla tristique facilisis. Donec eget sem sit amet ligula viverra gravida. Etiam vehicula urna vel turpis. Suspendisse sagittis ante a urna.

Morbi a est quis orci consequat rutrum. Nullam egestas feugiat felis. Integer adipiscing semper ligula. Nunc molestie, nisl sit amet cursus convallis, sapien lectus pretium metus, vitae pretium enim wisi id lectus. Donec vestibulum. Etiam vel nibh. Nulla facilisi. Mauris pharetra. Donec augue. Fusce ultrices, neque id dignissim ultrices, tellus mauris dictum elit, vel lacinia enim metus eu nunc.

Proin at eros non eros adipiscing mollis. Donec semper turpis sed diam. Sed consequat ligula nec tortor. Integer eget sem. Ut vitae enim eu est vehicula gravida. Morbi ipsum ipsum, porta nec, tempor id, auctor vitae, purus. Pellentesque neque. Nulla luctus erat vitae libero. Integer nec enim.

7

4. If you want to add padding to the divs, the method changes depending on the required value. If you're adding padding on a percentage basis, you add it in the same way as the margin in step 3, removing relevant values from the width settings. (For example, if you set the padding to 1% for both divs, this would mean there would be 1% of padding on each side, so 2% would need to be removed from each width value to keep the combined width of the two divs under 100%.)

However, if you want to add pixel-based padding values, things become a little more complex, because there's no way of specifying something like 39% - 20px for a width. The most sensible workaround is to use nested divs: add a content div within each of the two existing divs, and then set padding for those nested divs to a pixel value. In HTML, you end up with the following:

```
<div id="divOne">
  <div class="columnContent">
    [content]
  </div>
</div>
<div id="divTwo">
  <div class="columnContent">
    [content]
  </div>
</div>
```

You then apply a padding value to .columnContent in the CSS.

Note that, clearly, liquid layouts can have widths lower than 100%; this example showed that percentage because it's the most common width used for liquid layouts and has the most problems to overcome. Also, rounding errors can cause problems with liquid layouts when the width values add up to 100%—see the "Dealing with rounding errors" section in Chapter 9 for more on this.

Placing columns within wrappers and clearing floated content

The heading of this section is a bit of a mouthful, but it makes sense at this point to combine the two things it mentions—placing columns within wrappers and clearing floated content—because once you've started working with columns, that's what you'll likely next have to do. Placing columns within a wrapper enables you to position the overall layout (for example, centering it within the browser window) and restrict its width to a set size in pixels or a liquid measurement. Clearing floated content is an important concept to understand, because floated content appears outside of the normal document flow; subsequent content then wraps around floated content. Therefore, float an object left and subsequent content will stack to its right. Also, backgrounds don't appear behind floated content if it isn't cleared, because browsers consider floated elements to technically take up no height.

Placing columns within a wrapper

Required files	Files from two-divs-starting-point in the chapter 7 folder as a starting point.
What you'll learn	How to use two structural divs to create a two-column fixed-width layout, using both pixel- and percentage-based values.
Completed files	using-wrappers-to-contain-columns in the chapter 7 folder.

1. Add a wrapper. Open the HTML document and place a div around the web page's content, and give the div an id value of wrapper.

```
<body>
  <div id="wrapper">
    [web page content]
  </div>
</body>
```

2. Amend the body rule. Because the page will be fixed and centered, there's no longer a need for horizontal padding on the body element; therefore, amend the body rule in the CSS file as follows:

```
body {
   font: 62.5%/1.5 Verdana, Arial, Helvetica, sans-serif;
   padding: 20px 0;
}
```

3. Add the following rule to center the wrapper, per the "Creating a fixed-width wrapper" exercise earlier in this chapter:

```
#wrapper {
   width: 700px;
   margin: 0 auto;
}
```

4. Finally, add the following two rules to float the columns, set their widths, and then place a margin between them (by adding a margin-right setting to the left-hand column).

```
#divOne, #divTwo {
   float: left;
   width: 340px;
}
#divOne {
   margin-right: 20px;
}
```

Working with two divs

Div one

Lorem ipsum dolor sit amet, consectetuer adipiscing elit. Morbi commodo, ipsum sed pharetra gravida, orci magna rhoncus neque, id pulvinar odio lorem non turpis. Nullam sit amet enim.

Suspendisse id velit vitae ligula volutpat condimentum. Aliquam erat volutpat. Sed quis velit. Nulla facilisi. Nulla libero. Vivamus pharetra posuere sapien. Nam consectetuer. Sed aliquam, nunc eget euismod ullamcorper, lectus nunc ullamcorper orci, fermentum bibendum enim nibh eget ipsum.

Donec porttitor ligula eu dolor. Maecenas vitae nulla consequat libero cursus venenatis. Nam magna enim, accumsan eu, blandit sed, blandit a, eros. Quisque facilisis erat a dui. Nam malesuada ornare dolor. Cras gravida, diam sit amet rhoncus ornare, erat elit consectetuer erat, id egestas pede nibh eget odio.

Div two

Proin tincidunt, velit vel porta elementum, magna diam molestie sapien, non aliquet massa pede eu diam. Aliquam iaculis. Fusce et ipsum et nulla tristique facilisis. Donec eget sem sit amet ligula viverra gravida. Etiam vehicula urna vel turpis. Suspendisse sagittis ante a urna.

Morbi a est quis orci consequat rutrum. Nullam egestas feugiat felis. Integer adipiscing semper ligula. Nunc molestie, nisl sit amet cursus convallis, sapien lectus pretium metus, vitae pretium enim wisi id lectus. Donec vestibulum. Etiam vel nibh. Nulla facilisi. Mauris pharetra. Donec augue. Fusce ultrices, neque id dignissim ultrices, tellus mauris dictum elit, vel lacinia enim metus eu nunc.

Proin at eros non eros adipiscing mollis. Donec semper turpis sed diam. Sed consequat ligula nec tortor. Integer eget sem. Ut vitae enim eu est vehicula gravida. Morbi ipsum ipsum, porta nec, tempor id, auctor vitae, purus. Pellentesque neque. Nulla luctus erat vitae libero. Integer nec enim.

No matter the size of the browser window, the two-column design sits centrally horizontally.

Note that the fixed-width values for the two columns can be replaced with percentages:

```
#divOne, #divTwo {
  float: left;
  width: 49%;
}
#divOne {
  margin-right: 2%;
}
```

In such cases, the width of each div (and the margin) is a percentage of the parent element—the wrapper div—rather than the browser window.

> When using percentages to size columns, it makes sense to use them also to size the gutters and margins between them. If you don't, you'll have a hard time trying to match up column widths in percentages and margins in pixels.

Clearing floated content

Required files	Files from using-wrappers-to-contain-columns in the chapter 7 folder as a starting point.
What you'll learn	How to clear floated content, thereby making a wrapper's background display behind the content within it.
Completed files	clearing-floated-content in the chapter 7 folder.

1. To highlight issues with content that doesn't clear floated content, you need to make some quick changes to the HTML and CSS from the using-wrappers-to-contain-columns folder. First, add a paragraph of text after the closing tag of the wrapper div:

```
      </div>
    </div>
    <p>Subsequent content...</p>
  </body>
</html>
```

Next, add a background color to the #wrapper rule in the CSS, and change the width and margin-right settings of the #divOne, #divTwo and #divOne rules, as shown following:

```
#wrapper {
  width: 700px;
  margin: 0 auto;
  background: #bbbbbb;
}
#divOne, #divTwo {
  float: left;
  width: 300px;
}
#divOne {
  margin-right: 20px;
}
```

Upon previewing the amended page, you'll see that the subsequent content stacks to the right of the floated content; also, the background color for the wrapper doesn't extend behind the floated content. Both of these issues can be fixed by clearing the floated content.

Working with two divs

Div one

Lorem ipsum dolor sit amet, consectetuer adipiscing elit. Morbi commodo, ipsum sed pharetra gravida, orci magna rhoncus neque, id pulvinar odio lorem non turpis. Nullam sit amet enim.

Suspendisse id velit vitae ligula volutpat condimentum. Aliquam erat volutpat. Sed quis velit. Nulla facilisi. Nulla libero. Vivamus pharetra posuere sapien. Nam consectetuer. Sed aliquam, nunc eget euismod ullamcorper, lectus nunc ullamcorper orci, fermentum bibendum enim nibh eget ipsum.

Donec porttitor ligula eu dolor. Maecenas vitae nulla consequat libero cursus venenatis. Nam magna enim, accumsan eu, blandit sed, blandit a, eros. Quisque facilisis erat a dui. Nam malesuada ornare dolor. Cras gravida, diam sit amet rhoncus ornare, erat elit consectetuer erat, id egestas pede nibh eget odio.

Div two

Proin tincidunt, velit vel porta elementum, magna diam molestie sapien, non aliquet massa pede eu diam. Aliquam iaculis. Fusce et ipsum et nulla tristique facilisis. Donec eget sem sit amet ligula viverra gravida. Etiam vehicula urna vel turpis. Suspendisse sagittis ante a urna.

Morbi a est quis orci consequat rutrum. Nullam egestas feugiat felis. Integer adipiscing semper ligula. Nunc molestie, nisl sit amet cursus convallis, sapien lectus pretium metus, vitae pretium enim wisi id lectus. Donec vestibulum. Etiam vel nibh. Nulla facilisi. Mauris pharetra. Donec augue. Fusce ultrices, neque id dignissim ultrices, tellus mauris dictum elit, vel lacinia enim metus eu nunc.

Proin at eros non eros adipiscing mollis. Donec semper turpis sed diam. Sed consequat ligula nec tortor. Integer eget sem. Ut vitae enim eu est vehicula gravida. Morbi ipsum ipsum, porta nec, tempor id, auctor vitae, purus. Pellentesque neque. Nulla luctus erat vitae libero. Integer nec enim.

Subsequent content...

7

Note that Internet Explorer's behavior is different from other browsers here: the wrapper isn't being collapsed, so the background extends fully, and the paragraph of text added after the wrapper doesn't flow around the floated divs, presumably because the wrapper isn't collapsing.

2. Clear the floated content. There are two main methods for clearing floated content, both of which are worth having in your arsenal. The first was initially developed by Tony Aslett of CSS Creator (http://csscreator.com) and subsequently expanded by the folks at Position Is Everything (see www.positioniseverything. net/easyclearing.html for a full overview of the technique). First, add a class value of clearFix to the container of the floated content (the wrapper div, in this example), and then add the following rule in CSS:

```css
.clearFix:after {
  content: ".";
  display: block;
  height: 0;
  clear: both;
  visibility: hidden;
}
```

Working with two divs

Div one

Lorem ipsum dolor sit amet, consectetuer adipiscing elit. Morbi commodo, ipsum sed pharetra gravida, orci magna rhoncus neque, id pulvinar odio lorem non turpis. Nullam sit amet enim.

Suspendisse id velit vitae ligula volutpat condimentum. Aliquam erat volutpat. Sed quis velit. Nulla facilisi. Nulla libero. Vivamus pharetra posuere sapien. Nam consectetuer. Sed aliquam, nunc eget euismod ullamcorper, lectus nunc ullamcorper orci, fermentum bibendum enim nibh eget ipsum.

Donec porttitor ligula eu dolor. Maecenas vitae nulla consequat libero cursus venenatis. Nam magna enim, accumsan eu, blandit sed, blandit a, eros. Quisque facilisis erat a dui. Nam malesuada ornare dolor. Cras gravida, diam sit amet rhoncus ornare, erat elit consectetuer erat, id egestas pede nibh eget odio.

Div two

Proin tincidunt, velit vel porta elementum, magna diam molestie sapien, non aliquet massa pede eu diam. Aliquam iaculis. Fusce et ipsum et nulla tristique facilisis. Donec eget sem sit amet ligula viverra gravida. Etiam vehicula urna vel turpis. Suspendisse sagittis ante a urna.

Morbi a est quis orci consequat rutrum. Nullam egestas feugiat felis. Integer adipiscing semper ligula. Nunc molestie, nisl sit amet cursus convallis, sapien lectus pretium metus, vitae pretium enim wisi id lectus. Donec vestibulum. Etiam vel nibh. Nulla facilisi. Mauris pharetra. Donec augue. Fusce ultrices, neque id dignissim ultrices, tellus mauris dictum elit, vel lacinia enim metus eu nunc.

Proin at eros non eros adipiscing mollis. Donec semper turpis sed diam. Sed consequat ligula nec tortor. Integer eget sem. Ut vitae enim eu est vehicula gravida. Morbi ipsum ipsum, porta nec, tempor id, auctor vitae, purus. Pellentesque neque. Nulla luctus erat vitae libero. Integer nec enim.

Subsequent content...

The magic of this method is in the CSS rule. By using the :after pseudo-selector, content is added after the element the class is applied to (in this case, a period is added after the wrapper div), and said content is set to clear the element, have no height, and be rendered as invisible. The genius of the method is that you need no extra markup to clear floats.

3. Use an alternate method. The clearFix method is great for when you have content following a containing wrapper. In some cases, you may not have this, though. For example, place your subsequent content within the wrapper div, as shown:

```
      </div>
      <p>Subsequent content...</p>
    </div>
  </body>
</html>
```

The clearFix method won't work here, because the content is now *inside* the div that has the `clearFix` rule applied to it. Various options are open; the first is to wrap the floated elements in an internal wrapper and apply the `clearFix` class to that. In many cases, this will be fine, but you can end up with a case of divitis, where many nested divs impair the clean nature of the markup. An alternate option is to apply clearing directly to the element that follows the last piece of floated content. In HTML, this would look as follows:

```
<p class="ClearFloats">
```

In CSS, this is styled as follows:

```
.clearFloats {
  clear: both;
}
```

Generally, the clearFix method is considered superior to adding styles to specific elements, but on occasions when it doesn't work for your design, it's good to have a fallback, so be mindful of both clearing methods when working on your designs.

Working with sidebars and multiple boxouts

In this chapter so far, you've seen how to create web page columns and also how to fashion a boxout. In this section, two exercises will expand upon these ideas, showing how to create two different layouts that make use of sidebars. Sidebars are common in print, either for dividing up a page, thereby enabling a designer to show a main story and a smaller story, or for providing an area for ancillary content to the main story, but without having text wrapping underneath it (like in a boxout). The Pinkflag.com website (the official website of the rock band Wire) makes use of sidebars throughout the site. In the following image, a page from the Us section is shown. The main section of the page shows a photo of a band member, along with a short biography. In the sidebar is a selection of the subject's favorite tracks.

7

Based on what you've seen so far, you might think the best way to create such a layout would be to create a two-column layout and then add a border to one of the columns. However, in CSS, borders and backgrounds stop as soon as the content does. Therefore, if you add a border to the main content area, but the sidebar's content makes it taller than the main content area, the separating border stops short. What you therefore need to do is ensure that the two columns are placed in a wrapper, and then apply a vertically tiling background to the wrapper, thereby "faking" the column separator. This technique is commonly referred to as creating **faux columns**, and is explained fully in the following exercise.

Creating a sidebar with faux-column backgrounds

Required files	faux-columns-background.gif from the image folder and all files from using-wrappers-to-contain-columns (both in the chapter 7 folder) as a starting point.
What you'll learn	How to use two structural divs and a background image to create faux columns.
Completed files	faux-columns in the chapter 7 folder.

1. Clear the floated content, using the method outlined in step 2 of the "Clearing floated content" exercise.

2. Change the id values. When creating a website, you should amend your div id values to something appropriate for the content within them. Don't use generic names such as divOne and divTwo for a completed website. (They've been used for some exercises in this chapter just to make the exercises simpler to work through.) In both the HTML page and the CSS document, change all instances of divOne to mainContent and all incidences of divTwo to sidebar. Amend the two level-two headings in the web page accordingly, too.

3. Change the width settings for the columns, making sidebar narrower than mainContent.

```
#mainContent, #sidebar {
  float: left;
  width: 479px;
}
#mainContent {
  margin-right: 41px;
}
#sidebar {
  width: 180px;
}
```

4. Add the background image. Apply the background image (shown right) to the wrapper div, as shown following. The horizontal position is the width of the main content div, plus half the margin once 1 pixel is removed from that value (because the width of the "border" in the background image is a single pixel). By placing the background image 499 pixels from the left, it ends up exactly halfway between the content of the two divs.

```
#wrapper {
  width: 700px;
  margin: 0 auto;
  background: url(faux-columns-background.gif) 499px 0 repeat-y;
}
```

5. To make it easier to differentiate the two areas of text, change the size of the text in the sidebar, making it smaller.

```
#sidebar {
  width: 180px;
  font-size: 90%;
}
```

Using a percentage value is a quick way of doing this, with all values being based on those from the main content area. If you want to set specific values for each of the text elements within the sidebar, you could do so using contextual selectors (#sidebar h1, #sidebar p, etc.).

Working with two divs

Main content

Lorem ipsum dolor sit amet, consectetuer adipiscing elit. Morbi commodo, ipsum sed pharetra gravida, orci magna rhoncus neque, id pulvinar odio lorem non turpis. Nullam sit amet enim.

Suspendisse id velit vitae ligula volutpat condimentum. Aliquam erat volutpat. Sed quis velit. Nulla facilisi. Nulla libero. Vivamus pharetra posuere sapien. Nam consectetuer. Sed aliquam, nunc eget euismod ullamcorper, lectus nunc ullamcorper orci, fermentum bibendum enim nibh eget ipsum.

Donec porttitor ligula eu dolor. Maecenas vitae nulla consequat libero cursus venenatis. Nam magna enim, accumsan eu, blandit sed, blandit a, eros. Quisque facilisis erat a dui. Nam malesuada ornare dolor. Cras gravida, diam sit

Sidebar

Proin tincidunt, velit vel porta elementum, magna diam molestie sapien, non aliquet massa pede eu diam. Aliquam iaculis. Fusce et ipsum et nulla tristique facilisis. Donec eget sem sit amet ligula viverra gravida. Etiam vehicula urna vel turpis. Suspendisse sagittis ante a urna.

Morbi a est quis orci consequat rutrum. Nullam egestas feugiat felis. Integer adipiscing semper

> There is an alternate way to create faux columns as well—see step 5 of the "Creating flanking sidebars" exercise later in the chapter.

Boxouts revisited: Creating multiple boxouts within a sidebar

Required files	Files from `multiple-boxouts-starting-point` in the chapter 7 folder as a starting point.
What you'll learn	How to use faux columns, boxouts, and the cascade to create a page design with a sidebar that contains multiple boxouts.
Completed files	`multiple-boxouts-complete` in the chapter 7 folder.

1. Examine the code. Open the web page and CSS document from `multiple-boxouts-starting-point`, and also open the web page in a browser so you can see what it looks like. Lots of work has already been done here, but it's all stuff you already know. Essentially, this page is a combination of the "Creating a boxout" and "Creating a sidebar with faux-column backgrounds" exercises from earlier in the chapter. A few changes have been made, however. The boxout has been duplicated three times and placed within the sidebar, the `float: right` pair from `.boxout` has been deleted (because the boxouts no longer need to float—they are within a container that itself is floated), and some bottom padding has been added (to ensure there's a gap below the final paragraph of each boxout).

```
.boxout {
  width: 180px;
  padding: 0 10px 1px;
  margin: 0 0 20px;
  background: #e1e1e1 url(boxout-bottom.gif) 0 100% no-repeat;
}
```

Also, the background from the faux columns exercise isn't there, because the vertical line the boxouts create is enough to make the column visually distinct—another separator isn't necessary.

2. Add class values. While consistent style is good for a website, it's sometimes neat to offer multiple styles for an element. This can come in handy for categorization—for example, each boxout in this design could contain information about a certain area of the website, and therefore color coding them and providing each with an icon (for those viewers with color vision difficulties) may help users navigate more easily. Because you can use multiple class values in CSS, it's possible to simply add a second class value to each of the boxout divs and then create an override rule for each in CSS.

```
<div class="boxout questionsHeader">
  [div content]
</div>
<div class="boxout chatHeader">
  [div content]
</div>
<div class="boxout toolsHeader">
  [div content]
</div>
```

3. Add new CSS rules. In the multiple-boxouts-starting-point folder, you'll find a bunch of images with the boxout-top- prefix. These are additional tops for the boxouts, each of which has a different color and icon. By using three contextual rules, overrides are created, setting a new background color and image for each of the three heading classes defined in step 2.

```
.questionsHeader h2 {
  background: #d72a49 url(boxout-top-questions.gif) no-repeat;
}
.chatHeader h2 {
  background: #2a84d7 url(boxout-top-chat.gif) no-repeat;
}
.toolsHeader h2 {
  background: #d72ab0 url(boxout-top-tools.gif) no-repeat;
}
```

Note that these rules must be placed after the .boxout h2 rule in the CSS, because the CSS cascade ensures that the rule closest to the element is applied. If these were placed above the .boxout h2 rule, they would be overridden by it, resulting in the boxouts all retaining their default appearance.

The following image shows what your page should now look like.

7

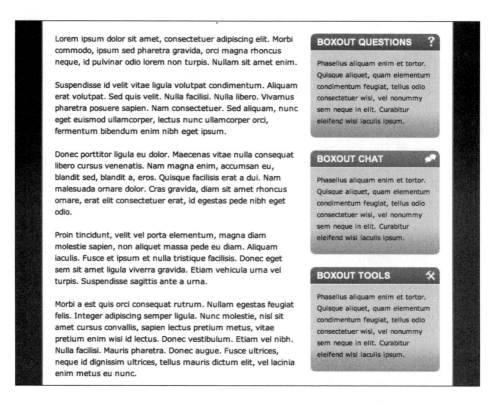

Creating flanking sidebars

Although some sites can be designed around a two-column model, you'll frequently need more. This can be achieved by adding further columns to the pages created in earlier exercises, or by nesting wrappers with two columns. (In other words, the first wrapper can contain a sidebar and a wrapper, which itself contains the main content and another sidebar.)

The only issue with this is that it doesn't allow for information to be provided in code in an order different from that shown on the screen. For users of alternate devices, a site with a sidebar (perhaps for navigation and advertising), followed by the main content, followed by another sidebar (perhaps for boxouts) would require them to wade through the first sidebar before accessing the main content. You can get around this by using a "skip to main content" link (as per the skip navigation link from Chapter 5), but you can also set the content in the order you want in the code (main content, first sidebar, second sidebar) and then use CSS to reorder the columns on the screen.

Creating flanking sidebars

Required files	Files from flanking-sidebars-starting-point in the chapter 7 folder as a starting point.
What you'll learn	How to create flanking sidebars for a content area, thereby enabling you to set content in one order in the code and another onscreen.
Completed files	flanking-sidebars-liquid and flanking-sidebars-fixed in the chapter 7 folder.

1. Check out the page. Open flanking-sidebars.html in a web browser and in a text editor. In the code, you have a wrapper that contains a masthead, followed by a wrapper for the columns, followed by a footer. Within the column wrapper are three divs: mainContent, leftSidebar, and rightSidebar. Each of these has a content wrapper (as per step 4 of the "Manipulating two structural divs for liquid layouts" exercise). In CSS, the page defaults and font styles are already set, as are styles for the masthead and footer. The clearFix method (see the "Clearing floated content" exercise) has also been used, since the three columns will be positioned by being floated. Note that for this exercise, the layout will be a liquid one, based on percentage values for widths and margins.

2. Add the column backgrounds. Add the following two rules, which supply two backgrounds for the divs. The first is applied to the column wrapper, setting the background to gray and adding a horizontally tiling drop-shadow image. The second is applied to the main content div, defining its background as white, and setting its own background. This will create a seamless shadow effect, but the main content will be differentiated from the sidebar via a brighter background.

```
#columnWrapper {
   background: #ebebeb url(assets/grey-shadow-top.gif) 0 0 repeat-x;
}
#mainContent {
   background: #ffffff url(assets/white-shadow-top.gif) 0 0 repeat-x;
}
```

3. Set column widths. Amend the #mainContent rule and add rules for the two sidebars, floating all of the columns left and setting width values. This is a liquid design, so percentages must be used, and they must add up to 100%.

```
#mainContent {
   background: #ffffff url(assets/white-shadow-top.gif) 0 0 repeat-x;
   float: left;
   width: 50%;
}
#leftSidebar {
   float: left;
   width: 30%;
}
```

```css
#rightSidebar {
  float: left;
  width: 20%;
}
```

PAGE TITLE

MAIN CONTENT

Lorem ipsum dolor sit amet, consectetuer adipiscing elit. Morbi commodo, ipsum sed pharetra gravida, orci magna rhoncus neque, id pulvinar odio lorem non turpis. Nullam sit amet enim. Suspendisse id velit vitae ligula volutpat condimentum. Aliquam erat volutpat. Sed quis velit. Nulla facilisi. Nulla libero. Vivamus pharetra posuere sapien. Nam consectetuer. Sed aliquam, nunc eget euismod ullamcorper, lectus nunc ullamcorper orci, fermentum bibendum enim nibh eget ipsum. Donec porttitor ligula eu dolor. Maecenas vitae nulla consequat libero cursus venenatis. Nam magna enim, accumsan eu, blandit sed, blandit a, eros.

Quisque facilisis erat a dui. Nam malesuada ornare dolor. Cras gravida, diam sit amet rhoncus ornare, erat elit consectetuer erat, id egestas pede nibh eget odio. Proin tincidunt, velit vel porta elementum, magna diam molestie sapien, non aliquet massa pede eu diam. Aliquam iaculis. Fusce et ipsum et nulla tristique facilisis. Donec eget sem sit amet ligula viverra gravida. Etiam vehicula urna vel turpis. Suspendisse sagittis ante a urna. Morbi a est quis orci consequat rutrum. Nullam egestas feugiat felis. Integer adipiscing semper ligula. Nunc molestie, nisl sit amet cursus convallis, sapien lectus pretium metus, vitae pretium enim wisi id lectus. Donec vestibulum. Etiam vel nibh. Nulla facilisi. Mauris pharetra. Donec augue. Fusce ultrices, neque id dignissim ultrices, tellus mauris dictum elit, vel lacinia enim metus eu nunc.

LEFT SIDEBAR

Proin at eros non eros adipiscing mollis. Donec semper turpis sed diam. Sed consequat ligula nec tortor. Integer eget Morbi ipsum ipsum, porta nec, tempor id, auctor vitae, purus. Pellentesque neque. Nulla luctus erat vitae libero. Integer nec enim. Phasellus aliquam enim et tortor. Quisque elit sit amet mi. Phasellus pellentesque, erat eget elementum volutpat, dolor nisl porta neque, vitae sodales ipsum nibh in ligula. Maecenas mattis pulvinar diam. Curabitur sed leo.

Nunc auctor bibendum eros. Maecenas porta accumsan mauris. Etiam enim enim, elementum sed, bibendum quis, rhoncus non, metus. Fusce neque dolor, adipiscing sed, consectetuer et, lacinia sit amet, quam. Suspendisse wisi quam, consectetuer in, blandit sed, suscipit eu, eros. Etiam ligula enim, tempor ut, blandit nec, mollis eu, lectus. Nam cursus. Vivamus iaculis. Aenean risus purus, pharetra in, blandit quis, gravida a, turpis. Donec nisl. Aenean eget mi. Fusce mattis est id diam. Phasellus faucibus interdum sapien. Duis quis nunc. Sed enim.

RIGHT SIDEBAR

Nunc auctor bibendum eros. Maecenas porta accumsan mauris. Etiam enim enim, elementum sed, bibendum quis, rhoncus non, metus. Fusce neque dolor, adipiscing sed, consectetuer et, lacinia sit amet, quam. Suspendisse wisi quam, consectetuer in, blandit sed, suscipit eu, eros. Etiam ligula enim, tempor ut, blandit nec, mollis eu, lectus. Nam cursus. Vivamus iaculis. Aenean risus purus, pharetra in, blandit quis, gravida a, turpis. Donec nisl. Aenean eget mi. Fusce mattis est id diam. Phasellus faucibus interdum sapien. Duis quis nunc. Sed enim.

This is the footer

4. Position the sidebars. At the moment, the columns are in the order specified in the code. However, via the use of margins, this order can be changed. For the main content div, set a margin-left value equal to the width of the left sidebar. Next, set a margin-left value for #leftSidebar that's the *negative* value of the sum of the width and left margin values of the main content area.

```css
#mainContent {
  background: #ffffff url(assets/white-shadow-top.gif) 0 0 repeat-x;
  float: left;
  width: 50%;
  margin-left: 30%;
}
#leftSidebar {
  float: left;
  width: 30%;
  margin-left: -80%;
}
#rightSidebar {
  float: left;
  width: 20%;
}
```

PAGE TITLE

LEFT SIDEBAR

Proin at eros non eros adipiscing mollis. Donec semper turpis sed diam. Sed consequat ligula nec tortor. Integer eget sem. Ut vitae enim eu est vehicula gravida. Morbi ipsum ipsum, porta nec, tempor id, auctor vitae, purus. Pellentesque neque. Nulla luctus erat vitae libero. Integer nec enim. Phasellus aliquam enim et tortor. Quisque elit sit amet mi. Phasellus pellentesque, erat eget elementum volutpat, dolor nisl porta neque, vitae sodales ipsum nibh in ligula. Maecenas mattis pulvinar diam. Curabitur sed leo.

Nunc auctor bibendum eros. Maecenas porta accumsan mauris. Etiam enim enim, elementum sed, bibendum quis, rhoncus non, metus. Fusce neque dolor, adipiscing sed, consectetuer et, lacinia sit amet, quam. Suspendisse wisi quam, consectetuer in, blandit sed, suscipit eu, eros. Etiam ligula enim, tempor ut, blandit nec, mollis eu, lectus. Nam cursus. Vivamus iaculis. Aenean risus purus, pharetra in, blandit quis, gravida a, turpis. Donec nisl. Aenean eget mi. Fusce mattis est id diam. Phasellus faucibus interdum sapien. Duis quis nunc. Sed enim.

MAIN CONTENT

Lorem ipsum dolor sit amet, consectetuer adipiscing elit. Morbi commodo, ipsum sed pharetra gravida, orci magna rhoncus neque, id pulvinar odio lorem non turpis. Nullam sit amet enim. Suspendisse id velit vitae ligula volutpat condimentum. Aliquam erat volutpat. Sed quis velit. Nulla facilisi. Nulla libero. Vivamus pharetra posuere sapien. Nam consectetuer. Sed aliquam, nunc eget euismod ullamcorper, lectus nunc ullamcorper orci, fermentum bibendum enim nibh eget ipsum. Donec porttitor ligula eu dolor. Maecenas vitae nulla consequat libero cursus venenatis. Nam magna enim, accumsan eu, blandit sed, blandit a, eros.

Quisque facilisis erat a dui. Nam malesuada ornare dolor. Cras gravida, diam sit amet rhoncus ornare, erat elit consectetuer erat, id egestas pede nibh eget odio. Proin tincidunt, velit vel porta elementum, magna diam molestie sapien, non aliquet massa pede eu diam. Aliquam iaculis. Fusce et ipsum et nulla tristique facilisis. Donec eget sem sit amet ligula viverra gravida. Etiam vehicula urna vel turpis. Suspendisse sagittis ante a urna. Morbi a est quis orci consequat rutrum. Nullam egestas feugiat felis. Integer adipiscing semper ligula. Nunc molestie, nisl sit amet cursus convallis, sapien lectus pretium metus, vitae pretium enim wisi id lectus. Donec vestibulum. Etiam vel nibh. Nulla facilisi. Mauris pharetra. Donec augue. Fusce ultrices, neque id dignissim ultrices, tellus mauris dictum elit, vel lacinia enim metus eu nunc.

RIGHT SIDEBAR

Nunc auctor bibendum eros. Maecenas porta accumsan mauris. Etiam enim enim, elementum sed, bibendum quis, rhoncus non, metus. Fusce neque dolor, adipiscing sed, consectetuer et, lacinia sit amet, quam. Suspendisse wisi quam, consectetuer in, blandit sed, suscipit eu, eros. Etiam ligula enim, tempor ut, blandit nec, mollis eu, lectus. Nam cursus. Vivamus iaculis. Aenean risus purus, pharetra in, blandit quis, gravida a, turpis. Donec nisl. Aenean eget mi. Fusce mattis est id diam. Phasellus faucibus interdum sapien. Duis quis nunc. Sed enim.

This is the footer

Internet Explorer may cause problems with this layout, making the right-hand sidebar sometimes appear beneath the others when the browser window is resized. This is caused by a rounding error (see the "Dealing with rounding errors" section in Chapter 9). Therefore, it's often useful to amend one of the percentages (and any related values), dropping them by 0.0001%—for example, change the width *value of* #mainContent *to 49.9999% and the* margin-left *value of* #leftSidebar *to 79.9999%.*

5. Fine-tune the design. Add the three rules in the following code block to finish off the layout and tidy things up.

```
.columnContentWrapper {
  padding: 30px 10px;
}
#mainContent, #leftSidebar, #rightSidebar {
  padding-bottom: 32767px !important;
  margin-bottom: -32767px !important;
}
#columnWrapper {
  overflow: hidden;
}
```

The first rule merely adds some padding to the column content wrappers. The next rule applies a large amount of padding to the bottom of each column and a negative margin of the same size, bringing the document flow back to the point where the padding begins. The use of overflow: hidden on the column container removes the overflow below the longest column's content. Note that the value used here is the *maximum* allowed by Apple's Safari. You can also use the second rule in the previous code block to control padding by reducing the `margin-bottom` value: the difference between the `padding-bottom` and `margin-bottom` values effectively becomes padding, although in this exercise, padding has been dealt with via the `.columnContentWrapper` rule.

PAGE TITLE

LEFT SIDEBAR

Proin at eros non eros adipiscing mollis. Donec semper turpis sed diam. Sed consequat ligula nec tortor. Integer eget sem. Ut vitae enim eu est vehicula gravida. Morbi ipsum ipsum, porta nec, tempor id, auctor vitae, purus. Pellentesque neque. Nulla luctus erat vitae libero. Integer nec enim. Phasellus aliquam enim et tortor. Quisque elit sit amet mi. Phasellus pellentesque, erat eget elementum volutpat, dolor nisl porta neque, vitae sodales ipsum nibh in ligula. Maecenas mattis pulvinar diam. Curabitur sed leo.

Nunc auctor bibendum eros. Maecenas porta accumsan mauris. Etiam enim enim, elementum sed, bibendum quis, rhoncus non, metus. Fusce neque dolor, adipiscing sed, consectetuer et, lacinia sit amet, quam. Suspendisse wisi quam, consectetuer in, blandit sed, suscipit eu, eros. Etiam ligula enim, tempor ut, blandit nec, mollis eu, lectus. Nam cursus. Vivamus iaculis. Aenean risus purus, pharetra in, blandit quis, gravida a, turpis. Donec nisl. Aenean eget mi. Fusce mattis est id diam. Phasellus faucibus interdum sapien. Duis quis nunc. Sed enim.

MAIN CONTENT

Lorem ipsum dolor sit amet, consectetuer adipiscing elit. Morbi commodo, ipsum sed pharetra gravida, orci magna rhoncus neque, id pulvinar odio lorem non turpis. Nullam sit amet enim. Suspendisse id velit vitae ligula volutpat condimentum. Aliquam erat volutpat. Sed quis velit. Nulla facilisi. Nulla libero. Vivamus pharetra posuere sapien. Nam consectetuer. Sed aliquam, nunc eget euismod ullamcorper, lectus nunc ullamcorper orci, fermentum bibendum enim nibh eget ipsum. Donec porttitor ligula eu dolor. Maecenas vitae nulla consequat libero cursus venenatis. Nam magna enim, accumsan eu, blandit sed, blandit a, eros.

Quisque facilisis erat a dui. Nam malesuada ornare dolor. Cras gravida, diam sit amet rhoncus ornare, erat elit consectetuer erat, id egestas pede nibh eget odio. Proin tincidunt, velit vel porta elementum, magna diam molestie sapien, non aliquet massa pede eu diam. Aliquam iaculis. Fusce et ipsum et nulla tristique facilisis. Donec eget sem sit amet ligula viverra gravida. Etiam vehicula urna vel turpis. Suspendisse sagittis ante a urna. Morbi a est quis orci consequat rutrum. Nullam egestas feugiat felis. Integer adipiscing semper ligula. Nunc molestie, nisl sit amet cursus convallis, sapien lectus pretium metus, vitae pretium enim wisi id lectus. Donec vestibulum. Etiam vel nibh. Nulla facilisi. Mauris pharetra. Donec augue. Fusce ultrices, neque id dignissim ultrices, tellus mauris dictum elit, vel lacinia enim metus eu nunc.

RIGHT SIDEBAR

Nunc auctor bibendum eros. Maecenas porta accumsan mauris. Etiam enim enim, elementum sed, bibendum quis, rhoncus non, metus. Fusce neque dolor, adipiscing sed, consectetuer et, lacinia sit amet, quam. Suspendisse wisi quam, consectetuer in, blandit sed, suscipit eu, eros. Etiam ligula enim, tempor ut, blandit nec, mollis eu, lectus. Nam cursus. Vivamus iaculis. Aenean risus purus, pharetra in, blandit quis, gravida a, turpis. Donec nisl. Aenean eget mi. Fusce mattis est id diam. Phasellus faucibus interdum sapien. Duis quis nunc. Sed enim.

This is the footer

For this layout to work in Internet Explorer 6, you need to use a style sheet attached via a conditional comment (see "Conditional comments" in Chapter 9) to set display *to* inline-block *for the* #columnWrapper *rule. Furthermore, that browser suffers from the double-float margin bug (see the "Double-float margin bug" section in Chapter 9); deal with this by setting* display: inline *to* #mainContent, *or by overriding the* margin-left *value of* #mainContent, *halving it via a style sheet attached via a conditional comment. The layout also suffers from a slight cosmetic glitch in Safari 2, with some space being shown above the footer's border. To fix this, you can add the following rule:* /**/#wrapper {display: block;}—*however, this should really be added in a Safari-specific style sheet attached using JavaScript (see the "Targeting other browsers" section in Chapter 9).*

6. Make the layout fixed. Amending the layout to a fixed one is simple. Because the layout will no longer span the window width, a border needs to be placed around the wrapper (otherwise the drop-shadow cutoffs at the left and right just look weird). Therefore, add a padding-bottom value of 20px to the body rule, and create the #wrapper rule shown following:

```
#wrapper {
  width: 700px;
  margin: 0 auto;
  border: 1px solid #555555;
  border-top: 0;
}
```

Next, update the `width` and `margin-left` values for the three rules shown in the following code, being mindful of the relationships mentioned in step 4 and the fact that the width values cannot exceed the value set for the wrapper's width in the previous step.

```
#mainContent {
  background: #ffffff url(assets/white-shadow-top.gif) 0 0 repeat-x;
  float: left;
  width: 400px;
  margin-left: 175px;
}
#leftSidebar {
  float: left;
  width: 175px;
  margin-left: -575px;
}
#rightSidebar {
  float: left;
  width: 125px;
}
```

The following image shows what your page should now look like.

7

Automating layout variations

The final exercise in this section shows how to automate page layouts in a similar manner to automating navigation, as described in Chapter 5 (e.g., in the "Creating a CSS-only tab bar that automates the active page" exercise). By defining a class value for the body element, contextual selectors can be used to amend the layout of a web page. This technique comes in handy when working on large sites that have many variations throughout, but some consistent elements. For example, the site's overall width, masthead, and footer may remain constant, but the number of columns on the page may change, or they may change widths.

Using body class values and CSS to automate page layouts

Required files	Files from faux-columns in the chapter 7 folder as a starting point.
What you'll learn	How to use body class values and contextual selectors to automate page layouts.
Completed files	automate-page-layouts in the chapter 7 folder.

1. Examine the files. The files from the "Creating a sidebar with faux-column backgrounds" exercise are used as the basis for this one. The web page has two divs, one for the main content (mainContent) and another for the sidebar (sidebar). The default setup is for the main content area to take up most of the width and for the sidebar to be narrow, with smaller text. During the next two steps, contextual selectors will be designed to create two alternate layouts, one of which will have a single column and one of which will split the columns evenly.

Working with two divs

Main content

Lorem ipsum dolor sit amet, consectetuer adipiscing elit. Morbi commodo, ipsum sed pharetra gravida, orci magna rhoncus neque, id pulvinar odio lorem non turpis. Nullam sit amet enim.

Suspendisse id velit vitae ligula volutpat condimentum. Aliquam erat volutpat. Sed quis velit. Nulla facilisi. Nulla libero. Vivamus pharetra posuere sapien. Nam consectetuer. Sed aliquam, nunc eget euismod ullamcorper, lectus nunc ullamcorper orci, fermentum bibendum enim nibh eget ipsum.

Donec porttitor ligula eu dolor. Maecenas vitae nulla consequat libero cursus venenatis. Nam magna enim, accumsan eu, blandit sed, blandit a, eros. Quisque facilisis erat a dui. Nam malesuada ornare dolor. Cras gravida, diam sit amet rhoncus ornare, erat elit consectetuer erat, id egestas pede nibh eget

Sidebar

Proin tincidunt, velit vel porta elementum, magna diam molestie sapien, non aliquet massa pede eu diam. Aliquam iaculis. Fusce et ipsum et nulla tristique facilisis. Donec eget sem sit amet ligula viverra gravida. Etiam vehicula urna vel turpis. Suspendisse sagittis ante a urna.

Morbi a est quis orci consequat rutrum. Nullam egestas feugiat felis. Integer adipiscing semper ligula. Nunc molestie, nisl sit amet

---

2. Create single-column rules. The way this method works is to create overrides for relevant rules. The contextual selectors will begin with a class selector that will be applied to the page's body start tag, followed by the rules that require overriding. For a single column, the wrapper no longer needs a background, the main content area needs to be as wide as the wrapper (700 pixels), and the sidebar doesn't need

to be displayed. Also, the default `margin-right` value for `#wrapper` needs to be overridden, otherwise the main content area will end up 700 pixels wide *plus* 41 pixels of margin.

```
.singleColumn #wrapper {
  background: none;
}
.singleColumn #mainContent {
  width: 700px;
  margin-right: 0;
}
.singleColumn #sidebar {
  display: none;
}
```

This style can be applied to the web page by setting the body element's class value to `singleColumn`.

```
<body class="singleColumn">
```

Working with two divs

Main content

Lorem ipsum dolor sit amet, consectetuer adipiscing elit. Morbi commodo, ipsum sed pharetra gravida, orci magna rhoncus neque, id pulvinar odio lorem non turpis. Nullam sit amet enim.

Suspendisse id velit vitae ligula volutpat condimentum. Aliquam erat volutpat. Sed quis velit. Nulla facilisi. Nulla libero. Vivamus pharetra posuere sapien. Nam consectetuer. Sed aliquam, nunc eget euismod ullamcorper, lectus nunc ullamcorper orci, fermentum bibendum enim nibh eget ipsum.

Donec porttitor ligula eu dolor. Maecenas vitae nulla consequat libero cursus venenatis. Nam magna enim, accumsan eu, blandit sed, blandit a, eros. Quisque facilisis erat a dui. Nam malesuada ornare dolor. Cras gravida, diam sit amet rhoncus ornare, erat elit consectetuer erat, id egestas pede nibh eget odio.

Note that when using designs such as this, be sure to empty the contents of non-displayed divs—*any content left within them is just a waste of bandwidth.*

3. Create an equal-column-split rule. For an equal column split, the column widths need to be amended to the same value. But because the `margin-right` setting defined earlier is 41px, the sidebar has been set to 1 pixel narrower than the main content area. (An alternate option would have been to set both column widths to 330px and set `margin-right` in `.equalSplitColumns #mainContent` to 40px.) The `background-position` horizontal value needs changing to reflect the new column positions. Finally, because both columns command equal prominence, the `font-size` setting for the sidebar is set to 100% in `.equalSplitColumns #sidebar`.

```
.equalSplitColumns #wrapper {
  background-position: 350px 0;
}
.equalSplitColumns #mainContent {
```

7

```
    width: 330px;
}
.equalSplitColumns #sidebar {
    width: 329px;
    font-size: 100%;
}
```

This style can be applied to the web page by setting the body element's class value to equalSplitColumns.

```
<body class="equalSplitColumns">
```

Working with two divs

Main content

Lorem ipsum dolor sit amet, consectetuer adipiscing elit. Morbi commodo, ipsum sed pharetra gravida, orci magna rhoncus neque, id pulvinar odio lorem non turpis. Nullam sit amet enim.

Suspendisse id velit vitae ligula volutpat condimentum. Aliquam erat volutpat. Sed quis velit. Nulla facilisi. Nulla libero. Vivamus pharetra posuere sapien. Nam consectetuer. Sed aliquam, nunc eget euismod ullamcorper, lectus nunc ullamcorper orci, fermentum bibendum enim nibh eget ipsum.

Sidebar

Proin tincidunt, velit vel porta elementum, magna diam molestie sapien, non aliquet massa pede eu diam. Aliquam iaculis. Fusce et ipsum et nulla tristique facilisis. Donec eget sem sit amet ligula viverra gravida. Etiam vehicula urna vel turpis. Suspendisse sagittis ante a urna.

Morbi a est quis orci consequat rutrum. Nullam egestas feugiat felis. Integer adipiscing semper ligula. Nunc molestie, nisl sit amet cursus convallis, sapien lectus pretium metus, vitae pretium enim wisi id lectus.

As mentioned, this exercise works in a similar way to some of the navigation ones in Chapter 5. With a little thought, it should be easy enough to see how this automation method can assist when creating websites. As long as the site's structure has been carefully planned, you can usually get away with a single navigation bar and a single structure, but have multiple layouts, each one driven by the CSS variations and the body class value.

Scrollable content areas

Scrolling is a matter of fact on the Web. Although designers should be careful not to make users scroll too much (or in multiple directions—sites that force both horizontal and vertical scrolling tend to be awkward and annoying to use), some scrolling is inevitable with the vast majority of websites. In the past, some designers created fixed sites that sat in the middle of the browser window, content restricted by the viewing area. Various techniques later enabled designers to get around this limitation, creating in-page scrollable content areas. First came frames, and later came CSS-driven scrolling areas. Both enable you to create in-page scrollable content, but although such things are explored in the final part of this chapter, scrollable areas should be used with care—if you need a user to see something right away, don't hide it "under the fold," and remember that if you create a centered, fixed-view window, test it out using many different screen resolutions to ensure it looks and works OK for all of your users.

Working with frames

Elsewhere in this book, I mostly refer to web pages that comprise single documents, with external files adding presentation information (CSS) or functionality (JavaScript or CSS). Frames are different, requiring an HTML document called a **frameset**, which acts as a container for a number of frames. The frameset has no actual content of its own—it's just a container used to order and place the frames. The frames are standard HTML documents. Therefore, you use a frameset to carve up the available space in a browser window and display several HTML documents simultaneously, each of which has the ability to scroll independently.

Today, frames are considered a relic, disrupting the logical structure of your site because of the way they're created. Each frame is a separate HTML document, and everything is stitched together with yet another HTML document—the frameset. This causes problems: users of alternate devices may find a frame-based site hard to navigate; all users may come across orphaned pages (pages outside of their framesets); bookmarking saves the frameset, not its pages; and design across frames isn't possible. Also, because of the increase in usage of design applications with templating features, and of PHP and server-side includes, the ease-of-development aspect of frames is no longer relevant. Because of these issues, the rest of this subsection is primarily here for the sake of completeness.

Although a frameset is still an HTML page, it requires a specific frameset DTD, which looks like this:

```
<!DOCTYPE html PUBLIC "-//W3C//DTD XHTML 1.0 Frameset//EN"
          "http://www.w3.org/TR/xhtml1/DTD/xhtml1-frameset.dtd">
```

The frameset page lacks a body element (although it still requires head and `title` elements, along with defining the character set) and instead uses a `frameset` element, which sets the attributes for how the frames are positioned. The `frameset` element houses `frame` elements, which define the location and attribute of each frame. Note that this DTD should only be used for the frameset and not for the individual pages that will be loaded into the frameset—they should use whatever DTD is relevant to their content.

A basic two-column frameset may use a code block like the following one, the `cols` attribute defining the width of each frame (values can be numerals for a pixel value, a percentage, or a wildcard *, which sets the dimension to whatever space remains). For each `frame` element, the `src` attribute defines the web page that will be displayed inside the frame.

```
<frameset cols="150,*">
  <frame src="frame-one.html" />
  <frame src="frame-two.html" />
</frameset>
```

7

To change the alignment of the frames and split the browser window horizontally, replace the cols attribute in the frameset element with a rows attribute:

```
<frameset rows="150,*">
```

To add more frames in either case, just add more frame elements, but ensure that your cols or rows values don't add up to more than 100%.

You can also nest framesets, to create a combination of columns and rows:

```
<frameset rows="120,*">
  <frame src="frame-one.html" />
  <frameset cols="150,*">
    <frame src="frame-two.html" />
    <frame src="frame-three.html" />
  </frameset>
</frameset>
```

The following list describes some of the attributes that can be added to the frame element, most of which amend the look of the frames:

- frameborder: This attribute defines whether the frame's border is displayed or not—via a value of 1 or 0, respectively. Turning off the frame borders prevents users from resizing frames.

- marginheight **and** marginwidth: These define the margins within the frame and are best set to 0; page content padding should be defined in CSS.

- scrolling: This attribute sets parameters for the use of scroll bars—it can be set to yes (scroll bars always on), no, or auto (scroll bars appear if required).

- noresize: In XHTML, this attribute takes its own name for its value (noresize). When set, the relevant frame can't be resized. Beware of using this—if the content is too big for the frame, users won't be able to easily access the information.

There are two other attributes of note: longdesc and name. longdesc enables you to set a URL with a long description of the frame's contents (for browsers that don't support frames). The name attribute enables you to assign a unique name to the frame, which is used for link-targeting purposes via the target attribute in anchors (the _top value replaces the frameset with the linked document, while the value myFrame would open a link in a frame with the name value of myFrame). However, this is not valid within XHTML Strict, and therefore requires any documents that use it to be reverted to XHTML Transitional.

For non-frames-compatible devices, use the noframes element (<noframes></noframes>) to provide accessible content. This is placed inside the outermost frameset element, after all the frames.

Working with internal frames (iframes)

The only type of frames in general use today are iframes. These enable you to update a page section without reloading the rest of it. Popular sites using iframes include Newstoday (www.newstoday.com/) and Pixelsurgeon (www.pixelsurgeon.com/), the latter of which uses a small inline frame to display its news feed.

In a more general sense, this can be handy for enabling users to update a portion of a site's design without touching the rest of the design, and without resorting to a costly content management system. However, there are superior and more accessible alternatives to this system, as you'll see later in the chapter.

An iframe can be placed anywhere within a web page. Its available attributes are outlined in Appendix A (XHTML Reference), but two worth mentioning here are width and height, which define the dimensions of the iframe. Set these with caution, because it's annoying if an iframe is bigger than the viewable area, or if the content of the iframe is too big for its defined dimensions. Note that these attributes can be omitted from HTML and instead defined in CSS (by way of an iframe tag selector or by applying a class to the iframe).

Here's some example code for an iframe:

```
<iframe src="internal_news.html" name="news" width="200" height="200"
➥ scrolling="yes" frameborder="0">Your browser doesn't support
➥ iframes. Please <a href="internal_news.html">click here
➥ to see the iframe's content</a>.</iframe>
```

Note the succinct content for the iframe, which enables non-frames-compatible devices to directly access the content of the iframe—compliant devices ignore this.

7

Scrollable content areas with CSS

Although iframes can be useful for practical reasons, many designers use them for aesthetic reasons, in order to provide a lot of information on a single page. For example, iframes are popular for lists of news items because they enable many hundreds of lines of text to be contained in a small area. However, if this is your reason for using an iframe, you're better off replacing it with a div and using CSS to control the overflow. If you use this method, the content will remain part of the web page, which is better for accessibility and site maintenance.

To do this, create a div with a unique class value:

```
<div class="scrollableContent">
  [content...]
</div>
```

Then style it in CSS—the rule provides the div's dimensions and determines how the div's overflow works:

```
.scrollableContent {
  width: 200px;
  height: 200px;
  overflow: auto;
}
```

When overflow is set to auto, scroll bars only appear when the content is too large for the set dimensions of the div. Other available values are hidden (display no scroll bars), scroll (permanently display both scroll bars), and visible (render content outside of the defined box area). Adding some padding, especially at the right-hand side of the scrollable content box, helps improve the area aesthetically, ensuring that content doesn't hug the scroll bar.

```
.scrollableContent {
  width: 200px;
  height: 200px;
  overflow: auto;
  padding: 0 10px 0 0;
}
```

Note that by also using PHP includes (see *PHP Solutions*, by David Powers, for more on those), you can even make scrollable content separate from the main web page, thereby emulating another aspect of an iframe, but without resorting to using frames at all.

```
<div class="scrollableContent">
  <?php @include $_SERVER['DOCUMENT_ROOT'] .
  ➥ "/include/document-name.php"; ?>
</div>
```

In this code block, @ suppresses errors, so if it didn't work, you'd receive no indication—removing @ would show any errors. Also, the document root setting sets the include to take the HTML/document root instead of the server root as the starting point for looking for the included file (when the file path starts with a /), so be aware of that when defining paths. An alternative would be to use a relative path, such as include/document-name.php. This would work without pointing to the server at the document root (so long as the path was correct).

Another more accessible option than using iframe elements is to use the object element to embed an external HTML document within a region of the page—when combined with the scrolling div method shown in this section, it pretty much provides all the benefits of an iframe with very few of the drawbacks (the content is on the page, unlike with frames and iframes—their content remains external).

The following code block shows how an object element can be added to the page. Note the alternate content within the object element, displayed if the browser cannot show the object. This can be used to directly link to the file in the data attribute.

```
<object data="a-file.html" type="text/html">
  <p>[alternate content]</p>
</object>
```

Like other elements, the object element can be styled using CSS, although Internet Explorer adds a border, so you need to overwrite existing border settings using conditional comments (see Chapter 9 for more on those) to prevent a double border. Also, if the content is too large for the object dimensions, it will scroll in whatever direction is needed, unless you explicitly set overflow to hidden; however, this setting doesn't work in Internet Explorer and Opera.

7

Name

Email address

Telephone number

Book title/ISBN

Reason for contacting us

publisher co-edition request

Comments/message

CONTACTS

Our office hours are from 10 a.m. to 6 p.m.
Thursday and 10 a.m. to 1 p.m. on Fridays.
the means below.

TELEPHONE
+44 (0) 1252 622 352

POST
Snub Communications, c/o Craig Grannell
29 Darset Avenue, Fleet, Hampshire, GU51 3

EMAIL
All fields are optional. However, please prov
details if you would like a reply.

hCard Creator

hCard-o-matic

given name

middle name

family name

organization

street

city

In this chapter:

- Creating forms and adding fields and controls
- Styling forms in CSS
- Configuring a mailform CGI script
- Sending forms using PHP
- Creating a layout for a user feedback page
- Creating an online business card using microformats

Introducing user feedback

One of the main reasons the Web has revolutionized working life and communications is its immediacy. Unlike printed media, websites can be continually updated at relatively minimal cost and also be available worldwide on a 24/7 basis. However, communication isn't one-way, and the Web makes it very easy to enable site users to offer feedback.

Using mailto: URLs

One of the most common methods of providing immediate user feedback is by using mailto: URLs within anchor tags. Instead of the anchor tag's value being a file name or URL, it begins with mailto: and is immediately followed by the recipient e-mail address.

```
<a href="mailto:someone@your.domain">Click to email!</a>
```

It's possible to take this technique further. You can define multiple recipients by using a comma-separated list, and by placing a question mark immediately after the final recipient address, you can add further parameters, such as a subject and recipients to carbon copy (cc) and blind carbon copy (bcc). If using more than one parameter, you must separate them with encoded ampersands (&). Note that spaces within the subject should also be encoded (as %20).

```
<a href="mailto:someone@your.domain,someoneelse@your.domain?subject=
➥Contact%20from%20website&amp;cc=bigboss@your.domain">Click
➥ to email!</a>
```

> There should be no spaces in a mailto: value. Therefore, don't place spaces before or after colons, commas, or the ? and = symbols.

Although this may sound great, there are several problems with such a system. First, e-mail addresses online are often harvested by spambots. Second, a mailto: link relies on the user having a preconfigured e-mail client ready to go—something that people working on college and library machines most likely won't have. Third, not all browsers support the range of options explained earlier.

A way to combat the spambots is presented in the next section. For the second issue (the `mailto:` link's reliance on a preconfigured mail client), I recommend using forms for any complex website feedback, which we will come to later on in this chapter. For the third issue (browser support for the more advanced `mailto:` options), I recommend just keeping things simple. Place your e-mail address online as a `mailto:` and enable the user to fill in any other details, such common as the subject line.

Scrambling addresses

In my experience, having an e-mail address online for just a few days is enough to start receiving regular spam. A workaround is to encrypt e-mail addresses using a bulletproof concoction of JavaScript. The Enkoder form from Hivelogic is a neat way of going about this, and produces decent results.

This online form at www.hivelogic.com/enkoder/form enables you to create a `mailto:` link that's composed of complex JavaScript. Although in time, spambots will likely break this code, as they have with simpler encoders, it's the best example I've seen, and the results I've had with it have been good. Beware, though, that any users with JavaScript disabled won't see the address, so ensure that you cater to them by including some other means of contacting the site owner.

> *Enkoder is also available as a plug-in for Ruby on Rails.*

8

Working with forms

In this section, we'll work through how to create a form and add controls. We'll also look at how to improve form accessibility by using the `tabindex` attribute, and the `label`, `fieldset`, and `legend` elements.

As suggested earlier in the chapter, the best way of getting user feedback is through an online form that the user fills in and submits. Fields are configured by the designer, enabling the site owner to receive specific information. However, don't go overboard: provide users with a massive, sprawling online form and they will most likely not bother filling it in, and will go elsewhere.

Similarly, although you can use JavaScript to make certain form fields required, I'm not a fan of this technique, because it annoys users. Some sites go overboard on this, "forcing" users to input a whole bunch of details, some of which may simply not be applicable to the user. In such cases, users will likely either go elsewhere or insert fake data, which helps no one.

So, keep things simple and use the fewest fields possible. In the vast majority of cases, you should be able to simply create name, e-mail address, and phone number fields, and include a text area that enables users to input their query.

Creating a form

Form controls are housed within a form element, whose attributes also determine the location of the script used to parse it (see the "Sending feedback" section later in the chapter). Other attributes define the encoding type used and the method by which the browser sends the form's data to the server. A typical start tag for a form therefore looks like this:

```
<form action="http://www.yourdomain.com/cgi-bin/FormMail.cgi"
➥ method="post">
```

> The preceding form start tag includes attributes that point at a CGI script, but alternative methods of sending forms exist, including PHP, ASP, and ColdFusion. Check with your hosting company about the methods available for sending forms, and use the technology supported by your ISP.

Adding controls

Some form controls are added using the input element. The type attribute declares what kind of control the element is going to be. The most common values are text, which produces a single-line text input field; checkbox and radio, which are used for multiple-choice options; and submit, which is used for the all-important Submit button.

Other useful elements include select, option, and optgroup, used for creating pop-up lists, and textarea, which provides a means for the user to offer a multiple-line response (this is commonly used in online forms for a question area). The basic HTML for a form may therefore look like the following, producing the page depicted in the following screen grab.

```
<form action="http://www.yourdomain.com/cgi-bin/FormMail.cgi"
➥ method="post">
  <p><strong>Name</strong><br />
  <input type="text" name="realname" size="30" /></p>
  <p><strong>Email address</strong><br />
  <input type="text" name="email" size="30" /></p>
  <p><strong>Telephone</strong><br />
  <input type="text" name="phone" size="30" /></p>
  <p><strong>Are you a Web designer?</strong><br />
  <input type="radio" name="designer" value="yes" />Yes |
  ➥ <input type="radio" name="designer" value="no" />No</p>
  <p>What platform do you favor?<br />
  <select name="platform">
    <option selected="selected">Windows</option>
    <option>Mac</option>
    <option>Linux</option>
    <option>Other</option>
```

```
    </select></p>
    <p><strong>Message</strong><br />
    <textarea name="message" rows="5" cols="30"></textarea></p>
    <p><input type="submit" name="SUBMIT" value="SUBMIT" /></p>
</form>
```

The bulk of the HTML is pretty straightforward. In each case, the name attribute value labels the control, meaning that you end up with the likes of Telephone: 555 555 555 in your form results, rather than just a bunch of answers. For multiple-option controls (check boxes and radio buttons), this attribute is identical, and an individual value attribute is set in each start tag.

By default, controls of this type—along with the select list—are set to off (i.e., no values selected), but you can define a default option. I've done this for the select list by setting selected="selected" on the Windows option. You'd do the same on a radio button to select it by default, and with a check box you'd set checked="checked".

Some of the attributes define the appearance of controls: the input element's size attribute sets a character width for the fields, while the textarea's rows and cols attributes set the number of rows and columns, again in terms of characters. It's also worth noting that any content within the textarea element is displayed, so if you want it to start totally blank, you must ensure that there's *nothing*—not even whitespace—between the start and end tags. (Some applications that reformat your code, and some website editors, place whitespace here, which some browsers subsequently use as the default value/content of the textarea. This results in the textarea's content being partially filled with spaces, and anyone trying to use it may then find their cursor's initial entry point partway down the text area, which can be off-putting.)

Long-time web users may have noticed the omission of a Reset button in this example. This button used to be common online, enabling the user to reset a form to its default state, removing any content they've added. However, I've never really seen the point in having it there, especially seeing as it's easy to click by mistake, resulting in the user having to fill in the form again, hence its absence from the examples in this chapter. However, if you want to add such a button, you can do so by using the following code:

```
<input type="reset" name="RESET" value="RESET" />
```

> *A full list of controls is available in Appendix A (XHTML Reference).*

Improving form accessibility

Although there's an onscreen visual relationship between form label text and the controls, they're not associated in any other way. This sometimes makes forms tricky to use for those people using screen readers and other assistive devices. Also, by default, the Tab key cycles through various web page elements in order, rather than jumping to the first form field (and continuing through the remainder of the form before moving elsewhere). Both of these issues are dealt with in this section.

The label, fieldset, and legend elements

The label element enables you to define relationships between the text labeling a form control and the form control itself. In the following example, the Name text is enclosed in a label element with the for attribute value of realname. This corresponds to the name and id values of the form field associated with this text.

```
<p><label for="realname">Name</label><br />
<input type="text" name="realname" id="realname" size="30" /></p>
```

Most browsers don't amend the content's visual display when it's nested within a label element, although you can style the label in CSS. However, most apply an important accessibility benefit: if you click the label, it gives **focus** to the corresponding form control (in other words, it selects the form control related to the label). Note that the id attribute—absent from the form example earlier in the chapter—is required for this. If it's absent, clicking the text within the label element won't cause the browser to do anything.

The fieldset element enables you to group a set of related form controls to which you apply a label via the legend element.

```
<fieldset>
  <legend>Personal information</legend>
  <p><label for="realname">Name</label><br />
  <input type="text" id="realname" name="realname" size="30" /></p>
  <p><label for="email">Email address</label><br />
  <input type="text" id="email" name="email" size="30" /></p>
  <p><label for="phone">Telephone</label><br />
  <input type="text" id="phone" name="phone" size="30" /></p>
</fieldset>
```

As you can see from the previous screenshot, these elements combine to surround the relevant form fields and labels with a border and provide the group with an explanatory title.

> *Note that each browser styles forms and controls differently. Therefore, be sure to test your forms in a wide range of browsers and don't be too concerned with trying to make things look exactly the same in each browser.*

Adding tabindex attributes

The tabindex attribute was first mentioned in Chapter 5 (in the "Using accesskey and tabindex" section). For forms, it's used to define the page's element tab order, and its value can be set as anything from 0 to 32767. Because the tabindex values needn't be sequential, it's advisable to set them in increments of ten, enabling you to insert others later, without having to rework every value on the page. With that in mind, you could set tabindex="10" on the realname field, tabindex="20" on the email field, and tabindex="30" on the phone field (these field names are based on their id/name values from the previous example). Assuming no other tabindex attributes with lower values are elsewhere on the page, the realname field becomes the first element highlighted when the Tab key is pressed, and then the cycle continues (in order) with the email and phone fields.

> *The reason for starting with 10 rather than 1 is because if you ignore the last digit, the tabindex values become standard integers, starting with 1. In other words, remove the final digits from 10, 20, and 30, and you end up with 1, 2, and 3. This makes it easier to keep track of the tabindex order.*

Note that whenever using tabindex, you run the risk of hijacking the mouse cursor, meaning that instead of the Tab key moving the user from the first form field to the second, it might end up highlighting something totally different, elsewhere on the page. What's logical to some people in terms of tab order may not be to others, so always ensure you test your websites thoroughly, responding to feedback. Generally, it makes sense to use the value only for form fields, and then with plenty of care.

CSS styling and layout for forms

Earlier, we covered how to lay out a form using paragraphs and line breaks. In this section, you'll see how tables and CSS can also be used to produce a more advanced layout.

Adding styles to forms

Form fields can be styled, enabling you to get away from the rather clunky default look offered by most browsers. Although the default appearance isn't very attractive, it does make obvious which elements are fields and which are buttons. Therefore, if you choose to style forms in CSS, ensure that the elements are still easy to make out.

A simple, elegant style to apply to text input fields and text areas is as follows:

```
.formField {
  border: 1px solid #333333;
  background-color: #dddddd;
  padding: 2px;
}
```

In HTML, you need to add the usual class attribute to apply this rule to the relevant element(s):

```
<input class="formField" tabindex="11" type="text" id="realname"
➥ name="realname" size="30" />
```

This replaces the default 3D border with a solid, dark gray border, and it also sets the background color as a light gray, thereby drawing attention to the form input fields. Note that browsers that support :hover and :focus on more than just anchors can have these states styled with different backgrounds, thereby providing further prompts. For example, upon focusing a form field, you might change its background color, making it more obvious that it's the field in focus.

Because the border in the previous code is defined using a class, it can be applied to multiple elements. The reason we don't use a tag selector and apply this style to all input fields is that radio buttons and check boxes look terrible with rectangular borders around them. However, applying this style to the select element can work well.

Note that the background color in this example is designed to contrast slightly with the page's background color, but still provide plenty of contrast with any text typed into the form fields; as always, pick your colors carefully when working with form styles.

The default Submit button style can be amended in a similar fashion, and padding can also be applied to it. This is usually a good idea because it enables the button to stand out and draws attention to the text within.

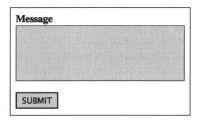

Should you desire a more styled Submit button, you can instead use an image:

```
<input type ="image" src="submit.gif" height="20" width="100"
➥ alt="Submit form" />
```

Along with the fields and controls, it's also possible to style the elements added in the previous section "The label, fieldset, and legend elements." The fieldset rule applies a 1-pixel dashed line around the elements grouped by the fieldset element, along with adding some padding and a bottom margin. The legend rule amends the legend element's font and the padding around it, and sets the text to uppercase; it also adds a background color so that the dotted line of the fieldset won't be shown behind the legend text in Internet Explorer. Note that not all browsers treat margins on legend elements in the same way, so if you add a margin value, be sure to thoroughly test your page. The screenshot that follows also includes the styles included in the default CSS document from the basic-boilerplates folder.

```
fieldset {
  border: 1px dashed #555555;
  padding: 10px;
  margin-bottom: 10px;
}
legend {
  padding: 0 10px;
  font-family: Arial, Helvetica, sans-serif;
  color: #000000;
  background: #ffffff;
  text-transform: uppercase;
}
```

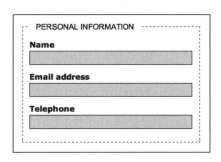

8

A final style point worth bearing in mind is that you can define styles for the form itself. This can be useful for positioning purposes (e.g., controlling the form's width and its bottom margin); the width setting can prove handy, since the fieldset border stretches to the entire window width, which looks very odd if the form labels and controls take up only a small area of the browser window. Reducing the form's width to specifically defined dimensions enables you to get around this. Alternatively, you can set a fixed width on the fieldset itself (or float it, enabling you to display fieldsets side by side.

You can also color the form's (or fieldset's) background in addition to or instead of the input fields, thereby making the entire form prominent. This is a device I've used on various versions of the Snub Communications website's contacts page, as shown in the following screenshot.

Regardless of the form styles you end up using, be sure to rigorously test across browsers, because the display of form elements is not consistent. Some variations are relatively minor—you'll find that defining values for font sizes, padding, and borders for input fields doesn't always result in fields of the same height, and that text fields and Submit buttons don't always align. A more dramatic difference is seen in versions of Safari prior to 3.0, which ignore many CSS properties for forms, instead using the Mac OS X "Aqua" look and feel—see the following screenshot for how the Snub Communications form looks in that browser. Form functionality is not affected by this, but layouts can be.

Advanced form layout with CSS

A common way of laying out forms is to use a table to line up the labels and form controls, although with the output being non-tabular in nature, this method is not recommended (CSS should be used for presentation, including positioning elements on a web page)—it's provided here to show a (partial) table layout that can be replicated in CSS. For our first three fields, a table-based form may have something like this:

```
<fieldset>
  <legend>Personal information</legend>
  <table class="formTable" cellpadding="0" cellspacing="0" border="0"
➥   summary="A contact details form.">
    <tr>
      <th scope="row">
      <label for="realname">Name</label></th>
      <td><input class="formField" type="text" id="realname"
➥ name="realname" size="30" /></td>
    </tr>
    <tr>
      <th scope="row"><label for="email">Email address</label></th>
      <td><input class="formField" type="text" id="email" name="email"
➥ size="30" /></td>
    </tr>
    <tr>
      <th scope="row"><label for="phone">Telephone</label></th>
      <td><input class="formField" type="text" id="phone" name="phone"
➥ size="30" /></td>
    </tr>
  </table>
</fieldset>
```

8

Because a class value was added to the table, the contextual selector .formTable th can be used as the selector for styling the form labels, defining the text-align property, along with other CSS properties such as font-weight. Applying a padding-right value to these cells also produces a gap to the right of the label cells. Another contextual selector, .formTable td, can then be used to style the cells—for example, to add padding at the bottom of each cell. The image to the right shows these styles applied to the various elements in the previous code block, along with the styles shown in the "Adding styles to forms" section.

```
.formTable td {
  padding: 0 0 5px 0;
}
.formTable th {
  padding-right: 10px;
  text-align: right;
  font-weight: bold;
}
```

> Note that the fieldset and legend elements must surround the table containing the relevant fields. If using these elements, you may need multiple tables for your form.

Although forms are not tabular in nature, using a table to create a form can result in a pleasing visual appearance, with the labels right-aligned and placed next to their associated labels. This kind of layout can be replicated using CSS, via a structure built from divs to replace the table rows. This method retains semantic integrity, via the semantic relationship created by the label and associated field's id. Using CSS for form layout also brings with it the benefit of being able to rapidly restyle and move form components.

> This isn't a complete form—it's just a guide to using this method. This example lacks, for instance, a Submit button and many of the controls in the example from earlier in the chapter.

```
<form action="http://www.yourdomain.com/cgi-bin/FormMail.cgi"
➥ method="post">
  <fieldset>
    <legend>Personal information</legend>
    <div class="row clearFix">
      <label for="realname">Name</label> <input class="formField"
      ➥ type="text" id="realname" name="realname" size="30" />
    </div>
    <div class="row clearFix ">
```

```
    <label for="email">Email address</label> <input class="formField"
    ➥ type="text" id="email" name="email" size="30" />
  </div>
  <div class="row clearFix ">
    <label for="phone">Telephone</label> <input class="formField"
    ➥ type="text" id="phone" name="phone" size="30" />
  </div>
</fieldset>
</form>
```

> *Note the use of the clearing device, the* clearFix *class value, as outlined in Chapter 7's "Placing columns within wrappers and clearing floated content" section.*

Various styles are then defined in CSS. The form itself has its width restricted, and label elements are floated left, the text within aligned right, and the font-weight property set to bold. The width setting is large enough to contain the largest of the text labels.

```
form {
  width: 350px;
}
label {
  float: left;
  text-align: right;
  font-weight: bold;
  width: 95px;
}
```

The form controls—the input elements—are floated right. Because only input elements within the div rows should be floated (rather than all of the input elements on the page), the contextual selector .row input is used. (The containing divs have a class value of row.) The width setting is designed to provide a gap between the labels and input elements.

```
.row input{
  float: right;
  width: 220px;
}
```

Finally, to make a gap between the rows, a .row class is added and given a margin-bottom value.

```
.row {
  margin-bottom: 5px;
}
```

8

PERSONAL INFORMATION
Name
Email address
Telephone

The method works fine in all browsers except Internet Explorer, which doesn't apply margin-bottom correctly. However, the slightly different layout in Internet Explorer can largely be fixed by adding the following in a style sheet attached via an IE-specific conditional comment:

```
.row {
  clear: both;
  margin-top: 5px;
}
```

Alternatively, add the following:

```
.clearFix {
  display: inline-block;
}
```

> *Example forms for the sections in this chapter are available in the* chapter 8 *folder of the download files.*

Sending feedback

In this section, you'll check out how to send form data using a CGI script and PHP. Once users submit information, it needs to go somewhere and have a method of getting there. Several techniques are available for parsing forms, but we're first going to cover using a server-side CGI script. Essentially, this script collects the information submitted, formats it, and delivers it to the addresses you configure within the script.

FormMail, available from Matt's Script Archive (www.scriptarchive.com), is probably the most common, and a number of web hosts preconfigure this script in their web space packages. However, FormMail does have flaws, and it hasn't kept up with current technology. A better script is nms FormMail (available from http://nms-cgi.sourceforge.net/ and described next)—it emulates the behavior of FormMail but takes a more modern and bug-free approach.

Configuring nms FormMail

The thought of editing and configuring scripts gives some designers the willies, but nms FormMail takes only a couple of minutes to get up and running. First, you need to add some more input elements to your web page, after the form start tag:

```
<input type="hidden" name="subject" value="Contact form from
➥ website" />
<input type="hidden" name="redirect"
➥ value="http://www.yourdomain.com/contact-thanks.html" />
```

Note that some browsers display an outline where hidden fields are if input *elements are set to* display *as* block. *In such cases, you can apply a* class *value of* hidden *to the relevant fields, with* display *set to* none.

Obviously, the values in the preceding elements need changing for your site. The subject value can be whatever you like—just make it obvious, so you or your clients can use an e-mail package to filter website form responses efficiently.

The redirect value isn't required, but it's good to provide positive feedback to users, not only to confirm that their form has been sent, but also to communicate that their query will be dealt with as soon as possible. Many "thank you" pages online tend to look a little barren, with a single paragraph of text. That's why I tend to make this page a duplicate of my standard contact page, but with the confirmation paragraph above the form. The script itself needs only minimal editing. Because CGI scripts tend to break with slight errors, I highly recommend editing them in a text editor that doesn't affect document formatting, such as HTML-Kit for Windows (www.chami.com) or BBEdit for Mac (www.barebones.com).

The first line of the script defines the location of Perl on your web host's server. Your hosting company can provide this, so you can amend the path accordingly.

```
#!/usr/bin/perl -wT
```

Elsewhere, you only need to edit some values in the user configuration section. The $mailprog value defines the location of the sendmail binary on your web host's server. You can find this out from your web host's system admin.

```
$mailprog = '/usr/lib/sendmail -oi -t';
```

The $postmaster value is the address that receives bounced messages if e-mails cannot be delivered. It should be a different address from that of the intended recipient.

```
$postmaster =  'someone@your.domain';
```

The @referers value lists IP addresses or domain names that can access this script, thereby stopping just anyone from using your script and your server resources. For instance, the Snub Communications mail form has snubcommunications.com and the site's IP address for this value (as a space-delimited list). If you use localhost, that enables local testing, if you have the relevant software set up on your PC.

```
@referers = qw(dave.org.uk 209.207.222.64 localhost);
```

The @allow_mail_to value contains the addresses to which form results can be sent, again as a space-delimited list. If you include just a domain here, then any address on that domain is valid as a recipient. If you're using only one address, set the $max_recipients value to 1 to increase security.

```
@allow_mail_to = qw(you@your.domain some.one.else@your.domain
➡ localhost);
```

8

Multiple recipients

You can also use the script to e-mail multiple recipients. To do so, an additional hidden input element is needed in the HTML:

```
<input type="hidden" name="recipient" value="emailgroup" />
```

And in the script itself, two lines are changed. The @allow_mail_to value is removed, because it's catered for by the newly amended %recipient_alias. Both are shown here:

```
@allow_mail_to = ();
%recipient_alias = ('emailgroup =>
➥ 'your-name@your.domain,your-name@somewhere-else.domain');
```

Should a script be used for multiple groups of recipients, you need a unique value for each in the HTML and to amend the %recipient_alias value accordingly:

```
%recipient_alias = ('emailgroup1' => 'your-name@your.domain,your-name@
➥somewhere-else.domain', 'emailgroup2' => 'foo@your.domain');
```

Script server permissions

Upload the script to your site's cgi-bin. Once there, the script's permissions must be set. Exactly how this is achieved depends on what FTP client you're using. Some enable you to right-click and "get info," while others have a permissions or CHMOD command buried among their menus. Consult your documentation and find out which your client has. If you can, use the CHMOD command to set the octal numbers for the script (thereby altering the file permissions) to 755. If you have to manually set permissions, do so as per the screenshot to the right. Check that the script's file extension matches that in your form element's action attribute (.pl or .cgi—the latter is usually preferred by servers). Also, you might want to amend your script's name (and update the form element's action value accordingly), in an attempt to outfox automated spammers. (This explains the rather odd name of the script in the adjacent screenshot.)

Not all hosts require you to place CGI scripts in a cgi-bin *directory: some prefer a* cgi *directory, and some enable you to place such scripts anywhere on the server. If in doubt, talk to your web host's support people about the specific requirements for your account. Also note that not all hosts enable CGI support, and so if you want to use such a script, check that it's possible with your host before you spend a load of time trying to set something up that's not permitted and won't run anyway.*

Sending form data using PHP

If your hosting company offers support for PHP, the most widely used server-side technology, there is no need to install a CGI script such as FormMail. Everything can be done with PHP's built-in mail() function. As a minimum, the function requires the following three pieces of information:

- The address(es) the mail is being sent to
- The subject line
- The message itself

An optional fourth argument to mail() permits you to send additional information in the e-mail headers, such as from, cc, and bcc addresses, and to specify a particular character encoding (if, for instance, you need to include accented characters or an Asian language in the e-mail). Unfortunately, spammers frequently exploit this ability to add extra e-mail headers, so you need to check the form input for suspicious content and stop the e-mail from being sent if any is found. A script written by my fellow friends of ED author, David Powers, does this for you automatically. Even if you have no experience working with PHP, the following instructions should have you up and running quickly:

1. Copy process_mail.inc.php from the download files to the same folder (directory) as the page containing the form. This is the PHP script that does all the hard work. You don't need to make any changes to it.

2. Save the page containing the form with a PHP extension—for instance, feedback.php. Amend the opening form tag like this:

   ```
   <form action="<?php echo $_SERVER['PHP_SELF']; ?>" method="post">
   ```

3. At the top of the page, insert the following PHP code block above the DOCTYPE. Although I've warned you elsewhere in the book never to place any content above the DOCTYPE, it's perfectly safe to do so in this case, because the PHP code doesn't produce any HTML output.

   ```php
   <?php
   if (array_key_exists('SUBMIT', $_POST)) {
     //mail processing script
     $to = 'me@example.com'; // use your own email address
     $subject = 'Feedback from website';

     // list expected fields
     $expected = array('realname', 'email', 'phone', 'message');
     // set required fields
     $required = array('realname', 'email', 'message');
     $headers = 'From: My website<feedback@example.com>';
     $process = 'process_mail.inc.php';
     if (file_exists($process) && is_readable($process)) {
       include($process);
       }
     else {
       $mailSent = false;
   ```

8

```
    mail($to, 'Server problem', "$process cannot be read", $headers);
  }
 }
?>
```

4. This script begins by checking whether the PHP $_POST array has been set. This happens only when a user clicks the form's Submit button, so this entire block of code will be ignored when the page first loads. It sets the address to which the e-mail is to be sent and the subject line. It then checks that all required fields have been filled in, and sends the form input for processing by process_mail.inc.php. If the mail processing file can't be found, the script e-mails an error message to you.

To adapt this script to your own form, you need to change some of the values, as explained in upcoming steps.

> PHP is case sensitive. Make sure that you use the same combination of uppercase and lowercase in the PHP script as in the name attributes in the form. Also be careful to copy the script exactly. Missing semicolons, commas, or quotes will cause the script to fail, and may result in ugly error messages or a blank screen.

5. Change SUBMIT in the second line of the script to the same value as the name of the form's Submit button.

6. Replace me@example.com with the e-mail address that the feedback is to be sent to. Make sure the address is in quotes, and that the line ends with a semicolon.

If you want to send the e-mail to multiple addresses, separate them with commas like this:

$to= 'me@example.com, **him@example.com, her@example.com**';

7. Replace the content inside the quotes in the following line (Feedback from website) with whatever you want the subject line to say.

8. Next, list the name attributes of each form element as a comma-separated list between the parentheses in the following line:

$expected = array('**realname**', '**email**', '**phone**', '**message**');

This tells the script what form input you're expecting. *This is very important*, as it prevents malicious users from trying to pass unexpected—and possibly danger-ous—data through your form. Any form field not included in this list will be ignored, so make sure you update the list whenever you add a new field to a form.

Note that the commas go outside the quotes. You can use single or double quotes. It doesn't matter as long as each set of quotes is a matching pair.

9. The next line of code looks very similar:

$required = array('realname', 'email', 'message');

This is used to check whether all required fields have been filled in. You'll notice that I've omitted phone from the list, so the script will treat it as optional. The order of items in the $expected and $required arrays is not important, but it makes maintenance easier if you use the same order as they appear in the form.

10. The next line looks like this:

```
$headers = 'From: My website<feedback@example.com>';
```

This sets the e-mail's From: header. Change My website <feedback@example.com> to the name and e-mail address that you want the e-mail to be sent from.

There are many additional headers you can add to an e-mail, such as Cc, or Bcc. You can also set the encoding to UTF-8 (for messages that require accents or Asian languages). The following example shows how to add a cc address and UTF-8 encoding:

```
$headers = "From: My website<feedback@example.com>\r\n";
$headers .= "Cc: copycat@example.com\r\n";
$headers .= "Content-type: text/plain; charset=UTF-8";
```

There are a couple of important points to note about this code. First, the headers are enclosed in double quotes. This is because each header must be on a separate line, and the characters \r\n at the end of the first two lines represent a carriage return and new line when enclosed in double quotes. You need these two characters at the end of each header *except* the last one. Second, there's a period in front of the equal sign in the second and third lines. This has the effect of stringing all the values together so the script treats the headers as a single block.

One nice touch with e-mail headers is to put the user's e-mail address in the Reply-to field of the e-mail, so all the user has to do is click Reply in their e-mail program to send a message back to the right person. Unfortunately, this is frequently used by spammers to inject malicious code into your script. The code in process_mail.inc.php filters out potential attacks and inserts the sender's e-mail address only if it's safe to do so. Consequently, there is no need to add a Reply-to header yourself; it's done automatically by the script.

If you want to use a special encoding, such as UTF-8, for your e-mails, make sure the web page containing the form uses the same encoding in its meta tag.

You don't need to use all these headers. Just remove the complete line for any you don't want.

11. You don't need to make any other changes to the code you inserted in step 3.

12. The script in process_mail.inc.php processes the form input and sends the e-mail if there are no problems. The final stage is to let the user know what happened.

Immediately above the form in the main part of your page, insert the following code:

```
<?php
if ($_POST && isset($missing) && !empty($missing)) {
?>
  <p class="warning">Not all required fields were filled in.</p>
<?php
```

```
       }
    elseif ($_POST && !$mailSent) {
    ?>
       <p class="warning">Sorry, there was a problem sending your message.
    Please try later.</p>
    <?php
       }
    elseif ($_POST && $mailSent) {
    ?>
       <p><strong>Your message has been sent. Thank you for your feedback.
    </strong></p>
    <?php } ?>
```

This block of code displays an appropriate message depending on the outcome. Put whatever messages you like in place of the ones shown here, and add the following rule to your style sheet:

```
.warning {
  font-weight: bold;
  color: #ff0000;
}
```

If you're using a visual HTML editor like Dreamweaver, all three messages will appear to be displayed at once. However, when you load the page onto your website, the PHP conditional logic hides all the messages, and only the appropriate one is displayed after the user submits the form.

13. Save the page and upload it to your hosting company, together with process_ mail.inc.php. Test it. In a few moments, you should receive the test message in your inbox. That's all there is to it!

   If you get error messages or a blank screen, it means you have made a mistake in the script. Check the commas, quotes, and semicolons carefully. If you get a message saying that process_mail.inc.php cannot be read, it probably means that you have forgotten to upload it, or that it's not in the same folder as the form.

Although these instructions should be sufficient to help you get a PHP form working successfully, server-side coding can seem intimidating if you've never done it before. If you would like to learn more about working with PHP and Dreamweaver, see The Essential Guide to Dreamweaver CS3 with CSS, Ajax, and PHP, *by David Powers; or you can check out* PHP Solutions, *also by David Powers, for a very approachable non–Dreamweaver-specific book on PHP.*

Using e-mail to send form data

In rare cases, it may not be possible to set up a form to send form data (although even most free web hosts tend to provide users with some kind of form functionality, even if it's a shared script that doesn't allow a great deal of customization). If you find yourself in this sticky situation, it's possible to use a `mailto:` URL for the form's action attribute value. This causes browsers to e-mail the form parameters and values to the specified address.

```
<form method="post" action="mailto:anemailaddress@somewhere.com"
➥ enctype="text/plain">
```

This might seem a simpler method than messing around with CGI scripts, but it has major shortfalls:

- Some browsers don't support `mailto:` as a form action.
- The resulting data may arrive in a barely readable (or unreadable) format, and you have no control over this.
- This method isn't secure.
- The user won't be redirected and may therefore not realize data has been sent.

That last problem can be worked around by adding a JavaScript alert to the form start tag:

```
<form method="post" action="mailto:anemailaddress@somewhere.com"
➥ enctype="text/plain" onsubmit="window.alert('This form is being
➥ sent by email. Thank you for contacting us.')">
```

Of course, this relies on JavaScript being active on the user's browser—but, then again, this is a last resort.

> Note the `enctype` *attribute in the previous code block. This defines the MIME type used to encode the form's content before it's sent to the server, so it doesn't become scrambled. By default, the attribute's value is* `application/x-www-form-urlencoded`, *which is suitable for most forms; however,* `multipart/form-data` *is available for when the user is able to use a form to upload files.*

A layout for contact pages

Once you've completed a form, you need to integrate it into your site in a way that most benefits the site's visitors. I've always been of the opinion that it's a good idea to offer users multiple methods of contact on the same page. This makes it easy for them to contact you, as it requires fewer clicks than the fairly common presentation of a form and link to other contact details.

8

The following images show a couple of example layouts. The first is from the Thalamus Publishing website, which has the contact form on the right (with a minimum of fields); to the left is the other contact information—address, telephone number, fax number, e-mail, and so on, along with other addresses and details relevant to this organization (such as sales representatives).

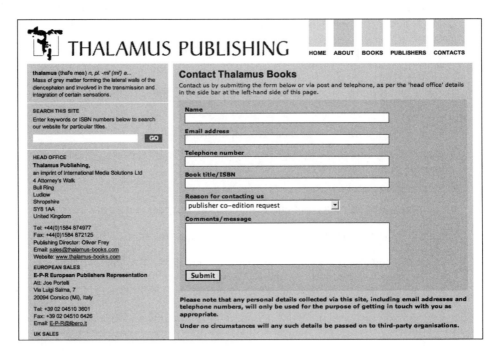

With this company having plenty of contact information, this two-column approach makes a lot of sense, and the prominence of the form is handy, because many queries can be dealt with more efficiently via e-mail.

For Snub Communications, my own site, things are simpler—I don't have a preference as to how people contact me, so all possibilities have pretty much the same prominence. The form area is made to stand out slightly more (thereby giving all contact details relatively equal prominence) by way of its background color.

Again, everything is in one place, rather than spread out over several pages, which makes sending feedback to and/or getting in contact with the organization convenient for the end user. The Snub Communications site doesn't require a map, but if it did, a link to it would appear on this page, too. The map page itself would likely resemble this one to some extent, but with the map in place of the form and image—in other words, the page would still include a telephone number and other contact details; after all, it's frustrating to have a map to an organization's location, get lost, and then discover you don't have the organization's details!

We're not going to dwell on exactly how to create these layouts, because we've already covered the techniques in the previous chapter—it's just a question of creating a two-column layout and cutting in the form (and other details) as appropriate.

Using microformats to enhance contact information

As shown in the previous section, user feedback may come in the form of a telephone call or letter, rather than an e-mail, and therefore you should always add other forms of contact details to a website—even if the site is an online store, customers will need other ways to get in touch (faceless multinational organizations, take note). In the most basic sense, these can be marked up by using some headings and paragraphs, as follows:

```
<h1>Contact details</h1>

<h2>Mail</h2>
<p><strong>Company name</strong><br />
  00, Street Name<br />
  Town or City<br />
  County or Region<br />
  Postal/ZIP code<br />
  Country name</p>

<h2>Telephone/fax</h2>
  Tel: +1 (0)0000 555555<br />
  Fax: +1 (0)0000 555556<br />
  Mobile/cell: +1 (0)7000 555555</p>
```

Now, there's nothing at all wrong with the previous block of code: it's valid, it does the job perfectly well, and it's semantically sound, which also means it's easy enough to style using CSS. However, by utilizing **microformats**, the page's functionality can be enhanced without compromising the markup.

More about microformats can be found at the microformats website at www. microformats.org, and in the book *Microformats: Empowering Your Markup for Web 2.0*, by John Allsopp, so I won't dwell on them too much. In short, though, microformats provide a way of adding commonly used semantics to web pages, working with common technologies, such as XHTML. For the example, you're going to see how to take a basic set of contact details and then use microformats to provide users with a means of efficiently downloading and storing the information as a vCard—the vCard format being that commonly used by address books). The semantic information is also of use to any other application that is microformat-aware—for example, some Firefox plug-ins are able to auto-detect microformat information on any web page and enable a user to browse and manipulate it.

Using microformats to enhance contact details

Required files	The files from using-microformats-starting-point in the chapter 8 folder.
What you'll learn	How to use microformats to enhance a set of contact details.
Completed files	using-microformats-completed in the chapter 8 folder.

1. Add a surrounding div. Open using-microformats. html, and place a div with a class value of vcard around the contact details content, as shown (truncated) following:

```
<h1>Contact details</h1>
  <div class="vcard">
    <h2>Mail</h2>
      [...]
    Mobile/cell: +1 (0)7000 555555</p>
  </div>
```

Contact details

Mail

Company name
00, Street Name
Town or City
County or Region
Postal/ZIP code
Country name

Telephone/fax

Tel: +1 (0)0000 555555
Fax: +1 (0)0000 555556
Mobile/cell: +1 (0)7000 555555

2. Structure the address. Marking up the address is fairly simple, and few changes are required to the general structure of the code. However, because each individual set of information requires its own container, and the best way of creating a container for the address is to place it within a block element of its own, the company name and the address each need their own paragraphs, rather than a line break separating the two. The organization's paragraph is then given a class value of fn org. Here, fn stands for "full name" and org defines that the name belongs to an organization, rather than a person.

The address paragraph's class value is adr, and each line of the address is placed within a span element. The various class values assigned to the spans denote which element of the address the content refers to, and those are all straightforward to understand. However, address books—and therefore microformats—enable you to distinguish between different types of data. For example, you can have a work address or a home address. This can be defined by adding the relevant word (e.g., work) and wrapping it in a span with a class value of type, thereby defining the type for the parent property. In this case, the address is being defined as a work address.

For cases when you don't want this information shown on the web page (which will likely be most of the time—after all, adding a lowercase "work" in front of the street name hardly looks great), add a second class value, hidden. Later, CSS will be used to make content with a hidden value invisible.

```
<h2>Mail</h2>
<p class="fn org">Company name</p>
<p class="adr">
  <span class="type hidden">work</span>
  <span class="street-address">00, Street Name</span><br />
```

8

337

```
<span class="locality">Town or City</span><br />
<span class="region">County or Region</span><br />
<span class="postal-code">Postal/ZIP code</span>
<span class="country-name">Country name</span>
</p>
```

3. Structure the telephone/fax details. Each definition for a telephone number requires its own container, and so the single paragraph must be split into three, as shown in the following code block. Each paragraph's class value should be tel. As with the address, a span with a class value of type hidden is used to define the type for each parent property. For tel, there are various options available, including work, home, fax, cell, pager, and video. Should duplicate types be required (such as for a work fax), two type spans are added. As for the contact number itself, that's placed in a span element with a class value of value.

```
<h2>Telephone/fax</h2>
<p class="tel">
  Tel: <span class="type hidden">work</span>
  <span class="value">+1 (0)0000 555555</span></p>
<p class="tel">
  Fax: <span class="type hidden">fax</span>
  <span class="type hidden">work</span>
  <span class="value">+1 (0)0000 555556</span></p>
<p class="tel">
  Mobile/cell: <span class="type hidden">cell</span>
  <span class="value">+1 (0)7000 555555</span></p>
```

> Note that with some address books, only a limited amount of data seems to get exported—specifics about work and home phone numbers may not. As always, test your work on a range of platforms and applications.

4. Style headings and paragraphs. The style sheet, using-microformats.css, already has some defined styles, which do the usual removal of margins and padding and setting of the default font size. The body rule also adds some padding to the page content so that it doesn't hug the browser window edges. To this, add the following three rules, which style the headings and paragraphs. Both headings are rendered in uppercase Arial, helping them to stand out, aiding visual navigation of the contact details.

```
h1 {
  font: bold 1.5em/1.2em Arial, Helvetica
  ➥ sans-serif;
  margin-bottom: 1.2em;
  text-transform: uppercase;
}
```

CONTACT DETAILS

MAIL
Company name

work 00, Street Name
Town or City
County or Region
Postal/ZIP code
Country name

TELEPHONE/FAX
Tel: work+1 (0)0000 555555

Fax: faxwork+1 (0)0000 555556

Mobile/cell: cell+1 (0)7000 555555

```
h2 {
  font: bold 1.25em/1.44em Arial, Helvetica sans-serif;
  text-transform: uppercase;
}
p {
  font-size: 1.2em;
  line-height: 1.5em;
  margin-bottom: 1.5em;
}
```

5. Hide hidden elements. As noted in steps 2 and 3, some information requires a type to be defined for it, but as you can see in the previous image, this is displayed onscreen like any other content. This is why the hidden value was also applied to the relevant span elements. By adding the following rule, these spans are made invisible.

```
.hidden {
  display: none;
}
```

6. Deal with margin issues. Because the telephone details are each in an individual paragraph, they each have a bottom margin, and this makes the layout look awful. The same problem also affects the company name paragraph. However, because each paragraph has its own class attribute value, it's easy to remove the bottom margins from the relevant paragraphs using the following rule:

```
.tel, .fn {
  margin-bottom: 0;
}
```

> **CONTACT DETAILS**
>
> **MAIL**
> Company name
> 00, Street Name
> Town or City
> County or Region
> Postal/ZIP code
> Country name
>
> **TELEPHONE/FAX**
> Tel: +1 (0)0000 555555
> Fax: +1 (0)0000 555556
> Mobile/cell: +1 (0)7000 555555

7. Embolden the company name. Balance-wise, the company name could do with standing out more. This is within a paragraph that has a class value of org, so making the contents bold is child's play—just add the following rule.

```
.org {
  font-weight: bold;
}
```

8. Finally, style the vcard div via the following rule. This sets a background color, width, border, and padding, but perhaps the most important property here is margin-bottom. This is required because the margins from paragraphs with a tel class were removed in step 6. When you add a bottom margin to the vcard div, the typical spacing you'd expect after a paragraphs returns.

```
.vcard {
  width: 200px;
  background: #eeeeee;
  border: 1px solid #cccccc;
```

```
    padding: 8px;
    margin-bottom: 1.5em;
}
```

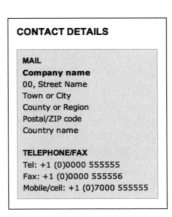

Note that further simplification of some elements of the code shown in the exercise is possible. For example, where you have the Fax line, the type span could be directly wrapped around the relevant label, and the hidden class removed.

Where before you had the following:

```
<p class="tel">
  Fax: <span class="type hidden">fax</span>
  <span class="type hidden">work</span>
  <span class="value">+1 (0)0000 555556</span></p>
```

you'll now have this:

```
<p class="tel">
  <span class="type">Fax</span>:
  <span class="type hidden">work</span>
  <span class="value">+1 (0)0000 555556</span></p>
```

The same is also true for the Mobile/cell line.

Note also that this is a relatively new technology, so it's not without its drawbacks. As mentioned earlier, some details are not carried through to some address books. Also, the need to hide extra data is problematic, since under some circumstances (such as in text readers), it will be displayed, which could lead to confusion. However, with the popularity of microformats increasing all the time, they're still worthy of investigation, hence my including this example in this book.

Online microformat contacts resources

If you decide to use microformats to enhance your site's contact details, there are two websites you need to bookmark. The first is Technorati's Contacts Feed Service, at www.technorati.com/contacts. This enables you to input the URL of a page with hCard information (i.e., the sort of page created in the previous exercise) and get a vCard out of it, which can be added to your address book.

Add hCard contacts to your address book `BETA`

Enter the URL of a page with hCard contact information (**What is hCard?**) to automatically add the contact information on that page into your address book application.

URL: `http://technorati.com/about/contact.html`   Get hCard Contacts

Get hCards favelet

Favelets let you take the power of the Technorati Contacts Feed Service with you wherever you go. Drag the following Get hCard Contacts link into your bookmarks / favorites bar, and use it when viewing a page with hCards to add them to your address book automatically.

- **Get hCard Contacts** - Add hCard contacts from the page you're on to your address book.

For more information on the hCard microformat, see the **hCard specification**.

The Technorati Contacts Feed Service is currently beta.

« **Technorati Home**

Usefully, the site's system enables you to automate the system via the kind of web page created earlier. If you upload a page like the one created in the previous exercise, and then add the following code (amending the URL after contacts/), you'll have a link on the contacts page that uses the microformat information to create a vCard that users can download.

```
<p><a href="http://technorati.com/contacts/http://yourdomain.com/
➥yourcontactpageurl.html">Download vCard</a>. (<em>This process
➥ may take a few seconds.</em>)</p>
```

A second handy resource is Tantek Çelik's hCard creator (amusingly titled the hCard-o-matic), at www.microformats.org/code/hcard/creator. This enables you to automate much of the process from the previous exercise—you put your values into the field on the left, and the code is built live in the field at the right of the page.

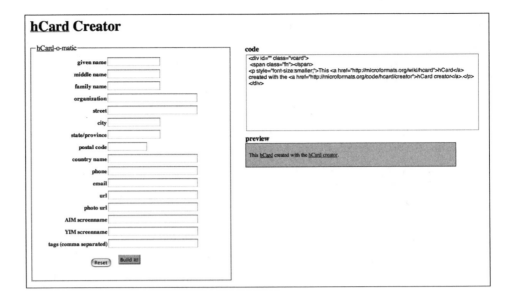

Contact details structure redux

In this chapter, and in the microformats exercise, the address and other contact details were styled using paragraphs and line breaks. An alternative structure, which perhaps has greater integrity from a semantic standpoint, is to use a definition list, with further nested definition lists within. At the top level, the term is Contact details and the definition is the actual contact details. At the next level, there are two terms, Mail and Telephone/fax, each with respective definitions. For the latter, the definition has a third definition within, providing term/definition pairs for the different types of telephone and fax numbers.

```
<dl>
  <dt>Contact details</dt>
  <dd>
    <dl class="vcard">
      <dt>Mail</dt>
      <dd>
        <address>
        <strong>Company name</strong><br />
        00, Street Name<br />
        Town or City<br />
        County or Region<br />
        Postal/ZIP code<br />
        Country name
        </address>
      </dd>
      <dt>Telephone/fax</dt>
      <dd>
        <dl>
```

```
      <dt>Tel:</dt>
      <dd>+1 (0)0000 555555</dd>
      <dt>Fax:</dt>
      <dd>+1 (0)0000 555556</dd>
      <dt>Mobile/cell:</dt>
      <dd>+1 (0)7000 555555</dd>
     </dl>
    </dd>
   </dl>
  </dd>
 </dl>
```

For the CSS, use the existing rules from using-microformats.css in the using-microformats-starting-point folder, *and* the .vcard rule from the previous exercise. The following rules can then be used to style the definition list and its contents.

First, the dt rule is used to style the Contact details text (as per the h1 element in the previous exercise), with the dd dt rule providing override styles for dt elements within a dd element. This rule is aimed to style the equivalent of the h2 elements from the previous exercise: the Mail and Telephone/fax text. The dd dd dt rule provides a third level of override, styling the dt elements within the telephone/fax definition list. Also, because the dt/dd pairs are displayed in a linear fashion by default, the dd dd dt rule floats the telephone/fax list dt elements to the left, enabling the dd elements to stack to the right in each case.

```
dt {
    font: bold 1.5em/1.2em Arial, Helvetica sans-serif;
    margin-bottom: 1.2em;
    text-transform: uppercase;
}
dd dt {
    font: bold 1.2em/1.5em Arial, Helvetica sans-serif;
    text-transform: uppercase;
    margin-bottom: 0;
}
dd dd dt {
    float: left;
    padding-right: 5px;
    display: block;
    text-transform: none;
}
```

The next two rules deal with formatting and fine-tuning of the text. The address rule adds the gap between the bottom of the address and the telephone/fax heading, along with reverting the address element content to normal text (it's italic by default). The second rule in the following code block defines a font for the address element content and the content of the telephone/fax definition list's term and definition.

8

```
address {
  padding-bottom: 1.5em;
  font-style: normal;
}
address, dd dd dt, dd dd dd {
  font: 1.2em/1.5em Verdana, Arial, sans-serif;
}
```

With these styles added, the contact details look virtually identical to those in the exercise. At this point, you can add hooks for the vCard as per steps 2 and 3 of the "Using micro-formats to enhance contact details" exercise. See contact-details-structure-redux.css and contact-details-structure-redux.html in the chapter 8 folder for the completed files.

We've covered plenty of ground here, so now it's time to leave the subject of collecting user feedback and progress to the next chapter, which explores how to test your websites and deal with common browser bugs.

9 DEALING WITH BROWSER QUIRKS

In this chapter:

- Weeding out common web page errors
- Creating a browser test suite
- Installing multiple versions of Internet Explorer
- Catering for unruly web browsers
- Common fixes for Internet Explorer bugs
- Targeting other browsers with JavaScript

The final test

One time web designers envy designers in other fields is when it comes to testing websites. Although we're a long way from the "design a site for each browser" mentality that afflicted the medium in the late 1990s, we've still not reached the holy grail of "author once, display anywhere."

The methods outlined in this book take you most of the way there, providing a solid foundation for websites that should need little tweaking to get them working across all web browsers. However, to say such sites will never need any amendments is naïve in the extreme. Therefore, unless authoring for an internal corporate environment where everyone uses exactly the same browser, designers must always ensure they thoroughly test sites in a range of browsers.

Weeding out common errors

Testing in browsers isn't everything; in fact, you may find that your site fails to work for no reason whatsoever, tear your hair out, and then find the problem lurking in your code somewhere. With that in mind, you should either work with software that has built-in and current validation tools (many have outdated tools, based on old versions of online equivalents), or bookmark and regularly use the W3C's suite of online tools: the Markup Validation Service (http://validator.w3.org/), CSS Validation Service (http://jigsaw. w3.org/css-validator/), Feed Validation Service (http://validator.w3.org/feed/), Link Checker (http://validator.w3.org/checklink), and others (www.w3.org/QA/Tools/) as relevant.

Other useful online services include WDG Link Valet (www.htmlhelp.com/tools/valet/), WDG HTML Validator (www.htmlhelp.com/tools/validator/), and Total Validator (www. totalvalidator.com/). Accessibility-oriented services include HP's Color Contrast Verification Tool (www.hp.com/hpinfo/abouthp/accessibility/webaccessibility/color_tool.html); Etre's Colour Blindness Simulator (www.etre.com/tools/colourblindsimulator/); and the Cynthia Says Portal Tester (www.cynthiasays.com/fulloptions.asp), which can aid you in Section 508 and WAI (Web Accessibility Initiative—see www.w3.org/WAI/) compliance.

Here are some of the more common errors you might make that are often overlooked:

- **Spelling errors**: Spell a start tag wrong and an element likely won't appear; spell an end tag wrong and it may not be closed properly, wrecking the remaining layout. In CSS, misspelled property or value names can cause rules—and therefore entire layouts—to fail entirely. British English users should also remember to check for and weed out British spellings—setting *colour* won't work in CSS, and yet we see that extra *u* in plenty of web pages (which presumably have their authors scratching their heads, wondering why the colors aren't being applied properly).

- **Incorrect use of symbols in CSS**: If a CSS rule isn't working as expected, ensure you've not erred when it comes to the symbols used in the CSS selector. It's a simple enough mistake to use # when you really mean . and vice versa.

9

- **Lack of consistency**: When working in XHTML, all elements and attributes must be lowercase. In CSS, tag selectors should also be lowercase. However, user-defined id and class values can be in whatever case the author chooses. Ultimately, decide on a convention and stick to it—always. If you set a class value to myvalue in CSS and myValue in HTML, chances are things won't work. For the record, I prefer lowerCamelCase, but there's no reason for choosing a particular case.

- **Not closing elements, attributes, and rules**: An unclosed element in HTML may cause the remainder of the web page (or part of it) to not display correctly. Similarly, not closing an HTML attribute makes all of the page's content until the next double quote part of the attribute. Not closing a CSS rule may cause part or all of the style sheet to not work. Note that CSS pairs that aren't terminated with a semicolon may cause subsequent rules to partially or wholly fail. A good tip to avoid accidentally not closing elements or rules is to add the end tag/closing bracket immediately after adding the start tag/opening bracket. This also helps to avoid incorrect nesting of elements.

- **Multiple rule sets**: In CSS, ensure that if you use a selector more than once, any overrides are intentional. It's a common error for a designer to duplicate a rule set and have different CSS property values conflicting in different areas of the CSS.

- **Errors with the head and body elements**: As stated earlier in the book, HTML content should not appear outside of the html element, and body content should not appear outside of the body element. Common errors with these elements include placing content between the closing head element tag (</head>) and the body start tag (<body>), and including multiple html and body elements.

- **Inaccessible content**: Here, we're talking in a more general sense, rather than about accessibility for screen reader users. If you create a site with scrollable areas, ensure users can access the content within, even if browser settings aren't at their defaults. Problems mostly occur when overflow is set to hidden. Similarly, textarea elements that don't have properly marked-up cols and rows settings will often be tiny when viewed without CSS (these attributes are functional as well as presentational). The same is true for text input fields without a defined size attribute.

- **Dead links**: These can take on many forms, such as a link to another page being dead, an image not showing up, or external documents not being accessible by the web page. If a JavaScript function isn't working for some reason, try checking to see whether you've actually linked it—in some cases, the simpler and most obvious errors are the ones that slip through the net. Also, if things aren't working on a live site, check the paths—you may have accidentally created a direct link to a file on your local machine, which obviously won't be accessible to the entire Internet. Spaces within href values or the original file names can also be accidentally overlooked.

- **Whitespace errors**: In CSS, do not place whitespace between class/id indicators and the selector name, or between numerals and units for measurements. However, do not omit whitespace from between contextual selectors, otherwise you'll "combine" them into a new, probably unknown, one.

- **Using multiple units**: In CSS, a value can only accept a single unit—the likes of 50%px can cause a rule to partially or wholly fail.

A browser test suite

Appendix E (Browser Guide) details when various browsers were created, their *approximate* share of the market, and the major problems they cause. However, it's important to note that the market is in continual change—just a quick look at Netscape's fortunes should be enough to prove that. Utterly dominant during the period when the Web first started to become mainstream, its share of the market was decimated by the then-upstart Internet Explorer, and it's now all but vanished. The point, of course, is that you cannot predict how the browser market will change, and although Internet Explorer is sitting proud today, its share of the market has been hit hard in recent years by Firefox, and this downward trend for Microsoft's browser could continue . . . or not. Also, each year sees new releases of web browsers, with new features and updated—but usually incomplete—standards support.

All of this is a roundabout way of saying that you need to think hard about browsers when you're creating your work. Don't only test sites in a single browser, and don't use the most popular for your starting point if it's not the most standards-compliant. Instead, use a browser with a good grasp of web standards for your first line of tests, until you've got your templates working. I personally use the Gecko engine as a starting point—more specifically, I favor Firefox as an initial choice of browser. Opera is also a decent choice, and Mac users can probably get away with using Safari for initial tests.

Once the basic structure is up and running, I test in a range of alternate web browsers, typically in the following order:

1. **The other compliant browsers**: Typically, I use Firefox as a starting point, although sometimes I use Safari. Whichever one you choose to start in, it's a good idea to test in the other compliant browsers first. Sometimes, one will pick up a coding error the others don't, and it's a good sanity check to ensure everything's working well. If you're lucky, everything will work fine right away in all of these browsers, on both Mac and Windows.

2. **A browser in text mode**: What I mean by this is testing the site without CSS, which is a way of somewhat figuring out if it's usable on alternate devices. Old hands might use Lynx for this, but I instead use the Accessibility layout option of Opera's User mode (see the following screenshot). The Firefox Web Developer toolbar (www.chrispederick.com) offers similar options.

3. **Internet Explorer 7 for Windows**: Although this release of Internet Explorer is a vast improvement over previous efforts, it's not as standards-compliant as the other mainstream browsers. Therefore, tests need to be done to ensure everything's working properly, not least because Internet Explorer 7 is the most popular browser in terms of market share. If things aren't working right, conditional comments need to be used (see the "Dealing with Internet Explorer bugs" section later in the chapter).

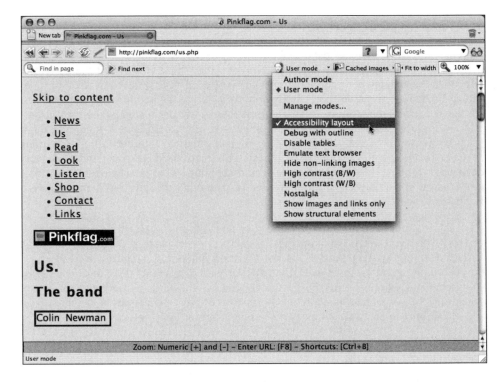

4. **Internet Explorer 6 for Windows**: Previously the most popular browser, this release is still in heavy use. Fairly compliant, it nonetheless has a raft of bugs, and complex CSS layouts will almost certainly need a little tweaking to work properly, again via the use of conditional comments. Note that because only Windows XP users can upgrade from Internet Explorer 6 to 7 (7 being the native browser for Windows Vista), a fair number of users—those with an earlier version of Windows—will likely use 6 for some time to come.

5. **Internet Explorer 5.5 for Windows**: How far you go back, in terms of versions of Internet Explorer, depends on your target market, the client's budget, and general expectations. Typically, I test the most recent three major versions of Microsoft's browser, due to their heavy usage. Internet Explorer 5.0 can be considered almost extinct, however. Overall, Internet Explorer 5.5 has more problems than Internet Explorer 6, although most of them are easy enough to work around. Generally, I don't aim to get sites working perfectly in this browser—a few cosmetic oddities are acceptable, in my opinion, because there's no point in compromising a totally compliant site to make it more compatible for an aging browser whose market share is in rapid decline. Ensuring content is accessible in the browser is essential, however, and the primary concern when dealing with obsolete browsers.

6. **Everything—all over again**: When any major changes are made, you need to go back through your browsers and make sure the changes haven't screwed anything up.

There are other browsers out there, but the preceding list will deal with the vast majority of your users. However, always try to find out the potential audience for a website to ascertain whether you should place more focus on a particular browser. For example, if authoring a site for a mostly Mac-based audience, it might make sense to use Safari as the basis for testing, and perhaps even wheel out the long-canceled Internet Explorer 5 for Mac, just to make sure your site works in it.

At each stage of testing, I recommend that you save HTML and CSS milestones on a very regular basis. If something fails in a browser, create a copy of your files and work on a fix. Don't continually overwrite files, because it's sometimes useful—and, indeed, necessary—to go back to previous versions.

Whichever browsers you test in, it's important to not avoid the "other side." Windows users have long seen the Mac as being inconsequential, but at the time of writing Safari now counts for about 4% of all web users, and the trend for Mac sales (as a percentage of the market) is upward. Usefully, there's now a version of Safari for Windows, but even the Mac and Windows versions of Firefox show slight differences in the way sites are handled (mostly regarding text). Even worse, many Mac-based designers don't test on a Windows PC or in Internet Explorer, which has the bulk of the market. If you're a Windows user, grab a cheap Mac that's capable of running Mac OS X (such as a second-hand iBook or a Mac mini), and if you're a Mac user, either grab a cheap Windows PC to test with or run Windows as a virtual machine (via Parallels Desktop or VMware Fusion) on an Intel Mac or using Virtual PC if you have a PPC-based machine. (You can also use Boot Camp on an Intel Mac, but that requires booting back and forth between Windows and Mac OS X, so using a virtual environment is more efficient unless you have two computers.) Linux users also have a range of browsers to test on. Firefox is popular on that platform, and Safari is a rough analog for Konqueror. It is worth noting, however, that the default fonts with Linux vary considerably from those that you'd expect on a Mac or Windows PC—so you should always define fallback fonts accordingly, and test in Linux if possible. See Chapter 3 for more on font stacks.

9

Installing multiple versions of browsers

One of the big problems when it comes to web design testing is that some browser manufacturers don't enable you to run multiple versions of their products. The two biggest culprits here are, unsurprisingly, Microsoft and Apple, who presumably argue that as their browsers rely on system-level code, they can't provide standalone testing environments for older releases. Luckily, enterprising developers have proven this to not be the case. Online, there are now a number of sites that enable you to install standalone versions of previous incarnations of Internet Explorer. By far the best is Tredosoft's effort, which packages everything up into a no-nonsense installer. This enables you to install standalones for Internet Explorer versions from 6 way back to 3 (the following image shows an example of three versions of Internet Explorer running simultaneously). Usefully, conditional comments work fine, too, which wasn't the case with earlier standalones. Download the installer from www.tredosoft.com/Multiple_IE. Alternatively, you can manually install the versions you require from Evolt (http://browsers.evolt.org/) and use the information at Position Is Everything (www.positioniseverything.net/articles/multiIE.html) to repair lost functionality.

In a similar vein, Michel Fortin has produced standalone versions of Safari for the Mac, available from www.michelf.com/projects/multi-safari/. However, because of the nature of WebKit (the application framework that's the basis for Safari), there are limitations regarding which versions of the browser can be run on which versions of Mac OS X. David Hellsing of David's Kitchen also notes in his "Browser Suite for Developers" article (www.monc.se/kitchen/91/browser-suite-for-developers) that you can use the WebKit nightly builds instead of the public downloads, in order to test in multiple versions of Safari. Links are available from the article.

Elsewhere, things are simpler. For Firefox, different versions can happily live on the same machine, although they can't be run simultaneously, unless you start each version with a different profile—see "Geek to Live: Manage Multiple Firefox Profiles," by Gina Trapani (www.lifehacker.com/software/firefox/geek-to-live--manage-multiple-firefox-➡ profiles-231646.php), for how to do this on Windows; and "Running Multiple Firefox Versions Concurrently," by Jeroen Coumans (www.jeroencoumans.nl/journal/multiple-firefox-versions), for how to do this on Mac OS X. Opera is even simpler: you can install multiple versions and run them without having to do anything special.

Dealing with Internet Explorer bugs

As mentioned elsewhere, Microsoft made a huge leap forward with Internet Explorer 7, but it's still not without its problems. Also, because Microsoft's browser enjoyed such an immense market share for so long, older versions remain in use for years, sometimes enjoying a share of the market that manages to eclipse every other browser apart from the latest release of Internet Explorer. With this in mind, along with the sad fact that Microsoft's browser has been the least compliant one out there for a long time now, this section is dedicated to exploring how to deal with the most common Internet Explorer bugs. These are all worth committing to memory, because if you're working on CSS layouts, these bugs *will* affect your designs at some point, and yet most of the fixes are extremely simple.

Outdated methods for hacking CSS documents

Historically, web designers have resorted to exploiting parsing bugs in order to get around Internet Explorer problems. Perhaps the most famous of these is Tantek Çelik's box model hack, designed to get around Internet Explorer 5.x's inability to correctly deal with the box model: it places padding and borders within the defined content dimensions of a box, rather than on the outside. In other words, a box with a width setting of 300px and padding of 20px should take up a total width of 340 pixels in a compliant browser, but in IE 5.x, it only takes up 300 pixels. Also, only 260 pixels are available for content, due to the 40-pixel padding being placed inside the defined width of the box.

Tantek's hack works by exploiting a CSS-parsing bug. In the following code block, padding is set in the rule, along with a width for Internet Explorer 5.x, which terminates the rule in the voice-family lines. Compliant browsers continue reading, thereby using the second width value to override the first. The net result is that all browsers show the box at the correct width.

```
.box {
  padding: 20px;
  width: 340px;
  voice-family: "\"}\"";
  voice-family: inherit;
  width: 300px;
}
```

A further rule is added by some designers to cater for Opera's then-inability to read past the voice-family lines—the "be nice to Opera" hack took advantage of Internet Explorer 5.x not understanding child selectors, and therefore used one to set the correct width in that browser:

```
html>body .box {
  width: 300px;
}
```

The box model hack itself was later simplified further, to the simplified box model hack (or SBMH), which involved using a single backslash in the second pair to get Internet Explorer 5.x to terminate the rule:

```
.box {
  padding: 20px;
  width: 340px;
  w\idth: 300px;
}
```

9

In a sense the opposite of the box model hack, the star HTML hack is also often seen, in order to make only Internet Explorer see a rule:

```
* html .box {
  background: #000000;
}
```

There are myriad other CSS hacks out there, but they won't be explored here. Not only do hacks mess up your otherwise clean and compliant style sheet, but they're also not future-proof, as evidenced when the star HTML hack stopped working upon the release of Internet Explorer 7. Also, hacks often need overrides, as evidenced by the "be nice to Opera" hack. A far better and more future-proof method is to ditch CSS hacks entirely, instead making a totally clean style sheet for a website, and using conditional comments to fix bugs in Internet Explorer.

Conditional comments

Conditional comments are proprietary code that's only understood by Microsoft browsers from version 5 onward, but as they're wrapped up in standard HTML comments, they don't affect other browsers, and they are also considered perfectly valid by the W3C's validation services. What conditional comments enable you to do is target either a specific release of Internet Explorer or a group of releases by way of expressions. An example of a conditional comment is shown in the following code block:

```
<!--[if IE 6]>
[specific instructions for Internet Explorer 6 go here]
<![endif]-->
```

Anything placed inside this comment will only be shown in Internet Explorer 6—all other browsers ignore the content. This is most useful for adding IE-specific style sheets to a web page, within which you can place overrides. For example, rather than using the box model hack shown earlier in the chapter, you would have a clean style sheet, and then override specific values in a separate style sheet for Internet Explorer 5.x, attached within a conditional comment.

Generally, problems with Internet Explorer fall into the following camps: rare issues with Internet Explorer 7, problems that affect versions 6 and below, and problems that specifically affect version 5.x. With that in mind, I mostly add three IE-specific style sheets to my web pages, with the newest release at the top. Conditional comments are generally added after the "default," or clean, style sheets (which in this case are the main style sheet added using a style element, and a print style sheet added using a link element).

```
<style type="text/css" media="screen">
/* <![CDATA[ */
@import url(x.css);
/* ]]> */
</style>
<link rel="stylesheet" rev="stylesheet" href="x-print.css"
➥ type="text/css" media="print" />
```

```
<!--[if IE 7]>
<link rel="stylesheet" type="text/css" href="ie-7-hacks.css"
  media="screen" />
<![endif]-->
<!--[if lte IE 6]>
<link rel="stylesheet" type="text/css" href="ie-6lte-hacks.css"
  media="screen" />
<![endif]-->
<!--[if lt IE 6]>
<link rel="stylesheet" type="text/css" href="ie-5-hacks.css"
  media="screen" />
<![endif]-->
```

Within the comments, lte IE 6 means "less than or equal to Internet Explorer 6," so anything added to ie-6lte-hacks.css affects Internet Explorer 6 and below; lt IE 6 means "less than Internet Explorer 6," so anything added to ie-5-hacks.css affects versions of Internet Explorer *below* 6. An alternate way of attaching a style sheet for Internet Explorer 5 would be to use the syntax if IE 5. Since the cascade still affects the rules within style sheets attached inside conditional comments, it makes sense to fix things for Internet Explorer 6 and below first, and then work backward to Internet Explorer 5.x to fix the few remaining things that need sorting out.

> *See* http://msdn2.microsoft.com/en-us/library/ms537512.aspx *for more on conditional comments. The hasLayout site—*www.haslayout.net—*also offers useful information on conditional comments.*

Note that the preceding code block also includes a link to a print style sheet—print style sheets are covered in Chapter 10.

> *The advanced boilerplates from the download files (in the* advanced-boilerplates *folder) include the preceding code block.*

Let's now examine the example from earlier, which has the following code hack to deal with the box model issues that affect versions of Internet Explorer below 6:

```
.box {
  padding: 20px;
  width: 340px;
  voice-family: "\"}\"";
  voice-family: inherit;
  width: 300px;
}
```

When using conditional comments, you'd make the rule in the default style sheet clean, with no hacks:

```
.box {
  padding: 20px;
  width: 300px;
}
```

You'd then add a rule to your style sheet that only Internet Explorer versions below 6 can see (the one within the conditional comment that references lt IE 6 in the large code block shown earlier).

```
.box {
  width: 340px;
}
```

Compliant browsers read the rule in the clean style sheet. Internet Explorer versions below 6 then override the width value, thereby displaying the box as intended. Unlike when using a CSS hack, however, the CSS hasn't been compromised in any way. The majority of problems detailed in the "Common fixes for Internet Explorer" sections later in the chapter are to do with CSS, and therefore require conditional comments when they're being dealt with.

Dealing with rounding errors

Problem: In liquid layouts with floated elements, rounding errors sometimes cause the widths of the elements to add up to more than 100%. This causes one of the floated elements to wrongly stack under the others. This problem is known to affect all versions of Internet Explorer. For an example, see the following image (from the "Creating flanking sidebars" exercise in Chapter 7), in which the right-hand sidebar is wrongly sitting underneath the left-hand sidebar.

Solution: As explained in the focus point within the "Creating flanking sidebars" exercise, rounding errors can be dealt with by reducing one of the percentage values of a column by as little as 0.0001%, although sometimes this reduction needs to be increased.

Alt text overriding title text

Problem: If you have an image with alt text nested inside a link that has a `title` element, the `title` element will be overridden. This is largely due to Internet Explorer wrongly displaying the content of the `alt` attribute as a tooltip.

Solution: The only way around this problem is to duplicate the `title` attribute and place a copy of it within the `img` element. This is superfluous markup, but it fixes the issue in Internet Explorer and does not adversely affect other web browsers.

```
<a href="sunset.html" title="Click to view a larger image"><img
➥ title="Sunset in Reykjav&iacute;k" src="sunset.jpg" alt="Sunset in
➥ Reykjav&iacute;k" width="400" height="300" /></a>
```

Common fixes for Internet Explorer 5.x

A few major problems are known to affect Internet Explorer 5.x specifically, and were fixed in versions 6 and above. When using any of the fixes from the following **Solution** sections, add them to an IE 5–specific style sheet (see the conditional comment earlier that begins `<!--[if lt IE 6]>`).

Box model fixes (5.x)

Problem: Internet Explorer 5.x wrongly applies padding and border values within the defined dimensions of a box (which is what the box model specifies). In the following example, the overall width taken up by the box should be the sum of its border, padding, and width values (420px). (Note that when using shorthand, you need to be mindful that the amount of space they take up is double the value. In other words, if you set padding to 50px, 50 pixels of padding is applied to *both* horizontal edges. Therefore, in the following code block, the sum to find the overall width of the values in the rule is 300 + 50 + 50 + 10 + 10.) However, in Internet Explorer 5.x, the box is only 300 pixels wide—the padding and border are placed inside the defined width, leaving only 180 pixels for content. This issue tends to affect most CSS-based layouts.

```
.boxout {
  width: 300px;
  padding: 50px;
  border: 10px solid #000000;
}
```

Solution: Override the width setting by setting a new value in the style sheet attached via a conditional comment. The value should take into account the shortcomings listed previously and therefore needs to equal the value of the relevant dimension (depending on whether you're defining a `width` or a `height`), along with the relevant padding and border values.

```
.boxout {
  width: 420px;
}
```

9

Centering layouts

Problem: The browser doesn't understand margin: auto, so when, for example, a wrapper is horizontally centered using the following code block, the resulting layout will be incorrectly aligned to the left of the browser window.

```
#wrapper {
  width: 700px;
  margin: 0 auto;
}
```

Solution: A workaround for this problem is to use the text-align property to align everything within the page body centrally. You then set the alignment back to the default of left in your wrapper (or wrappers, if you've used more than one). If you've used other/additional layout elements that have been centered (e.g., if you have separate masthead, content, and footer containers, rather than your entire page structure placed within a single wrapper), those elements will also need the text-align: left override.

```
body {
  text-align: center;
}
#wrapper {
  text-align: left;
}
```

The text-transform bug

Problem: The browser ignores a text-transform value if line-height is defined in the same rule.

```
h1 {
  font: bold 1.2em/1.4em Arial, Helvetica, sans-serif;
  text-transform: uppercase;
}
```

Solution: Reconfirm the text-transform value in the style sheet linked via a conditional comment.

```
h1 {
  text-transform: uppercase;
}
```

Font-size inheritance in tables

Problem: When using relative units, text within table cells may be displayed at the wrong size (too large).

Solution: Set font-size to 100% in a table rule in a style sheet linked via a conditional comment.

```
table {
  font-size: 100%;
}
```

Common fixes for Internet Explorer 6 and 5

Internet Explorer 6 was a step up by Microsoft, away from the disaster (from a standards point of view) that was Internet Explorer 5.x. That said, it still had plenty of shortcomings of its own, the vast majority of which were dealt with when Internet Explorer 7 finally jumped on in. Any fixes from the **Solution** sections that follow should be added to an IE 6-and-below-specific style sheet (see the conditional comment earlier that begins `<!--[if lte IE 6]>`).

Fixing min-width and max-width

Problem: The browser does not understand `min-width` and `max-width`, thereby causing problems with semiliquid layouts that have minimum and maximum widths, rather than set width values.

```
#wrapper {
  min-width: 700px;
  max-width: 1100px;
}
```

Solution: Use a proprietary IE expression to enable Internet Explorer to emulate the functionality of `min-width` and `max-width`. In the code, the expression essentially states that if the browser window width is less than 702 pixels, set the wrapper width to 700px (these values—702 pixels and 700px—are numerically different to prevent Internet Explorer 6 from freezing); if it's more than 1102 pixels, set the wrapper width to 1100px; and otherwise set it to auto.

```
#wrapper {
width: expression(document.body.clientWidth < 702? "700px" :
➥ document.body.clientWidth > 1102? "1100px" : "auto");
}
```

Double-float margin bug

Problem: The browser doubles the value of any margin in the same direction as a float. For example, in the following code, the right-floated boxout with a `margin-right` value of 30 pixels would actually be shown in Internet Explorer 6 and below to have a 60-pixel `margin-right` value. Note that this problem only occurs for the first float in any float row.

```
.boxout {
  width: 300px;
  float: right;
  margin-right: 30px;
}
```

9

Solution: Override the `margin-right` value, and halve it.

```
.boxout {
  margin-right: 15px;
}
```

Alternatively, if appropriate, `display: inline` can be defined in the original CSS rule, which results in the IE-specific override becoming unnecessary.

Expanding boxes

Problem: An element with a string that's too wide for it doesn't break out of its container; instead, the browser stretches the container to contain it.

Solution: Use the `word-wrap` property with the `break-word` value, assigning it to the relevant container.

```
#sidebar {
  word-wrap: break-word;
}
```

Note that this is a CSS 3 property that's not particularly well supported, and while it fixes the layout, it doesn't emulate the correct standards-compliant approach of the string breaking out of the box—instead, it breaks the string into a number of separate lines. An alternative is to set `overflow` on the container to `hidden`, thereby hiding the overflow and returning the layout to normal, at the expense of not being able to see the long string. Generally, when you come up against this problem, it makes sense to rework your string, because while the layout won't be affected in standards-compliant browsers, it will still look bad.

Internet Explorer 5.x sometimes also expands a box when italics are used for some of the text, although the problem is somewhat random. Setting `overflow` to `visible` for the container often fixes the problem. Alternatively, setting the value to `hidden` crops the unruly few extra pixels.

The 3-pixel text jog

Problem: Inline content next to a floated element is pushed away by 3 pixels. In the depicted example, the content in the dotted line has a 3-pixel jog in the text that appears under the floated element.

Solution: Apply the "Holly hack," a 1% height value to the relevant containing element(s). See three-pixel-jog.html in the chapter 9 folder of the download files. Try removing `height: 1%;` from `#textWrapper` to see how the page looks without the hack.

Whitespace bugs in styled lists

Problem: The browser wrongly interprets whitespace in the code as actual space in styled navigation lists, thereby placing space between lists and list items. This affects lists such as that created in Chapter 5's "Using HTML lists and CSS to create a button-like vertical navigation bar" exercise.

Solution: There are several solutions to this problem, the most drastic of which is to remove whitespace from the relevant portions of code (between the list items). You can also leave a space between the last character of the link text and the closing </a> tag, assuming this doesn't compromise your layout in any way. Otherwise, use *one* of the following rules:

```
li {
    display: inline;
}
li {
    float: left;
    width: nnnpx;
}
li a {
    display: block;
    float: left;
    clear: left;
    width: nnnpx;
}
```

Note that in the preceding code, where *nnn*px is shown, *nnn* should be replaced with a numerical value.

Problems with iframes

Problem: Internet Explorer spawns both horizontal and vertical scroll bars when content is larger than the declared width or height. This means that if your iframe is 200 pixels high, but your content is 400 pixels high, you'll end up with a vertical scroll bar *and* a horizontal one, even if your content is narrower than the iframe dimensions. Other browsers don't make this mistake, displaying only the relevant scroll bar. Also, styling iframes can cause problems. Turning off the default border is a good move, because it looks clunky. Adding a border using CSS should be possible by applying it directly to the iframe (via a class or iframe tag selector); in practice, however, this partially fails in Internet Explorer versions 6 and below, creating an ugly gap between your scroll bars and iframe borders (which happens to be the same size as the defined border).

Solution: If you know your iframe content is always going to be too large for the iframe, set scrolling="yes" in the iframe start tag. Alternatively, add a conditional comment in the head of the iframe content document, with the following code, experimenting with the width property until the scroll bar disappears. If you use similar iframes on a number of pages, you should instead assign a class value to the body element of the relevant pages and define the html, body rule in an IE 6-and-below-specific style sheet.

9

```
<!--[if lte IE 6]>
<style type="text/css">
  html, body {margin:0; width:180px;}
</style>
<![endif]-->
```

For border styles, you can work around the problem in one of two ways: you can override the original border value, setting it to 0 for Internet Explorer 6 and below; or you can nest the iframe in a div and provide the div with a border instead.

Ignoring the abbr element

Problem: The browser does not recognize the abbr element, completely ignoring it.

Solution: Use JavaScript to fix the behavior (at least for those users who have JavaScript enabled), as shown in "<ABBR> Support in IE," by Jason Davis (www.browserland.org/scripts/abbrhack/). Note that since Internet Explorer 7 does not exhibit this behavior, the script should be targeted at earlier versions of the browser only, by using conditional comments.

PNG replacement

Problem: The browser does not display PNG transparency—rather than a background showing through a semitransparent PNG, the transparency is shown as solid white.

Solution: For backgrounds, use the AlphaImageLoader filter as shown. Here's the clean CSS:

```
.boxout {
  background: url(an-image.png);
}
```

And here's the override CSS for the IE style sheet:

```
.boxout {
  filter: progid:DXImageTransform.Microsoft.AlphaImageLoader
  ➥(src='an-image.png',sizingMethod='scale');
  background: none;
}
```

For individual images, either put up with old versions of Internet Explorer not displaying them as intended, or create some additional content for Internet Explorer that can be swapped out for the PNG image.

Here's the HTML:

```
<img src="an-image.png" width="300" height="300" alt="An image"
➥ class="pngImage" />
<img src="shim.gif" width="300" height="300" alt="An image"
➥ class="IEImage" />
```

Here's the clean CSS:

```
.IEImage {
  display: none;
}
```

And here's the override CSS for the IE style sheet:

```
.pngImage {
  display: none;
}
.IEImage {
  filter: progid:DXImageTransform.Microsoft.AlphaImageLoader
  ➥(src='an-image.png',sizingMethod='scale');
  background: none;
}
```

Note that shim.gif should be a transparent GIF with no content.

> *Replacing PNG images manually is a tedious task if you've got more than a couple on your site. If you regularly work with PNG transparency, it's worth investigating JavaScript alternatives (such as the one shown at www.bjorkoy.com/past/2007/4/8/ the_easiest_way_to_png/) for automating the method shown in this section.*

Problems with CSS hover menus (drop-downs)

Problem: The browser supports :hover only on links, rather than on any element, thereby making drop-downs like that in Chapter 5's "Creating a drop-down menu" exercise fail.

Solution: Use some kind of JavaScript fallback system. There are various options for this, but the simplest is the solution offered by Peter Nederlof at www.xs4all.nl/~peterned/ csshover.html. All you need to do is download either csshover.htc or csshover2.htc, place it somewhere within your site's hierarchy, and then link to it through a rule in a style sheet linked via a conditional comment.

```
body {
behavior: url(csshover2.htc);
}
```

Another solution is to use HTML Dog's Suckerfish Dropdowns (www.htmldog.com/ articles/suckerfish/dropdowns/), which works nicely all the way back to Internet Explorer 5, and uses perfectly valid CSS.

Fixing hasLayout problems (the peekaboo bug)

Problem: Due to the archaic nature of some aspects of the Internet Explorer rendering engine, it sometimes serves up some rather odd bugs, and perhaps the most irritating of these is the so-called peekaboo bug, also known as the disappearing content bug. Fairly

9

common (but also fairly random as to whether it occurs), it typically affects layouts that use floats and clearing divs, and it can cause elements to partially disappear below a given point, or for content to flicker on and off as a page is scrolled.

The problem occurs due to a proprietary Internet Explorer concept called "layout," which refers to how elements render their content and interact with other elements. Some elements have layout by default, others don't, and some CSS properties (irreversibly) trigger it. Any property that gains layout in some way has Microsoft's proprietary hasLayout property set to true. If an element doesn't have layout, the property is set to false. Unfortunately, there's no way to *directly* set hasLayout for any element, even in an IE-specific style sheet, and yet hasLayout is the cause of many layout problems in Internet Explorer.

The hasLayout-trigger.html document within the hasLayout folder from the chapter 9 folder of the download files always exhibits the peekaboo bug. The page's structure is extremely simple: a wrapper has within it three divs; the first is floated right and given a 50% width, the second has no style applied, and the third is a clearing div. By default, when the page is loaded, the second div cannot be seen in Internet Explorer 6 or below (see the following left-hand image)—only by scrolling, selecting content, or resizing the window can you make the "missing" content reappear. In a compliant browser, however, this problem doesn't occur (see the following right-hand image).

Note that hasLayout *issues still affect Internet Explorer 7, although they are thankfully rarer than in previous versions of Microsoft's browser.*

Solution: Should you come across this problem when working on your own sites, the solution is to give layout to the containing div. The best method for doing this is to set the proprietary zoom property to 1 in a style sheet linked via a conditional comment.

Try doing this for the #wrapper rule in the ie6-lte-hacks.css file (see the following code block), and you'll see that the hasLayout problem no longer affects the page—the content that wasn't initially visible should now be displayed properly.

```
#wrapper {
  zoom: 1;
}
```

> *It's probably worth noting that* zoom, *like some of the other things mentioned in the Internet Explorer fixes, will not validate. However, as far as I'm concerned, there's no real urgency or reason to make IE-specific style sheets validate. Keep your main style sheet clean and valid, and then add whatever you need to get things working in Internet Explorer—although always use as few additions as possible, even when working with conditional comments. In some cases, however,* height: 1% *should provide the same effect, and this is valid CSS.*

Targeting other browsers

Generally, targeting browsers other than Internet Explorer is unnecessary. All other currently shipping browsers are pretty well behaved. However, under extreme circumstances, there are exceptions. For users who still have to deal with Internet Explorer for Mac, you can create overrides by importing a style sheet via a style element, but omitting url and leaving no space between @import and the opening bracket:

```
<style type="text/css" media="screen">
/* <![CDATA[ */
@import("ie-mac-hacks.css");
/* ]]> */
</style>
```

This can be placed in the same style element as the import line for the clean style sheet:

```
<style type="text/css" media="screen">
/* <![CDATA[ */
@import url(clean.css);
@import("ie-mac-hacks.css");
/* ]]> */
</style>
```

For any other overrides, you need to resort to JavaScript, which isn't an ideal solution—after all, there are still plenty of people out there who routinely turn off JavaScript—but it's the best we've got.

9

For targeting a specific platform, you can use a script like this, added to an external JavaScript file:

```
if (navigator.platform.indexOf('Mac')!= -1) {
  var cssNode = document.createElement('link');
  cssNode.setAttribute('rel', 'stylesheet');
  cssNode.setAttribute('type', 'text/css');
  cssNode.setAttribute('href', 'mac-hacks.css');
  document.getElementsByTagName('head')[0].appendChild(cssNode);
}
```

In this case, if the user has a Mac, the style sheet mac-hacks.css will be linked to, but if the user has a different operating system, it won't. (Win and Linux are values for other popular operating systems that you may wish to target.)

To target specific browsers, use the following code block, replacing BrowserName with Firefox, IE (for Internet Explorer, although conditional comments are a better bet for dealing with IE issues), Mozilla, Netscape, OmniWeb, Opera, or Safari. Obviously, you also need to change the file name of the CSS document in the href line, too, from hacks-file.css to the relevant CSS document for your chosen browser in the first line of the script.

```
if (navigator.userAgent.indexOf('BrowserName')!= -1) {
var cssNode = document.createElement('link');
  cssNode.setAttribute('rel', 'stylesheet');
  cssNode.setAttribute('type', 'text/css');
  cssNode.setAttribute('href', 'hacks-file.css');
  document.getElementsByTagName('head')[0].appendChild(cssNode);
}
```

10 PUTTING EVERYTHING TOGETHER

In this chapter:

- Combining methods to create website designs
- Creating a blog layout
- Creating a storefront layout
- Creating a homepage layout
- Creating an online gallery
- Working with style sheets for print output

Putting the pieces together

The majority of this book intentionally works in a modular manner. The idea is that you can work on the various components as you wish and then combine them to form all manner of websites. This chapter shows how this process can work. Three layouts will be explored, and elements from each one will be heavily based on exercises from elsewhere in this book. You'll see the Photoshop mock-up, a breakdown of its structure, and instructions for how the completed files were put together—mostly using techniques you've already worked with in this book. In all cases, the completed files are available in the download files (in the chapter 10 folder). Note that these layouts are mock-ups of websites, with a single page designed, not complete websites. However, there's enough material here to use as the basis for your own designs, although you shouldn't use them as is—after all, you're not the only person with a copy of this book!

> Note that in the following sections, there are references to exercises elsewhere in the book, stating that the code was more or less copied and pasted. In all cases, ensure you check the paths to any linked files—mostly, the book has used a totally flat structure for files. In this chapter, images are always placed in an assets folder. Therefore, paths to images need updating accordingly when using portions of exercises from elsewhere in the book.

Managing style sheets

In the download files, there are two sets of boilerplates. The basic-boilerplates folder is the one used for the exercises throughout the book. The XHTML document contains only a single wrapper div, while the CSS document has a handful of rules that are designed to reset margins and padding and define a default font. Projects in this chapter are instead based on the documents from the advanced-boilerplates folder. This contains a more complex web page and a style sheet that uses CSS comments to split the document into sections. The "Creating boilerplates" section in Chapter 2 provided an overview of the reasoning behind this technique, and the "CSS boilerplates and management" section in Appendix D (CSS Reference) does largely the same thing. However, because this section will examine CSS rules within certain sections of each style sheet, a brief overview is required here, too.

Essentially, you can use CSS comments for writing notes within a style sheet—whatever's between CSS comments (which begin /* and end */) is ignored by browsers. Comments can be multiline or single-line, and you can therefore use comments to create sections in the style sheet for various "groups" of rules. For example, you can use the following to introduce a group of rules on forms:

```
/* ---------- forms ---------- */
```

Taking things further, a multiline comment can be added at the start of the document. This can include a table of contents, and the various section headers within the style sheet can be numbered, thereby making navigation and editing even easier. As also explained elsewhere, I indent both property/value pairs *and* the closing quote of the declaration, as shown in the following code block (with a tab being represented by four spaces):

```
#sidebar {
    float: right;
    }
```

This makes it simpler to scan the left-hand side of the document for selectors. Note that although the rules within the remainder of this chapter are not formatted in this manner, the rules within the download file style sheets are.

Creating a portfolio layout

This section will show how I created a layout for an online portfolio, suitable for a designer or photographer (professional or otherwise) to show off their wares. The Photoshop file for the document is gallery-layout.psd, in the PSD mock-ups folder within the chapter 10 folder of the download files. The completed web page (along with associated files) is within the gallery-website folder, within the chapter 10 folder. The following image shows the Photoshop mock-up of the page.

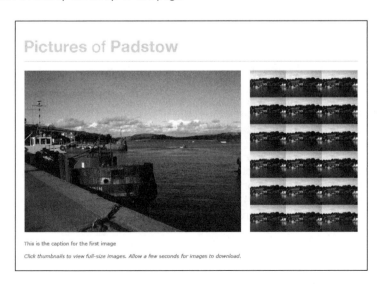

About the design and required images

As you can see from the previous screenshot, this page has a simple structure. The fixed-width layout has a masthead that contains the name of the portfolio and is bordered on the bottom, creating a visual separator between the site's name and its contents. The main content area is split into two columns. On the right are thumbnail images, and on the left are the main image, a caption, and basic instructions regarding how to use the page.

From the mock-up, only one image was exported: the site's heading from the masthead. Although it would be possible to approximate this in HTML text, the size of the heading and the nonstandard font used (Helvetica Neue) means it made more sense to export it as a GIF. Image replacement was used to ensure the heading remains accessible. The other images—the thumbnails and full-size ones—aren't in the mock-up, but were fine-tuned, optimized, and exported separately and placed in the assets folder, along with the heading image. Note that I used a convention for file names: thumbnails share the name of their full-size parent, but with -t appended.

Putting the gallery together

When putting this page together, techniques were used from the following exercises and sections in this book:

- Creating a fixed-width wrapper (Chapter 7)
- Placing columns within a wrapper (Chapter 7)
- Manipulating two structural divs for fixed-width layouts (Chapter 7)
- Styling semantic markup: A traditional example with serif fonts and a baseline grid (Chapter 3)
- Image-replacement techniques (Chapter 3)
- Switching images using JavaScript (Chapter 5)
- Adding captions to your image gallery (Chapter 5)

I also took on board various techniques discussed in Chapter 4 regarding working with images.

Open index.html and examine the code. The head section imports a style sheet, uses a conditional comment to link to an IE 5–specific style sheet (because once the layout was done, there were layout issues in Internet Explorer 5.5) and the JavaScript file gallery.js. The JavaScript document is identical to the one from the "Adding captions to your image gallery" exercise in Chapter 5.

The page's basic structure is simple: the page is contained within a wrapper div. Within that, there is a masthead and a content area, the latter of which has two columns, formed from div elements with id values of mainImageContainer and thumbnailsContainer. If the content were removed, this structure would look like that in the following code block:

```
<div id="wrapper">
  <div id="masthead"></div>
  <div id="content">
    <div id="mainImageContainer"></div>
    <div id="thumbnailsContainer"></div>
  </div>
</div>
```

If you've read through Chapter 7, you'll see that this layout is formed using techniques shown in the "Creating a fixed-width wrapper," "Placing columns within a wrapper," and "Manipulating two structural divs for fixed-width layouts" exercises.

Within the masthead div is a level-one heading with an empty span element. This is as per the image-replacement method shown in the "Image-replacement techniques" section of Chapter 3. The CSS applied to the elements (shown later in this section) effectively places the span over the text and sets the heading image exported from the mock-up as its background.

```
<h1 class="mainHeading"><span></span>Pictures of Padstow</h1>
```

In the mainImageContainer div, there's an image, a caption, and explanatory text. Note the id value for the image—this is a hook for both the JavaScript and CSS, as explained in the "Switching images using JavaScript" and "Adding captions to your image gallery" exercises in Chapter 5.

The thumbnailsContainer div contains an unordered list, each item from which contains a linked thumbnail image, and an example of which is shown in the following code block:

```
<li><a href="assets/boat.jpg" onclick="javascript:swapPhoto
➥('boat.jpg','A docked boat, with distant clouds rolling in.');
➥ return false;"><img src="assets/boat-t.jpg" alt="A docked
➥ boat." width="80" height="60" /></a></li>
```

Again, the various elements of the code are explained in the aforementioned exercises from Chapter 5. The only difference here is the use of the list, which is used to provide structure for the 18 images—as you've seen elsewhere in the book, CSS makes it possible to style lists in any manner of ways.

Styling the gallery

The pictures-of-padstow.css document contains the styles for this layout, and these styles are arranged into sections, as explained earlier in the chapter. The defaults section includes two rules. The first is the universal selector (*), used to remove padding and margins (as per the "Zeroing margins and padding on all elements" section in Chapter 2). The second is a body rule with a commented-out background pair. If you remove the CSS comments and load the web page into your browser, you'll see a background grid, as shown in the following screenshot (the baseline grid's height is 20 pixels per line). It's worth leaving

10

the rules in place when working with baseline grids, because if you make changes to your page later, you can temporarily turn the grid back on to ensure rhythm is being maintained. Having a commented-out property/value pair in your CSS makes no noticeable difference to file download times anyway.

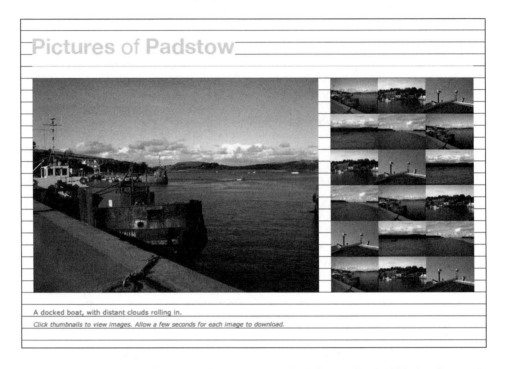

A docked boat, with distant clouds rolling in.

Click thumbnails to view images. Allow a few seconds for each image to download.

In the structure section of the CSS, the #wrapper rule defines a fixed width for the page's wrapper, and the margin property value of 0 auto centers the page in the browser window (as explained in Chapter 7's "Creating a fixed-width wrapper" exercise). The #masthead rule sets some padding at its top (to place some space above the heading), adds a single-pixel bottom border, and adds a bottom margin, again for spacing reasons. Note that the values within this rule, taken in combination with the height of the heading (23 pixels) ensure that the vertical rhythm is maintained. The two other rules in the section style the two columns, floating them, giving them fixed widths, and adding some space between them, as per the "Manipulating two structural divs for fixed-width layouts" exercise in Chapter 7.

In the fonts section of the CSS, the default font size is set using the html and body rules, as per the "Setting text using percentages and ems" section in Chapter 3. The h1.mainHeading and h1.mainHeading span rules are the image-replacement technique in full swing, as per the "Image-replacement techniques" section in Chapter 3. Note the h1.mainHeading rule's font-size value, which ensures that the text doesn't spill out from behind the image in Internet Explorer when zooming the page. While defining font size in pixels is generally a bad idea, it's largely irrelevant here, because the HTML text is only likely to be seen if the CSS isn't shown. (For anyone surfing with images off, a portfolio is kind of useless, and even if they're determined to press on regardless, the 20px value ensures that the heading text is likely to be legible for them anyway.)

```
h1.mainHeading {
  position: relative;
  width: 342px;
  height: 28px;
  overflow: hidden;
  padding-bottom: 19px;
  font-size: 20px;
  line-height: 1em;
}
h1.mainHeading span {
  position: absolute;
  background: #ffffff url(assets/pictures-of-padstow.gif) no-repeat;
  width: 100%;
  height: 100%;
}
```

The p rule sizes the paragraph, and the line-height value is determined by dividing the baseline grid line height (2em, derived from the 20 pixel target—see the "Styling semantic markup: A traditional example with serif fonts and a baseline grid" exercise in Chapter 3 for the thinking behind this) by the font-size value: 2.0 divided by 1.1 equals 1.81818181 (recurring, but you can stop after a half-dozen or so decimal places in CSS).

```
p {
  font: 1.1em/1.81818181em Verdana, Arial, Helvetica, sans-serif;
  color: #898989;
}
```

The p em rule reduces the font-size value for the emphasized text in the instructions paragraph, while the #thumbnailsContainer li rule displays the list items within the thumbnailsContainer div inline, stacking them horizontally.

```
#thumbnailsContainer li {
  display: inline;
}
```

The final section in the style sheet is for images, and the three rules are as follows: a img, which removes borders from linked images; #imgPhoto, which defines the margin under the main image; and #thumbnailsContainer img, which floats the images within the thumbnailsContainer div, ensuring there's no space between them.

The completed page is shown in the following image.

10

Pictures of Padstow

A docked boat, with distant clouds rolling in.
Click thumbnails to view images. Allow a few seconds for each image to download.

Hacking for Internet Explorer

As mentioned earlier, there's also a style sheet for Internet Explorer 5, attached using a conditional comment. This document, ie-5-hacks.css, has four rules. The body and #wrapper rules deal with that browser not centering the site (see the "Centering layouts" section in Chapter 9). The h1.mainHeading rule adds extra padding to the bottom of the heading to cater for Internet Explorer 5's poor handling of the box model (again, see Chapter 9), while the final rule deals with the browser placing margins around the thumbnail images. The defined negative horizontal margins (shown in the following code block) pull the thumbnails back into position.

```
#thumbnailsContainer img {
  margin: 0 -3px;
}
```

Creating an online storefront

This section will detail how I created a layout for an online storefront, providing the user with a quick and simple means of accessing a number of product categories by way of a multicolumn drop-down menu. The Photoshop file for the document is store-front-layout.psd, in the PSD mock-ups folder within the chapter 10 folder of the download files. The completed web page (along with associated files) is within the store-website folder, within the chapter 10 folder. The following image shows the Photoshop mock-up of the page.

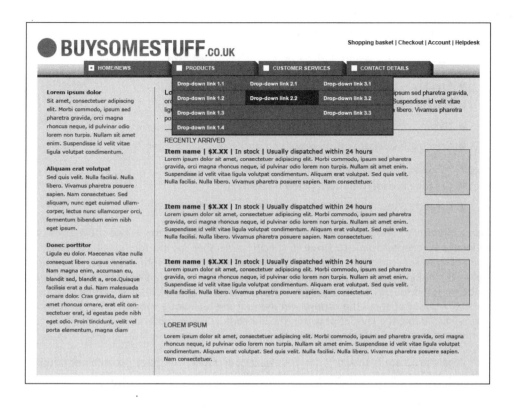

About the design and required images

Prior to working on this design, I decided that it would be a semi-liquid layout, with a maximum width of around 1000 pixels and a minimum width slightly larger than the width of the four tabs (which total 740 pixels). This explains the use of the blue gradient behind the tabs, providing a transition between the dark orange stripe and the white masthead area when the site is displayed wider. Without this, the jolt between these two elements would be too harsh. This also explains the lack of fixed-width elements elsewhere in the design—images are floated right and recently added items are displayed in a linear fashion. With a liquid layout, displaying these three containers as columns wouldn't be entirely straightforward (although it could be done by replacing the images with divs that have background images large enough to cater for changes in column width; however, at narrow widths, the images would be cropped).

In terms of imagery, the logo was exported, as was a portion of the gradient image (which was tiled horizontally). Had I been working entirely from scratch on this layout, the tab states would also have been included in and exported from the mock-up, but I took those directly from the drop-down exercise from Chapter 5. The inline images in the document are all just a single gray square saved as temporary-image.gif. Clearly, in an actual site, all of those images would show items for sale!

10

Putting the storefront together

When working on this layout, I made use of techniques shown in the following exercises:

- Creating a maximum-width layout (Chapter 7)
- Placing columns within a wrapper (Chapter 7)
- Manipulating two structural divs for liquid layouts (Chapter 7)
- Creating a sidebar with faux-column backgrounds (Chapter 7)
- Creating a boxout (Chapter 7)
- Creating breadcrumb navigation (Chapter 5)
- Creating a multicolumn drop-down menu (Chapter 5)

Open index.html and examine the code. The head section imports a style sheet, uses conditional comments to link to three IE-specific style sheets (one for Internet Explorer in general, one for Internet Explorer 6 and below, and one for Internet Explorer versions below 6), and attaches the JavaScript file store.js. The JavaScript document is not going to be explored fully. The reason for its inclusion at all is because Internet Explorer prior to version 7 does not show the drop-down menu if the technique shown earlier in the book is used. By adding the JavaScript within the linked document, behavior in all generally used versions of Internet Explorer becomes identical.

The page's structure is shown in the following code block. The page is contained within a wrapper div. Within that, there is a masthead that contains a logo div and a navContainer div (which itself contains a navigation div). After the masthead is a content div that contains two columns, formed from div elements with id values of sidebar and mainContent.

```
<div id="wrapper">
  <div id="masthead">
    <div id="logo"></div>
    <div id="navContainer">
      <div id="navigation"></div>
    </div>
  </div>
  <div id="content">
    <div id="sidebar"></div>
    <div id="mainContent"></div>
  </div>
</div>
```

In the masthead, prior to the logo div, is an unordered list with an id value of pullNav. This is used for the pull-navigation at the top right of the design (including the shopping basket, checkout, account, and helpdesk links).

```
<ul id="pullNav">
  <li><a href="#">Shopping basket</a></li>
  <li><a href="#">Checkout</a></li>
  <li><a href="#">Account</a></li>
  <li><a href="#">Helpdesk</a></li>
</ul>
```

The logo div contains a linked image (linked to # in this example, but in a live site, this would be linked to the website's home page). The navContainer contents are literally identical to those in Chapter 5's "Creating a multicolumn drop-down menu" exercise.

In the content area, the sidebar div contents are straightforward: level-two headings are twice followed by unordered lists full of links (intended for links to top sellers and items coming soon), and a third heading is followed by a paragraph of text. In the mainContent div, a level-one heading is followed by an introductory paragraph and a horizontal rule. Next are the page's recently arrived item highlights. These each take the form of a containing div (with an id value of itemContainer), and each of these containers contains two divs, itemImage (which houses an image) and itemDetails. Each itemDetails div contains an unordered list for the name, price, stock notification and dispatch details, along with a paragraph of descriptive text. Two of the list items have class values, which are used as hooks for CSS styles.

```
<div class="itemContainer">
  <div class="itemImage">
    <a href="#"><img src="assets/temporary-image.gif" alt="[temporary
    ➥ image]" width="100" height="100" /></a>
  </div>
  <div class="itemDetails">
    <ul>
      <li class="itemName"><a href="#">Item name</a></li>
      <li class="itemCost">£X.XX</li>
      <li>In stock</li>
      <li>Usually dispatched within 24 hours</li>
    </ul>
    <p>Lorem ipsum dolor […]</p>
  </div>
</div>
```

After the three-item container blocks is a second horizontal rule, and then the main content area's final content: a level-two heading and a paragraph of text. Because the item containers each have a bottom border style assigned in CSS, the second horizontal rule results in a double border. Because of its semantic significance, it needs to remain, which leaves the choice of making it invisible by CSS or making the final item container's bottom border invisible, which is what's been done. (If you look at the class attribute of the third itemContainer div, it has a second value, lastItemContainer.)

Finally, after the two columns, but inside the content div, is a single footer paragraph containing a copyright statement.

Styling the storefront

The store.css document contains the styles for this layout, arranged into sections, as noted earlier in the chapter. The defaults section includes two rules. The first is the universal selector (*), used to remove padding and margins (as per the "Zeroing margins and padding on all elements" section in Chapter 2). The second is a body rule, which adds some top and bottom padding to the web page, ensuring that there's always some whitespace around the design.

10

In the structure section are a number of rules for styling the page's structural elements. The #wrapper rule provides both a maximum and minimum width for the site wrapper, along with centering the site via the margin value.

```
#wrapper {
  max-width: 1000px;
  min-width: 760px;
  margin: 0 auto;
}
```

The #masthead rule adds a large bottom border of 18 pixels to the masthead.

```
#masthead {
  border-bottom: 18px solid #eeeeee;
}
```

At this point, the reasoning for the #masthead rule won't be apparent, so I'll explain. The design as a whole has 18 pixels of padding around the content area. It also uses faux columns (as outlined in Chapter 7's "Creating a sidebar with faux-column backgrounds" exercise) to apply a vertical separator stripe between the two columns (the sidebar and the main content area). However, from a design standpoint, it looks much nicer if the column doesn't start right from the top of the content area, and there's instead some space above it. Because the background is applied to the content div, the background image by default starts from the top of the content area. To avoid this, one option would be to add further markup that "covers" a portion of the separator stripe (via a div with a background color, a fixed height, and a width that spans the entire content div's width). However, adding a border to the bottom of the masthead that has the same color as the content area's background has the same effect. Sure, this is kind of a hack, but it doesn't cause any problems from a structural standpoint, and no semantics are affected. If you do this sort of thing, however, always remember where the various elements of the visual design lie in CSS, and use comments to remind yourself, if you need to.

Anyway, onward. The #logo rule is much simpler, adding some padding at the bottom and left of the div that houses the site logo. The reason for adding padding at the left is because otherwise the logo would abut the browser window edge at a screen resolution of 800×600. The #content rule adds some horizontal padding, along with the column-stripe.gif image as a vertically tiling background image (the aforementioned faux-column technique). Note the horizontal position of 27%. This is designed to sit roughly within the margin to the right of the sidebar div—see the following code block for the width and margin-right values of the sidebar and mainContent divs. Logically, a value of 26% should be set, because that would be the width of the sidebar, plus half of the margin-right value. However, the padding value of #content messes with that calculation somewhat, because the two columns don't span the entire width that the content div background occupies, since that stretches to the edge of the padding, which is 18 pixels on each horizontal edge. A setting of 26% therefore results in the vertical stripe appearing too far to the left; adding 1% results in a more pleasing position for the background.

```
#content {
  padding: 0 18px;
  background: #eeeeee url(assets/column-stripe.gif) 27% 0 repeat-y;
```

```
}
#sidebar {
  float: left;
  width: 24%;
  margin-right: 4%;
}
#mainContent {
  float: left;
  width: 72%;
}
```

Next, the .itemContainer rule defines a border and margin at the bottom of the itemContainer divs. This is overridden for the last of the three containers by the .lastItemContainer rule to avoid a double underline (as explained earlier). The .itemContainer:after rule is essentially the same as the clearFix rule (see the "Clearing floated content" exercise in Chapter 7), clearing floated content so that the itemContainer divs don't stack incorrectly. The .itemImage rule floats the divs containing the images right, adding some bottom and left margins so that other content doesn't abut them. Finally, the hr rule defines settings for the horizontal rule (although note that Internet Explorer deals with hr margins differently from other browsers, making them larger—this will be dealt with via conditional comments).

In the navigation section, the first three rules define colors for default, visited, and hover/focus link states, while the next three style the pull-navigation. The #pullNav rule floats the pull-navigation list right and adds some right padding, while #pullNav li sets the list items within to display inline, adding the vertical-bar.gif image as a background and some padding. The ul#pullNav li:first-child rule then removes the background from the first of the list items. The code is shown in the following block, and a full explanation is shown in the "Creating breadcrumb navigation" exercise in Chapter 5.

```
#pullNav {
  float: right;
  padding-right: 10px;
}
#pullNav li {
  display: inline;
  background: url(assets/vertical-bar.gif) 0 55% no-repeat;
  padding: 0 3px 0 8px;
}
ul#pullNav li:first-child {
  background: none;
}
```

The remainder of the rules are copied from Chapter 5's "Creating a multicolumn drop-down menu" exercise, and the path values to the css-tab-rollover-image.gif have been amended accordingly to take into account that the image is now being housed in an assets folder. There are two other changes as well, to cater for the layout the menu is being used with. First, #navContainer has a horizontally tiling background image (the gradient) applied, and the #navigation ul rule has width and margin values to center the list horizontally, in the same way the wrapper div was centered earlier.

10

```
#navContainer {
  height: 30px;
  border-bottom: 5px solid #ad3514;
  background: url(assets/nav-background.gif) repeat-x;
}
#navigation ul {
  list-style-type: none;
  width: 740px;
  margin: 0 auto;
}
```

Fonts and fixes for the storefront layout

In the fonts section of the CSS, the default font size is set using the html and body rules, as per the "Setting text using percentages and ems" section in Chapter 3. The h1 rule defines the lead heading, and I've done something that's not been done elsewhere in the book: the heading is floated left. This enables subsequent content to wrap around the heading, and is something I rarely do, but for this design, it made sense for the heading to be more of an introduction to the introductory paragraph itself, and displaying it inline was the way to do that. The padding-right value ensures there's some space before the subsequent paragraph. The line-height setting was calculated *after* the values for p and h1+p were defined, and the final figure was calculated in the same proportional manner as per h1+p (see later in the section).

```
h1 {
  float: left;
  padding-right: 0.3em;
  font: bold 1.4em/1.2571428em Arial, Helvetica, sans-serif;
}
```

The next three rules, h2, #sidebar h2, and p, style the level-two headings, level-two headings in the sidebar, and paragraphs, respectively. There's nothing of note here, but refer to Chapter 3 if there's something you're not familiar with. Next is the h1+p rule. This increases the font size of the paragraph that immediately follows the level-one heading, giving it more prominence. Because the font-size value has been increased, the line-height value has to be decreased proportionately in order for the text to all line up correctly. The p and h1+p rules are shown in the following code block.

```
p {
  font: 1.1em/1.6em Verdana, Arial, Helvetica, sans-serif;
  margin-bottom: 1.6em;
}
h1+p {
  font-size: 1.2em;
  line-height: 1.4666666em;
}
```

The next rule, #content ul, #pullNav, sets the default font and bottom margin for the two types of horizontally aligned list (the pull-navigation and the item details lists in the main content area). The three subsequent rules, #content .itemDetails ul, .itemDetails li, and .itemDetails li:first-child, style the lists in the itemContainer divs in pretty much the same way as for the pull-navigation. The main difference is the white background applied to the list items, which was added during the build stage in order to make the item details stand out more (see the detail below). This sort of thing happens all the time when I create sites—mock-ups should always be more a guideline than something to slavishly and exactly reproduce in the final site. If you can think of an improvement (and the client is happy with it, if you're working on a commercial project), then make changes!

The remaining rules in this section are all straightforward. The .itemName, .itemCost rule emboldens the text in the list items with the class values of itemName and itemCost, thereby making the name and cost stand out more. And p.footer styles the footer paragraph. In this rule, clear is set to both so that the footer clears the two floated columns, and the text is aligned right. However, the footer also serves other purposes of a more decorative nature. The background is set to white, an 18-pixel top border the same color as the content background is defined, and negative horizontal margins of 18px are set, along with padding of 18px. What this does is make the background of the footer white and span the entire width of the content div, including its padding. The top border deals with the faux-column separator in the same way as the bottom border on the masthead. A detail of the resulting footer is shown in the following image.

libero cursus venenatis. Nam magna
enim, accumsan eu, blandit sed,
blandit a, eros.Quisque facilisis erat
a dui. Nam malesuada ornare dolor.

GRAVIDA DIAM SIT AMET

Rhoncus ornare, erat elit consectetuer erat, id egestas pede nibh eget odio. Proin tincidunt, velit vel porta
elementum, magna diam molestie sapien, non aliquet massa pede eu diam. Aliquam iaculis. Fusce et ipsum
et nulla tristique facilisis.

© 200X BuySomeStuff.co.uk

The last three rules are in the images section. The first, a img, removes borders from linked images. The next, .itemImage img, adds a border to images within the itemImage divs, and .itemImage img:hover changes the border color on the hover state, indicating that the link is clickable (seeing as all of the item images are surrounded by links).

As mentioned earlier, this layout also has three style sheets linked via conditional comments to deal with Internet Explorer issues. The first, ie-hacks.css, has line-height overrides for h1 and h1+p, which line up the heading and paragraphs properly in Microsoft's browser. A rounding problem causes a horizontal scroll bar to appear at narrow browser window sizes, so the #mainContent rule's width value is overridden with a setting of 71.9%. Finally, the hr rule defines vertical margin values to make the horizontal rules in Internet Explorer behave in a similar manner to other browsers.

The ie-61te-hacks.css document has some fixes for Internet Explorer 6 and below. The #wrapper rule deals with Internet Explorer 6 and below not understanding max-width and min-width, and uses a Microsoft-proprietary expression to compensate for this failing. The #content rule is a hasLayout hack, which stops the entire layout from jolting when the tabs are rolled over. The #pullNav li, .itemDetails li rule removes the vertical bars from the inline lists, since Internet Explorer prior to version 7 doesn't understand the :first-child pseudo-class used to set specific values for the initial list item in each inline list. The next two rules, #dmenu li.over ul and #dmenu li li li, deal with issues relating to the drop-down menu. The first is a hook for the JavaScript, ensuring that the drop-down appears as expected in Internet Explorer 6 and below. The second removes the bottom borders from the list items, since they don't appear correctly in Internet Explorer versions below 7. Finally, because Internet Explorer 6 and below don't allow CSS :hover rules on anything other than links, a new rule is required to change the borders around the images on the hover state:

```
#content a:hover img {
   border: 1px solid #ad3514;
}
```

The ie-5-hacks.css style sheet contains rules for centering components and dealing with positioning issues.

The completed web page is shown in the following image, with the drop-down active.

Creating a business website

This section will detail how I created the third layout in this chapter, which is suitable for a business website. This makes use of the two-tier navigation system devised in Chapter 5, and although the entire design doesn't adhere strictly to a baseline grid, I decided that it would be good for the content area to do so, to create a more pleasing rhythm for the content area of the page. The Photoshop file for the document is sme-layout.psd, in the PSD mock-ups folder within the chapter 10 folder of the download files. The completed web page (along with associated files) is within the sme-website folder, within the chapter 10 folder. The following image shows the Photoshop mock-up of the page.

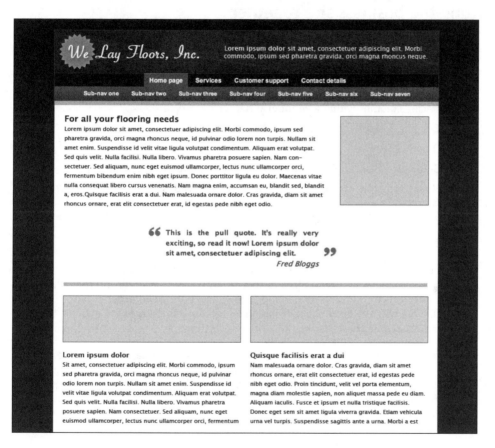

About the design and required images

This design is clean and modern. The site is fixed-width, with a dark background color for the overall page; a dark gradient from the top draws the attention toward the top of the page. The masthead contains the company logo, along with a short sentence regarding what the organization offers. Below that is the navigation, followed by the content area.

The content area is simple: an introductory heading and paragraph (with a floated image to the right) is followed by a client quote. Below that is a large horizontal rule, which is followed by two columns.

Image-wise, the masthead background was exported (with the sentence turned off—that was added in HTML text), as was the background gradient. Other images were sourced from elsewhere, the temporary image being the same one as in the previous layout example, and the navigation images being taken directly from the example created for Chapter 5.

Putting the business site together

When creating this layout, I made use of methods shown in the following exercises/sections:

- Creating a fixed-width wrapper (Chapter 7)
- Manipulating two structural divs for fixed-width layouts (Chapter 7)
- Placing columns within a wrapper (Chapter 7)
- Creating a two-tier navigation menu (Chapter 5)
- Using CSS to wrap text around images (Chapter 4)
- Gradients (Chapter 2, from the "Web page background ideas" section)
- Styling semantic markup: A traditional example with serif fonts and a baseline grid (Chapter 3)
- Creating a boxout (Chapter 7)
- Creating pull quotes in CSS (Chapter 3)

Open index.html and examine the code. The head section imports a style sheet and uses conditional comments to link to three IE-specific style sheets (one for Internet Explorer in general, one for Internet Explorer 6 and below, and one for Internet Explorer versions below 6). Note that the body element has an id value—this dictates the active tab, as per the method shown in the "Creating a two-tier navigation menu" exercise in Chapter 5.

The page's structure is shown in the following code block. The page is contained within a wrapper div. Within that, there is a masthead that contains a logo div and a navContainer div (which itself contains a navigation div and a subNavigation div). After the masthead is a content div. Without content, the skeleton structure looks like that shown in the following code block:

```
<div id="wrapper">
  <div id="masthead">
    <div id="logo"></div>
    <div id="navContainer">
      <div id="navigation"></div>
    </div>
  </div>
  <div id="content"></div>
</div>
```

In the logo div is the paragraph about the company, and the contents of the navContainer div are identical to those from "Creating a two-tier navigation menu" in Chapter 5.

The content div begins with a level-one heading, immediately followed by an image with a class value of leadImage. The image is positioned here because it will be floated right, and you need to place floated content before the content you want it to float left or right of (see the "Using CSS to wrap text around images" section in Chapter 4). This is followed by a paragraph of text and then a blockquote element, as per "Creating pull quotes in CSS" from Chapter 3.

Next, a horizontal rule provides a visual break from the introductory content, followed by two divs that have class values of columnLeft and columnRight. As you've no doubt guessed, these are the two columns; each contains an image, a level-two heading, and a paragraph. The final piece of code within the content div is a footer paragraph.

Styling the business website

The sme.css document contains the styles for this layout, arranged into sections, as per the discussion earlier in this chapter. The defaults section includes two rules. The first is the universal selector (*), used to remove padding and margins (as per "Zeroing margins and padding on all elements" in Chapter 2). The second is a body rule, which adds some vertical padding to the web page, ensuring there's always some space before and after the bordered content (having borders directly touch browser window edges makes for a cluttered and visually unappealing design), and defines the page background—a dark gray color (#333333) into which is blended the horizontally tiled background image page-background.gif.

```
body {
  padding: 20px 0;
  background: #333333 url(assets/page-background.gif) repeat-x;
}
```

10

In the structure section, the #wrapper rule defines a fixed width for the wrapper, horizontally centers it, and defines a one-pixel border around its edges. The #masthead rule defines the thick, light gray border under the masthead, and #logo sets the masthead-background. jpg image as a background for the logo div, along with setting the height of the div (which is the same height as the image) and adding a one-pixel bottom margin (otherwise the top border of the navigation items doesn't show).

Next, the #content rule sets 18 pixels of padding around the content area's contents, and defines the background color as white (otherwise the dark gray page background would show through). There's also a commented-out rule for the baseline grid image, added for the same reason as in the Pictures from Padstow example (see the first paragraph of the "Styling the gallery" section, earlier in this chapter). Note that 18 pixels is the target baseline grid line height for this design.

Next, the hr rule styles the horizontal rule, making it light gray and ensuring that it takes up a couple of "rows" in the grid (0.7em plus 2.9em is 3.6em, which because of the standard text sizing used throughout this book equates by default to 36px—twice the target line height of 18px).

```
hr {
    height: 0.7em;
    margin-bottom: 2.9em;
    background-color: #cccccc;
    color: #cccccc;
    border: none;
}
```

The final two rules in the section, .columnLeft, .columnRight (.columnLeft, .columnRight is a grouped selector, not two separate rules) and .columnLeft, float the two column divs, set fixed widths for them (equally, since this property is placed in the grouped selector), and define a margin-right value for the left-hand column so that there's space between the two columns.

The next section, links and navigation, is copied wholesale from Chapter 5's "Creating a two-tier navigation menu" exercise. There are no changes. Nothing to see here . . . move along.

Next is the fonts section. This section's all pretty straightforward, assuming you've read and digested the "Styling semantic markup: A traditional example with serif fonts and a baseline grid" exercise in Chapter 3. As usual, the html and body rules reset the font size, as per the "Setting text using percentages and ems" section in Chapter 3. The body rule also sets the preferred font to a Lucida variant (eventually falling back to Arial and Helvetica). The h1, h2, and p rules then set font-size, line-height, and margin-bottom values for their respective elements, line-height values being calculated by dividing 1.8 by the font-size value. (If you're going "wha?" the "Styling semantic markup: A traditional example with serif fonts and a baseline grid" exercise in Chapter 3 has all the answers.)

Override rules follow, with specific settings for the masthead paragraph defined via #masthead p—the color is set to white, and padding is used to position the block of text.

```
#masthead p {
    color: #ffffff;
    font-size: 1.2em;
    padding: 24px 20px 0 320px;
    line-height: 1.3em;
}
```

The p.footer rule is used to clear any floated content; the rule also aligns the text right and adds some top padding to shift it further away from other page content (ensuring the footer isn't a distraction). The various blockquote and cite rules are variants on the method shown in Chapter 3's "Creating pull quotes in CSS" exercise. Again, somewhat complex line-height and margin values are used to take into account the baseline grid.

Finally, the images section has four rules. The first, a img, removes borders from linked images. Next, #content img applies a one-pixel border to images within the content div. After that, the img.leadImage rule floats the image after the main heading right, adding some margins at the bottom and left edges to ensure there's some whitespace between the image and other content. And then .columnLeft img, .columnRight img sets the images within the columns to display as block, which removes the default overhang browsers that otherwise apply to images (as they do to text). The margin-bottom value ensures subsequent content is aligned with the baseline grid. Note that the height of the images, as defined in HTML, is 70 pixels. Add two pixels from the borders and you have 72, a multiple of 18, ensuring that the actual images adhere to the baseline grid, too—at least when browsers are at their default settings.

```
.columnLeft img, .columnRight img {
  display: block;
  margin-bottom: 1.8em;
}
```

In terms of Internet Explorer fixes, few things are needed for this layout. For ie-hacks.css, Internet Explorer's problems dealing with hr margins are dealt with by providing new margin-top and margin-bottom values. For the ie-lte6-hacks.css document (which affects Internet Explorer 6 and below), the blockquote, blockquote p rule removes the pull quote background images. Also, a hasLayout bug causes the background behind the navigation to show incorrectly. This is fixed by giving layout to the element by way of a width value.

```
#navigation {
  width: 100%;
}
```

In ie-5-hacks.css, the two rules center the layout in the browser window.

The completed layout is shown in the following screenshot.

Working with style sheets for print

This chapter's final section briefly looks at using CSS to create a printable version of a website layout. Printing from the Web is still a bit of a hit-and-miss affair, and even using CSS doesn't solve every problem, although browser support for print-oriented CSS is improving. If you omit a print style sheet, though, chances are the output will be significantly worse. Browsers may have varying opinions on how to present both fixed and liquid layouts, and you may end up with bizarre results. Most likely, however, if you omit a print style sheet, all of the elements on your web page will just be printed in a linear fashion, using system defaults for the fonts—not nice.

In the old days (and, frankly, in the not-so-old days, since the practice somehow survives), designers often worked on so-called printer-friendly sites, run in parallel with the main site. However, if you're using CSS layouts, it's possible to create a style sheet specifically for print, which you can use to dictate exactly which elements on the page you want to print, which you want to omit, and how you want to style those that can be printed.

As mentioned earlier in the book, a print style sheet is attached to web pages using the following HTML:

```
<link rel="stylesheet" type="text/css"media="print"
➥ href="print-style-sheet.css" />
```

The media attribute value of print restricts the CSS solely to print, and within the print style sheet, you define styles specifically for print, such as different fonts and margins. In the example in the download files, I've used a version of the business website, which you can access via the sme-website-print folder in the chapter 10 folder. The print style sheet is sme-print.css, and if you compare it to the main style sheet, you'll see that it's much simpler and massively honed down.

The defaults section houses a single body rule, defining padding (to take into account varying printer margins, 5% is a good horizontal padding to use), the background color (white is really the only choice you should use, and it's usually the default, but setting it explicitly ensures this is the case), the text color (black is best for contrast when printing), and the font. There's absolutely no point in trying to ape your onscreen design and typography in print—instead, use values that enhance the printed version. In the example's body rule (shown in the following code block), serif fonts are defined for font-family, because serifs are easier to read in print. Note that you're not only restricted to web-safe fonts at this point either—you can define choices based on fonts that come with the default install of Windows and Mac OS, hence the choices of Baskerville (Mac) and Palatino Linotype (Windows), prior to Times New Roman and Times.

```
body {
  padding: 0 5%;
  background: #ffffff;
  font-family: Baskerville, "Palatino Linotype", "Times New Roman",
  ➥ "Times", serif;
  line-height: 16pt;
}
```

In the structure section, the #masthead declaration sets display to none. That's because this area of the page is of no use for printed output—you simply don't need website masthead and navigation offline. (This is, of course, a generalization, and in rare cases this may not be applicable; however, in the vast, vast majority of websites I've created, the printed version has not required the masthead and navigation links.) Note that if other areas aren't required, just use a grouped selector instead of this rule with a lone selector, as shown in the following code block (which *isn't* in the example CSS):

```
#element1, #element2, .class1, .class2 {/* these items won't be
➥ printed */
  display: none;
}
```

10

Because pixel values don't tend to translate to print well, some settings may need to be redefined. An example in this case is the two-column section of the page. The widths and margins were initially defined in pixels, but in the print CSS, it makes more sense to define these values in percentages. (Note that the 9.99% value is there in case of rounding errors.)

```
.columnLeft, .columnRight {
  float: left;
  width: 45%;
}
.columnLeft {
  margin-right: 9.99%;
}
```

In the links and navigation section, only one rule remains. While links are of no real use offline, it's still a good idea to make it apparent what text-based content was originally a link, in order for people to be able to find said links should they want to, or for reasons of context. Just ensuring the default underline is in place should do, and that can be done via the following rule:

```
a:link, a:visited {
  text-decoration: underline;
}
```

For browsers other than Internet Explorer (although JavaScript workarounds exist for IE compatibility—e.g., see www.grafx.com.au/dik//printLinkURLs.html), you can also provide the href values alongside any printed links by using the following code:

```
a:link:after, a:visited:after {
  content: " (" attr(href) ") ";
  font-size: 90%;
}
```

In terms of fonts, keeping things simple makes sense. It's also worth noting that because you're working with print, sizes in points are more useful than sizes in pixels. (Note that in the body rule, the line-height value was 16pt, not 16px or 1.6em.) Therefore, the font-size values all reflect that. Note in the p.footer rule that floated content still needs clearing in the print style sheets.

The final section, images, is not changed much. The images within the columns were deemed superfluous, and so display has been set to none for .columnLeft img, .columnRight img. Elsewhere, the margins on the floated image have been set to values in centimeters (cm) and the border value for #content img is in millimeters (mm), since we're working in print. (Values in pixels are permitted, but they tend to be less accurate when working with print style sheets—for example, if elements have a one-pixel border, they may not all be even when printed.)

One final thing that's useful to know is how to create print-only content. In this example, removing the masthead from the print output has also removed the site's corporate ID. A cunning way to bring this back is to create a black-and-white version of the company logo, and add that as the first item on the web page, within a div that has an id value of printLogo.

```
<div id="printLogo">
  <img src="assets/we-lay-floors-bw-logo.gif" alt="Web Lay Floors,
  ➥ Inc. logo" width="267" height="70" />
</div>
```

Then, in the main style sheet, create a rule that displays this element offscreen when the page is loaded in a browser window.

```
#printLogo {
  position: absolute;
  left: -1000px;
}
```

The content will then show up in print, but not online. Note, however, that you should be mindful to not hide weighty images in this manner, otherwise you'll compromise download speeds for anyone using your website in a browser, only for making things slightly better for those printing the site. A small, optimized GIF should be sufficient.

If there's other content you want to hide in this manner, you can also create a generic printOnly class to apply to elements you want hidden in the browser, but visible in print. The following CSS rule applied to your screen style sheet would be sufficient for doing this:

```
.printOnly {
  display: none;
}
```

The reason for not using this generic method with the logo is because at the time of writing, Opera appears to only print images cached from the normal page view—in other words, if the image isn't displayed in the standard browser window, Opera won't print it. Therefore, if using the generic printOnly class, be aware that any images hidden won't print in Opera, but text will.

> *If you've used Internet Explorer expressions for fixing layout issues with IE 6 and lower (see Chapter 9), these may "leak" into the print version, regardless of whether you've attached the style sheet by using a* media *attribute of* screen. *In such cases, use a conditional comment to attach an IE-specific print CSS that overrides the expression value or values.*

An example of how the print style sheet looks is shown in the following screenshot.

10

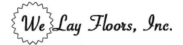

We Lay Floors, Inc.

For all your flooring needs

Lorem ipsum dolor sit amet, consectetuer adipiscing elit. Morbi commodo, ipsum sed pharetra gravida, orci magna rhoncus neque, id pulvinar odio lorem non turpis. Nullam sit amet enim. Suspendisse id velit vitae ligula volutpat condimentum. Aliquam erat volutpat. Sed quis velit. Nulla facilisi. Nulla libero. Vivamus pharetra posuere sapien. Nam consectetuer. Sed aliquam, nunc eget euismod ullamcorper, lectus nunc ullamcorper orci, fermentum bibendum enim nibh eget ipsum. Donec porttitor ligula eu dolor. Maecenas vitae nulla consequat libero cursus venenatis. Nam magna enim, accumsan eu, blandit sed, blandit a, eros. Quisque facilisis erat a dui. Nam malesuada ornare dolor. Cras gravida, diam sit amet rhoncus ornare, erat elit consectetuer erat, id egestas pede nibh eget odio.

This is the pull quote. It's really very exciting, so read it now! Lorem ipsum dolor sit amet, consectetuer adipiscing elit.

Fred Bloggs

Lorem ipsum dolor

Sit amet, consectetuer adipiscing elit. Morbi commodo, ipsum sed pharetra gravida, orci magna rhoncus neque, id pulvinar odio lorem non turpis. Nullam sit amet enim. Suspendisse id velit vitae ligula volutpat condimentum. Aliquam erat volutpat. Sed quis velit. Nulla facilisi. Nulla libero. Vivamus pharetra posuere sapien. Nam consectetuer. Sed aliquam, nunc eget euismod ullamcorper, lectus nunc ullamcorper orci, fermentum.

Quisque facilisis erat a dui

Nam malesuada ornare dolor. Cras gravida, diam sit amet rhoncus ornare, erat elit consectetuer erat, id egestas pede nibh eget odio. Proin tincidunt, velit vel porta elementum, magna diam molestie sapien, non aliquet massa pede eu diam. Aliquam iaculis. Fusce et ipsum et nulla tristique facilisis. Donec eget sem sit amet ligula viverra gravida. Etiam vehicula urna vel turpis. Suspendisse sagittis ante a urna.

© 2007 We Lay Floors, Inc.

Note that you can take things further in terms of layout, but it's best to keep it simple. Also, ensure that you use the Print Preview functions of your browser test suite to thoroughly test your print style sheet output and ensure that there are no nasty surprises for visitors to your site. Ultimately, it's worth the extra hassle—just amending the fonts and page margins and removing images and page areas that are irrelevant to the printed version of the site not only improves your users' experience, but also makes the site seem more professional.

A XHTML REFERENCE

This section of the reference guide details, in alphabetical order, generally supported elements and associated attributes. This is not intended as an exhaustive guide; rather, its aim is to list those elements important and relevant to current web design. Archaic deprecated elements such as font and layer are therefore ignored, as well as many attributes once associated with the body element, but the guide includes still occasionally useful deprecated and nonstandard elements and attributes such as embed and target.

> *Note that in the following pages, various styles are used for the attribute names and values. For the sake of clarity, quote marks have been omitted, but never forget that XHTML attributes must be quoted. Therefore, where you see the likes of* id=*name in this reference section, the final output would be* id="name".

Standard attributes

Standard attributes are common to many elements. For brevity, they are listed in full here rather than in the XHTML element table later in the chapter. For each element in the forthcoming table, I simply state which groups of standard attributes are applicable to the element.

Core attributes

Attribute	Description
class=*classname*	Specifies a CSS class to define the element's visual appearance.
id=*name*	Defines a unique reference ID for the element.
style=*style* (*deprecated*)	Sets an inline style. Deprecated in XHTML 1.1, so it should be used sparingly and with caution.
title=*string*	Specifies the element's title. Often used with links to provide a tooltip expanding on the link's purpose or the target's content.

> *Not valid in these elements:* base, head, html, meta, param, script, style, *and* title.

Keyboard attributes

Attribute	Description
accesskey=*character*	Defines a keyboard shortcut to access an element. The shortcut must be a single character. Most commonly used with navigation links. See also Chapter 5, "Using accesskey and tabindex."
tabindex=*number*	Defines the tab order of an element. Most commonly used with form input elements. Setting the value to 0 excludes the element from the tabbing order. The maximum value allowed is 32767. The tabindex values on a page needn't be consecutive (for instance, you could use multiples of 10, to leave space for later additions). See also Chapter 5, "Using accesskey and tabindex."

Language attributes

Attribute	Description
dir=*dir*	Specifies the text rendering direction: left-to-right (ltr, the default) or right-to-left (rtl).
lang=*language* (deprecated)	Specifies the language for the tag's contents, using two-letter primary ISO639 codes and optional dialect codes. Included for backward compatibility with HTML. Used together with xml:lang (see below) in XHTML 1.0, but deprecated in XHTML 1.1. Examples: lang="en" (English) lang="en-US" (US English) ISO639 codes include the following: ar (Arabic), zh (Chinese), nl (Dutch), fr (French), de (German), el (Greek), he (Hebrew), it (Italian), ja (Japanese), pt (Portuguese), ru (Russian), sa (Sanskrit), es (Spanish), and ur (Urdu).
xml:lang=*language*	Replaces lang in XHTML 1.1, but both should be used together in XHTML 1.0 to ensure backward compatibility with HTML and older browsers. xml:lang takes precedence over lang if set to a different value.

Not valid in these elements: base, br, frame, frameset, hr, iframe, param, *and* script.

Event attributes

As of HTML 4.0, it's been possible to trigger browser actions by way of HTML events. Again, these are listed in full here and referred to for the relevant elements of the XHTML element table. In XHTML, all event names must be in lowercase (e.g., onclick, not onClick).

Core events

Attribute	Description
onclick=*script*	Specifies a script to be run when the user clicks the element's content area
ondblclick=*script*	Specifies a script to be run when the user double-clicks the element's content area

A

continues

Attribute	Description
onkeydown=*script*	Specifies a script to be run when the user presses a key while the element's content area is focused
onkeypress=*script*	Specifies a script to be run when the user presses and releases a key while the element's content area is focused
onkeyup=*script*	Specifies a script to be run when the user releases a pressed key while the element's content area is focused
onmousedown=*script*	Specifies a script to be run when the user presses down the mouse button while the cursor is over the element's content area
onmousemove=*script*	Specifies a script to be run when the user moves the mouse cursor in the element's content area
onmouseout=*script*	Specifies a script to be run when the user moves the mouse cursor off the element's content area
onmouseover=*script*	Specifies a script to be run when the user moves the mouse cursor onto the element's content area
onmouseup=*script*	Specifies a script to be run when the user releases the mouse button on the element's content area

Not valid in these elements: base, bdo, br, frame, frameset, head, html, iframe, meta, param, script, style, *and* title.

Form element events

These events are generally restricted to form elements, although some other elements accept some of them.

Attribute	Description
onblur=*script*	Specifies a script to be run when the element loses focus
onchange=*script*	Specifies a script to be run when the element changes
onfocus=*script*	Specifies a script to be run when the element is focused

Attribute	Description
onreset=*script*	Specifies a script to be run when a form is reset
onselect=*script*	Specifies a script to be run when the element is selected
onsubmit=*script*	Specifies a script to be run when a form is submitted

Window events

These events are valid only in the following elements: body and frameset.

Attribute	Description
onload=*script*	Specifies a script to be run when the document loads
onunload=*script*	Specifies a script to be run when the document unloads

Although onresize *is part of DOM2, it's not recognized by the XHTML specification. If an* onresize *event is required, it cannot be applied directly to the* body *element. Instead, you must declare it in the document* head *using* window.onresize=functionName.

XHTML elements and attributes

The following pages list XHTML elements, associated attributes, and descriptions for all. Unless otherwise stated, assume an element is allowed in pages with XHTML Strict, XHTML Transitional, or XHTML Frameset DTDs. Do not use elements or attributes with DTDs that don't allow them. For instance, the target attribute cannot be used with XHTML Strict—doing so renders the page invalid.

Some elements are shown with a trailing forward slash. These are empty tags. Instead of having a start tag, content, and an end tag, these elements have a combined form. This takes the form of a start tag with an added trailing forward slash. Prior to the slash, a space is usually added. For instance, <br /> denotes a line break.

A

Element	Attribute	Description	Standard attributes
`<!-- ... -->`		Defines a comment. See also Chapter 2, "Commenting your work."	No attributes
`<!DOCTYPE>` *(required)*		Specifies a DTD for the document. This is required for a valid XHTML document. See also Chapter 2, "DOCTYPE declarations explained."	No attributes
`<a>`		Defines an anchor. Can link to another document by using the `href` attribute, or create an anchor within a document by using the `id` or `name` attributes. Despite the number of available attributes, some aren't well supported. Generally, `href`, `name`, `title`, and `target` are commonly used, along with `class` and `id` for use as CSS or scripting hooks. See also Chapter 5, "Creating and styling web page links."	Core attributes, keyboard attributes, language attributes Core events, `onblur`, `onfocus`
	`href=URL`	Defines the link target.	
	`name=name` *(deprecated)*	Names an anchor. Due to be replaced by `id` in future versions of XHTML. When defining a fragment identifier in XHTML 1.0, `id` must be used.	
	`rel=relationship`	Specifies the relationship from the current document to the target document. Common values include `next`, `prev`, `parent`, `child`, `index`, `toc`, and `glossary`. Also used within `link` elements to define the relationship of linked CSS documents (e.g., to establish default and alternative style sheets).	

Element	Attribute	Description	Standard attributes
	rev=*relationship*	Specifies the relationship from the target document to the current document. Common values include next, prev, parent, child, index, toc, and glossary.	
	target=*_blank|* *_parent|_self|* *_top|[name]* *(deprecated)*	Defines where the target URL opens. Primarily of use with frames, stating which frame a target should open in. Commonly used in web pages to open external links in a new window—a practice that should be avoided, because it breaks the browser history path. *Unavailable in XHTML 1.0, so cannot be used with XHTML 1.0 Strict documents. However,* target *is available in XHTML 1.1 using the target module.*	
	type=*MIME type*	Specifies the MIME type of the target. For instance, if linking to a plain text file, you might use the following: `<a href="document.txt` ➥ `type="text/plain">`	
`<abbr>`		Identifies the element content as an abbreviation. This can be useful for nonvisual web browsers. For example: `<abbr` ➥ `title="Doctor">Dr.</abbr>` See also Chapter 3, "Acronyms and abbreviations."	Core attributes, language attributes Core events

A

continues

Element	Attribute	Description	Standard attributes

`<acronym>`		Identifies the element content as an acronym. This can be useful for nonvisual web browsers. For example:
		
		`<acronym title="North`
		➥ `Atlantic Treaty`
		➥ `Organization">NATO`
		`</acronym>`
		
		See also Chapter 3, "Acronyms and abbreviations."
			Core attributes, language attributes
			
			Core events

`<address>`		Used to define addresses, signatures, or document authors. Typically rendered in italics, with a line break above and below (but no additional space). See also Chapter 8, "Contact details structure redux."	Core attributes, language attributes Core events
`<applet>` *(deprecated)*		Adds an applet to the web page. Deprecated in favor of the object element, but still required for embedding some Java applets. *This element cannot be used with an XHTML Strict* DOCTYPE. *Likewise, all of the element's attributes are deprecated and cannot be used with the XHTML Strict* DOCTYPE.	Core attributes, keyboard attributes, language attributes Core events
	`align=`*position*	Defines text alignment around the element. Possible values are `left`, `right`, `top`, `middle`, and `bottom`.	
	`alt=`*string*	Alternate text for browsers that don't support applets.	
	`archive=`*URL*	Defines a list of URLs with classes to be preloaded.	

Element	Attribute	Description	Standard attributes
	code=*URL* (required)	Specifies either the name of the class *file* that contains the applet's compiled applet subclass or the path to get the class *file*, including the class file itself.	
		This attribute is required if the object attribute is missing, and vice versa. If both are present, they must use the same class name. Note: the value is case-sensitive.	
	codebase=*URL*	Base URL of the applet.	
	height=*number* (required)	Pixel height of the applet. This attribute is *required*.	
	hspace=*number*	Sets horizontal space around the applet.	
	name=*name*	Sets a unique name for this instance of the applet, which can be used in scripts.	
	object=*name*	Defines a resource's name that contains a serialized representation of the applet.	
	vspace=*number*	Sets vertical space around the applet.	
	width=*number* (required)	Pixel width of the applet. This attribute is *required*.	
<area />		Defines a clickable area within a client-side image map. Should be nested within a map element (see separate <map> entry).	Core attributes, keyboard attributes, language attributes
			Core events, onblur, onfocus
		See also Chapter 5, "Image maps."	
	alt=*string* (required)	Provides alternate text for nonvisual browsers. This attribute is *required*.	

continues

A

Element	Attribute	Description	Standard attributes
	coords= *coordinates list*	Specifies coordinates for the clickable image map area. Values are defined as a comma-separated list. The number of values depends on the shape attribute value:	
		For rect, four values are required, defining the coordinates on the x and y axes of the top-left and bottom-right corners.	
		For circle, three values are required, with the first two defining the x and y coordinates of the hot-spot center, and the third defining the circle's radius.	
		For poly, each pair of x and y values defines a point of the hot-spot's.	
	href=*URL*	The link target.	
	nohref=*nohref*	Enables you to set the defined area to have no action when the user selects it. nohref is the only possible value of this attribute.	
	shape=*rect*| *circle*|*poly*| *default*	Defines the shape of the clickable region.	
	target=*_blank*| *_parent*|*_self*| *_top*|*[name]* *(deprecated)*	Defines where the target URL opens. *Cannot be used in XHTML Strict.*	

Element	Attribute	Description	Standard attributes
`<b>`		Renders text as bold. This element is a physical style, which defines what the content looks like (presentation only), rather than a logical style, which defines what the content is (which is beneficial for technologies like screen readers). It's recommended to use the logical element `<strong></strong>` in place of `<b></b>` (see separate `<strong>` entry). See also Chapter 3, "Styles for emphasis (bold and italic)."	Core attributes, language attributes Core events
`<base />`		Specifies a base URL for relative URLs on the web page.	
	`href=`*URL* *(required)*	Defines the base URL to use. This attribute is *required*.	
	`target=`*_blank|* *_parent|_self|* *_top|[name]* *(deprecated)*	Defines where to open page links. Can be overridden by inline target attributes. *Cannot be used in XHTML Strict.*	
`<bdo>`		Overrides the default text direction.	Core attributes, language attributes
	`dir=`*ltr|rtl* *(required)*	Defines text direction as left to right (ltr) or right to left (rtl). This attribute is *required*.	

continues

A

409

Element	Attribute	Description	Standard attributes
`<big>`		Increments text size to the next size larger as compared to surrounding text. Because the size differential is determined by the browser, precise text size changes are better achieved via span elements and CSS. Some browsers misinterpret this tag and render text as bold. See also Chapter 3, "The big and small elements."	Core attributes, language attributes Core events
`<blockquote>`		Defines a lengthy quotation. To validate as XHTML Strict, enclosed content must be set within a block-level element (such as `<p></p>`). Although it is common for web designers to use this element to indent content, the W3C strongly recommends using CSS for such things. See also Chapter 3, "Block quotes, quote citations, and definitions," and "Creating drop caps and pull quotes using CSS."	Core attributes, language attributes Core events
	cite=*URL*	Defines the online location of quoted material.	
`<body>` *(required)*		Defines the document's body and contains the document's contents. This is a *required* element for XHTML web pages. (In HTML, it is optional and implied when absent. However, it's good practice to always include the element.)	Core attributes, language attributes Core events, onload, onunload
` `		Inserts a single line break.	Core attributes

Element	Attribute	Description	Standard attributes

`<button>`		Defines a push button element within a form. Works similarly to buttons created with the input element, but offers greater rendering scope. This is because all content becomes the content of the button, enabling the creation of buttons with text and images. For example:
		
		`<button type="submit">`
		`Order now! <img`
		➥ `src="go.gif" alt="Go"`
		`/>`
			Core attributes, keyboard attributes, language attributes
			
			Core events, onblur, onfocus

	`disabled=`*`disabled`*	Disables the button. disabled is the only possible value of this attribute.	
	`name=`*`name`*	Defines the button's name.	
	`type=`*`button`*`|`*`reset`*`|`*`submit`*	Identifies the button's type.	
	`value=`*`string`*	Defines the button's initial value.	
`<caption>`		Defines a caption for a table. Seldom used, but recommended because it enables you to associate a table's title with its contents. Omitting the caption may mean the table's contents are meaningless out of context. See also Chapter 6, "Captions and summaries."	Core attributes, language attributes Core events
`<cite>`		Defines content as a citation. Usually rendered in italics. See also Chapter 3, "Block quotes, quote citations, and definitions."	Core attributes, language attributes Core events

A

continues

411

Element	Attribute	Description	Standard attributes
`<code>`		Defines content as computer code sample text. Usually rendered in a monospace font. See also Chapter 3, "Logical styles for programming-oriented content," and the "Displaying blocks of code online" exercise.	Core attributes, language attributes Core events

`<col />`		Defines properties for a column or group of columns within a colgroup. Attributes defined within a col element override those set in the containing colgroup element. col is an empty element that contains attributes only. The following example sets the column widths of the table's first three columns to 10, 30, and 50 pixels, respectively:
		
		`<colgroup span="3">`
		  `<col width="10"></col>`
		  `<col width="30"></col>`
		  `<col width="50"></col>`
		`</colgroup>`
		
		See also the `<colgroup>` entry.
			Core attributes, language attributes
			
			Core events

	align=*left*|*right*|*justify*|*center* *(deprecated)*	Defines the horizontal alignment of table cell content. It's recommended that you use the CSS `text-align` property instead (see its entry in the CSS reference) to do this.	

	span=*n*	Defines how many successive columns are affected by the col tag. Use only when the surrounding colgroup element does not specify the number of columns.
		
		The following example creates a colgroup with five columns, with each of the middle three columns 30 pixels wide:
		
		`<colgroup>`
		  `<col width="10" />`
		  `<col width="30" span="3" />`
		  `<col width="50" />`
		`</colgroup>`	

Element	Attribute	Description	Standard attributes
	valign=*top*|*middle*| *bottom*|*baseline* *(deprecated)*	Specifies the vertical alignment of table cell content. It's recommended that you instead use the CSS vertical-align property (see its entry in the CSS reference) to do this.	
	width=*percentage/* *number*	Defines the width of the column. Overrides the width settings in colgroup.	
<colgroup>		Defines a column group within a table, enabling you to define formatting for the columns within. See the <col /> entry for examples. See also Chapter 6, "Scope and headers."	Core attributes, language attributes Core events
	align=*left*|*right*| *justify*|*center* *(deprecated)*	Defines the horizontal alignment of the table cell content within the colgroup. It's recommended that you instead use the CSS text-align property (see its entry in the CSS reference) to do this.	
	span=*number*	Defines how many columns the colgroup should span. Do not use if any of the col tags within the colgroup also use span, because a colgroup definition will be ignored in favor of span attributes defined within the col elements.	
	valign=*top*|*middle*| *bottom*|*baseline* *(deprecated)*	Specifies the vertical alignment of the table cell content within the colgroup. It's recommended that you instead use the CSS vertical-align property (see its entry in the CSS reference) to do this.	

A

continues

413

Element	Attribute	Description	Standard attributes
	width=*percentage/ number*	Defines the width of columns within the colgroup. Can be overridden by the width settings of individual col elements.	
`<dd>`		Defines a definition description within a definition list. See the `<dl>` entry for an example. See also Chapter 3, "Definition lists," and the "Displaying blocks of code online" exercise.	Core attributes, language attributes Core events
`<del>`		Indicates deleted text. Usually appears in strikethrough format. See also Chapter 3, "Elements for inserted and deleted text."	Core attributes, language attributes Core events
	cite=*URL*	Defines the URL of a document that explains why the text was deleted.	
	datetime=*date*	Defines the date and time that the text was amended. Various formats are possible, including YYYY-MM-DD and YYYY-MM-DDThh:mm:ssTZD (where TZD is the time zone designator). See www.w3.org/ TR/1998/NOTE-datetime- 19980827 for more date and time formatting information.	
`<dfn>`		Defines enclosed content as the defining instance of a term. Usually rendered in italics. See also Chapter 3, "Block quotes, quote citations, and definitions."	Core attributes, language attributes Core events

Element	Attribute	Description	Standard attributes
`<div>`		Defines a division within a web page. Perhaps one of the most versatile but least understood elements. Used in combination with an id or class, the div tag element allows sections of a page to be individually styled and is the primary XHTML element used for the basis of CSS-based web page layouts. See also Chapter 7, "Workflow for CSS layouts."	Core attributes, language attributes Core events

`<dl>`		Defines a definition list. Contains pairs of term and definition elements, as follows:
		
		`<dl>`
		`  <dt>Windows</dt>`
		`  <dd>Operating system`
		`➥ made by Microsoft.</dd>`
		`  <dt>Mac OS</dt>`
		`  <dd>Operating system`
		`➥ made by Apple.</dd>`
		`</dl>`
		
		See also Chapter 3, "Definition lists," and the "Displaying blocks of code online" exercise.
			Core attributes, language attributes
			
			Core events

`<dt>`		Defines a definition term within a definition list. See the `<dl>` entry for an example. See also Chapter 3, "Definition lists," and the "Displaying blocks of code online" exercise.	Core attributes, language attributes Core events

A

continues

415

Element	Attribute	Description	Standard attributes
`<em>`		Defines enclosed content as emphasized. Generally renders as italics in a browser and is preferred over the use of `<i></i>`. See separate `<i>` entry. See also Chapter 3, "Block quotes, quote citations, and definitions."	Core attributes, language attributes Core events
`<embed>` *(nonstandard)*		Embeds an object. Nonstandard and not supported by any XHTML DOCTYPE. If this is included in a web page, the page will not validate. Poor browser support for the W3C preferred alternative, object, left developers with little choice other than to use this nonstandard element when embedding Flash or other multimedia into a web page. Support for object has now improved, although embed may still be required in some circumstances.	
	`align=left|right| top|bottom`	Defines the alignment of the embedded object in relation to the surrounding text.	
	`height=number`	Defines the height of the object in pixels.	
	`hidden=yes|no`	Hides the player or media file when set to yes. Defaults to no.	
	`hspace=number`	Sets horizontal space around the object.	
	`name=name`	Sets a name for the object.	
	`pluginspage=URL`	Defines a URL for information on installing the relevant plug-in.	

Element	Attribute	Description	Standard attributes
	src=*URL* (required)	Provides the location of the object to be embedded. This attribute is *required*.	
	type=*MIME type*	Specifies the MIME type of the plug-in required to run the file.	
	vspace=*number*	Sets vertical space around the object.	
	width=*number*	Defines the width of the object in pixels.	
`<fieldset>`		Creates a group of related form elements by nesting them within the fieldset element. Usually used in tandem with the legend element to enhance form accessibility (see the `<legend>` entry for more information). See also Chapter 8, "Improving form accessibility."	Core attributes, language attributes Core events
	accesskey= *character*	Defines a keyboard shortcut to access an element.	
`<form>`		Indicates the start and end of a form. Cannot be nested within another form element. Generally, the method and action attributes are most used. See also Chapter 8, "Working with forms."	Core attributes, language attributes Core events, onreset, onsubmit
	accept=*content- type list*	Specifies a comma-separated list of MIME types that the server processing the form can handle correctly.	
	accept- charset=*charset list*	Specifies a comma-separated list of character sets for form data.	

A

continues

Element	Attribute	Description	Standard attributes
	action=*URL* (required)	The URL of the form processing application where the data is sent once the form is submitted. This attribute is *required*.	
	enctype=*encoding*	The MIME type used to encode the form's content before it's sent to the server, so it doesn't become scrambled. Defaults to application/x-www-form-urlencoded. Other options are multipart/form-data, which can be used when the user is able to upload files, and text-plain, which can be used when using a mailto: value for the action instead of a server-side script to parse the form data.	
	method=*get*|*post*	Specifies the http method used to submit the form data. The post value is most commonly used.	
	name=*name* (deprecated)	Defines the form's name. *Cannot be used in XHTML Strict.*	
	target=*_blank*| *_parent*|*_self*| *_top*|*[name]* (deprecated)	Defines where the target URL is opened. *Cannot be used in XHTML Strict.*	
`<frame>`		Defines a frame. *This element and its attributes must only be used with the XHTML Frameset DTD, and not with XHTML Strict or XHTML Transitional.* See also Chapter 7, "Working with frames."	Core attributes

Element	Attribute	Description	Standard attributes
	frameborder=*0*|*1*	Defines whether frame borders are present (frameborder="1") or not (frameborder="0").	
	longdesc=*URL*	Defines a URL for a long description of the frame contents for non-frames-compatible browsers.	
	marginheight=*number*	The vertical space between the frame edges and its contents (measured in pixels).	
	marginwidth=*number*	The horizontal space between the frame edges and its contents (measured in pixels).	
	name=*name* (deprecated)	Defines a name for the frame.	
	noresize=*noresize*	Stops the user from resizing the frame. The only available value is noresize.	
	scrolling=*auto*|*no*|*yes*	Specifies whether scroll bars appear when the frame contents are too large for the visible area. The yes value mean permanent scroll bars are shown; no means scroll bars don't appear, even if the content is too large for the frame; and auto means scroll bars appear when the content is too large for the frame.	
	src=*URL*	Defines the location of the frame's default HTML document.	

continues

A

Element	Attribute	Description	Standard attributes
`<frameset>`		Defines a frameset. Must have either a cols *or* a rows attribute. *This element and its attributes must only be used with the XHTML Frameset DTD, and not with XHTML Strict or XHTML Transitional.*	Core attributes onload, onunload
		`<frameset cols="150,* ">` `<frame src=` ➥`"frame-one.html" />` `<frame src=` ➥`"frame-two.html" />` `</frameset>`	
		See also Chapter 7, "Working with frames."	
	cols=*percentage/ number"**	Defines the number and sizes of columns (vertical frames). When setting the value to *, the frame it's applied to takes up all remaining browser window space for that dimension. If more than one value is *, the remaining space is split between those frames the * value is assigned to.	
	rows=*percentage/ number"**	Defines the number and sizes of rows (horizontal frames). See the preceding entry for an explanation of how the * value works.	

Element	Attribute	Description	Standard attributes
`<hn>`		Defines enclosed contents as a heading. Available levels are 1 to 6. Note that although h4 through h6 tend to be displayed smaller than body copy by default, they are not a means to create small text; rather, they are a way to enable you to structure your document. This is essential, because headings help with assistive technology, enabling the visually impaired to efficiently surf the Web. See also Chapter 3, "Paragraphs and headings."	Core attributes, language attributes Core events
`<head>` *(required)*		Defines the header of the HTML file. Houses information-based elements, such as base, link, meta, script, style, and title. This is a *required* element for XHTML web pages. (It's optional for HTML, but implied when absent. However, it's good practice to always include a head element in web pages.)	Language attributes
	profile=*URL*	The location of a metadata profile for this document. Not commonly used.	
`<hr />`		Inserts a horizontal rule.	Core attributes, language attributes Core events

continues

A

421

Element	Attribute	Description	Standard attributes
`<html>` *(required)*		Defines the start and end of the HTML document. This is a *required* element for XHTML web pages. (It's optional for HTML, but implied when absent. However, it's good practice to always include a head element in web pages.) No HTML content should be placed before the html start tag or after the html end tag.	Language attributes
	`xmlns=namespace`	Defines the XML namespace (e.g., `http://www.w3.org/1999/xhtml`). See also Chapter 2, "Document defaults."	
`<i>`		Renders text as italic. This element is a physical style, which defines what the content looks like (presentation only), rather than a logical style, which defines what the content is (which is beneficial for technologies like screen readers). It's generally preferable to use the logical element `<em></em>` in place of `<i></i>`. See the preceding `<em>` entry. See also Chapter 3, "Styles for emphasis (bold and italic)."	Core attributes, language attributes Core events
`<iframe>`		Defines an inline frame. Content within the element is displayed only in browsers that cannot display the iframe. *This element and its attributes cannot be used in XHTML Strict.* See also Chapter 7, "Working with internal frames (iframes)."	

Element	Attribute	Description	Standard attributes
	frameborder=*0|1*	Defines whether a frame border is present (frameborder="1") or not (frameborder="0").	
	height=*percentage/ number*	Defines the iframe's height.	
	longdesc=*URL*	Defines a URL for a long description of the iframe's contents for non-frames-compatible browsers.	
	marginheight= *number*	The vertical space (in pixels) between the iframe's edges and its contents.	
	marginwidth= *number*	The horizontal space (in pixels) between the iframe's edges and its contents.	
	name=*name* *(deprecated)*	Defines a name for the iframe.	
	scrolling=*auto| no|yes*	Specifies whether scroll bars appear when the iframe's contents are too large for the visible area. The yes value means permanent scroll bars are shown; no means scroll bars don't appear, even if the content is too large for the frame; and auto means scroll bars appear when the content is too large for the frame.	
	src=*URL*	Defines the location of the iframe's default HTML document.	
	width=*percentage/ number*	Defines the iframe's width.	

continues

A

Element	Attribute	Description	Standard attributes
`<img />`		Inserts an image. Both the `src` and `alt` attributes are required; although many web designers omit the `alt` attribute, it's essential for screen readers. The height and width values are recommended, too, in order to assist the browser in rapidly laying out the page. The border value, despite common usage, is deprecated and should be avoided. Use CSS to determine whether images have borders. See also Chapter 4, "Working with images in XHTML."	Core attributes, language attributes Core events
	`alt=text` (required)	Provides alternate text for nonvisual browsers. Should provide an indication of an image's content or, if it's a link, its function. When an image has no visual semantic significance, include it via CSS. If that's not possilbe, use `alt=""`. This attribute is required.	
	`border=number` (deprecated)	Defines a border. Despite its common usage, this attribute is deprecated and cannot be used in XHTML Strict. Instead, use CSS to set borders on images. See also Chapter 4, "Applying CSS borders to images."	
	`height=number`	Defines the image's height in pixels.	
	`ismap=URL`	Defines the image as a server-side image map. The image must be contained within an anchor tag. Server-side image maps require specialized setup and are rarely used. Do not confuse this attribute with usemap (see the upcoming usemap entry).	

Element	Attribute	Description	Standard attributes
	longdesc=*URL*	Provides the location of a document containing a long description of the image.	
	src=*URL* (*required*)	The URL of the image to be displayed. This attribute is *required*.	
	usemap=*URL*	Defines the image as a client-side image map. See also Chapter 5, "Image maps."	
	width=*number*	Defines the image's width in pixels.	
`<input />`		Defines a form input field. See also Chapter 8, "Adding controls."	Core attributes, keyboard attributes, language attributes Core events, onblur, onchange, onfocus, onselect
	accept=*list*	A list of MIME types that can be accepted by this element. *Only used with type="file".*	
	alt=*text*	Provides alternate text for nonvisual browsers. *Only used with type="image".*	
	checked=*checked*	Sets input element's default state to checked. The only value for this attribute is checked. *Only used with type="checkbox" and type="radio".*	
	disabled=*disabled*	Disables the input element. The only value for this attribute is disabled. *Cannot be used with type="hidden".*	
	maxlength=*number*	Defines the maximum number of characters allowed. *Only used with type="text".*	

A

continues

Element	Attribute	Description	Standard attributes
	name=*name* (*required**)	Defines a name for the input element.	
		* Required for the following types: button, checkbox, file, hidden, image, password, text, and radio.	
	readonly=*readonly*	Indicates the input element is read-only and cannot be modified. The only value for this attribute is readonly. *Only used with* type="text" *and* type="password".	
	size=*number*	Defines in characters (*not* pixels) the width of the input element. (For pixel-defined widths, use CSS.)	
		Cannot be used with type="hidden".	
	src=*URL*	Defines the URL of the image to be displayed. *Only used with* type="image".	
	type=*button|* *checkbox|file|* *hidden|image|* *password|radio|* *reset|submit|text*	Defines the input element type. Defaults to *text*.	
	value=*string* (*required when* *type=checkbox and* *type=radio*)	When type="button", type="reset", or type="submit", it defines button text.	
		When type="checkbox" or type="radio", it defines the result of the input element; the result being sent when the form is submitted.	
		When type="hidden", type="password", or type="text", it defines the element's default value.	
		When type="image", it defines the result of the field passed to the script. *Cannot be used with* type="file".	

Element	Attribute	Description	Standard attributes

`<ins>`		Defines inserted text. Usually appears in underline format, which can be confusing because links are also underlined. It's therefore recommended that you use CSS to change the underline color.
		
		`ins {`
		`text-decoration: none;`
		`border-bottom: 1px solid red;`
		`}`
		
		See also Chapter 3, "Elements for inserted and deleted text."
			Core attributes, language attributes
			Core events

	`cite=URL`	Defines the URL of a document that explains why the text was inserted.	
	`datetime=date`	Defines the date and time that the text was amended. Various formats are possible, including YYYY-MM-DD and YYYY-MM-DDThh:mm:ssTZD (where TZD is the time zone designator). See `www.w3.org/TR/1998/NOTE-datetime-19980827` for more date and time formatting information.	
`<kbd>`		Defines "keyboard" text (text inputted by the user). Usually rendered in a monospace font. See also Chapter 3, "Logical styles for programming-oriented content."	Core attributes, language attributes Core events

continues

A

Element	Attribute	Description	Standard attributes
`<label>`		Assigns a label to a form control, enabling you to define relationships between text labels and form controls. For example: `<p><strong><label for=` ➥ `"realname">Name</label>` ➥ `</strong> ` `<input type="text"` ➥ `name="realname"` ➥ `id="realname" size="30"` ➥ `/></p>` See also Chapter 8, "The label, fieldset, and legend elements."	Core attributes, language attributes Core events, onblur, onfocus
	accesskey= *character*	Defines a keyboard shortcut to access an element.	
	for=*text*	Defines the form element that the label is for. Value must be the same as the associated control element's id attribute value.	

`<legend>`		Defines a caption for a fieldset. Must be nested within a fieldset element. For example:
		
		`<fieldset>`
		`<legend>Caption for this`
		`fieldset</legend>`
		`[form labels/controls]`
		`</fieldset>`
		
		See also Chapter 8, "The label, fieldset, and legend elements."
			Core attributes, language attributes
			
			Core events

	accesskey= *character*	Defines a keyboard shortcut to access an element.	
`<li>`		Defines a list item. Must be nested within `<ol>` or `<ul>` elements (see the separate `<ol>` and `<ul>` entries). See also Chapter 3, "Working with lists."	Core attributes, language attributes Core events

Element	Attribute	Description	Standard attributes
	type=*format* *(deprecated)*	Specifies the list type for the list item. (See the <ol> and <ul> entries for possible values.) *Cannot be used in XHTML Strict.*	
	value=*number* *(deprecated)*	Defines the number of the item in an ordered list. *Cannot be used in XHTML Strict.*	
<link />		Defines the relationship between two linked documents. Must be placed in the head section of a document. Mainly used for attaching external style sheets and favicons to a document. Also, modern blogging systems use link elements to define relationships between the current document and others, such as XML feeds, next and previous pages, and archives. When used fully, link elements can have considerable accessibility and usability benefits; for example, some modern browsers use the data to provide extra navigation toolbars/options. See also Chapter 2, "Attaching external CSS files: The link method," and "Attaching favicons and JavaScript."	Core attributes, language attributes Core events
	charset=*charset*	Defines the character set of the target document.	
	href=*URL*	The URL of the target.	
	hreflang= *language code*	Defines the language of the linked document.	

continues

A

Element	Attribute	Description	Standard attributes
	media=*media type list*	Defines the target medium for the linked document (all, aural, braille, handheld, print, projection, screen, tty, or tv). More than one medium can be combined in a comma-delimited list.	
	rel=*relationship*	Specifies the relationship from the current document to the target document (alternate, appendix, bookmark, chapter, contents, copyright, glossary, help, index, next, prev, section, start, stylesheet, or subsection). More than one relationship can be combined in a space-separated list.	
	rev=*relationship*	Specifies the relationship from the target document to the current document (see the preceding entry for values).	
	target=*_blank| _parent|_self| _top|[name]* *(deprecated)*	Defines where the target URL opens. *Cannot be used in XHTML Strict.*	
	type=*MIME type*	Specifies the target's MIME type, such as text/css or text/javascript.	
`<map>`		Contains client-side image map specifications. Contains one or more area elements (see preceding `<area />` entry). See also Chapter 5, "Image maps."	Core attributes, keyboard attributes, language attributes Core events, onblur, onfocus
	id=*name* *(required)*	Defines a unique name for the map. This attribute is *required*.	
	name=*name* *(deprecated)*	Defines a unique name for the map. (Superseded by id, but can be used for backward compatibility.)	

Element	Attribute	Description	Standard attributes
`<meta />`		Provides meta information about the document. Must be placed inside the HTML page's head section. Each meta element requires a content attribute and also an http-equiv or a name attribute. Most commonly used to define the character set, and to set keywords and descriptions for search engines (increasingly ineffective, as search engines now pay more attention to page content and links than to meta tags). See also Chapter 2, "meta tags and search engines," and "What about the XML declaration?"	Language attributes
	content=*string* (*required*)	Defines the value of the meta tag property.	
	http-equiv=*string*	Specifies the http equivalent name for the meta information. Examples are content-type, expires, refresh, and set-cookie.	
	name=*string*	Specifies a name for the meta information. Examples are author, description, generator, and keywords.	
	scheme=*string*	Specifies the metadata profile scheme.	
`<noembed>` (*nonstandard*)		Nested within embed elements and displayed only when the browser cannot display the embedded object. Nonstandard and not supported by any XHTML DOCTYPE. If this is included in a web page, the page will not validate.	

continues

A

Element	Attribute	Description	Standard attributes
<noframes>		Defines content to be displayed in non-frames-compatible browsers. Should be placed inside a frameset element. *Intended for use with XHTML Frameset DOCTYPE only.*	Core attributes, language attributes
<noscript>		Defines content to be displayed in browsers that don't support scripting. This is considered a "block-level" element, so it cannot be nested in an element that accepts only inline content, such as a paragraph, heading, or preformatted text. Can be used inside a div, form, or list item.	Core attributes, language attributes
<object>		Defines an embedded object. See also Chapter 7, "Scrollable content areas with CSS."	Core attributes, keyboard attributes, language attributes Core events
	archive=*URL*	Defines a list of URLs to resources used by the object.	
	border=*number* (deprecated)	Sets the object's border width. *Cannot be used in XHTML Strict.*	
	classid=*URL*	Defines the URL of the object.	
	codebase=*URL*	Defines the base URL of the object.	
	codetype=*MIME type*	Defines the object's MIME type.	
	data=*URL*	Defines the URL of the object's data.	
	declare=*declare*	Declares an object but does not download it until the object is used. The only value for this attribute is declare.	
	height=*number*	Defines the object's height in pixels.	

Element	Attribute	Description	Standard attributes
	name=*name*	Sets a unique name for this instance of the object, which can be used in scripts.	
	standby=*text*	Defines text to display while the object is downloading.	
	type=*MIME type*	Defines the object data's MIME type.	
	usemap=*URL*	Specifies the client-side image map to use with the object.	
	width=*number*	Defines the object's width in pixels.	
`<ol>`		Defines the start and end of an ordered list. Contains one or more li elements. (see preceding `<li>` entry). See also Chapter 3, "Ordered lists."	Core attributes, language attributes Core events
	start=*number* *(deprecated)*	Starts the list numbering at the defined value instead of 1. *Cannot be used in XHTML Strict.*	
	type=*1|A|a|I|I* *(deprecated)*	Specifies the list numbering system (1=default numerals, A=uppercase letters, a=lowercase letters, I=uppercase Roman numerals, and i=lowercase Roman numerals). *Cannot be used in XHTML Strict.*	

continues

A

Element	Attribute	Description	Standard attributes
`<optgroup>`		Defines a form option group, enabling you to group related options in a select element. Beware: display output varies between browsers. Some italicize optgroup label values to highlight them, while others highlight them by inverting the optgroup label value. Others display them as per option values.	Core attributes, language attributes Core events

		`<select name="">`
		`<optgroup label="fruits">`
		`<option value="Apple">`
		➥ `Apple</option>`
		`<option value="Pear">`
		➥ `Pear</option>`
		`</optgroup>`
		`<optgroup label="vegetables">`
		`<option value="Carrot">`
		➥ `Carrot</option>`
		`<option value="Turnip">`
		➥ `Turnip</option>`
		`</optgroup>`
		`</select>`
		
		See also Chapter 8, "Adding controls."	

	`disabled=disabled`	Disables the option group. The only value for this attribute is disabled.	
	`label=string` *(required)*	Defines a label for the optgroup. This attribute is *required*.	
	`tabindex=number`	Defines the tab order of an element.	
`<option>`		Defines an option within a drop-down list. Nested within a select element and can be placed within optgroup elements. (See separate `<select>` and `<optgroup>` entries.) See also Chapter 8, "Adding controls."	Core attributes, language attributes Core events
	`disabled=disabled`	Disables the option. The only value for this attribute is disabled.	

Element	Attribute	Description	Standard attributes
	label=*string*	Defines a label for this option.	
	selected=*selected*	Sets the option as the default. The only value for this attribute is *selected*.	
	value=*string*	Defines the value of the option to be sent when the form is submitted.	
`<p>`		Defines a paragraph. See also Chapter 3, "Paragraphs and headings."	Core attributes, language attributes Core events
`<param>`		Supplies parameters for applets and objects. Must be enclosed within an applet or object element, and must come at the start of the content of the enclosing element.	
	id=*name*	Defines a unique reference ID for the element.	
	name=*name*	Defines a unique name for the element.	
	type=*MIME type*	Specifies the MIME type for the element.	
	value=*string*	Defines the element's value.	
	valuetype=*data|object|ref*	Specifies the MIME type of the value as data, ref (the value of a URL pointing to the data), or object (the value of an object within the document).	
`<pre>`		Defines enclosed contents as preformatted text, thereby preserving the formatting from the HTML document. Usually displayed in a monospace font. Cannot contain images, objects, or any of the following tags: big, small, sub, and sup.	Core attributes, language attributes Core events

A

continues

Element	Attribute	Description	Standard attributes
	width=*number* (*deprecated*)	Defines the maximum number of characters per line. This attribute is deprecated; use CSS to define the element width instead. *Cannot be used in XHTML Strict.*	
<q>		Defines enclosed content as a short quotation. Some browsers automatically insert quote marks. See also Chapter 3, "Block quotes, quote citations, and definitions."	Core attributes, language attributes Core events
	cite=*URL*	Defines the location of quoted online material.	
<s> (*deprecated*)		Defines strikethrough text. This element is deprecated and cannot be used in XHTML Strict. It's recommended to use the <del> element (see separate <del> entry) instead.	Core attributes, language attributes Core events
<samp>		Defines enclosed content as a computer code sample. Usually rendered in a monospace font. See also Chapter 3, "Logical styles for programming-oriented content."	Core attributes, language attributes Core events
<script>		Inserts a script into the document. See also Chapter 2, "Attaching favicons and JavaScript."	
	charset=*charset*	Defines the script's character set.	
	defer=*defer*	Indicates the script doesn't generate document content. This attribute's only value is defer. This allows the browser to delay parsing the script until after the page has loaded. Although this may speed up loading, it will generate script errors if user interaction results in a call to a script that still hasn't been parsed. Use with care.	

Element	Attribute	Description	Standard attributes
	language=*encoding* *(deprecated)*	Specifies the scripting language. Superseded by the type attribute, and no longer required. *Cannot be used in XHTML Strict.*	
	src=*URL*	Provides the URL of an external script.	
	type=*MIME type* *(required)*	Defines the MIME type of the scripting language, such as text/javascript or text/vbscript. This attribute is *required*.	
<select>		Creates a drop-down menu or scrolling list (depending on whether multiple has been set). This element is a container for option and optional optgroup elements. (see separate <option> and <optgroup> entries). See also Chapter 8, "Adding controls."	Core attributes, keyboard attributes, language attributes Core events, onblur, onchange, onfocus
	disabled=*disabled*	Disables the element. The only value for this attribute is disabled.	
	multiple=*multiple*	Specifies that multiple items can be selected. If absent, only single options can be selected. If included, the select element displays as a scrolling list rather than a drop-down menu. The only value for this attribute is multiple.	
	name=*name*	Defines a name for the element.	
	size=*number*	Sets the element to a pop-up menu when the value is 1, or a scrolling list when the value is greater than 1.	

A

continues

Element	Attribute	Description	Standard attributes
`<small>`		Reduces text size as compared to the surrounding text. Because the browser determines the size differential, precise text size changes are better achieved via span elements and CSS. See also Chapter 3, "The big and small elements."	Core attributes, language attributes Core events
`<span>`		Identifies a span of inline elements for applying styles to. For example: `<p>Use span elements to create` ⮕ `<span class="styleName">styled` ⮕ `inline text</span>.</p>`	Core attributes, language attributes Core events
`<strike>` *(deprecated)*		Defines strikethrough text. This element is deprecated and cannot be used in XHTML Strict. It's recommended to use the `<del>` element (see separate `<del>` entry) instead.	Core attributes, language attributes Core events
`<strong>`		Defines enclosed content as strongly emphasized. Generally renders as bold text in browsers and is preferred over `<b></b>`. (see separate `<b>` entry). See also Chapter 3, "Logical and physical styles."	Core attributes, language attributes Core events
`<style>`		Used to embed CSS rules in the head of a web page or to import CSS files. `<style type="text/css"` ⮕ `media="all">` `@import url(stylesheet.css);` `.thisPageOnly {` `color: #de3de3;` `}` `</style>` See also Chapter 2, "Attaching CSS files: The @import method."	Language attributes

Element	Attribute	Description	Standard attributes
	media=*list* (required)	Defines target media on which this style can be rendered. Possible values are all, aural, braille, handheld, print, projection, screen, tty, and tv.	
	title=*string*	Specifies the element's title.	
	type=*MIME type* (required)	Defines the MIME type of the style's contents. The only currently viable value is text/css, although this may change in the future. The value text/javascript is also allowed.	
<sub>		Defines contents as subscript text. See also Chapter 3, "Teletype, subscript, and superscript."	Core attributes, language attributes Core events
<sup>		Defines contents as superscript text. See also Chapter 3, "Teletype, subscript, and superscript."	Core attributes, language attributes Core events
<table>		Defines the start and end of a table. See also Chapter 6, "How tables work."	Core attributes, language attributes Core events
	border=*number*	Defines the table border width.	
	cellpadding= *percentage|number*	Defines the space between cell edges and contents.	
	cellspacing= *percentage\number*	Defines the space between table cells.	
	summary=*string*	Provides a summary of the table contents for nonvisual browsers.	
	width=*percentage| number*	Defines the table's width in pixels or as a percentage of the available space within its parent element.	
<tbody>		Defines the table body. See also Chapter 6, "Row groups" and "Building a table."	Core attributes, language attributes Core events

A

continues

Element	Attribute	Description	Standard attributes
	align=*left*|*right*| *justify*|*center* *(deprecated)*	Defines the horizontal alignment of table cell content. It's recommended that you use the CSS text-align property instead (see its entry in the CSS reference) to do this.	
	valign=*top*|*middle*| *bottom*|*baseline* *(deprecated)*	Specifies the vertical alignment of table cell content. It's recommended that you instead use the CSS vertical-align property (see its entry in the CSS reference) to do this.	
<td>		Defines a table cell. See also Chapter 6, "How tables work" and "Building a table."	Core attributes, language attributes Core events
	align=*left*|*right*| *justify*|*center* *(deprecated)*	Defines the horizontal alignment of table cell content. It's recommended that you use the CSS text-align property instead (see its entry in the CSS reference) to do this.	
	axis=*name*	Provides a name for a related group of cells. Not commonly used. (Note: any td cells containing the axis attribute are/should be treated as table header cells by the user agent.)	
	colspan=*number*	Defines how many columns the cell spans. See also Chapter 6, "Spanning rows and cells."	

	headers=*id list*	A list of cell IDs that provide header information for this cell, thereby enabling nonvisual browsers to associate header information with the cell. If more than one value is used, values are space separated. Example:
		
		`<th id="theTitle"`
		`➥ scope="col">The title</th>`
		`<th id="price"`
		`➥ scope="col">Price</th>`
		`<td headers="theTitle">A new`
		`➥ book</td>`
		`<td headers="price">$29.99</td>`	

Element	Attribute	Description	Standard attributes
	height=*number* (*deprecated*)	Defines the height of a cell in pixels. This attribute is deprecated—use CSS to define cell dimensions. *Cannot be used in XHTML Strict.*	
	nowrap=*nowrap* (*deprecated*)	Disables text wrapping. The only value for this attribute is nowrap. *Cannot be used in XHTML Strict. Use the CSS* white-space *property (see its entry in the CSS reference) instead.*	
	rowspan=*number*	Defines how many rows the cell spans. See also Chapter 6, "Spanning rows and cells."	
	valign=*top|middle| bottom|baseline* (*deprecated*)	Specifies the vertical alignment of table cell content. It's recommended that you instead use the CSS vertical-align property (see its entry in the CSS reference) to do this.	
	width=*number* (*deprecated*)	Defines the width of a cell in pixels. This attribute is deprecated—use CSS to define cell dimensions. *Cannot be used in XHTML Strict.*	
<textarea>		Defines a text area within a form. Any element content is displayed as the textarea's default value, and that includes spaces. Therefore, if you want a blank textarea, avoid having any spaces between the start and end tags. Although the cols and rows attributes are required, you can override these settings by using CSS. See also Chapter 8, "Adding controls."	Core attributes, language attributes Core events, onblur, onchange, onfocus
	cols=*number* (*required*)	Specifies the visible width in characters of the textarea. This attribute is *required*.	
	disabled=*disabled*	Disables the element. The only value for this attribute is disabled.	
	name=*name*		

continues

Element	Attribute	Description	Standard attributes
	readonly=*readonly*	Indicates the textarea is read-only and cannot be modified. The only value for this attribute is readonly.	
	rows=*number* *(required)*	Specifies the visible height (expressed as a number of rows) of the textarea. This attribute is *required*.	
<tfoot>		Defines a table footer. See also Chapter 6, "Row groups" and "Building a table."	Core attributes, language attributes Core events
	align=*left*|*right*| *justify*|*center* *(deprecated)*	Defines the horizontal alignment of table cell content. It's recommended that you use the CSS text-align property instead (see its entry in the CSS reference) to do this.	
	valign=*top*|*middle*| *bottom*|*baseline* *(deprecated)*	Specifies the vertical alignment of table cell content. It's recommended that you instead use the CSS vertical-align property (see its entry in the CSS reference) to do this.	
<th>		Defines a table header cell. See also Chapter 6, "How tables work" and "Building a table."	Core attributes, language attributes Core events Core attributes, language attributes Core events
	abbr=*string*	Provides an abbreviation of the cell's contents. Browsers can then choose to use this if they are short on space or to aid accessibility. Not commonly used, but particularly potentially useful for screen readers.	
	align=*left*|*right*| *justify*|*center* *(deprecated)*	Defines the horizontal alignment of table cell content. It's recommended that you instead use the CSS text-align property (see its entry in the CSS reference) to do this.	
	axis=*name*	Provides a name for a related group of cells. Not commonly used.	

Element	Attribute	Description	Standard attributes
	colspan=*number*	Defines how many columns the cell spans. See also Chapter 6, "Spanning rows and cells."	
	headers=*id list*	A list of cell IDs that provide header information for this cell, thereby enabling nonvisual browsers to associate header information with the cell. If more than one value is used, values are space separated. Example: `<th id="theTitle"` ➡ `scope="col">The title</th>` `<th id="price"` ➡ `scope="col">Price</th>` `<td headers="theTitle">A new` ➡ `book</td>` `<td headers="price">$29.99</td>`	
	height=*number* (deprecated)	Defines the height of a cell in pixels. This attribute is deprecated—use CSS to define cell dimensions. *Cannot be used in XHTML Strict.*	
	nowrap=*nowrap* (deprecated)	Disables text wrapping. The only value for this attribute is nowrap. *Cannot be used in XHTML Strict. (Use CSS whitespace instead.)*	
	rowspan=*number*	Defines how many rows the cell spans. See also Chapter 7, "Spanning rows and cells."	
	scope=*col| colgroup|row| rowgroup*	States whether the cell provides header information for the rest of the row, column, rowgroup, or colgroup that contains it. (See the headers description.)	
	valign=*top|middle| bottom|baseline* (deprecated)	Specifies the vertical alignment of table cell content. It's recommended that you instead use the CSS vertical-align property (see its entry in the CSS reference) to do this.	

A

continues

Element	Attribute	Description	Standard attributes
	width=*number* (*deprecated*)	Defines the width of a cell in pixels. This attribute is deprecated—use CSS to define cell dimensions. *Cannot be used in XHTML Strict.*	
<thead>		Defines a table header. See also Chapter 6, "Row groups" and "Building a table."	Core attributes, language attributes Core events
	align=*left*|*right*| *justify*|*center* (*deprecated*)	Defines the horizontal alignment of table cell content. It's recommended that you use the CSS text-align property instead (see its entry in the CSS reference) to do this.	
	valign=*top*|*middle*| *bottom*|*baseline* (*deprecated*)	Specifies the vertical alignment of table cell content. It's recommended that you instead use the CSS vertical-align property (see its entry in the CSS reference) to do this.	
<title> (*required*)		Defines the title of a document. This is a *required* element for web pages. See also Chapter 2, "Page titles."	Core attributes, language attributes
<tr>		Defines a table row. See also Chapter 6, "How tables work" and "Building a table."	Core attributes, language attributes Core events
	align=*left*|*right*| *justify*|*center* (*deprecated*)	Defines the horizontal alignment of table cell content. It's recommended that you instead use the CSS text-align property (see its entry in the CSS reference) to do this.	
	valign=*top*|*middle*| *bottom*|*baseline* (*deprecated*)	Specifies the vertical alignment of table cell content. It's recommended that you instead use the CSS vertical-align property (see its entry in the CSS reference) to do this.	
<tt>		Renders as teletype (monospaced) text. See also Chapter 3, "Teletype, subscript, and superscript."	Core attributes, language attributes Core events

Element	Attribute	Description	Standard attributes
`<ul>`		Defines the start and end of an unordered list. Contains one or more li elements (see separate `<li>` entry). See also Chapter 3, "Unordered lists."	Core attributes, language attributes Core events
`<var>`		Defines contents as a variable name. Usually rendered in italics. See also Chapter 3, "Logical styles for programming-oriented content."	Core attributes, language attribute Core events

A

B WEB COLOR REFERENCE

This section of the reference guides provides an overview of how to write color values for the Web, as well as a full list of supported color names. See the "Color theory" section in Chapter 4 for a discussion of color theory.

Color values

On the Web, colors are displayed by mixing red, green, and blue (RGB) light. Values range from 0 to 255 and can be written as such (e.g., rgb(5,233,70)), but they are more commonly written in hexadecimal. Colors written in hex consist of a hash sign (#) followed by six digits. The six digits are made up of pairs, representing the red, green, and blue color values, respectively.

- #XXxxxx: Red color value
- #xxXXxx: Green color value
- #xxxxXX: Blue color value

Hexadecimal notation is a numbering system that has 16, rather than 10, as its base. Digits range from 0 to f, with 0 to 9 representing the same value as ordinary numbers, and the letters a to f representing 10 to 15. The letters can be either uppercase or lowercase. If you set the first two digits to their highest value (ff) and the others to null, you get #ff0000, which is the hex color value for red. If you write #00ff00, you get green, and if you write #0000ff, you get blue. If all are set to full, you get white (#ffffff), and if all are null values, you get black (#000000).

Hexadecimal can also be written in shorthand if the six-digit value is composed of pairs in which both numbers are the same. For instance, #ff6600 (orange) can be written as #f60, and #ffffff (white) can be written as #fff. All three pairs must consist of equal numbers. For instance, you cannot use shorthand for #ffff01. Also, although hexadecimal can be written in shorthand, many designers choose not to do so, because when all color values are written in full, it tends to be easier to scan CSS files for specific values.

Web-safe colors

The 216-color web-safe palette uses hex combinations of the following hex value pairs only: 00, 33, 66, 99, cc, and ff—for example, #cc6699, #33ff66, and #ff0000.

Using these pairs provides you with 216 colors that are said to not dither on Macs and Windows PCs that have 8-bit monitors (256 colors). Because the vast majority of monitors sold since 2000 are able to display thousands or millions of colors, this palette is now rarely used and is generally considered archaic and obsolete.

Color names

Although a significant number of HTML color names are supported by major browsers, the CSS standard only recognizes the following 17.

Color name	Color hex value	Shorthand hex	RGB
Aqua	#00ffff	#0ff	0,255,255
Black	#000000	#000	0,0,0
Blue	#0000ff	#00f	0,0,255
Fuchsia	#ff00ff	#f0f	255,0,255
Gray (or Grey)	#808080	n/a	128,128,128
Green	#008000	n/a	0,128,0
Lime	#00ff00	#0f0	0,255,0
Maroon	#800000	n/a	128,0,0
Navy	#000080	n/a	0,0,128
Olive	#808000	n/a	128,128,0
Orange	#ffa500	n/a	255,165,0
Purple	#800080	n/a	128,0,128
Red	#ff0000	#f00	255,0,0
Silver	#c0c0c0	n/a	192,192,192
Teal	#008080	n/a	0,128,128
White	#ffffff	#fff	255,255,255
Yellow	#ffff00	#ff0	255,255,0

Although each color name in the preceding table begins with a capital letter (for book style purposes), color names are case insensitive, and lowercase is most commonly used. However, most designers ignore color names entirely, using hex all the time for consistency's sake—a practice that the W3C recommends.

B

C ENTITIES REFERENCE

Generally speaking, characters not found in the normal alphanumeric set must be added to a web page by way of **character entities**. These take the form &#n;, with n being a two- to four-digit number. Many entities also have a name, which tends to be more convenient and memorable; these are also listed. However, entities are case sensitive, so take care when adding them to your web pages.

Although most browsers display nonalphanumeric characters when the relevant encoding is specified, it's sometimes necessary to use entities to ensure your page displays as intended across a large range of machines.

Most reference guides tend to list entities in numerical order, but I find it more useful to browse by grouped items, so I list entities alphabetically within sections such as "Common punctuation and symbols" and "Characters for European languages." (The exception is for Greek characters, which I've listed in the order of the Greek alphabet, rather than in alphabetical order from an English language perspective.)

Characters used in XHTML

The less-than and ampersand characters are used in XHTML markup, and to avoid invalid and broken pages, these should be added to your web pages as entities. It's also common (although not required) to add greater-than and quotation marks as entities.

The ampersand character is commonly used in URL query strings (particularly when working with server-side languages), and in such cases, the & must be replaced by the entity name or number (it will still be correctly interpreted by the browser).

Character	Description	Entity name	Entity number
"	Quotation mark (straight)	&quot;	&#34;
&	Ampersand	&amp;	&#38;
<	Less-than sign	&lt;	&#60;
>	Greater-than sign	&gt;	&#62;

Punctuation characters and symbols

Although many web designers tend to get around punctuation character limitations by using double hyphens (--) in place of em dashes (—), triple periods (. . .) in place of an ellipsis (...), and straight quotation marks ("") instead of "smart" quotes (""), XHTML supports many punctuation characters as character entities. Likewise, plenty of symbols are supported in XHTML, so you needn't write (c) when the copyright symbol is available.

This section lists all such characters and is split into four subsections: quotation marks, spacing and nonprinting characters, punctuation characters, and symbols.

Quotation marks

Character	Description	Entity name	Entity number
'	Left single	&lsquo;	&#8216;
'	Right single	&rsquo;	&#8217;
"	Left double	&ldquo;	&#8220;
"	Right double	&rdquo;	&#8221;
‹	Single left angle	&lsaquo;	&#8249;

Character	Description	Entity name	Entity number
›	Single right angle	›	›
«	Double left angle	«	«
»	Double right angle	»	»
‚	Single low-9	‚	‚
„	Double low-9	„	„

Spacing and nonprinting characters

> On Windows, zero-width joiner and zero-width nonjoiner may be displayed by default as a vertical bar with an x on top and a vertical bar, respectively. To display these as nonprinting characters, you may need to install the Arabic language pack.

Character	Description	Entity name	Entity number
	Em space		
	En space		
Nonprinting	Left-to-right mark	‎	‎
	Nonbreaking space		
	Overline	‾	‾
Nonprinting	Right-to-left mark	‏	‏
	Thin space		
Nonprinting	Zero-width joiner	‍	‍
Nonprinting	Zero-width nonjoiner	‌	‌

C

Punctuation characters

Character	Description	Entity name	Entity number
¦	Broken vertical bar	&brvbar;	&#166;
•	Bullet point	&bull;	&#8226;
†	Dagger	&dagger;	&#8224;
‡	Double dagger	&Dagger;	&#8225;
″	Double prime, seconds, inches	&Prime;	&#8243;
…	Ellipsis	&hellip;	&#8230;
—	Em dash	&mdash;	&#8212;
–	En dash	&ndash;	&#8211;
/	Fraction slash	&frasl;	&#8260;
¡	Inverted exclamation mark	&iexcl;	&#161;
¿	Inverted question mark	&iquest;	&#191;
′	Prime, minutes, feet	&prime;	&#8242;
-	Soft hyphen	&shy;	&#173;

Symbols

Character	Description	Entity name	Entity number
ℑ	Blackletter capital I, imaginary part	&image;	&#8465;
ℜ	Blackletter capital R, real part	&real;	&#8476;
©	Copyright symbol	&copy;	&#169;
ª	Feminine ordinal	&ordf;	&#170;

Character	Description	Entity name	Entity number
º	Masculine ordinal	&ordm;	&#186;
¬	Not sign	&not;	&#172;
¶	Paragraph sign	&para;	&#182;
‰	Per mille symbol	&permil;	&#8240;
®	Registered trademark symbol	&reg;	&#174;
§	Section sign	&sect;	&#167;
™	Trademark symbol	&trade;	&#8482;
℘	Script capital P, power set	&weierp;	&#8472;

Characters for European languages

For any characters that have accents, circumflexes, or other additions, entities are available. However, many of these entities have their roots in the days when ASCII was the only available encoding method. These days, as long as you use the appropriate input method, and the page is correctly encoded, you may not need to use these entities. They are still listed here, though, for times when you just want to be on the safe side.

Take care when adding these, because case is important. In most cases, capitalizing the first letter of the entity name results in an uppercase character, but this isn't always so (notably the Icelandic characters "eth" and "thorn," the uppercase versions of which require the entire entity name to be in uppercase).

Character	Description	Entity name	Entity number
´	Acute accent (no letter)	&acute;	&#180;
¸	Cedilla (no letter)	&cedil;	&#184;
ˆ	Circumflex spacing modifier	&circ;	&#710;
¯	Macron accent	&macr;	&#175;

continues

C

Character	Description	Entity name	Entity number
·	Middle dot	`&middot;`	`&#183;`
˜	Tilde	`&tilde;`	`&#732;`
¨	Umlaut	`&uml;`	`&#168;`
Á	Uppercase A, acute accent	`&Aacute;`	`&#193;`
á	Lowercase a, acute accent	`&aacute;`	`&#225;`
Â	Uppercase a, circumflex accent	`&Acirc;`	`&#194;`
â	Lowercase a, circumflex accent	`&acirc;`	`&#226;`
À	Uppercase A, grave accent	`&Agrave;`	`&#192;`
à	Lowercase a, grave accent	`&agrave;`	`&#224;`
Å	Uppercase A, ring	`&Aring;`	`&#197;`
å	Lowercase a, ring	`&aring;`	`&#229;`
Ã	Uppercase A, tilde	`&Atilde;`	`&#195;`
ã	Lowercase a, tilde	`&atilde;`	`&#227;`
Ä	Uppercase A, umlaut	`&Auml;`	`&#196;`
ä	Lowercase a, umlaut	`&auml;`	`&#228;`
Æ	Uppercase AE ligature	`&AElig;`	`&#198;`
æ	Lowercase ae ligature	`&aelig;`	`&#230;`
Ç	Uppercase C, cedilla	`&Ccedil;`	`&#199;`
ç	Lowercase c, cedilla	`&ccedil;`	`&#231;`
É	Uppercase E, acute accent	`&Eacute;`	`&#201;`

Character	Description	Entity name	Entity number
é	Lowercase e, acute accent	é	é
Ê	Uppercase E, circumflex accent	Ê	Ê
ê	Lowercase e, circumflex accent	ê	ê
È	Uppercase E, grave accent	È	È
è	Lowercase e, grave accent	è	è
Ë	Uppercase E, umlaut	Ë	Ë
ë	Lowercase e, umlaut	ë	ë
Ð	Uppercase eth	Ð	Ð
ð	Lowercase eth	ð	ð
Í	Uppercase I, acute accent	Í	Í
í	Lowercase i, acute accent	í	í
Î	Uppercase I, circumflex accent	Î	Î
î	Lowercase i, circumflex accent	î	î
Ì	Uppercase I, grave accent	Ì	Ì
ì	Lowercase i, grave accent	ì	ì
Ï	Uppercase I, umlaut	Ï	Ï
ï	Lowercase i, umlaut	ï	ï

continues

C

457

Character	Description	Entity name	Entity number
Ñ	Uppercase N, tilde	&Ntilde;	&#209;
ñ	Lowercase n, tilde	&ntilde;	&#241;
Ó	Uppercase O, acute accent	&Oacute;	&#211;
ó	Lowercase o, acute accent	&oacute;	&#243;
Ô	Uppercase O, circumflex accent	&Ocirc;	&#212;
ô	Lowercase o, circumflex accent	&ocirc;	&#244;
Ò	Uppercase O, grave accent	&Ograve;	&#210;
ò	Lowercase o, grave accent	&ograve;	&#242;
Ø	Uppercase O, slash	&Oslash;	&#216;
ø	Lowercase o, slash	&oslash;	&#248;
Õ	Uppercase O, tilde	&Otilde;	&#213;
õ	Lowercase o, tilde	&otilde;	&#245;
Ö	Uppercase O, umlaut	&Ouml;	&#214;
ö	Lowercase o, umlaut	&ouml;	&#246;
Œ	Uppercase OE ligature	&OElig;	&#338;
œ	Lowercase oe ligature	&oelig;	&#339;
Š	Uppercase S, caron	&Scaron;	&#352;
š	Lowercase s, caron	&scaron;	&#353;
ß	Lowercase sz ligature	&szlig;	&#223;

Character	Description	Entity name	Entity number
Þ	Uppercase thorn	&THORN;	&#222;
þ	Lowercase thorn	&thorn;	&#254;
Ú	Uppercase U, acute accent	&Uacute;	&#218;
ú	Lowercase u, acute accent	&uacute;	&#250;
Û	Uppercase U, circumflex accent	&Ucirc;	&#219;
û	Lowercase u, circumflex accent	&ucirc;	&#251;
Ù	Uppercase U, grave accent	&Ugrave;	&#217;
ù	Lowercase u, grave accent	&ugrave;	&#249;
Ü	Uppercase U, umlaut	&Uuml;	&#220;
ü	Lowercase u, umlaut	&uuml;	&#252;
Ý	Uppercase Y, acute accent	&Yacute;	&#221;
ý	Lowercase y, acute accent	&yacute;	&#253;
Ÿ	Uppercase Y, umlaut	&Yuml;	&#376;
ÿ	Lowercase y, umlaut	&yuml;	&#255;

C

Currency signs

Although the dollar sign is supported in XHTML, other common currency symbols are not. However, several can be added by way of entities, as shown in the following table.

Character	Description	Entity name	Entity number
¢	Cent	¢	¢
¤	General currency sign	¤	¤
€	Euro	€	€
£	Pound	£	£
¥	Yen	¥	¥

Mathematical, technical, and Greek characters

This set of entities combines mathematical and technical symbols and the Greek alphabet (which is commonly used in scientific work). For ease of use, this section is divided into three subsections: common mathematical characters (fractions and the most commonly used mathematical symbols), advanced mathematical and technical characters (characters of interest to those marking up technical documents or anything other than basic mathematical text), and Greek characters.

Common mathematical characters

Character	Description	Entity name	Entity number
°	Degree sign	°	°
÷	Division sign	÷	÷
½	Fraction—one half	½	½
¼	Fraction—one quarter	¼	¼
¾	Fraction—three quarters	¾	¾
>	Greater-than sign	>	>

Character	Description	Entity name	Entity number
≥	Greater-than or equal to sign	&ge;	&#8805;
<	Less-than sign	&lt;	&#60;
≤	Less-than or equal to sign	&le;	&#8804;
−	Minus sign	&minus;	&#8722;
×	Multiplication sign	&times;	&#215;
¹	Superscript one	&sup1;	&#185;
²	Superscript two	&sup2;	&#178;
³	Superscript three	&sup3;	&#179;

Advanced mathematical and technical characters

Character	Description	Entity name	Entity number
ℵ	Alef symbol, first transfinite cardinal	&alefsym;	&#8501;
≈	Almost equal to, asymptotic to	&asymp;	&#8776;
∠	Angle	&ang;	&#8736;
≅	Approximately equal to	&cong;	&#8773;
∗	Asterisk operator	&lowast;	&#8727;
⊕	Circled plus, direct sum	&oplus;	&#8853;
⊗	Circled times, vector product	&otimes;	&#8855;
∋	Contains as member	&ni;	&#8715;
·	Dot operator	&sdot;	&#8901;

continues

Character	Description	Entity name	Entity number
∈	Element of	&isin;	&#8712;
∅	Empty set, null set, diameter	&empty;	&#8709;
∀	For all	&forall;	&#8704;
ƒ	Function, florin (Latin small f with hook)	&fnof;	&#402;
≡	Identical to	&equiv;	&#8801;
∞	Infinity	&infin;	&#8734;
∫	Integral	&int;	&#8747;
∩	Intersection, cap	&cap;	&#8745;
⌈	Left ceiling	&lceil;	&#8968;
⌊	Left floor	&lfloor;	&#8970;
∧	Logical and, wedge	&and;	&#8743;
∨	Logical or, vee	&or;	&#8744;
µ	Micro sign	&micro;	&#181;
∇	Nabla, backward difference	&nabla;	&#8711;
∏	N-ary product, product sign	&prod;	&#8719;
∑	N-ary summation	&sum;	&#8721;
∉	Not an element of	&notin;	&#8713;
⊄	Not a subset of	&nsub;	&#8836;
≠	Not equal to	&ne;	&#8800;
∂	Partial differential	&part;	&#8706;
±	Plus-minus sign, plus-or-minus sign	&plusmn;	&#177;

Character	Description	Entity name	Entity number
∝	Proportional to	&prop;	&#8733;
⌉	Right ceiling	&rceil;	&#8969;
⌋	Right floor	&rfloor;	&#8971;
√	Square root, radical sign	&radic;	&#8730;
⊂	Subset of	&sub;	&#8834;
⊆	Subset of or equal to	&sube;	&#8838;
⊃	Superset of	&sup;	&#8835;
⊇	Superset of or equal to	&supe;	&#8839;
∃	There exists	&exist;	&#8707;
∴	Therefore	&there4;	&#8756;
~	Tilde operator, varies with, similar to, approximately	&sim;	&#8764;
∪	Union, cup	&cup;	&#8746;
⊥	Up tack, orthogonal to, perpendicular	&perp;	&#8869;

Greek characters

Character	Description	Entity name	Entity number
A	Uppercase alpha	&Alpha;	&#913;
α	Lowercase alpha	&alpha;	&#945;
B	Uppercase beta	&Beta;	&#914;
β	Lowercase beta	&beta;	&#946;
Γ	Uppercase gamma	&Gamma;	&#915;

continues

C

Character	Description	Entity name	Entity number
γ	Lowercase gamma	&gamma;	&#947;
Δ	Uppercase delta	&Delta;	&#916;
δ	Lowercase delta	&delta;	&#948;
E	Uppercase epsilon	&Epsilon;	&#917;
ε	Lowercase epsilon	&epsilon;	&#949;
Z	Uppercase zeta	&Zeta;	&#918;
ζ	Lowercase zeta	&zeta;	&#950;
H	Uppercase eta	&Eta;	&#919;
η	Lowercase eta	&eta;	&#951;
Θ	Uppercase theta	&Theta;	&#920;
θ	Lowercase theta	&theta;	&#952;
I	Uppercase iota	&Iota;	&#921;
ι	Lowercase iota	&iota;	&#953;
K	Uppercase kappa	&Kappa;	&#922;
κ	Lowercase kappa	&kappa;	&#954;
Λ	Uppercase lambda	&Lambda;	&#923;
λ	Lowercase lambda	&lambda;	&#955;
M	Uppercase mu	&Mu;	&#924;
μ	Lowercase mu	&mu;	&#956;
N	Uppercase nu	&Nu;	&#925;
ν	Lowercase nu	&nu;	&#957;
Ξ	Uppercase xi	&Xi;	&#926;
ξ	Lowercase xi	&xi;	&#958;
O	Uppercase omicron	&Omicron;	&#927;

Character	Description	Entity name	Entity number
ο	Lowercase omicron	&omicron;	&#959;
Π	Uppercase pi	&Pi;	&#928;
π	Lowercase pi	&pi;	&#960;
Ρ	Uppercase rho	&Rho;	&#929;
ρ	Lowercase rho	&rho;	&#961;
ς	Lowercase final sigma	&sigmaf;	&#962;
Σ	Uppercase sigma	&Sigma;	&#931;
σ	Lowercase sigma	&sigma;	&#963;
Τ	Uppercase tau	&Tau;	&#932;
τ	Lowercase tau	&tau;	&#964;
Υ	Uppercase upsilon	&Upsilon;	&#933;
υ	Lowercase upsilon	&upsilon;	&#965;
Φ	Uppercase phi	&Phi;	&#934;
φ	Lowercase phi	&phi;	&#966;
Χ	Uppercase chi	&Chi;	&#935;
χ	Lowercase chi	&chi;	&#967;
Ψ	Uppercase psi	&Psi;	&#936;
ψ	Lowercase psi	&psi;	&#968;
Ω	Uppercase omega	&Omega;	&#937;
ω	Lowercase omega	&omega;	&#969;
ϑ	Small theta symbol	&thetasym;	&#977;
ϒ	Greek upsilon with hook	&upsih;	&#978;
ϖ	Greek pi symbol	&piv;	&#982;

C

Arrows, lozenge, and card suits

Character	Description	Entity name	Entity number
↵	Carriage return	&crarr;	&#8629;
↓	Down arrow	&darr;	&#8595;
⇓	Down double arrow	&dArr;	&#8659;
←	Left arrow	&larr;	&#8592;
⇐	Left double arrow	&lArr;	&#8656;
↔	Left-right arrow	&harr;	&#8596;
⇔	Left-right double arrow	&hArr;	&#8660;
→	Right arrow	&rarr;	&#8594;
⇒	Right double arrow	&rArr;	&#8658;
↑	Up arrow	&uarr;	&#8593;
⇑	Up double arrow	&uArr;	&#8657;
◊	Lozenge	&loz;	&#9674;
♣	Clubs suit	&clubs;	&#9827;
♦	Diamonds suit	&diams;	&#9830;
♥	Hearts suit	&hearts;	&#9829;
♠	Spades suit	&spades;	&#9824;

Converting the nonstandard Microsoft set

The final table in this section lists the nonstandard Microsoft set and modern equivalents. Some older HTML editors, such as Dreamweaver 4, insert nonstandard entity values into web pages, causing them to fail validation. Here, we present the outdated nonstandard value and its corresponding approved alternatives (entity name and entity number, either of which can be used).

Character	Description	Nonstandard value	Entity name	Entity number
'	Single low-9 quote	`&#130;`	`&sbquo;`	`&#8218;`
ƒ	Lowercase Latin f with hook (florin)	`&#131;`	`&fnof;`	`&#402;`
„	Double low-9 quote	`&#132;`	`&bdquo;`	`&#8222;`
…	Ellipsis	`&#133;`	`&hellip;`	`&#8230;`
†	Dagger	`&#134;`	`&dagger;`	`&#8224;`
‡	Double dagger	`&#135;`	`&Dagger;`	`&#8225;`
ˆ	Circumflex spacing modifier	`&#136;`	`&circ;`	`&#710;`
‰	Per mille symbol	`&#137;`	`&permil;`	`&#8240;`
Š	Uppercase S, caron	`&#138;`	`&Scaron;`	`&#352;`
<	Less-than sign	`&#139;`	`&lt;`	`&#60;`
Œ	Uppercase OE ligature	`&#140;`	`&OElig;`	`&#338;`
'	Left single quote	`&#145;`	`&lsquo;`	`&#8216;`
'	Right single quote	`&#146;`	`&rsquo;`	`&#8217;`
"	Left double quote	`&#147;`	`&ldquo;`	`&#8220;`
"	Right double quote	`&#148;`	`&rdquo;`	`&#8221;`
•	Bullet point	`&#149;`	`&bull;`	`&#8226;`
–	En dash	`&#150;`	`&ndash;`	`&#8211;`
—	Em dash	`&#151;`	`&mdash;`	`&#8212;`
~	Tilde	`&#152;`	`&tilde;`	`&#732;`
™	Trademark symbol	`&#153;`	`&trade;`	`&#8482;`

continues

C

Character	Description	Nonstandard value	Entity name	Entity number
š	Lowercase s, caron	&#154;	&scaron;	&#353;
>	Greater-than sign	&#155;	&gt;	&#62;
œ	Lowercase oe ligature	&#156;	&oelig;	&#339;
Ÿ	Uppercase Y, umlaut	&#159;	&Yuml;	&#376

D CSS REFERENCE

This section includes a table listing CSS properties and values. In many cases, properties have specific values, which are listed in full. However, some values are common across many properties. These are outlined in the "Common CSS values" section, and in the CSS properties and values table these values are shown in italics. The end of the section includes information on basic selectors, pseudo-classes, pseudo-elements, CSS boilerplates, and CSS management.

The CSS box model

In CSS, every element is considered to be within its own box, and you can define the dimensions of the content and then add padding, a border, and a margin to each edge as required, as shown in the following image.

THE CSS BOX MODEL HIERARCHY

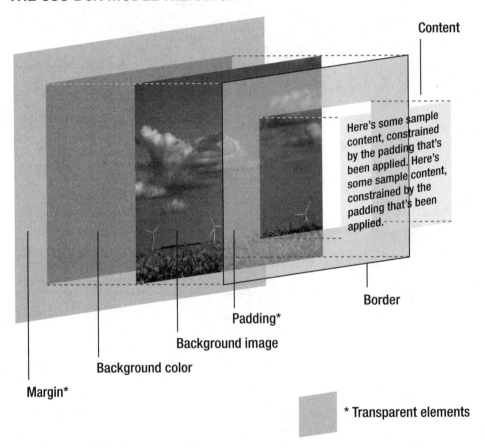

Here's some sample content, constrained by the padding that's been applied. Here's some sample content, constrained by the padding that's been applied.

Content

Border

Padding*

Background image

Background color

Margin*

* Transparent elements

© Jon Hicks (www.hicksdesign.co.uk)

Padding, borders, and margins are added to the set dimensions of the content, so the sum of these elements is the overall space that they take up. For example, a 100-pixel-wide element with 20 pixels of padding will take up an overall width of 140 pixels, not 100 pixels with 20 pixels of padding within.

Note that the top and bottom margins on adjacent elements collapse. For example, if you set the bottom margin to 50px on an element, and set a top margin of 100px on the element below, the margin between the two elements will be 100 pixels, not 150 pixels.

Internet Explorer 5.x for Windows gets the box model wrong, placing padding and borders inside the defined dimensions of an element. The bug is explained in Chapter 9, which also offers workarounds to fix layouts that get broken in aging versions of Microsoft's browser.

Common CSS values

In addition to the values listed in the following table, a property may have a value of inherit, whereupon it takes the same value as its parent. Some properties are inherited by default—see the CSS properties and values table for more information.

D

Value	Formats
color	Color name. See Appendix B (Color Reference) for information on available CSS color names. rgb(n,n,n): Where n is a value from 0 to 255 or a percentage. #rrggbb: Hexadecimal color format (preferred).
length	An optional sign (+ or -), followed by a number and one of the following units (there should be no whitespace between the number and unit): %: A percentage. cm: Centimeters. em: One em is equal to the font size of the parent or current element (see following focus point for elaboration). ex: One ex is, in theory, equal to the font size of the x character of the current element. Most browsers render ex as half an em. in: Inches. mm: Millimeters. pc: Picas. 1pc = 12pt. pt: Points. 1pt = 1/72in. px: Pixels. For zero values, the unit identifier may be omitted. Generally, px, em, and % are the best units for screen design, and pt is best for print fonts.
number	An optional sign (+ or -) followed by a number.
percentage	An optional sign (+ or -) followed by a number, immediately followed by the percentage symbol.
url	The word url immediately followed by parentheses, within which is placed a URL. The URL can optionally be enclosed in single or double quotes.

> When setting element dimensions (width, height, margins, etc.), one em is equal to the font size of that element. However, when setting font sizes for an element, one em is equal to the font size of its parent element. In both cases, this is measured relative to the dimensions of the M character.

CSS properties and values

In the tables within this section, default values are listed in bold and shorthand properties are shaded in gray. A number of tables online list browser compatibility with regard to CSS. Some good examples of these and related resources can be found at the following URLs:

- www.westciv.com/style_master/academy/browser_support/index.html: CSS support for most browsers

- www.webdevout.net/browser-support-css: CSS support for Internet Explorer, Firefox, and Opera

- www.quirksmode.org/css/contents.html: Concentrates on quirks

- www.macedition.com/cb/resources/macbrowsercsssupport.html: CSS2 support in *old* Mac browsers—note: not updated since 2004

- www.macedition.com/cb/resources/abridgedcsssupport.html: CSS2 support chart for *old* browsers—note: not updated since 2004

- www.css3.info/selectors-test/: Live CSS3 support testing of your browser

- http://devedge-temp.mozilla.org/toolbox/sidebars/: Useful sidebar reference tools for Gecko browser users

Remember that such charts are guides only, are sometimes out of date, and should not be considered a replacement for thorough testing in a range of web browsers.

To inherit a parent element's style for a property, use the value `inherit`. To raise a property's weight in the cascade, use `!important`. Important declarations override all others.

```
p {color: red !important;}
```

Add comments to CSS files as follows:

```
/*
This is a comment in CSS
*/

/* This is a single-line comment */
```

Property	Values	Description	Inherited
background		Shorthand for defining background property values in a single declaration. Values can be any of those from background-attachment, background-color, background-image, background-position, and background-repeat, in any order. Example: background: #ffffff ➥ url(background.gif) fixed left ➥ repeat-y; See also Chapter 2, "Web page backgrounds in CSS" and "CSS shorthand for web backgrounds."	No
background-attachment	**scroll** | fixed	Determines whether a background image is fixed or scrolls with the page. See also Chapter 2, "background-attachment."	No
background-color	**transparent** | *color*	Defines an element's background color. See also Chapter 2, "background-color."	No
background-image	**none** | *url*	Sets an element's background image. Example: background-image: ➥ url(background_image.jpg); See also Chapter 2, "background-image."	No
background-position	*length* | *percentage* | top | center | bottom | left | right	Defines the initial position of the background image. Defaults to 0,0. Values are usually paired: x,y. Combinations of keyword, length, and percentage are permitted, although combining keywords with either length or percentages is buggy in some browsers. If only one keyword is provided, the other defaults to center. If only one length or percentage is given, it sets the horizontal position, and the vertical position defaults to 50%. See also Chapter 2, "background-position."	No

D

Continued

475

Property	Values	Description	Inherited
background-repeat	**repeat** | repeat-x | repeat-y | no-repeat	Defines how the background image tiles. See also Chapter 2, "background-repeat."	No
border		Shorthand for defining border property values in a single declaration. Values can be any of those from border-width, border-style, and border-color. Borders are drawn on top of a box's background. Example: border: 1px solid #000000; See also Chapter 4, "Applying CSS borders to images," and Chapter 6, "Styling a table."	No
border-bottom		Shorthand for defining bottom border property values (see border).	No
border-bottom-color	*color* | transparent	Sets the bottom border color.	No
border-bottom-style	(See border-style.)	Sets the bottom border style.	No
border-bottom-width	(See border-width.)	Sets the bottom border width.	No
border-collapse	collapse | **separate**	Defines a table's border model. In the separate border model, which is the default, each table cell has its own distinct borders, but in the collapsed border model, adjacent table cells share borders. See also Chapter 6, "Adding borders to tables."	Yes
border-color	*color* | transparent	Defines the element's border color. Defaults to the element's color.	No
border-left		Shorthand for defining left border property values (see border).	No
border-left-color	*color* | transparent	Sets the left border color.	No
border-left-style	(See border-style.)	Sets the left border style.	No
border-left-width	(See border-width.)	Sets the left border width.	No

Property	Values	Description	Inherited
border-right		Shorthand for defining right border property values (see border).	No
border-right-color	*color* | transparent	Sets the right border color.	No
border-right-style	(See border-style.)	Sets the right border style.	No
border-right-width	(See border-width.)	Sets the right border width.	No
border-spacing	*length length*	Defines the distance between borders or adjacent table cells when using the separated borders model. (See border-collapse.) If a single length is given, it's used for horizontal and vertical values; if two lengths are provided, the first is used for the horizontal spacing and the second for the vertical spacing. Negative values are not permitted.	Yes
border-style	dashed | dotted | double | groove | inset | **none** | outset | ridge | solid	Sets the style of an element's borders. Can work as shorthand, with one style per edge, from the top clockwise. Example: border-style: solid dashed dotted ↪ groove; Not all styles are supported in all browsers. Notably, Internet Explorer 5 and 6 render dotted as dashed when a border is 1 pixel in width.	No
border-top		Shorthand for defining top border property values (see border).	No
border-top-color	*color* | transparent	Sets the top border color.	No
border-top-style	(See border-style.)	Sets the top border style.	No
border-top-width	(See border-width.)	Sets the top border width.	No
border-width	*length* | medium | thick | thin	Sets the width of an element's borders. Can work as shorthand: border-width: 1px 2px 3px 4px; See also Chapter 4, "Applying CSS borders to images."	No

D

Continued

Property	Values	Description	Inherited
bottom	**auto** | *length* | *percentage*	Determines the vertical offset of the element's bottom edge from the bottom edge of its parent element if the parent is positioned; if not, then offset is determined from the first positioned ancestor. Must be used with a position value of relative, absolute, or fixed.	No
caption-side	bottom | **top**	Specifies the position of table caption elements with relation to the table element box.	Yes
clear	both | left | **none** | right	Moves the element down until its margins are clear of floated elements to its left, right, or both sides. (See the float entry.) See also Chapter 7, "Placing columns within wrappers and clearing floated content."	No
clip	**auto** | (shape)	Creates a clipping area for an absolute positioned element to determine the visible area. As of CSS 2.1, the only available shape is rect. Example: clip: rect(5px, 60px, 15px, 20px); As per the preceding code block, dimensions are stated as a comma-separated list, and percentage lengths are not permitted. The dimensions are, as per typical CSS shorthand, in the following order: top, right, bottom, left. The top and bottom values specify offsets from the top border edge of the box. The left and right measurements specify offsets from the left border edge of the box in left-to-right text and from the right border edge of the box in right-to-left text. The defined region clips out any aspect of the element that falls outside the clipping region. The preceding example creates a window 40 pixels wide and 10 pixels high, through which the content of the clipped element is visible. Everything else is hidden. See also www.w3.org/TR/CSS21/visufx.html#propdef-clip.	No

Property	Values	Description	Inherited
color	*color*	Sets an element's foreground color (i.e., the color of the text).	Yes

content	**normal** | (*string*) | *url* | counter(*name*) | counter(*name*, list-style-type) | counters(*name*, *string*) | counters(*name*, *string*, list-style-type) | open-quote | close-quote | no-open-quote | no-close-quote | attr(X)	Generates content to attach before or after a CSS selector, using the :before and :after pseudo-elements. Example:
		
		#users h2:before {
		content: "Username: ";
		display: inline;
		}
		
		See also Chapter 7, "Placing columns within wrappers and clearing floated content."
			No

counter-increment	**none** | *identifier number*	Increments a counter when the current selector is encountered. The *identifier* defines the selector, ID, or class that is to be incremented; the optional *number* defines the increment amount. Used in conjunction with content. Browser support for this property is poor.	No
counter-reset	**none** | *identifier number*	Defines a new value for the specified counter whenever the current selector is encountered.	No
cursor	**auto** | crosshair | default | help | pointer | move | progress | text | wait | n-resize | ne-resize | e-resize | se-resize | s-resize | sw-resize | nw-resize | w-resize | *url*	Defines the cursor type to be displayed. Can be a comma-separated list. Cursors vary by system, so use this property with care. Also, if using custom cursors via the url value, include a generic cursor at the end of the list, in case of compatibility problems. Note: Internet Explorer 5.x for Windows does not recognize pointer, the correct CSS value for displaying a hand-shaped cursor. Instead, it uses the nonstandard value hand, which can be applied using a style sheet attached via a conditional comment.	Yes

D

Continued

Property	Values	Description	Inherited
direction	**ltr** | rtl	Sets the direction of text flow. ltr: Left to right. rtl: Right to left.	Yes
display	block | inline | list-item | none | run-in | inline-block | table | inline-table | table-caption | table-cell | table-column | table-column-group | table-footer-group | table-header-group | table-row | table-row-group | table-row	States how an element is displayed on the page. The most common values are none, block, and inline, which all happen to be well supported. See several of the exercises in Chapters 5 and 7 for more on this property.	No
empty-cells	hide | **show**	Determines whether empty table cell borders show when using the separated borders model. (See border-collapse.)	Yes
float	left | **none** | right	Defines whether an element floats left or right (allowing other content to wrap around it) or displays inline (by using the none value). See also Chapter 7, "The float property."	No
font		Shorthand for defining font properties in a single declaration. Values can include any or all of the following: font-style, font-variant, font-weight, font-size, line-height, and font-family. Any omitted values revert to default settings, but font-size and font-family are mandatory. If font-style, font-weight, and font-variant values are included, they should appear at the start of the rule, prior to the font-size value.	Yes

Property	Values	Description	Inherited
font (continued)		When using line-height, you must combine it with the font-size property using the syntax font-size/line-height (e.g., 12px/18px). Examples (using selected values): font: bold 12px/16px Verdana, ➥ sans-serif; font: 85%/1.3em Georgia, serif; See also Chapter 3, "Styling text using CSS" and "CSS shorthand for font properties." Additional values for the font property are also available: caption, icon, menu, message-box, small-caption, status-bar. These set the font to system fonts, or the nearest equivalent, and are not available via font-family. However, these values are rarely, if ever, used.	Yes
font-family	(*family name*) | (*generic family*)	Defines the font family of an element. Takes the form of a prioritized comma-separated list, which should terminate in a generic family name (cursive, fantasy, monospace, serif, or sans-serif). Multiple-word font-family names must be quoted (e.g., "Times New Roman"). Readers used to American typographical conventions should take care not to put commas inside the closing quotes. Example: font-family: Georgia, "Times New ➥ Roman", serif; See also Chapter 3, "Defining fonts."	Yes
font-size	xx-small | x-small | small | **medium** | large | x-large | xx-large | smaller | larger | *length* | *percentage*	Sets the size of a font. See also Chapter 3, "Defining font size and line height."	Yes

Continued

Property	Values	Description	Inherited
font-style	italic | **normal** | oblique	Sets the font's style. See also Chapter 3, "Defining font-style, font-weight, and font-variant."	Yes
font-variant	**normal** | small-caps	Sets the font to display in small caps. See also Chapter 3, "Defining font-style, font-weight, and font-variant."	Yes
font-weight	lighter | **normal** | bold | bolder | *number*****	Sets the font weight. * When using a number, it must be a multiple of 100 between 100 and 900 inclusive. The value 700 is considered equivalent to bold, and 400 is synonymous with normal. In practice, numbers are supported inconsistently and poorly in browsers. See also Chapter 3, "Defining font-style, font-weight, and font-variant."	Yes
height	**auto** | *length* | *percentage*	Sets the content height of an element.	No
left	**auto** | *length* | *percentage*	Determines the horizontal offset of the element's left edge from the left edge of its parent element if the parent is positioned; if not, then offset is determined from the first positioned ancestor. Must be used with a position value of relative, absolute, or fixed. See also the Chapter 7 exercise, "Using absolute positioning to center a box onscreen."	No
letter-spacing	*length* | **normal**	Amends kerning (i.e., the space between characters). Positive and negative values are permitted. Relative values are determined once and then inherited. See also Chapter 3, "Setting letter-spacing and word-spacing."	Yes

Property	Values	Description	Inherited
line-height	**normal** | *length* | *number* | *percentage*	Controls the element's leading. When the line-height value is larger than the font-size value, the difference (which is the leading) is halved, and this new value is applied to the top and bottom of the element's inline box. See also Chapter 3, "Setting line height."	Yes
list-style		Shorthand for defining list properties in a single declaration. Values can be those from list-style-type, list-style-position, and list-style-image. See also Chapter 3, "Styling lists with CSS" and "List style shorthand."	Yes
list-style-image	**none** | *url*	Defines an image for list bullet points.	Yes
list-style-position	inside | **outside**	Determines whether the bullet point appears as the first character of the list item content (inside) or in default fashion (outside).	Yes
list-style-type	none | **disc** | circle | square | decimal | decimal-leading-zero | lower-alpha | upper-alpha | lower-greek | lower-latin | upper-latin | lower-roman | upper-roman | armenian | georgian	Sets the bullet point style. If a browser doesn't understand an ordered list value, it defaults to decimal. Generally, none, circle, square, decimal, and the alpha and roman values are best supported. The W3C recommends using decimal for ordered lists whenever possible.	Yes

D

Continued

Property	Values	Description	Inherited
margin		Shorthand for defining margin properties in a single declaration. Examples: margin: 0; (sets all margins to 0) margin: 0 10px 20px 30px; (sets individual margins for each edge) See also Chapter 2, "Content margins and padding in CSS" and "Working with CSS shorthand for boxes."	No
margin-bottom	auto | *length* | *percentage*	Sets the bottom margin. Defaults to 0. Note that browsers usually override the zero value by applying default margins to most block elements. Set margins explicitly to 0 to cancel the browser's default. See Chapter 2, "Zeroing margins and padding on all elements."	No
margin-left	auto | *length* | *percentage*	Sets the left margin. Defaults to 0. Note that browsers usually override the zero value by applying default margins to most block elements. Set margins explicitly to 0 to cancel the browser's default. See Chapter 2, "Zeroing margins and padding on all elements."	No
margin-right	auto | *length* | *percentage*	Sets the right margin. Defaults to 0. Note that browsers usually override the zero value by applying default margins to most block elements. Set margins explicitly to 0 to cancel the browser's default. See Chapter 2, "Zeroing margins and padding on all elements."	No
margin-top	auto | *length* | *percentage*	Sets the top margin. Defaults to 0. Note that browsers usually override the zero value by applying default margins to most block elements. Set margins explicitly to 0 to cancel the browser's default. See Chapter 2, "Zeroing margins and padding on all elements."	No
max-height	**none** | *length* | *percentage*	Sets the maximum height of an element. Does not apply to table elements.	No

Property	Values	Description	Inherited
max-width	**none**	*length*	*percentage*	Sets the maximum width of an element. Does not apply to table elements. See also the Chapter 7 exercise, "Creating a maximum-width layout."	No
min-height	**none**	*length*	*percentage*	Sets the minimum height of an element. Does not apply to table elements.	No
min-width	**none**	*length*	*percentage*	Sets the minimum width of an element. Does not apply to table elements.	No
orphans	*number*	Defines the number of lines of a paragraph that must be left at the bottom of a page when printing. Defaults to 2. Defined number must be an integer. Very poorly supported.	Yes

outline		Shorthand for defining outline properties in a single declaration. Outlines are rendered outside the border edge and do not affect document flow. Example:
		
		`.highlight {`
		`outline: 1px dotted #ff0000;`
		`}`
		
		Not supported by Internet Explorer up to and including version 7.
			No

outline-color	*color*	**invert**	Sets the color of an outline. Defaults to invert, which inverts the color of the pixels onscreen, ensuring the outline is visible.	No
outline-style	dashed	dotted	double	groove	inset	**none**	outset	ridge	solid	Sets the style of an outline.	No
outline-width	*length*	**medium**	thick	thin	Sets the width of an outline.	No

Continued

D

Property	Values	Description	Inherited
overflow	auto | hidden | scroll | **visible**	Determines what happens when content is too large for the defined dimensions of the element. auto: If content is clipped, the browser displays a scroll bar. hidden: Content is clipped, and content outside the element's box is not visible. scroll: Content is clipped, but a scroll bar is made available. visible: Content is not clipped and may be rendered outside of the element's containing box. See also Chapter 7, "Scrollable content areas with CSS."	No
padding		Shorthand to define padding properties in a single declaration. Examples: padding: 0; (sets padding on all sides to 0) padding: 0 10px 20px 30px; (sets individual padding for each edge) See also Chapter 2, "Content margins and padding in CSS" and "Working with CSS shorthand for boxes."	No
padding-bottom	*length* | *percentage*	Sets the bottom padding of an element.	No
padding-left	*length* | *percentage*	Sets the left padding of an element.	No
padding-right	*length* | *percentage*	Sets the right padding of an element.	No
padding-top	*length* | *percentage*	Sets the top padding of an element.	No
page-break-after	**auto** | always | avoid | left | right	Determines whether a page break should appear after the element when printing. Poorly supported.	No
page-break-before	**auto** | always | avoid | left | right	Determines whether a page break should appear before the element when printing. Poorly supported.	No
page-break-inside	**auto** | avoid	Determines whether a page break should appear inside the element when printing. Poorly supported.	Yes

Property	Values	Description	Inherited
position	absolute | fixed | relative | **static**	Determines the positioning method used to render the element's box: absolute: Element is placed in a specific location outside of normal document flow, using the top, right, bottom, and left properties. fixed: As per absolute, but the element remains stationary when the screen scrolls. Poorly supported by some browsers. relative: Offset from the static position by the values set using top, right, bottom, and left properties. static: The default. The top, right, bottom, and left properties do not affect the element if this value is set. The element is not removed from the document's normal flow. Various examples of this property in use are found in Chapters 5 and 7.	No
quotes	none | *string string*	Determines the type of quote marks to be used for embedded quotations. The string contains paired quoted values, which determine each level of quote embedding. The default depends on the user agent (browser).	Yes
right	**auto** | *length* | *percentage*	Determines the horizontal offset of the element's right edge from the right edge of its parent element if the parent is positioned; if not, then offset is determined from the first positioned ancestor. Must be used with a position value of relative, absolute, or fixed.	No
table-layout	**auto** | fixed	Controls the layout algorithm used to render tables. Using fixed, table columns are based on analysis of the first row and rendered accordingly. This can speed up processing time, but may lead to columns that are too narrow for subsequently downloaded content.	No

Continued

D

Property	Values	Description	Inherited
text-align	center | justify | **left*** | right	Sets the text alignment for an element. * The default is left in left-to-right languages and right in right-to-left languages such as Arabic, Hebrew, and Urdu. Should be used instead of the HTML align attribute.	Yes
text-decoration	blink | line-through | **none** | overline | underline	Adds decoration to text. Values may be combined in a space-separated list, and the default depends on the element in question. Note that browsers may ignore blink but still be considered compliant. Examples: text-decoration: underline; text decoration: underline ➥ line-through; See also Chapter 5, "Editing link styles using CSS."	No
text-indent	*length* | *percentage*	Sets the horizontal indent of an element's first line of text. Defaults to 0.	Yes
text-transform	capitalize | lowercase | **none** | uppercase	Sets the case of an element's text. See also Chapter 3, "Controlling case with text-transform."	Yes
top	**auto** | *length* | *percentage*	Determines the vertical offset of the element's top edge from the top edge of its parent element if the parent is positioned; if not, then offset is determined from the first positioned ancestor. Must be used with a position value of relative, absolute, or fixed. See also the Chapter 7 exercise, "Using absolute positioning to center a box onscreen."	No

Property	Values	Description	Inherited
unicode-bidi	bidi-override | embed | **normal**	Enables overrides for text direction. The embed value forces text to be displayed with regard to the associated direction property. The bidi-override value also overrides the default Unicode ordering scheme. This is a complex subject concerned with inserting elements of right-to-left text in blocks of left-to-right text (such as embedding Arabic or Hebrew in English, or vice versa). For details about working with bidirectional text, see www.w3.org/International/resource-index.html#bidi.	No
vertical-align	*length* | *percentage* | **baseline** | bottom | middle | top | sub | super | text-bottom | text-top	Determines the vertical alignment of an element. Applies to inline elements and those within table cells. Should be used in place of the HTML valign attribute. If a percentage value is used, that refers to the element's line-height value.	No
visibility	collapse | hidden | **visible**	Sets the visibility of an element. When hidden is used, the element box is invisible but still affects page layout (use display: none for an element to not affect document flow). When collapse is used, results are similar to hidden, except for spanned table cells, which may appear clipped.	Yes
white-space	**normal** | nowrap | pre | pre-wrap | pre-line	Determines how whitespace within an element is handled. Browser support for pre-line and pre-wrap is poor.	Yes
widows	*number*	Defines the number of lines of a paragraph that must be left at the top of a page when printing. Defaults to 2. Defined number must be an integer. Very poorly supported.	Yes

Continued

D

Property	Values	Description	Inherited
width	**auto** | *length* | *percentage*	Sets the content width of an element.	No
word-spacing	*length* | **normal**	Provides space between words in addition to the default settings. See also Chapter 3, "Setting letter-spacing and word-spacing."	Yes
z-index	**auto** | *number*	Changes an element's position in the stack. Higher numbers are "closer" and lower numbers are "further away." Negative values are permitted, but will result in content not being displayed in some browsers.	No

Basic selectors

This section outlines the most commonly used selectors, along with their syntax. Note that selectors for pseudo-classes and pseudo-elements are covered in the following two sections, rather than being duplicated.

> *Some selectors are not fully supported in all browsers. Notably, child and adjacent selectors are not supported by versions of Internet Explorer prior to 7. See* www.webdevout.net/browser-support-css *for an overview of basic selector support.*

Selector type	Syntax	Description
Universal	*	Matches any element. Can be used in context to attach a rule to all elements within another element (e.g., #sidebar *).
Type	*element*	Matches any element of type *element*. For example: h1.
Class	.*value*	Matches an element with a class value of *value*.
ID	#*value*	Matches an element with an id value of *value*.

Selector type	Syntax	Description
Descendant	*element descendant*	Matches a *descendant* element that is a descendant of the element of type *element*. For example, div p targets paragraphs that are descendants of div elements.
Child	*element>child*	Matches an element that is a child of another element. Similar to but more precise than descendant selectors, rules are applied to elements that are direct children of the parent only. For example, div p matches all paragraphs within all divs. div>p only matches paragraphs that are direct children of divs, and so would not match a paragraph within a table within a div.
Adjacent	*element1+element2*	Matches *element2*, adjacent to *element1*. For example, h1+h2 matches any h2 element that directly follows an h1 element within the web page, with no other elements in between.
Attribute	*element[attribute]*	Matches an element of type *element* that has an attribute of type *attribute*. Further clarification can be added via the syntax *element[attribute="value"]* (targets *element* with *attribute* with value equal to *value*), *element[attribute~="value"]* (targets *element* with *attribute* that has a list of space-separated values, of which one is equal to *value*), *element[lang=value]* (targets *element* with a lang attribute equal to *value*).

> Note that the word element *in the preceding table refers to a general element on the web page, rather than a de facto HTML element.*

Pseudo-classes

Pseudo-classes initially provided additional styles relating to a selector's state, but now also include those that apply styles to conceptual document components.

Pseudo-class	Description
:active	The state when an element is active (e.g., when a link is being clicked)
:first-child	Affects the first descendant of an element
:focus	The state when an element is focused to accept keyboard input
:hover	The state when the pointer is over an element
:lang	Applies to elements with the specified language (defined using xml:lang)
:link	Applies to an unvisited link
:visited	Applies to a visited link

Pseudo-elements

Pseudo-elements enable generated content that's not in the document source and the styling of conceptual document components.

Pseudo-element	Description
:after	Used in conjunction with content to generate content after an element. For example: h1:after {content: url(bleep.wav);}
:before	Used in conjunction with content to generate content before an element.
:first-letter	Styles the first letter of an element.
:first-line	Styles the first rendered line of a "block-level" element.

CSS boilerplates and management

By using CSS comments and a monospace font when editing CSS, it's possible to create clear sections within the style sheet and a table of contents, enabling you to more easily manage rules. A full example is available in the advanced-boilerplates folder of the download files. An example of a table of contents is shown following:

```
/*

STYLE SHEET FOR [WEB SITE]
Created by [AUTHOR NAME]
[URL OF AUTHOR]

ToC

        1. defaults
        2. structure
        3. links and navigation
        4. fonts
        5. images
        6. tables
        7. forms

Notes

*/
```

An example of a section of a boilerplate is shown following, with empty rules waiting to be filled. Here, a single tab is represented by eight spaces. Note how the property/value pairs and closing curly quotes are indented equally. This makes it easier to scan the far-left side of the document for selectors.

```
/* ---------- 4. fonts ---------- */

html {
        font-size: 100%;
        }

body {
        font-size: 62.5%;
        }

h1, h2, h3, h4, p, ul {
        }

h1 {
        }

h2 {
        }

h3 {
        }

h4 {
        }
```

D

```
p {
        }

ul {
        }
```

The use of the CSS comment to introduce the section, with a string of hyphens before and after the section name, provides a useful visual separator for when directly editing code. Subsections are best added by indenting them the same amount as the property/value pairs; rule-specific comments are best placed after the opening curly quote; pair-specific comments are best placed after the pair. See the following for examples.

Sub-section introduction:

```
        /* --- sidebar headings --- */
#sidebar h2 {
        }

#sidebar h3 {
        }
```

Rule-specific comment:

```
.boxoutProducts {/* used on sales and purchase pages */
        }
```

Pair-specific comment:

```
body.advert h2 {
        font-size: 1.5em;
        text-transform: uppercase; /* over-ride for ad pages only */
        }
```

> Note that the indents in this section are different from those shown elsewhere in this book. This is intentional, in order to provide a close match to the code in the actual style sheet, rather than something that works better on the printed page.

Modular style sheets

From a management perspective, I find it easiest to work with a single style sheet, albeit one that already has a number of elements prewritten. However, you can also work in a modular manner, creating a number of small boilerplate documents (e.g., to reset margins and padding and define font size defaults) and area-specific style sheets (for navigation, layout, forms, etc.), and then importing them into your CSS via an @import line. As an example, you could save the clearFix rule (shown following, and used in various exercises throughout the book, notably in Chapter 7's "Clearing floated content" exercise) in its own style sheet as clearfix.css.

```
.clearFix:after {
  content: ".";
  display: block;
  height: 0;
  clear: both;
  visibility: hidden;
}
```

This could then be imported into your main style sheet as follows:

```
@import url(clearfix.css);
```

You can import as many style sheets as you want, depending on how modular you want to be, and how you want to organize your CSS. For example, at the time of writing, this book's technical editor, David Anderson, imports all of his CSS, using eight @import lines to do so, and separating out his CSS into categories such as "generic," "navigation," and "forms". How you decide to work is up to you.

D

E BROWSER GUIDE

This appendix provides a brief overview of the mainstream browsers in general use at the time of writing, including a little history about them, estimated market share, and how standards-compliant they are (along with whether they pass the Web Standards Project Acid2 Browser Test, at www.webstandards.org/action/acid2/). Note that new versions of browsers are regularly released, so this section is intended only as a guide. Details are accurate as of October 2007.

Firefox

- **Full name**: Mozilla Firefox.
- **Initial year of release**: 2004 (as 1.0).
- **OS**: Windows, Mac OS X, Linux (unofficial ports to various other systems exist).
- **Website**: www.mozilla.com/firefox/.
- **Market share estimate**: 10–15%.
- **Trend**: Steady growth.
- **Engine**: Gecko.
- **Compliance**: High. Firefox makes an excellent base for development, although as of 2.0, it fails a few advanced elements of the Acid2 Browser Test.
- **Comments**: Initially devised as an unofficial branch of the Mozilla project, Firefox's aim was to be a compact, speedy browser, devoid of the feature-creep evident in its parent. Initially innovative, bringing tabbed browsing and incremental find (find-as-you-type) functionality to the masses, Firefox's market share rapidly grew as standards-aware websites formed an aggressive switch marketing campaign, designed to tear complacent users away from Internet Explorer. Should you work with Firefox, I highly recommend you install Chris Pederick's Web Developer toolbar, available from www.chrispederick.com/work/web-developer/.

Internet Explorer

- **Full name**: Windows Internet Explorer.
- **Initial year of release**: 1995.
- **OS**: Microsoft Windows.
- **Website**: www.microsoft.com/ie.
- **Market share estimate**: Around 80%. (This figure is combined, split more or less evenly between Internet Explorer 7 and Internet Explorer 6, with a low and diminishing number of users running version 5.x.)
- **Trend**: Slow decline.
- **Engine**: Trident.

- **Compliance**: Reasonable for version 7, although it dramatically fails Acid2. Poor for version 6 and before, which require fixes for many advanced CSS properties and values.

- **Comments**: Despite being initially ignored, Microsoft's Mosaic-derived browser became embroiled in the infamous browser wars of the late 1990s, regularly adding new features and capabilities to eclipse rival Netscape Navigator. With the battle won by 1999, Microsoft's browser seemingly lapsed into a semicomatose state. Version 5's standards support was dire (unlike the Mac version, which was later canceled), and while version 6 was an improvement, it still lagged behind its rivals, including the then-new Firefox, resulting in its previously all-dominant market share (which rose to a high of around 95%) being hit hard for nearly two years. In late 2006, the final public release of version 7 appeared, with much-improved standards support (although this aspect remains inferior to that of its rivals) and features available in rival browsers (such as tabbed browsing). A Microsoft-produced developer toolbar is available for version 7 of Internet Explorer; it's available from www.microsoft.com/downloads/details.aspx?familyid= e59c3964-672d-4511-bb3e-2d5e1db91038&displaylang=en.

Opera

- **Full name**: Opera.

- **Initial year of release**: 1996 (first public release).

- **OS**: Windows, Mac OS X, Mac OS, Linux, BeOS, Solaris, and others.

- **Website**: www.opera.com/.

- **Market share estimate**: Under 2%.

- **Trend**: Stable.

- **Engine**: Presto.

- **Compliance**: Excellent. Passes Acid2, making it an excellent alternative to Firefox for a development base.

- **Comments**: Starting life as a research project for a Norwegian telecom company, Opera has grown into a feature-packed, standards-compliant browser. Its innovative features—some of which are of direct benefit to developers—often lead its rivals, although the browser has been hampered over the years by a cluttered and superficially complex interface, and the browser for a long time identifying itself as Internet Explorer. Because of this, market share figures for Opera were—and indeed possibly still are—artificially low. However, in terms of reach, Opera has plenty of potential: there are versions of the browser for a massive range of systems, including for handheld devices. A developer toolbar is available from www.operawiki.info/WebDevToolbar.

E

499

Safari

- **Full name**: Safari.
- **Initial year of release**: 2003.
- **OS**: Mac OS X, Windows.
- **Website**: www.apple.com/safari/.
- **Market share estimate**: About 4%.
- **Trend**: Slow growth.
- **Engine**: KHTML.
- **Compliance**: Excellent, with reservations (see comments). Passes Acid2, making it suitable for a development base.
- **Comments**: Most likely developed as a reaction to Microsoft axing Internet Explorer for Mac, Safari rapidly became the primary browser for Mac users. Its clean interface complements the KHTML engine, which is one of the most compliant in existence. (Indeed, Safari was the first browser to pass Acid2.) Although initially available to Mac users only, June 2007 saw the first beta of Safari for Windows, primarily intended as an aid to Windows-based developers creating content for Apple's iPhone. Safari has some shortcomings regarding JavaScript support, and its method of anti-aliasing text is significantly different to other browsers. Prior to version 3, CSS borders and colors for form fields and buttons were ignored, the Mac OS Aqua equivalents instead being "forced."

Other browsers

A number of other web browsers exist, although their market share is so minimal as to be considered all but insignificant. A possible exception to this is Linux-based Konqueror, although with its KHTML engine, you should expect similar results to those in Safari. Elsewhere, some browsers are based on Gecko (such as SeaMonkey/Mozilla and Flock), some on Trident (such as AOL Explorer/OpenRide), and one on both (Netscape Browser).

Opinions on the merit of software tools are usually pretty subjective. This chapter isn't supposed to be some kind of definitive guide on web design software and each application's pros and cons—instead, it aims to provide an overview of the most popular solutions on the market, along with insight into the tools I myself use on a daily basis.

Web design software

Adobe Dreamweaver (www.adobe.com/products/dreamweaver/) is the market leader for web design software on both Windows and Mac platforms. Formerly a Macromedia product, the application joined the Adobe stable after Adobe acquired Macromedia in 2005. Dreamweaver's position at the top of the pile is no accident: for several versions now, it has concentrated on standards-compliance and lean code, but has also provided a flexible interface that enables designers to take either a code-based or a layout-based approach to web page design and the creation of dynamic websites. Although the CS3 update was underwhelming, Dreamweaver remains the only WYSIWYG web design tool that I recommend to people with any enthusiasm.

Adobe GoLive (www.adobe.com/products/golive/), formerly the Mac-only CyberStudio, was unceremoniously ousted from Adobe's Creative Suite bundles once Dreamweaver CS3 arrived. Taking a more graphic-design approach, many of the tools in GoLive 9 are seemingly derived from Adobe's desktop publishing application, InDesign. Although the application is fairly easy to use, it pales beside Dreamweaver when it comes to working with CSS-based sites and web standards, and using its control panel tends to result in unwieldy span-infested markup and a document littered with inline styles.

Microsoft Expression Web (www.microsoft.com/products/expression/en/expression-web) arrived on the scene in very late 2006, and after the disaster that was Microsoft FrontPage, was a surprisingly strong effort from Microsoft. While weaker than Dreamweaver, it managed—at the time of release—to provide some CSS tools superior to Adobe's application, and although its workflow is inferior to Dreamweaver's, it's a surprisingly capable and user-friendly application. Unfortunately, Microsoft Expression Web is hampered by a lack of support for PHP (it concentrates primarily on Microsoft-originated technologies) and the lack of a Mac OS X release. However, for Windows-based web designers only interested in static sites, and those who develop ASP.NET-based sites, it's worth a look.

Other applications in this area are more extreme in terms of working method than those discussed so far, either relying on a purely layout-based approach, or being based around hand-coding. An example of a purely layout-oriented application is the Mac-only **Softpress Freeway** (www.softpress.com/), which is even more geared toward print designers than GoLive and has an interface akin to QuarkXPress. Software geared toward hand-coding includes **BBEdit** (Mac OS X, www.barebones.com/), **TextMate** (Mac OS X, www.macromates.com/), **HomeSite** (Windows, www.adobe.com/products/homesite/), **HTML Kit** (Windows, www.chami.com/html-kit/), and **TopStyle Pro** (Windows, www.newsgator.com/Individuals/TopStyle/Default.aspx).

Graphic design software

Adobe Photoshop (www.adobe.com/products/photoshop/) is a Mac and Windows application that's pretty much ubiquitous in the print design world. Immensely powerful and surprisingly user-friendly once you get to grips with the interface, more recent versions have provided a number of tools geared toward web designers, including a decent Save for Web function. Now part of the same suite as Dreamweaver, Photoshop integrates with the popular web design application, and if you can afford it, the application is pretty much unbeatable for bitmap editing.

Adobe Photoshop Elements (www.adobe.com/products/photoshopel) is also available for Mac and Windows, and is a cut-down consumer-oriented version of Photoshop. Although not as feature-rich as its bigger brother, Elements nonetheless has enough useful tools to warrant purchase for any designer on a tight budget. Note that the Mac and Windows versions of Elements are significantly different in terms of feature set, with the Mac version lacking a number of the extras from the Windows version (although many of those deal with asset organization, a task iPhoto can deal with on Mac OS X).

Adobe Fireworks (www.adobe.com/products/fireworks/) is a Mac and Windows application formerly part of Macromedia's suite of web design tools. Previously something of a web-focused rival to Photoshop, Adobe has repositioned Fireworks as a tool primarily aimed at rapidly working up mockups of websites. However, its tool set is such that it's just as capable as Photoshop for working up entire layouts. (In fact, the vector tools within Fireworks are generally considered superior to Photoshop's equivalents), and at a much lower cost.

Corel Paint Shop Pro (www.corel.com/) is a Windows-only graphics editor, which has historically been seen as a low-budget alternative to Photoshop. Enabling users to edit both bitmap and vector graphics, previous versions of the application were well suited to web design, and its price point—significantly lower than Photoshop's—made it a good choice for designers on a tight budget. More recent versions have seen the application focus rather more significantly on photo editing, however.

GIMP (www.gimp.org/)—the GNU Image Manipulation Program—is the closest open source equivalent to Photoshop, and is available in various flavors for Linux, Windows, and Mac OS X (although the main Mac version requires X11 to run, with native ports being rather flaky by comparison). Primarily a bitmap editor, the application includes a surprising range of tools equivalent to those found in Adobe's market-leading application, although it lacks strong color model support, and the omission of a free transform tool is a disappointment.

Adobe Illustrator (www.adobe.com/products/illustrator/) is a Mac and Windows application for working with vector graphics. Although the majority of web graphics are bitmap-based, there's nothing to stop you from using a vector-oriented application for crafting the initial design, and Illustrator's tools prove flexible when creating sites with clean lines and large blocks of color. Usefully, the application has a modicum of tools for web publishing.

505

The author's toolbox

I often get asked what hardware and software I use, so here is a quick list:

- **Hardware**: I use a Mac Pro, with lots of extra RAM and several hard drives for daily and weekly backups, along with a MacBook as a backup machine. I personally prefer Mac OS X over Windows, but with Intel Macs, the real advantage is being able to design on the Mac, test on Mac *and* Windows, and host stuff locally for testing on the built-in Apache server.

- **Design software**: I mostly use **Adobe Photoshop** for layout design, although **Adobe Illustrator** is wheeled out occasionally. **Color Consultant Pro** (www.code-line.com/software/colorconsultantpro.html) assists with color schemes, while **Color Oracle** (http://colororacle.cartography.ch/) and **Sim Daltonism** (www.michelf.com/projects/sim-daltonism/) both enable me to check whether designs are usable for people who are color blind.

- **Authoring software**: This will likely come as no surprise if you've read this book, but I tend to favor a code-based approach to creating site templates. However, I don't like wasting time, so applications that speed up code creation are a must. **CSSEdit** (www.macrabbit.com/cssedit/) is my weapon of choice for CSS, and it's perhaps the best piece of shareware available for the Mac (worth the entry price just for its preview override function, which enables you to override a live site's CSS with a local file). For code, I tend to flit between **BBEdit** and **TextMate**. For managing content and sites, I sometimes use Dreamweaver, and for uploading everything, Panic's **Transmit** (www.panic.com/transmit/) is unbeatable.

- **Miscellaneous software**: A few bits of shareware provide supporting roles when I'm working: **ImageWell** (www.xtralean.com/IWOverview.html) is handy for batch processing images without requiring you to open up Photoshop; **Paparazzi** (www.derailer.org/paparazzi/) makes it simple to take full-page grabs of any website—handy for the portfolio; **Headdress** (http://headdress.twinsparc.com/) makes virtual hosting a breeze, removing the need to muck about with config files; and **SuperDuper** (www.shirt-pocket.com/SuperDuper/) is essential for creating system clones, which suddenly become extremely important on those inevitable days when my main hard drive decides to keel over and die.

INDEX

Numbers and symbols

A

B

D

- **Write strong web content**
- **Maximize your search engine marketing**
- **Learn how accessibility and web standards apply to corporate sites**

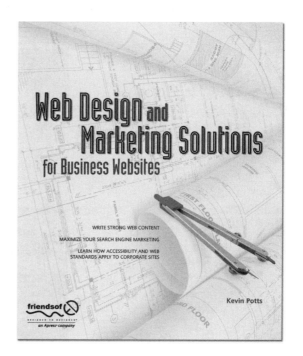

Web Design and Marketing Solutions
for Business Websites

By Kevin Potts

ISBN-10: 1-59059-839-3 | ISBN-13: 978-1-59059-839-9

Published August 2007

400 Pages

- **Be inspired by 10 web design lessons from 10 of the world's best web designers**
- **Get creative with cutting-edge XHTML, CSS, and DOM scripting techniques**
- **Learn breathtaking design skills while remaining standards-compliant**

Web Standards Creativity
Innovations in Web Design with XHTML, CSS, and DOM Scripting

Cameron Adams, Mark Boulton, Andy Clarke, Simon Collison, Jeff Croft, Derek Featherstone, Ian Lloyd, Ethan Marcotte, Dan Rubin, Rob Weycher

Introduction by Andy Budd

ISBN-10: 1-59059-803-2 | ISBN-13 978-1-59059-803-0

Published March 2007

288 Pages